THE
AGE OF MINERVA

VOLUME 2

*Cognitive Discontinuities
in Eighteenth-Century Thought*

THE
AGE OF MINERVA

VOLUME 2

Cognitive Discontinuities
in Eighteenth-Century Thought

FROM BODY TO MIND IN PHYSIOLOGY
AND THE ARTS

PAUL ILIE

University of Pennsylvania Press

Philadelphia

Library of Congress Cataloging-in-Publication Data
Ilie, Paul, 1932-
   The age of Minerva / Paul Ilie.
      p.   cm.
   Includes bibliographical references and indexes.
   Contents: v. 1. Counter-rational reason in the eighteenth century — v. 2. Cognitive
discontinuities in eighteenth-century thought.
   ISBN 0-8122-3307-7 (v. 1 : alk. paper). — ISBN 0–8122-3308-5 (v. 2 : alk. paper)
   1. Europe—Intellectual life—18th century.   2. Philosophy, Modern—18th century.
I. Title.
B802.I36   1995
190'.9'033—dc20
                                                                              95-38671
                                                                              CIP

To my wife, MARIE-LAURE,
. . . for bringing me to this vast
quarry

Contents

Figures

"Quick, from the Mind's imperial Mansion shed
With *lively Tension* spins the *nervous Thread*
With Flux of animate Effluvia stor'd,
And Tubes of nicest Perforation bor'd,
Whose *branching Maze* thro' ev'ry Organ tends.;
And Unity of conscious Action *lends*;
While Spirits thro' the *wandring Channels* wind,
And wing the Message of informing Mind;
Or Objects to th' ideal Seat convey;
Or dictate Motion with internal Sway

           —Henry Brooke, *Universal Beauty*

Introduction
Methodological Orientation—
Paradigims, Polyps, and Poets

In the previous volume, *Counter-Rational Reason in the Eighteenth Century*, I described the nonrational modes of expression that are symptomatic of cognitive discontinuity. Casting Reason in the role of a guarantor of philosophical connectedness or continuity, I showed how Reason could also harbor aberration and foster discontinuity in what I called the Age of Minerva. The evidence for a "counter-rational" Reason consisted of Western European texts interpreted through the lens of Goya's *Capricho 43* ("The Sleep/Dream of Reason Produces Monsters," Fig. 1). Although my interpretation approached the borderline of science and pseudoscience, the history of biology seemed tangential to this goal. My notion was that dreaming was a nonlinguistic mode of cognition for Goya's contemporaries, a way of apprehending the metamorphic reality that eludes empirical Reason. Dream cognition, so to speak, was held intuitively to originate in the neurophysiology of an imagination set free from Reason. I planned a second book (this one) that would discuss Goya's universal dream language and its relation to animal spirits and to what I would call the epistemology of aether. The writing of this book progressed in an unforeseen manner, however. It began to encroach upon a scientific-literary framework that became alarming because of the unexpected new materials that insisted on being included. The result turned "progress" into a forced march along the landscape of eighteenth-century treatises on anatomy and physiology.

Meanwhile, there arose a scholarly complaint over scientific models that I'll describe shortly, a complaint which is pertinent to this methodological orientation and which exposed the uncertain nature of evidence. Given the divergent positions among eighteenth-century natural philosophers, it was unclear what weight should be given to writings that described competing scientific models. Specifically, why cite this particular

Figure 1. Francisco de Goya. *Capricho 43*. "El sueño de la razón produce monstruos" (The Sleep/Dream of Reason Produces Monsters). 1798–99. Courtesy of the Norton Simon Foundation, Pasadena, California.

author or text rather than others, or in these proportions and not different ones? The assumption here was that a consensus exists among historians of biology and medicine that can guide literary and intellectual historians to the models that are paradigmatic, as distinct from merely marginal. Regarding my own study, could I safely ignore the works of naturalists who, for other reasons, had come to my notice unexpectedly—Jean-Baptiste Robinet, John Needham, Claude-Nicolas Le Cat, and Charles Bonnet? In Needham's case, although his experiments offered a "unique view . . . of the kinds of philosophical, religious, and social concerns that lay at the heart of much eighteenth-century biology," according to historian of science Shirley Roe, his flawed theories "appear not to have been accepted by any major biological figure during his lifetime" (Roe, "John Turberville Needham," 182, 184). Such a naturalist would not seem to have major significance for nonspecialists seeking an authoritative scientific model.

The problem of weighing evidence was intense with respect to studying the psychological processes. Eighteenth-century psychology depended ultimately on the biological sciences, which in turn shared with intellectual history a common denominator that is best called *sensibility*. The word "sensibility," however, entails more than the literary concept of "feeling." It includes the genesis of material sensibility in post-Cartesian science, especially in the empirical origins of biology and psychology. Because science plays a crucial role in the history of culture, it is arguable that eighteenth-century authors cannot stand apart from the Lockean, Newtonian, and lesser paradigms that were developing in the sciences. This position has been championed for literature by George S. Rousseau in his approach to the interface between neurophysiology and the psychology of literary sensibility. It would seem useful, therefore, for nonspecialists to know whether biology specialists consider Thomas Willis or Albrecht von Haller the authority for the reigning model for eighteenth-century sensibility; that is, whether nerve vibrations (Willis) or animal spirits (Haller) trace images along tracks upon the brain and thereby affect the intensity of imagination. Again, however, it is assumed that a consensus exists about paradigms, an assumption that prompted the scholarly complaint just mentioned.

In the "Forum" section of *Eighteenth-Century Studies* in 1984, Joseph Musser testified to the manner in which his manuscript ran afoul of one editorial consultant who, by favoring the "Haller paradigm" for literary sensibility, objected to Musser's unquestioning acceptance of the "Willis paradigm," which Musser had gleaned from Rousseau's research. Rousseau describes the neurophysiological model of animal spirits but does not prescribe it in absolute terms. Indeed, historian of science Duchesneau writes otherwise: "the new physiological theory . . . is illustrated in a paradigmatic fashion by Hermann Boerhaave (1668–1738), who annexes Harvey's discovery to the methodological framework of mechanism" ("D'Alembert et la physiologie," 81). The term "paradigm" ordinarily refers to Thomas Kuhn's concept of a scientific community's dominant theory, and should not be confused with competing schools that prefer different models prior to a general consensus (*The Structure of Scientific Revolutions*, 10–12). Strictly speaking, a historian of science might say that the only paradigm in the eighteenth century is Newtonian; however, it is fair to add that John Locke's psychology was paramount or "paradigmatic," pushing aside earlier Cartesian and Scholastic paradigms even though the coexisting models of Père Nicolas de Malebranche and Abbé Étienne Bonnot de Condillac exerted their own presence.

What troubled me about Musser's frustration was the discrepancy among authorities. I had already formed my own opinions about whether flowing animal spirits or vibrating fibers had held sway in the age of Goya, Diderot, and Samuel Richardson, which is to say, in Western Europe, but I had not yet completed my research. As a historian of ideas, I would have preferred to rely on historians of science instead of digging into the primary sources without benefit of their expertise. This incertitude is the most debilitating of procedures in research, although it is seldom acknowledged.

My first response to the crisis of scholarly authorities, was defensive. Was my work really affected by the Willis-Haller debate and the interpretive disagreement between scholarly consultants? The plaintiff Musser had accepted one paradigm as being dominant, presumably in the sense intended by Kuhn. But any discussion of dominant and minor hypotheses must keep in mind Stephen Toulmin's explanation. Paradigms and peripheries surely exist in scientific discovery, but they are functions of social forces and institutionalized activities as well as disciplinary criteria (*Human Understanding*, 227, 300–302). All human understanding, including today's scholarship, is constituted by assertions from diverse communities that do not always acknowledge one another's persuasive authority. Our own scholarly assertions about eighteenth-century paradigms are akin to the competing models themselves: they group themselves into stronger and weaker influential forces within the full scholarly community. The sociology of knowledge as presented by Toulmin drove home to me the enduring issue raised by Musser's rejected manuscript. The issue is not whether Haller's or Willis's model governed sensibility, or even whether Professor

Rousseau's or Consultant X's history of science is the more valid for "the rest of us" to follow. Both either/or choices are more complex than they appear, and in the end they are reconcilable.

The deeper issue is stated candidly by Lester King in his preface to *The Road to Medical Enlightenment* (1970), where he confesses to the selective bias that shaped his book. King was interested in the theories of Friedrich Hoffmann, and so he decided first to understand key predecessors. Because he chose to study authors (scientists) P, Q, R, and S, he decided not to study authors J, K, L, and M. He goes on to state that a study of J, K, L, and M would probably result in a configuration quite different from the one he is presenting, and that his book does not make any claim to an exclusive truth about the "real" road to the medical enlightenment mentioned in his title. This frank preface confronted me with one of four problems that I describe briefly in the next pages. Notwithstanding King's disclaimer, his synthesizing books have no competitors as yet, so he remains the authority that scholars unaffiliated with the history of science must cite. Suppose, therefore, that one such outsider—a historian of ideas, for instance—configures materials from the authors omitted by King. He deviates on the grounds cited by Roe, namely, the unique view the materials offer of the period's central concerns. Is that scholarly outsider also obliged to reconcile his group of authors with King's group, given that King did not reconcile his own original group, and its models, with the omitted group now studied? What privileges the expert after he renounces his authority?

Granted that I do want to recognize scholarly authorities, there is nevertheless a limit in anyone's ability to credit their findings. The limiting influence on scholars with my particular profile is national scope. Much of King's evidence and all Musser's and Rousseau's sources originate in Great Britain. And yet these scholars generalize implicitly for all of Europe by using phrases like "seventeenth- and eighteenth-century physiologists," and "paradigms guiding eighteenth-century research." Don't they really mean "British physiologists" and "British research"? Why are French and Spanish sources omitted?

Assume, for purposes of comparison, that a Western European sphere of cultural forces exists after the War of the Spanish Succession (1704–11). May the historian of science then proceed to generalize about scientific communities? The answer is yes, provided that local or national criteria for these communities do not exist, as they do for "the independence of the Genevan scientific tradition from of the French" (Dawson, *Nature's*

Enigma, 12). The path Peter Gay chose to take in his preface to *The Science of Freedom* is to speak of "families" of thinkers in two concentric Enlightenments, one narrow and the other wide. But what Gay refers to as affinities and divergences—sometimes contradictory, partly friendly, and partly hostile—is a condition of discontinuity that connective metaphors tend to obscure.

The problem of the relative status of community or national paradigms brought me face to face with a second problem. What constitutes compelling evidence about sensibility that might guide the interdisciplinarian outsider? My work on Goya had led me to search for texts that describe dreaming. My note-taking was not guided by scholarly authority because the subject was not documented beyond the French sources outlined by Lester Crocker ("L'analyse des rêves"). I seized on any book that might mention dreams. How "important" were these primary sources with respect to reflecting a so-called paradigm? Would it not be appropriate to give special weight to sources that fulfilled such conditions of prominence as a printing history that went beyond a single edition and a prestige manifested by translation into other languages?

My procedure was in fact to begin with works on psychology, physiology, and anatomy written in French, because France and Spain had close intellectual ties. To round things out, I also read what I believed to be key British authors of the eighteenth century: I read William Cheselden because nine editions of his work were published by 1768. I read William Cullen's version of Haller, because it had been translated into French and also because his prose seemed remarkably precise when compared with my French readings. I read David Hartley because British-oriented research mentions him so often. I read Needham because of his international collaboration with Comte de Buffon. And I studied Hume rather than Locke because the faculty of imagination is so important in Hume's philosophy, as it is in dreaming.

What I began to realize is that Musser's discomfort over contradictory authorities supported his suggestion that perhaps eighteenth-century physiology is pre-paradigmatic after all. The best summary of competing positions is Thomas Hankins's chapter on natural history and physiology in *Science and the Enlightenment* (113–57). Problem three, therefore, was the absence of criteria for spotting dominance and marginality in eighteenth-century models. With respect to dreaming within Western European sensibility, I could find no measure of overriding influence that might entail brain anatomy and neurophysiology, the sciences pertinent to my research. Not only were the differences complicated from one nation or another, but also local influences varied in particular literary authors such as Samuel Richardson, José Cadalso, or Baculard d'Arnaud.

In the end, it seemed pointless to think in terms of scientific paradigms. I would instead adhere to a striking proposition in King's preface, that what counts is the *kind* of question asked by historians. King draws an analogy with stamp collecting. The conventional collector (or specialist) will arrange stamps by country and date, whereas a newcomer might want to classify them iconically, say, according to the faces or flowers pictured on the stamps. The outsider's perspective is not wrong, but it violates unexamined expectations as to what is "right." From this standpoint, problem four became clear to me. How could I sidestep the debate about sensibility and its physiological paradigm in favor of evidence related to the original question that brought this debate to my attention in the first place? To deal with Goya's enigma of "the dream of Reason" and "Universal Language" required research into the biology of cognition during his era. This path uncovered numerous speculative issues in the philosophy of science, issues that, although discontinuous among themselves, all stemmed from a single inquiry into the roots of human perception and knowledge. One issue in particular appeared to involve scientific matters but in reality transcended all of them. Goya's enigma posed the issue of a pre-linguistic form of cognition. Was such a nonverbal cognition implied on both sides of the debate between the vibrationists and the fluidists? This question was independent of the scholarly debate itself, which turned on the problem of whose version of nerve physiology dominated in the eighteenth century.

In contrast, my cognitive question was related to a quite different scientific commotion, not among scholars but among scientists and literary figures like Needham, Bonnet, and Diderot, a commotion that made anatomy and physiology irrelevant. The merely anatomical question had forced a choice between nerve fibers that were always in a state of keen irritability because they had no cavity, or hollow nerve fibers that caused sensation through the action of nerve fluid or spirits. Diderot recorded both these models in his *Elements of Physiology* because, as a philosopher and a poet, he hesitated in the face of uncertain scientific findings. Clearly there was no dominant model to sway this intensely thoughtful Encyclopedist. Diderot went further by asserting, "I regard the simple fiber, without any cavity, to be an animal, a worm" (*Éléments*, 9:279), and he repeated elsewhere, "Everything is explained by considering the fiber as a worm" (9:312).

The commotion in Diderot's day was that the retreat from worm to polyp meant hardly any difference at all in neurophysiological terms. They both were said to have a core of spiritous or medullary substance, the soft pulp identified as "the origin of animal force" (9:318). Both organisms were also capable of regeneration while lacking a brain. The polyp especially, more than any other single organic curiosity, focused attention on what might be called *functional* cognition. Its irritability invoked the organizing principles of life that could not be implemented as conscious knowledge, but entailed pre-linguistic signals that permit vital functions. The polyp's transcending significance, as Dawson has intimated, resides in the way it reformulates the mind-body problem so as to supersede the Cartesian soul without eliminating the original dualism. In Diderot's phrase, polyps epitomize "the spontaneous self-ordering life force in matter" (Vartanian, "La Mettrie and Diderot," 162). Indeed, Diderot's friend and scientist, Théophile de Bordeu, compared the nervous system with the polyp, "whose roots or mouths extend to the sense organs and to all the parts, giving each a kind of sensibility and activity" (*Éléments* [1964], 89).

As an outsider to these matters, I preferred to shift the question from the mechanics of sensation and vital force by turning attention toward the polyp's—or any organism's—medullary essence. Having read texts about the dream process, I took additional notes without regard for the physiological structure responsible for nerve signals. I was not concerned with how the transmission occurs, but rather with the nature of the signal. I was interested in how a material sensation becomes a nonmaterial perception, and how thereafter it is transformed into a kind of knowledge that is either rational or emotive or oneiric or even instinctual. Obviously there are problems of definition in the terms "knowledge" and "instinct," even as far as the role of "language" and its character. But, admitting this, I was interested in the transformatory process in sensibility, or, more plainly, in the nature of the neural signal itself.

My task would take me from what Isaac Newton called "the sensible species of things [that] are carried through the nerves and brain" to the common sensorium, and from there to God and "his boundless uniform sensorium" (*Opticks*, 345, 379). In the *Opticks*, Newton elaborates on "a Being incorporeal, living, intelligent, omnipresent, who in infinite space, as it were in his Sensory, sees the things themselves intimately . . . and comprehends them wholly by their immense presence to himself; Of which things the images only [are] carried through the organs of sense into our little sensoriums." How this relates to Goya's universal dream language requires a journey that passes through the Enlightenment's submerged grottoes of Ancient philosophy, a landscape bathed in aether theory. For example, the Spanish alchemist and oneirologist Diego de Torres Villarroel understood the link between mind and the so-called subtle matters such as aether, electricity, magnetism, and effluvia, all of which descend from the ancient pneuma. Torres invents literary dreams that make allusion to a neurophysiological model of dream process. His dreams claim to be truth-statements that return us to Newton's reference to God's organless sensorium that makes all things directly present. Absolute knowledge, the Logos, is sensorially unmediated.

Concepts of aether in Ancient philosophy come down to the eighteenth century through various hermeticist strains, as Frances Yates and others have demonstrated. Alchemy, Neoplatonism, and astrology all seek the unity of cosmic substance. Aether is the purest part of Fire, and the children of aether are those who dream light, which ignites the imagination. The luminous imagination captures the sublime fire through dream, itself the fiery aether that is the fifth element in matter's need to rejoin intellectual light. In other words, between the physical light of the senses and the metaphysical light of knowledge there mediates the glorious light of dream, the inner world of imagination that reaches upward (Tuzet, *Cosmos*, 161–68, 216).

The broad physiology of dreams is well-known: the imagination responds to the vestigia traced on the brain by the subtle matter or animal spirits. According to the *Encyclopédie*, aether produces the elasticity of nerve fibers and its spiritous nature, in addition to being the cause of light emission. Newton himself related his mechanics to Neoplatonic air by way of aether, which in turn mediates in animal spirits. In such studies as Betty Dobbs's *Foundations of Newton's Alchemy* and King's discussion of Hoffmann, the role of aether belongs to a universe regarded as a living body, where aether is considered "a sort of prime mover" (*Road to Medical Enlightenment*, 189).

At this point the minute polyp reenters the picture. In Cartesian dualism and in the later vitalist dualism, an external Divine mind directs the inscrutable properties of living matter at the highest and lowest ends of the animal scale. These seemingly immaterial properties are inexplicable. The polyp fascinated Needham, Abraham Trembley, Bonnet, and Diderot because, lacking a soul or a nervous system or a sensorium, and possessing minimal spiritous matter, the polyp's self-regeneration and photosensitivity seemed to make it a prototype for higher forms of functionalism and cognition. Hartley believed that polypoid animals possessed a sensorium diffused through the medullary fluid. Diderot conceived of the polyp as being all sensorium. He also said it was "all eye" but equipped with a form of touchsight that could be considered the primal language of vital force, a "Universal Language."

The polyp's sensibility is a monoesthesia, and Diderot considers what this implies for the human analog. His verdict is rationalist when he declares that "the man who is reduced to a single sense would be mad. Nothing would remain except feeling [*sensibilité*], a blind quality in the living molecule. Nothing is more mad than this" (*Éléments*, 9:375). Sensibility begins with the kinesthetics of touch, but it also extends to the physical impact felt when experiencing a "touching" emotion. The blindness of "feeling" in these terms may be harmful and perhaps "mad," but is it without its insights? Goya's reply might be that the abyss of madness yawns wide, for the *Capricho 43* dissolves into dream. Knowledge then consorts with monsters, just as the mind consorts with the chaotic elements of reality before their rational ordering. What the polyp "knows" is an inchoate reality. Its cognitive medium is the same spirituous matter that produces dreams. This medium consists of the aethereal substance that flows throughout the entire Chain of Being that is present in the Divine sensorium.

The significance of eighteenth-century research on the polyp is that it brought the problem of soul into a single framework. Whether the soul is defined as the intelligent seat of generation or of sensibility or of general behavior is beside the point. The polyp framed the problem of soul as it governs vital functions for all animated forms of matter. If nothing else, the common factor in rational and subrational matter is intelligent animation. And the common denominator of intelligence in all living matter is orderly behavior directed by internal signifying codes that ensure the survival of organisms at their respective levels of complexity. If this common factor is considered in the all-encompassing polar terms of polyps and poets, then the polyps might be said to exhibit a preverbal sensibility at a primal but paradigmatic level. In the hypothesis of Jacques Monod regarding biological codes, language may well precede the emergence of a peculiarly human nervous system.

As for poets, they might exhibit the tenet formulated by Gregory Bateson and Claude Lévi-Strauss for all humanity: that "the heart has precise algorithms coded differently from verbal communication" (Bateson, 139). The heartfelt algorithms of sensibility are far from being a poetical formulation. They arise from what today are held to be strict neurochemical laws. The mind-body mystery is not solved thereby, but the implications of polypal "intelligence" shift the problem of spirit and soul away from the humanly rational perspective and toward the evolutionary perspective of encoded signals suggested in Monod's formula that language (however defined) precedes the nervous system. This book defers that idea to a future volume, except to suggest the importance of Goya's "Universal Language" as a concept that transcends rational speech by extending its range to all vital organisms.

The relevance of *Capricho 43*, "The Sleep/Dream of Reason Produces Monsters," to this alternative way of regarding language should be clear. When Jacques Derrida refers to the "gramme" as the significational factor in genetic programming, he may be too restrictive in his concept of language. Bateson points out that genetic programming entails a cybernetics where "it is possible that the paradigms of interaction which are basic to iconic signalling about relationship could serve as evolutionary models for the paradigms of verbal grammar" (423–24). The mention of "iconic signalling" returns the discussion to the neural mechanisms debated by vibrationists and fluidists, mechanisms that are responsible not only for mental "images" (however defined) but also for all vital messages.

I stated earlier that the choice between opposing paradigms of sensibility can be a conciliatory one. This is especially true when a Western European context frames the discussion. There seems to be no unequivocal evidence that either the vibrationist or the fluidist models dominated in Western Europe. The fluidist position is defended as early as 1715 by Raymond Vieussens, if not earlier, while the vibrationist theory is defended as late as 1761 by Robinet. But the terminologies of both positions are avoided in 1779 by Daniel Delaroche, a follower of Haller, and in 1802 by P. J. G. Cabanis. At mid-century (1749), Hartley speaks of medullary particles not easily disposed "to receive and communicate vibrations," and says that "vibrations which ascend along any sensory nerve affect the region of the brain which corresponds to this sensory nerve" (*Observations*, 1:23–24). On the other hand, Le Cat refutes vibrationist theory in 1767. Nevertheless, throughout the middle decades, Diderot oscillates between the two positions while Condillac expresses indifference regarding the origins of knowledge—whether animal spirits or vibrations.

There is also uncertainty in Great Britain. Jacques-Bénigne Winslow's French treatise of 1732 enjoyed a second edition of its translation in 1743, and Winslow accepts animal spirits while posing questions about nerve endings. Hume speaks of nerves and animal spirits without detail, and mentions our ignorance of the force or energy by which bodies and minds act on one another. Most intriguing of all is Cheselden's inconclusive report that accepts Alexander Monro's authority about "many small distinct threads running parallel, without any cavity observable in them" (Cheselden, *Anatomy*, 247–48).

Cheselden also states frankly that he is unable to side either with the vibrationists or with the fluidists, declaring that whereas the sensory role of nerves is indisputable, "how they convey those sensations to the brain is a matter of great dispute" (247). The adjective "great" appears in the fourth edition of 1730, and early editions record "the most general opinion" that nerves are "tubes to contain animal spirits, by whose motions these sensations are conveyed: and diligent inquiry has been made to discover their cavities, but hitherto in vain." He then conjectures that "if each nerve is distinct from its origin, as I have endeavored to show, and too small to be the object of the best microscope, I do not see how such cavities are like to be discovered." In spite of all, Cheselden then qualifies: "Nevertheless, nerves may be tubes, and *possibly* a fluid, whose cohesion is very little, and whose parts, no finer than light, may move freely in them" (247–48). In a significant shift, the later 1760 edition states more directly: "However, I think the nerves may be tubes and *that* a fluid, whose cohesion is very little" (236–37, emphasis added).

This brief survey illustrates the type of question that makes the debate a concern for historians of science: "What anatomical structures and mechanisms mediate sensation?" At the same time, it bears remembering Condillac's indifference to such explanations with reference to the origins of knowledge. His psychological step toward the conversion of sensory signals prompts questions about the extent of his materialism. The lesson of the polyp is instructive in this regard. The simple cybernetic whole that is the polyp's organism was explained by René-Antoine Ferchault de Réaumur and Charles Bonnet in terms of a newly defined, non-Cartesian soul. But did this mean that the polyp's mechanical autoregulation could therefore be regarded as a primitive prototype of the self-directive process that Aram Vartanian reconciles with the concept of "l'homme machine"? (*La Mettrie's "L'homme machine,"* 135).

The advancing monism in eighteenth-century thought broke down mechanistic dualism in biology, but scientists perpetuated the mind-body split in other ways. They eliminated the teleology of soul by endowing matter with self-organizing powers, yet their account left intact the mystery of a designing intelligence. Their explanation was that organized matter displayed performative abilities, a performance that for subrational organisms indicates a special tier of sensory knowledge and, in beasts, of emotive capability. The primal unit for measuring a level or tier was the polyp's irritability and its soul-like aptitude for regenerating itself. The question to consider is whether these capacities comprise a form of pre-linguistic cognition.

The step from here to Goya's Universal Language of dream cognition is attempted, if not completed, in this volume. Instead of attending to the mechanics of sensory transmission, I ask about the nature of the neural signal itself. The emphasis is on transformation: the change of material sense data into immaterial perceptions and ideas. Posing the issue in this way shifts the focus to the phenomena of signals: neural, engrammic, and finally linguistic. Physiology continues to be a prime source of evidence in this volume, but the problem of transmission, while a part of the discussion, is exchanged for that of inscription. As an alternative issue, the signaling process shapes a reading of texts that differs from conventional studies in biology in a way that creates a new subject matter. For example, in Cheselden's previously cited account of nerve fiber activity, the newly interesting element is his rhetoric of qualification: "possibly a fluid . . . whose parts, no finer than light . . ." The word "light," a mere comparison, suddenly appears crucial, for it implies an aethereal matter. If he is assuming the presence of aether, then tubelike nerves would not be an obligatory conduit. The mechanism of passage ceases to be a foreground problem and interest can shift to the implications of aether theory, which extends to qualities and to esoteric powers that affect the nature of cognition and of reality itself. But I am getting ahead of my exposition.

1. The Discontinuity Beneath Continuity

> And indeed, since there is no connection between each sensation and the object that occasions it, or at least the object to which we relate it, it does not seem that any possible passage from one to the other can be found through reasoning. Only a kind of instinct, surer than reason itself, can compel us to leap so great a gap. . . . Therefore, let us believe without wavering that in fact our sensations have the cause outside ourselves which we suppose them to have.
>
> —d'Alembert, *Preliminary Discourse*

The preceding pages brought the unrelated entities of polyps and poets into the same context as Goya's *Capricho 43*, "The Sleep/Dream of Reason Produces Monsters." The shared feature of all three entities was sensibility, and this feature spread a conceptual canopy over frankly discontinuous fields of knowledge: biology, literature, and art. I suggested that to investigate the nature of sensibility would involve eventually seeking its neurophysiological roots. The object of inquiry in all cases thus would be fundamentally one and the same—the cognitive process—even though the surface fields of inquiry seem to have discontinuous boundaries. It is worth observing, furthermore, that my own reasoned discourse supplied connections that maintained the continuity of subject matters.

Reason therefore looms as the ideal guarantor of continuity, today and in past eras. This role explains why the emblems for the eighteenth-century concept of continuity were the Chain of Being and the clock. Each emblem invoked the unbroken intelligibility of a universe composed of perfectly fitting parts. This continuity, however, belonged to an ideal or generic order. The concrete performances of Reason were neither uniform nor consistent, as I argued in Volume 1, *Counter-Rational Reason in the Eighteenth Century*. Reason functioned polymorphically: the prudent, truth-bearing Minervan Reason of the Christian Enlightenment contended with aberrant forms of the rational faculty. Yet aberration did not necessarily mean error. Indeed, if Minerva was the authentic goddess of wisdom in all its forms, her Reason would connect everything and conceivably would encompass Unreason itself, the irrationality practiced by artists like Goya that also bore cognitive fruit.

The suggestion in these next chapters is that, regardless of Reason's shape, its goal has been the continuity of knowledge. The contents of cognition for a poet is of course qualitatively different from the "information" that a polyp commands. (The difference between the poet's abstract understanding and the polyp's physiological ability is addressed in Chapter 8.) At any level of vital performance, however, the organism performs an externalizing gesture. A material point of contact furnishes a sentient link between epidermis and environment. So too does a figurative continuity put the subjective mind in contact with an external object by means of postsensory signals and linguistic signs. Here, at the individual level of "mind," the material continuity seems to break down. The discontinuity resists repair despite the efforts of Reason or science to demonstrate unity in monist or materialist terms. The evidence of this failure resides in the literature of anatomy and physiology that will occupy many of the chapters that follow.

The core of this evidence concerns more fundamentally the signaling mechanism in the neurocerebral system. But even at speculative levels of discourse, eighteenth-century authors betray concern over the discontinuities between dissimilar realms. How, for instance, does one bridge the domains of science and art? In this perspective, the findings of rival biologists and natural philosophers grow less conflictive, just as today's scholarly disagreement over scientific paradigms diminishes in importance. The most encompassing paradigm of all is the motto "Universal Language" inscribed by Goya in his preliminary sketch for *Capricho 43* (Fig. 2). In this sketch, as Volume 1 described, the inscription "Universal Language" will become an erased concept for the final scene in *Capricho 43*. The inscription will be replaced by one that is more inclusive and that verbalizes the scene as "The Sleep/Dream of Reason Produces Monsters." Both works by Goya seek answers to the puzzle of how reality is to be defined, and on what cognitive grounds.

The place vacated by Reason in Goya's works is filled with discontinuity of several kinds: between text and picture, between one species of animal and another, and between a confidently perceived reality and the troubling uncertainty of irreality. More than ambiguity, the pictorial and textual elements signify partial meanings that defy connection. That the goddess of wisdom Minerva (the ultimate guarantor of cognitive continuity) now appears virtually unrecognizable in her symbolic metamorpho-

Figure 2. Francisco de Goya. *Sepia Two*. "Idioma universal" (Universal Language). 1797. Courtesy of the Museo del Prado, Madrid.

sis as a quartet of owls suggests that any assurance of continuity must offer more than the conventional Reason of waking life.

The difficulty Goya encountered in depicting a Universal Language of continuity parallels certain philosophical difficulties that defied empirical science in the eighteenth century. The intellectual milieu governed itself, in matters of scientific discovery, by a belief in the validity of an "encyclopedic tree," which the Encyclopedist d'Alembert adapted from Bacon. This metaphor needs to be viewed as the Enlightenment's unstated assumption about "the filiation of the parts of our knowledge" (*Preliminary Discourse* 5). If the figures of the Chain of Being and the clock stood for the unbroken intelligibility of the universe, the *Encyclopédie* stood for the age's faith that "it is readily apparent that the sciences and the arts are mutually supporting, and that consequently there is a chain that binds them together."

These meeting points proved to be poorly connected at the cognitive base where d'Alembert began to describe "the connection that discoveries have with one another." This base is biological, as suggested in the preceding chapter. Yet the more carefully we examine the physiological facts for the light they shed on basic life principles, the more disjoined facts and the significance of facts seem to be. They point to a fundamental discontinuity that lies beneath the self-assured air of unbroken relationships in what might be called the Age of Minerva, an age where the continuities of wisdom and Reason betray baffling fault-lines. That is, it is both accurate and misleading to think of "the connection that discoveries have with one another" as characteristic of natural philosophy. Scientific progress encouraged the belief in a continuous universe, including the liaisons of integrated knowledge. However, the advances beyond earlier biological science were marked by an increasingly sophisticated concept of science that took distance from its parent, natural philosophy, abandoning speculation about the nature of vitality, mentality, spirit, and other enigmatic principles. In this way, science inadvertently inherited theology's role as the authority for the expedient credence vested in larger unproven principles such as continuity.

The general confidence expressed in the advances made by Reason needs no proof. What seems important is that the scientific reports embodying such advances also reveal to us inadequate explanations for the assumptions behind reported facts. This inadequacy has nothing to do with any deficit relative to more modern findings. The explanations were inadequate on their own terms, on the basis of eigthteenth-century principles inferred from the reported facts. Many crucial terms asserted their scientific power by metaphorical means. Once those terms are analyzed as the metaphors they are, they elude empiricism and escape into another realm. A good example is the following passage from La Mettrie's *L'homme machine*:

> The body is but a clock, whose new pith [*suc*] is the clockmaker. When it enters the body, nature's first care is to excite a sort of fever that chemists who think only of ovens have taken for a fermentation. This fever procures a greater filtration of spirits that mechanically animate the muscles and the heart. . . . These are the causes or the forces of life. (138–39)

The woeful inadequacy here of both philosophical precision and physiological description is plain enough. La Mettrie does not distinguish between the "causes" of life and the "forces" that keep it going. Clocks do not have a "pith." How can heat work like a coiled spring? If these terms are analogous, can heat fit into a filtering model? What clock has a filter? What does "animate" mean and how does it differ from motion? If these activities are synonymous, why does a rolling stone lack "the forces of life"? And so on. Questions along these lines may have given La Mettrie and others pause, but their doubts do not seem to modulate the quotation, whose assertive style matches the confident tone of its explanation.

If such confidence were confined to a specialized discipline or sector, the breakdown of continuist beliefs in integrated knowledge would be less significant. But the inconsistency was reflected in eighteenth-century society at large, where such beliefs shaped the very signs of cultural discourse, and particularly the visual signs attached to intellectual communication. The aperture between empirical and speculative beliefs is noticeable in a certain class of illustrations for books on natural philosophy, as the next section shows. This iconological aperture permitted contemporary readers to expand their verbal understanding through visual means. But visual images also abet the irrational side of reading. Whereas diagrams might enhance rational understanding, other visual illustrations proved susceptible to less rational paths. The act of reading exerts its prerogatives, and readers might ponder text and picture in an imaginative way. Occasional lapses into private musings or subjective associations need not be unique to a given reader. Certain illustrations also lend themselves to allegory. Signs and conceptual associations slip into a collective domain of tacit communication and overtly exchanged beliefs. On the rare occasions when such cultural processes are captured allegorically by a paradigmatic statement of the sort inspired by Goya's *Capricho 43*, the statement gathers momentum from earlier interplays of image and word. These interplays were later condensed into richly nuanced pictorial enigmas.

A Subversive Allegory of Scientific Faith

One such condensed allegory is the frontispiece decorating the *Traité des sensations et des passions* (1767) by Claude-Nicolas Le Cat (Fig. 3). The assured tones of this treatise are brightened by the author's belief in the connectedness of things, but the brooding frontispiece throws a shadow on the idea of linkages. As an engraving, it is a richly detailed execution. It integrates the five senses into a circle of five scenes, a design that appears to illustrate the continuity of sense perception.

The illustration gleams at its summit. A pagan deity, his crown emanating rays of light, straddles an eagle whose beak sends out lightning bolts. These symbols of immortal clarity depict the world of abstract "Truth" placed at a zenith beyond the senses. Descending from the deity are a series of conventional allegories. Counterclockwise, "Sight" is represented as a female regarding her body in a mirror. Just below, "Taste" is a matron pouring liquor into the cup of a garlanded man. Via this route the eye reaches the lower portion of the page. Descending clockwise from the deity's left side are "Hearing" as a female lyre-player, and "Smell" burning fragrances that rise from an urn wreathed in flowers. The scene at the bottom of the circle, diametrically opposite the crowned deity of Truth presiding at the summit, shows a goddess sitting in her chariot, accompanied by a cherub and two doves. She accepts the gift of a helmet offered by a blacksmith.

It would seem that the bottommost scene completes the circle by allegorizing "Touch." If this were the case, the unbroken, clocklike progression would epitomize the harmonious connection of the senses within an orderly universe. The abstract deity of Truth would illuminate the celestial summit in a position of supremacy. However, several details undermine that ideal. The two most important senses, held conventionally to be "Sight" and "Hearing," appear on the deity's right and left. Yet the circle of scenes fixes the light-radiating deity in polar association with the allegory of "Touch," which enjoys a similar proximity to another divinity, this time the goddess of the helmet. No other sense occupies this doubly privileged spatial position relative to the gods.

But this bottommost scene involving a helmet does *not* directly allego-

Bacheley del. et sculp.

Figure 3. Untitled. (Allegory of the Five Senses.) Frontispiece to Claude-Nicolas le Cat, *Traité des sensations et des passions*. 1767. Courtesy of the Bibliothèque Nationale, Paris.

rize "Touch." By association with the Minerva-like goddess in the chariot, there is instead a deification of the tactile sense. Through Minerva's immortal power, the status of "Touch" rises above the other senses. The helmet and the blacksmith stand in a metonymous relation to that power.

Where then is the allegory of "Touch"? The real scene depiciting the sense of Touch has yet to be mentioned, and it breaks the circular symmetry prevailing thus far. At the bottom right of the engraving, in its darkest area, an underground scene discloses a forge, where three men beat out weaponry. Thus the tactile faculty is represented by *two* vignettes in Le Cat's frontispiece. The helmet presented to Minerva in one scene derives from the sunless region depicted outside the circle. The duplication elevates the sense of Touch to a privileged rank in the otherwise Newtonian universe of light, and this special ranking interrupts the continuous, circular order ruled by the refulgent deity above. A straight axis unites this celestial divinity with the subterranean materiality of existence. Put another way, the axis joins the abstract and the telluric poles of reality. This diametrical relationship breaks the presumed harmony of the senses. Now a Minervan deity enables direct communication between conventionally divine symbolism (light, knowledge, vital force) and earthly symbolism (darkness, matter, death). The circumvention of ordinary perceptual modes borders on the magical, if not the demonic. A Goyesque atmosphere surrounds the gloomy underworld where the primal activity of manual arts, aided by fire in a cavern deprived of sunlight, produces material artifacts destined for Minervan uses.

This iconic inkling of disruption beneath Le Cat's rational optimism also has its verbal sign. A Latin inscription from Virgil on the engraving reads: "Igneus est ollis vigor et celestis origo sensibus."[1] This tribute to the power of fire and sensory origins is paraphrased in French to mean, "The senses are a gift of the gods. Their power, their wisdom burst forth in each of them." This maxim is reversed by the blacksmith's offering to the goddess. His earthbound sense of Touch now gains primacy over the convention of a celestial origin of the senses. In fact, Touch *is* of celestial origin, now inverted by polarization with the zenith. Minerva, receiving the helmet, situates the divine place elsewhere. Her own divinity confers on

---

1. The phrase had several interpretations. In the Ancient Philosophy, according to one mythographer, Virgil said of souls "Igneus est ollis vigor, et celestis origo; qu'elles sont formées de ce feu actif qui brille dans les cieux, et qu'elles y retournent après leur séparation d'avec le corps. On retrouve le même doctrine dans le songe de Scipion." Charles François Dupuis, *Abrégé de l'origine de tous les cultes* (1794) (Paris: Lebigre Frères, 1836), 421.

Touch a supremacy equal to the abstract or nonsensory Truth, personified by the celestial deity above.

The diptychal vignette of Touch contrasts with the full sensory circle by its unusual access to the celestial place of abstract Truth. The conventional sensory circuit enjoys no direct link to this abstraction. The gap is manifest because the celestial scene is devoid of sensory references. In the contrasting telluric scene, no such gap disjoins the sensory from the abstract. The Minervan deity, an abstraction, communicates directly with materiality. This communication is a tactile event, and its symbolic meaning may be inferred. Touch clearly bypasses the natural ("clockwork") order of the senses and their coordinated relays. Touch brings a primordial immediate knowledge that can remain independent of the complete sensory circuit. Abstract knowledge, personified by the supreme deity, and the material world, embodied in the blacksmith, are brought into a symbolic subject-object relationship through tangibility. The result is stereognosis, or instantaneous cognition through the connection of surfaces. Touch replaces the delayed gathering of data that characterizes the circuit of five discrete senses. Whereas multiple sensory events are normally relayed in series and only thereafter coordinated, the information supplied tactilely is simultaneous with the physical contact of manual reception. This point will be amplified in later chapters on the language of Touch and the sensibility of polyps.

The privileging of Touch undercuts at least one function of the engraving. As a frontispiece, it ushers in a book about psychology that is marked by Le Cat's rational optimism. Yet the allegory of Touch depicts an extra-rational notion about the fires at the earth's center that are the force and divine origin of knowledge. That an artist might conceive of so imaginative an inaugural illustration for a book about the life sciences in the mid-eighteenth century may not be remarkable in itself. The discrepancy may be explained by absolving the author from responsibility for the book's confection; perhaps scientific publishing at this historical juncture could relax its rigor if an attractive frontispiece could increase sales. In any case, a distinguished scientist like Le Cat could feel uncompromised because he himself regarded extra-rational concepts without antipathy. Indeed, he could not have been unaware of the intellectual residues of Neoplatonic, Paracelsian, and occultist science that mingled with the more sophisticated notions prevailing in his day.

Evidence for the extra-rationalist vein in science may be found in Le Cat's preface, consisting of metaphorical principles that purported to explain natural events. The human body is portrayed as a masterpiece of mechanics, while its architect and creator is "the motor of all things," identified as a "Supreme Being." Le Cat strives to leave no doubt that the mechanist model of human physiology is perfectly integrated. It is "well known" that man is a machine resembling all things mechanical and hydraulic, just like the diverse constructions in physics. But man surpasses all other structures both in harmony and in something called "beauty," owing to an equally indefinable "motor principle" endowed with feelings and capable of spontaneous action. The outlook is elevated by a confident rationalism, and it undergirds Le Cat's materialism. But his attitude is also a foundation that supports metaphors and hypotheses about continuities and universal spirits.

Confident rationalism of this kind took several forms in scientific discourse. One involved the materialism that structured the emerging modern science. The materialist view could not conceive of permanent obstacles to the comprehensive integration of all the parts of knowledge. In this universalist outlook, order governed both the physical world and the moral world of feelings and values. As the respected psychologist P. J. G. Cabanis contended by 1800, the proof of that integrated order is the "secret force" that acts as an organizing agent. This force, said Cabanis, "always active, tends without respite to render this order more general and more complete" (*Rapports*, 2–3). Such a claim was encouraging, and he termed it "a truth" confirmed by the progressive perfectioning and stability of society in the process of realizing "its true goal." The data and mechanisms that permitted Cabanis to believe in this "truth" remained unaccounted for. Nevertheless, he produced a book dealing materialistically with the relations between the physical and the moral realms of man.

The sustaining belief in rational naturalism did not waver before acknowledged mystery. It held that the "force" did exist. The "force" provided material connectedness to sensory and perceptual events. This point of contact between body and mind closed the open circle of links and ties, yet the materialist contact remained a great scientific enigma, a truth that by 1800 persisted without confirmation and to this day is still debated in cybernetic circles. Cabanis admitted that "the manner whereby diverse parts of the nervous system communicate with one another, act upon organs, and determine their functions is still covered with a thick veil" (414). Perhaps the answer could be found in Volta's experiments with electricity, ventured Cabanis without great conviction. His candor is disarming, because it is unreasonable to expect science to penetrate every veil all at once. The effect has been recognized, a reader might say, even when the cause is unknown.

The transmission of vital "force" requires a communicative model in keeping with the premise of universal continuity. But how sound a model can it be when the materialist hypotheses of force and aethereal convection are unprovable? Vital force itself is as verifiable or unverifiable as any of the supernatural hypotheses. Nevertheless, Cabanis's show of self-awareness in regard to methods and procedures seduces the respectful reader. Theory must precede factual knowledge, he cautioned, since "we have not advanced very much in the knowledge of the true processes of Nature" (28). Here Cabanis resorted to a second metaphor, which he compounded by the unproven assumption of "secret threads that tie the disorders of organic parts to those of sensibility." By a "secret" process, emotional disorders are tied to material nerves, but those "threads" "have not always been well grasped." Optimism won out, nonetheless, as Cabanis concluded that "the intimate correspondence of these two types of phenomena" had become increasingly apparent.

The claim rests on the neurophysiological model of fibers, here extended into a vaguer metaphorical "thread." Further evidence is supposed in the experiments with polyps and zoophytes, organisms that represent the midway stages between plant and animal systems and preserve continuity in the full gamut of vital organisms. At the same time, they guarantee the uninterrupted transmission of the elusive "universal spirit" from external to internal states of being. The phenomena are demonstrable in themselves, although their causes remain mysteries formulated as hypothetical explanations. Scientific faith proceeds undeterred, in this instance sustained by Cabanis's vision of infinite progress in the evolution of matter. The "immense variety" of creatures, together with the specific organization of their faculties by species, permits

> all possible degrees of development, from the stupidest mollusk . . . to the eminent being who applies his sensibility to all objects of the universe . . . an organization that itself is subject to a continual and progressive perfecting that presages unknown marvels for us in the centuries ahead. (384–85)

The Cabanis who spoke as a material rationalist also spoke as a plain-spoken scientist. Cabanis was a member of the Medical Society of Paris and the Philosophical Society of Philadelphia. He addressed his post-Revolutionary readers as "citizens," and in 1802 he wrote in a historical vein about the science of his predecessors. Before the current era, useful research was feasible through "the art of reasoning." One could indicate the "general paths of truth," fix the "traits" that identify truth, and trace methods for penetrating the faculties of mind. Nevertheless, added Cabanis, to that day there still existed no precise notion either of

> the manner by which man communicates with the external world, or of the material nature of his ideas. Even less is known of the operations by which the sense organs and the brain receive impressions, much less how these are transformed into sensations or perceived impressions. (440–41)

It is important to note the location of this sketch on the limits of knowledge. It appears in Cabanis's book after he has already presented nine technical dissertations. His book proposes to speak of physiology and pathology in order to reveal the bond between physical life and moral life in human beings. And at the end, Cabanis makes the remarkable confession of ignorance regarding the cornerstone of that binding edifice. Having spoken assuredly of his subject while leaving its premises unexamined, the author now undertakes an unusual tenth dissertation that diverges from the tenor and contents of the preceding nine. Here he encroaches on the irrational world, first discussing sleep, then delirium, and finally what might be called the mechanisms of intangibility. At the time he was writing this, Goya's "Sleep/Dream of Reason" had been suppressed by censorship in Spain for several years, following an initial popularity.

The Scope of the Continuity-Discontinuity Problem

The end-of-century cognitive uncertainty reflected by Cabanis throws in sharp relief the earlier self-assurance of the influential psychologist Condillac, and particularly his belief in continuities, both intellectual and neurophysiological. The metaphorical value of continuity in Condillac's work exceeds its application to the connectedness of external and internal worlds. He uses the same word, "liaison," for distinct spheres of knowledge. "Liaison" is a term to describe scientific inquiry into truth, but it also figures the process of physical-mental exchanges. Repeated words like "combination" and "generation" refer indifferently to the investigation of knowledge or to sense perception. The shift from one to the other is subtle and even logical. Nevertheless, Condillac neglects the distinction between the internal organic process and the external intellectual categories resulting from that process. The inner-outer duality goes unremarked. Instead, the argument is that the sensory-intellectual apparatus produces a "suite of fields of knowledge that so strongly hang upon one another that we cannot reach the most distant ones except by those that precede them" (*Origine des connaissances*, 421). The suite's beginning can be traced to an originary thought, the thought that is generated at the juncture of sense perception and abstraction. Thus the "branches" of knowledge are more than a mere connecting series. They originate in a matrix that itself constitutes a combinatory power. In order to describe this, Condillac allows a single trope to govern the continuities of both neurophysiological transmission and the categories of knowledge. We must "begin by grasping ideas according to their widest liaison. I contend that this liaison is found in the same combination that applies to the very generation of things. We should therefore begin with the first idea that must have produced all the others" (434–35).

Condillac's return to a generative process occurred within the field of influences exerted by the concept of continuity. The pull of this concept was as strong as its repulsion was in Cabanis, for it warded off the spectre of cosmic discontinuity. Eighteenth-century continuity began with a universal scheme of linkages. Continuity also marked the subject-object relation signaled in the organic-sensory "language" of vital performance and survival. This external-internal materiality extended to the internal continuity of material senses and intangible emotions, according to Le Cat and Cabanis. In Condillac, the same metaphor applied both to human nature and to the progress of the mind. Condillac's essay on the origins of human knowledge proposed "the study of the human spirit: not in order to discover its nature but to know its operations, observe the art with which they combine, and how they should be managed by us" (*Origine*, x).

These words stressed a mental process, the organic infrastructure that Condillac studied elsewhere. But at a given point the product of that process becomes the issue. The cognitive process generated knowledge not merely for the individual organism but for the species and its evolving culture. Process at this higher level involved "human spirit" insofar as this means a collective "mind" in its cultural function. Here entered an abstraction that was discontinuous with material processes. The same belief in continuity was evidenced at this level by a concern for genealogy: "We must go back to the origin of our ideas, pursue their generation, follow them to the limits prescribed for them by Nature, and thereby fix the scope and boundaries of our knowledge." Nevertheless, we must note, such an origin could not help but be individual, and not collective, at its inception.

Discovery turned its direction toward the source. This direction, on the human scale, receded toward the internality of cognitive processes, while on the universal scale it looked outward to the cosmic hub of things. The initial step was "to discover a first experience that nobody can put in doubt and that suffices to explain all the others. It should demonstrate plainly what the source of knowledge is, what its materials are, what principle sets them into motion" (xi). Condillac focused on this human scale, and his first step toward discovering originary experience was to consider the human organism as a statue that gradually awakens into a sentient being. Let us note, nevertheless, that the human scale differs from the cosmic scale. It ranges only from the external senses to the physical brain, and thence to abstract mind or spirit, whereas the cosmic scale ranges from individual circumstance to Nature itself, and then to the primal stuff of reality from which they both spring.

At this point, two different paths beckon. As if to acknowledge subliminally the alternatives, Condillac and Goya responded accordingly. The cosmic and primal scale was the path taken by Goya's irrational exploration of reality and the perception of it. The human scale was the path back to neurophysiology, which belonged logically to Condillac's analysis of sensation. However, Condillac did not abandon dualism. He omitted a cerebro-neural explanation of simple and compound ideas, the doctrine held by his predecessor Locke. He went no further than to declare that the subject receives real knowledge of the object through a conversion process that transforms a series of sensory and apperceptive data into ever more abstract combinations of ideas. This account neglected a crucial element. It assumed that the mental representation of perceived objects is faithful, and that the fidelity is sealed by verbal language. The assumption would later come under assault by modern philosophers who deny any reality to the represented object other than a linguistic one. Indeed, Locke already expounded a linguistic "presence to the mind," as John Yolton has argued. In any such view, no material reality can be said to exist in verbal representation, and still less in the further remove that Jacques Derrida calls "Writing."

The assumption of representational fidelity was nevertheless confirmed in the materialist terms of Condillac's rationalizing epoch. The basis of that confirmation was the idea of material continuity, as I have indicated. A substantive "force," energy, or aether imbued the process of transmitting impulses from the perceived object to a coordinating intelligence. This unbroken materiality between subject and object, and from individual to cosmos, ensured unity throughout as well as concrete knowledge: the cognitive surety of real objects whose external presence can never be challenged.

The unbroken continuum was also a question of time as well as matter. The neurophysiologist Daniel Delaroche indicated as much when he refined perception by forming two sequential groups of sensations. Here, he implied a delay of some kind. The "sensations of consciousness" were sensations of the mind knowing that it experiences impressions. But these impressions are in fact earlier "sensations of apperception," which attend to ideas, memories, and desires. If thinking and feeling occur simultaneously, both with each other and also simultaneous with their origin in external stimuli, then the continuum can be said to be preserved in time no less than in aethereal matter. But all such guarantees depended on material continuity, making this concept a widespread preoccupation as well as an article of faith.

Preoccupation with continuity was justified because the hints of a threatening discontinuity troubled materialist explanations. In psychologist David Hartley's view, different aethereal densities "may almost be an Interruption or Discontinuity" of the medullary substance (*Observations*, 1:23). While Hartley believed in vibrations, their feebleness prevented him from being lured into the rational confidence manfiested by Cabanis and Le Cat. He noted that microscopic anatomy cannot trace out the nerve fibers that dissolve in the soft matter of the brain. And so "we must content ourselves with such conjectures as the phenomena shall suggest, trying them by one another, and admitting for the present those which appear more consistent on the whole, till farther light appears." The procedure was scientifically modern, although its empirical utility flickered wanly in "the same, or even a greater obscurity [that] attends all inquiries into the uses of the particular shape and protuberances of the medullary substance of the brain" (1:19).

At the macroscopic end of the universe, the concept of continuity was a question of cause and effect in nature. And here a comparable obscurity befell the natural history attempted by the great naturalist Buffon. In order to "pierce the night of past time," Buffon studied current phenomena by the method of comparison. His pronounced aim was to examine origins long since vanished and to pursue "the historical truth of shrouded events" (*Histoire naturelle*, ed. Varloot, 247). Buffon's scientific method is impeccable. He mocks the prestigious academician and entomologist Réaumur for describing bees as a social community, and he calls it a humanizing account. Because we cannot understand every connection, "even disorder itself, provided it is constant, seems to us a harmony when we are ignorant of the causes" (148). This is folly, and the solution is "to recognize an order that is relative to our own nature instead of making that order intrinsic to the things we study" (45).

In this way Buffon circumvented the rationalist self-assurance of materialism while remaining a skeptical optimist. The same metaphor of connectedness governed his vision of natural history. In this account, observed vestiges and monuments attest to the earliest epochs and traditions that are linked to subsequent ages. These observable facts bring us close to the origin of Nature, "after which we attempt to tie the entirety by analogies, and to form a chain that, from the peak of the ladder of time, descends down to us" (247). If these prospects for understanding causality seem bright, the descending "chain" remained for Buffon an idealistic glow. It only reminded him that even though "the weak light that guides us might become strong enough for us to perceive the general order of causes and effects," genius itself will never be brilliant enough to complete the connections. Knowledge of "first causes will always be hidden from us." In such moods, Buffon shied away from the rationalist confidence of his colleagues, without characterizing the unknown in the irrationalist terms of the older science. The problem of causality was the most baffling issue that he, along with Hume, had to confront. Behind the factual order of his discourse, a rare admission can be glimpsed:

> It will be as difficult for us to know the general results of these causes as to know the causes themselves. All that is possible for us is to perceive some particular effects . . . and in the end to recognize an order that is relative to our own nature. (45)

Mind Discontinuous from Matter

The history of science illustrates continuity nicely with Descartes's plenum, a space where aether particles are always in motion and there are no empty interstices. Movement entails the incessant collision and contact of particles throughout the entire closed "chain." By this model, as historian Edmond Whittaker explained, aether theory serves natural philosophy, which tried to account for actions transmitted between bodies not in contact with each other, as occurs in the effects of moontides and magnets. Despite the apparent disjunctions in such phenomena, the continuity truly existed for Descartes as a material condition.

The theory of aether, however, was not demonstrable empirically in the eighteenth century, certainly not for the purposes of the natural philosophers already cited who were concerned with cognitive physiology. The visible void between perceived objects, as well as the separation of subject from object, impressed their everyday reality on the enlightened observer. As noted, the illustrator of Le Cat's scientific world transformed the conventional premises behind scientific beliefs into an imaginative fantasy. The illustrator's allegory led to the edge of an esoteric rendition of sensory and cognitive understanding. His effort justifies further inquiry into the type of visual representation that might emerge when an artist ponders the dilemma of a continuity not corroborated by the senses. If such an artist disbelieved the reality of a continuous universe, his imagery might show disjunctions in symbolic juxtapositions as well as realistic ones. Or, if the artist did believe in continuity but could not represent it by ordinary sensorial representation, his imagery might resort to another form of perception, such as dreaming. These alternatives existed for artists engaged in manifold spheres of intellectual experience and creative response. They provide one avenue of interpretation for Goya's *Capricho 43*.

Goya's etching comprises three concentric domains. At the center is the sleeper or dreamer; a middle perimeter is ringed by the owls and the feline; this ring separates a wilder, outermost domain of bats removed from the human center. The three domains pose their theme of discontinuity in several ways. Are the beasts actually "out there" in the same space occupied by the human figure? If so, what connection can there be among the species in this nonempirical reality invented by Goya? The composition does in effect encourage interpretation along the lines of metamorphosis, as I suggest in a later chapter. But there remains the discontinuity between the insentient subject and the monsters around him. At the same time, the creatures might be images dreamed by the sleeper and projected into imaginary space for the spectator's benefit. If so, what sort of continuity permits these private representations to be viewed by our conscious perception? What connection is there between any two individuals' mental screens, whether unconscious or awake? How are the dreamed creatures connected to one another? Does the feline, for instance, occupy the same imaginary space as the owls? Is there no discontinuity between the owls and the bats by virtue of their species' difference and what this signifies?

Contemplated in this way, *Capricho 43* seriously challenges the ideal of continuism. This ideal has two formulations. If the eighteenth century's ambition was to devise a unifying system that embraces both matter and the ways of knowing matter, then Goya set an obstacle: he depicted phantasmal beings that defy materiality. His choice of animals poses the taxonomical problem facing Buffon. A further difficulty is the breach between standard animals and "monsters," as these creatures are termed by the inscription on the desk. Moreover, if the ideal of continuism aimed to integrate the perceived external space with the perceiving inner space, then Goya set the obstacle of incongruent perspectives and unequal time lapses.

If these obstacles were overcome, continuity would consist of the following synthesis. External and internal worlds emerge from the individual's perceptual act as a sensible totality, which itself is abstracted into a conception. The sum of all such conceptions is also a totality, made manifest by a unified system of human knowledge. This knowledge rises integrally from within the perceiving universe. In short, externality and internality relate to each other as an object that becomes involuted by the subject and is turned again outward in the guise of objective reality.

Such a synthesis is untenable, because of its inability to make connections in the philosophical and physiological areas, to be outlined in the chapters that follow. Connectedness can be schematized graphically by a descending scale of putative linkages, like the branches that grow out of each other in d'Alembert's diagrammed tree in the *Encyclopédie*. This knowledge is continuous with living matter by the simple fact that a human mind produces it. The mind inhabits a living organism that in turn is continuous with other organisms in its species. The generations of human species are continuous, as are the various species with one another down the evolutionary scale and through the plant kingdom, if not further into the mineral realm, as some theories claimed. In the individual organism, the physiological parts are linked within a single system: muscles are continuous with nerves, and some nerves seem to connect the epidermis to the brain. At this level the problems of discontinuity begin. At the epidermal surface, the object sensed and the sensation registered by the nerve ending are disconnected and mediated by space, except for the sense of touch. The sensory impulses from nerve to brain traverse an unmapped medullary terrain. Equally unknown is the connecting mechanism that synchronizes diverse sensations into one perception—the size, color, and scent of a rose. As for the conversion of this perception into an idea, where the word "rose" represents the thing in itself, its site is an unexplained space between those two events—one more discontinuity.

Among the empirical philosophers, Hume declared his ignorance of the connecting power, although he called it *belief*. Ideas are associated or linked in a series by the act of fixing attention on the succession of images, while the intervals between ideas are linked by a belief based on customary conjunctions derived or inferred from past experience. Such expectations are purely internal, and they occur without sensory intervention. Thus their mechanical aspect differs but little from the nonsensory act of dreaming, except that in one instance the subject is awake and is able to control the intensity of attention. The same attaching power or intensity was also cited in the *Encyclopédie*, which held separate entries for "Dream" and "Dreaming [To Dream]." The entry for the verb "Songer" bears the clarifying tag, "active verb, metaphysics," intended to alert us to the cognitive implications of the dreaming mechanism, as distinct from the dream that it produces. The article evokes Humean terminology by its reference to the mind's "application" to objects, akin to Hume's description of connecting power; the resemblance extends to its reference to the mind's manner of "attaching itself" or paying attention to the "suite of ideas."

Although the mind-body division was a classic dilemma, efforts to overcome it drew fresh impetus with the advent of eighteenth-century skepticism. Hume's stress on the nonsensory bridge of belief did not narrow the rift. A further insight could be gained from the parallel between dreamwork and nonsensory attention as it implicates this passage in Buffon:

> We can believe that there is something outside of us, but we are not sure, whereas we are assured of the real existence of everything within us. The real existence of our mind is thus certain, and that of our body seems doubtful, since we end by thinking that matter can well be nothing more than a mode of our mind, one of its ways of seeing. Our mind sees in this way when awake and that way during sleep, and it will see in yet a different way after our death. Everything, matter in general, that causes the sensations of mind today could very well no longer exist for it when our own body no longer exists for us. (Varloot, 112)

Here the objects of attention are focused with regard to their perceived existence, which in effect addresses the nature of reality itself. The question is how close to reality our mental experiences are when we depict matter. Buffon's version of how spirit asserts itself over matter gives the materialist little comfort. He points out that during sleep the mind is affected by sensations despite the objects' absence. If we consider this fact, he adds, we realize that such sensations often differ from those experienced when our waking senses are at work. This being the case, should we not affirm that the presence of objects is irrelevant to the nature of reality? As Goya suggested, the bats are no less real for being present in the dreamer's mind, even though they are not materially present. And conversely, the mind surely must exist independently of material objects, because it can conceive their existence in their absence.

Buffon concluded that, yes, mind is discontinuous from matter and can persist independently. In fact, "during sleep and after death, our bodies exist," although the mind no longer perceives the existence. That the *mind* might cease to exist did not enter Buffon's reasoning. Rather, in sleep and death the bodily existence "ceases to be for us." And if that was the case, if a thing first could be and then could cease to be, or if it affects us now in a way so different from what it was, then perhaps this thing is not real enough to confirm its existence. Reality enjoys a status that outranks material existence.

As a naturalist, Buffon proceeded on the assumption that matter exists, but he coincided with Diderot in denying that its existence is demonstrable. Rather than following George Berkeley in the open denial of material existence, Buffon paralleled the argument in Diderot's *Letter on the Blind* (Varloot, 322). We may add to this that Buffon introduced the nuance of cognitive belief. This premise, more than a working assumption at the level of scientific observation, operates philosophically as a believed hypothesis. The emphasis on the act of belief, rather than on plausibility, also dominated Hume's orientation, as noted earlier.

What Hume asked regarding an object, Goya asked regarding the bat: in what manner do we know an entity? Each microinstant is the occasion for our recording a sensory impression of the bat. The perceptual result in real space may derive from a series of epidermal sensations of batwings fanning the air around the head and temples, or from the sounds of whirring wings, or the sightings of a shape registered on the retina. Whatever the components of the sensory sequence, they are somehow fused into what the mind believes to be a single image whose abstract sign is "bat." But in fact the mind receives a succession of disconnected impressions, converted into as many "sub-images" that follow each other in time. The chain of bats in *Capricho 43* is the pictorial equivalent of what happens when impressions follow one another in a chain that soon will collapse into a single superimposition or compounded perception of the bat. The temporal sequence is imperceptible in human time, and it is represented by spacing: the same bat occupies a different location in the air, corresponding to different microinstants in the dream sequence.

The bats submit to other interpretations as well, but the one just advanced is relevant to Hume's recognition of discontinuity. Goya depicted a dream that operated no less extrasensorially than the Humean mechanism of belief. That is, a single bat, and not a squadron, forms the dream content, together with the row of owls, which represent a single owl undergoing transformation as the dream progresses in time (Fig. 4). One might ask about the direction of these transformations—whether from large to small in the case of the bat, or from calm to wild in the case of the owl, or the contrary—but the question is irrelevant here. Other digressive features arise directly from the Humean interpretation, and they should be noted briefly in passing. The process of metamorphosis also affects our understanding of the scene. First, for the owl to change from a mustachioed pedant into a wild creature implies a certain judgment about Reason, knowledge, and wisdom. Second, if the band of owls represents the progression of images experienced temporally by the dreamer, who is to say that the dream does not grow nightmarish by a metamorphosis of the fourth, rightmost owl into the owlish bat just above it? In that case, the ring of owls blending into the ranks of bats is a transformation that overcomes generic discontinuities of taxonomy and shape. Finally, although "images" is the term applied to these beings and events, the images are neither optical nor sensorial. The reality known through dreaming seems to be unmediated and direct. It might be said that a dream cognition surmounts the discontinuity between material and immaterial existence and preserves reality in its full presence.

The subject-object discontinuity just reviewed raises the issue of "presence." An object's "presence" is defined in terms of the subject's direct knowledge of its existence and qualities. The state of being of Goya's bat or any other object is present simultaneously both where it is and also fully and identically in the subject's mind. Such an event would appear impossible on two counts. First, it would split the concept of identity into two ontic modes, whereby the bat would "be" there and here at the same time. This state of being seems materially a contradiction, although it is conceivable in the immaterial circumstance of dreams. Second, the bat's full presence in the subject's mind is impossible from the standpoint of representational signs. Between the knowing mind and the object intervene stages of cognitive events, from sensory signals to percepts to verbal signs, all of which displace the object's presence. Nevertheless, this objection regards signs as a language that substitutes its own reality for that of the object. Goya's effort, in contrast, explores dreaming in a quest for a "Universal Language" that obeys quite another phenomenology.

The notion that mind is discontinuous from matter refers to the

Figure 4. Francisco de Goya. *Capricho 43*. Detail of owls. 1798–99. Courtesy of the Norton Simon Foundation, Pasadena, California.

waking reality, not to the reality that is "present" in the oneiric circumstance. Goya's perspective calls attention to what natural philosophy and neurophysiology sidestep—namely, that verbal language itself is responsible for such concepts as identity, subject, and object. Conventional signs block the presence of raw reality. Language is said to "represent" reality, but in truth it creates its own reality. It organizes the components of reality through signs and categories that constitute a distancing hierarchy that interferes with presence. Reality itself stands beyond language in its raw state of undifferentiated phenomena. In "raw" reality, there is no need for such concepts as identity, difference, and similitude. But waking language overlays reality with a taxonomical grid that organizes phenomena so as to conceal the naked chaos beneath.[2] As that chaos has no name, it cannot enter scientific discourse. Being accessible intuitively, however, as through Goya's dream or a poet's imagery, it may elicit an irrational treatment that resolves the problem of discontinuity in less rational terms.

Disjuncture and the Credent Imagination

The dualist rift that biology could not resolve was healed by an invigorated concept of imagination in art, poetry, and philosophy. The bias against the faculty of imagination that derived from Neoclassical doctrine and pietistic thinking survived throughout the eighteenth century. Even the sagacious Samuel Johnson declaimed against imagination in his works, notably *Rasselas*. Yet a concurrent favorable attitude also exerted wide appeal, so that the very concept of imagination came to depend on how this faculty functioned. From one standpoint, both artistic "good taste" and sound philosophical reasoning risked being harmed by an unchecked imagination. But from the standpoint of the psychological faculties, imagination played an indispensable role in combining simple ideas for conceptual ends. This associationist principle was reinforced by artistic and philosophical sources alike. David Hume cited the fortifying power of imagination in begetting "belief," which is the governing principle of judgment. Going further than skeptical philosophy, Goya furnished evidence of the superior power of an

2. This arbitrary grid has been analyzed by Foucault in *Les mots et les choses* (Paris: Gallimard, 1966) on the model of Borges's monstrous encyclopedia. It is Goya, however, who reveals the awesome truth about the veil concealing reality's presence. He depicts an oneiric reality in *Capricho 43* as a response to his quest for the cognitive mechanism that seals the rift between mind and matter.

unsupervised imagination in *Capricho 43*. The product of this faculty was a Minervan truth, a "dream of monsters" that exposed raw reality for the anarchy that it is after it is stripped of its epidermal rational continuity.

Imagination ultimately played opposing roles. On one hand it supplied the continuity that otherwise remained missing, and on the other it exposed the most radical discontinuity of all. But this opposition did not result from any defect in the imaginative faculty itself. Instead, mutually exclusive conceptions of reality came into conflict. The empirical community preserved its value system of rationally shared and communicable experiences. But another kind of experience, expressed tentatively by Goya, defined reality by more individual and intuitive perceptions that took rational communication to be ineffective. A reality conceived so haphazardly could in fact be discontinuous after all. So long as imagination is yoked to the categories of identity and difference, a bat is not an owl and the branchlike hierarchy of encyclopedias is preserved in its continuity. But the imagination free to perform in the wordless theater of dreams apprehends reality by rules that no longer correspond to the continuist ideal. No longer does a main trunk exist to support the branching specimens of dream knowledge. No connecting threads are attached to the coordinating center of Diderot's spider-brain universe.[3] If such a web exists at all, it attaches to the object's presence by means of an undiscovered dream mechanism.

What Goya freed from Reason's control in 1798 was an indifferent faculty—not a reconstructing agent that would duplicate Reason but a witness to Chaos. Imagination had not yet become a concept that Wordsworth in 1805 would call the "willful Fancy," the transcendent force that stabilizes thought around a "substantial centre." On the contrary, Goya's monsters resulted from his decentering the Enlightenment's perspective by means of the same faculty that Hume cited as responsible for that perspective's ideal. Whereas the continuist ideal surrendered presence for a representational reality mediated by rational signs, the Goyesque imagination fathomed the disorder underlying that reality. The surface that imposed order with the complicity of imagination in the employ of an empirical value system dissolved into another order judged "monstrous" by empirical values.

It is instructive to note briefly how Romanticism, following on the heels of Goya, channeled the power of imagination for the absolute harnessing of an anarchic universe. Wordsworth's "willful Fancy" was a con-

---

3. Denis Diderot, *Rameau's Nephew. D'Alembert's Dream*, trans. L. W. Tancock (Baltimore: Penguin, 1966), 183.

structive partner, with "engrafted far-fetched shapes on feelings bred / By pure imagination." A new duality marking the nonrational faculty gave access both to Chaos and to the centered ground that orders it. Despite "the fervent swarm / Of these vagaries," the poet had "forms distinct / To steady me: each airy thought revolved / Round a substantial center." He probes the blind turmoil of primal feeling aided by Fancy, a "busy Power" equipped with a "ready pupil turned / Instinctively to human passions, then / Least understood" (*The Prelude*, 8:421–31). Yet this cognitive role was more than personal. Imagination exposed the discontinuous essence of things, described in Wordsworth's metaphor of the cave of the mind where a "senseless mass" is reduced to order. His mental torch "sees the vault / Widening on all sides." The roof above him seems to materialize, but it unsettles quickly and recedes. There are shapes and shadows, but also "tendencies to shape / That shift and vanish, change and interchange / Like spectres,—to ferment silent and sublime!" (8:560–72). But this ended any resemblance to the Goyesque night of the mind.

The fearful apparitions that fermented in Goya's world inhered as an elusive condition of Nature. The Romantic cave, in contrast, secures uncertain knowledge, turning convulsion into synthesis. Between both perspectives was Diderot's ambivalent vision, less convulsive than Goya's without reaching the stabilized imagination of Wordsworth. In fact, the Romantic cave inverted Diderot's metaphor for securing knowledge, "a hole drilled suddenly into my door" (*Correspondance*, 9:246). Diderot faces a room shut off from sight, unlike the poet's first impression of a vault that widens its opening. The door is perforated by a word that produces an illuminating hole. Diderot knows the concealed chamber promptly, although briefly, through the luminous word, "like a sunbeam that suddenly lights up the depths of a cavern and dies out." Much the opposite is the perplexing canopy of Wordsworth's spectral knowledge, which at first glimpse is "Substance and Shadow, light and darkness, all / Commingled" (*The Prelude*, 8:568–69). An organic synthesis captures every imaginable shade of reality, on the premise that reality can be contained. Diderot's intelligible room grows instantly dark. Goya captures totality without knowing shades and oppositions, on the premise that reality escapes categories. Thus Wordsworth's "whole cave, so late a senseless mass, / Busies the eye with images and forms / Boldly assembled." Unlike the fixed nature of Goya's reality, which is a silent ferment, there issues a "sublime" and stable order.

The nineteenth-century transcendent imagination was prefigured by

Kant, as shown in Volume 1, *Counter-Rational Reason in the Eighteenth Century*. The unruly eighteenth-century phantoms of mind and matter were not readily dominated by this faculty. Only among the Romantics did confused reality reassemble its components intelligibly in conjunction with a superior mental force. For Diderot, sudden light dispersed the initial confusion that returns to darkness. No such confidence gladdened either Goya's insight into monstrous discontinuity or Diderot's firmer faith in language. Psychological theory was too ruffled by neurophysiological uncertainties for the Enlightenment to confer maximum authority on a single faculty of imagination. Goya's reality was "a senseless mass" empty of meaning and irretrievable amid the unreliable data of diminished senses. In contrast, reality for Wordsworth was "a variegated landscape," thanks to an intellectualizing imagination that was buttressed by what he called "fancy" and restored to its visionary or visual clarity. Just how indecisive the Newtonian, sight-oriented sensibility was with respect to the Romantic metaphors of light and eyesight can be observed by comparing it with the allegory of the senses in Le Cat's frontispiece. Wordsworth confronts "the projections, wrinkles, cavities" of reality and its "ghostly semblance" of animate creatures, as any eighteenth-century observer of a lively mind might. Yet the Romantic poet Wordsworth is able to impose order on the whole, comprehending it as a "Strange congregation!" but one to be viewed by natural light with "Eyes that perceive through minds that can inspire" (8:580–89). The subversion of light and eyesight in the frontispiece for Le Cat by the subterranean Minervan "touchsight"—to coin a term on which I elaborate in Chapter 8—bodes ill for the confidence vested in the harmonious systems of Newtonian and Lockean order. The eighteenth-century debates over eyesight, blindness, and touch also attest to the uncertain roots of perception.

The subsequent reversal of opinion about imagination, among other factors, arose because discontinuity was not a problem for the Romantics who exalted imaginational powers. Dream experience and nocturnal phenomena were intelligible mysteries of a Nature restored to the integrating "oversoul." The Western European Enlightenment cannot know this outcome because its cognitive theory lacks the Germanic concept of primary and secondary modes of imagination that serves the next century. The best that Enlighteners like Hume and La Mettrie could offer was a concept of imagination that made room for an inexplicable "force" that integrated mental and physical operations. Hume admitted to having "sought in vain for an idea of power or necessary connection" between events that seem conjoined. One billiard ball strikes another and the shock produces motion. One event follows the other without his

> being able to comprehend any force or power by which the cause operates or any connection between it and its supposed effect. The same difficulty occurs in contemplating the operations of mind on body, where we observe the motions of the latter to follow upon the volition of the former, but are not able to observe or conceive the tie which binds together the motion and volition. . . . There appears not, throughout all nature, any one instance of connection which is conceivable by us. All events seem entirely loose and separate. One event follows another, but we never can observe any tie between them. They seem *conjoined*, but never *connected* . . . the necessary conclusion *seems* to be that we have no idea of connection or power at all, and that these words are absolutely without any meaning. (*Human Understanding*, 84–85)

Hume reduces his explanation to the idea that the observer "*feels* these events to be connected in his imagination" (86). This feeling, based on previous experiences, is the origin of "belief," the irrational agent that corrects the "sublime" freedom of the imagination and permits us to distinguish fiction from valid beliefs (61–63, 71, 170).

Epistemological belief is a subset of connectedness. It is the adhesive mechanism for mental functions, just as its corresponding subset, aether, is the linking mechanism for material functions, as Chapter 9 indicates. Belief can be construed more narrowly, however. It is also the faith in a religious world view or an intellectual system. But this belief depends on the same adhesive power to bind the contents of thought into a psychological continuity with the subject. Again Goya illustrates the discontinuous eruptions beneath the surface. The dogmatic faith that dominated his cultural milieu produced a tight spiritual organization whose artistic ideology was the Counter-Reformational and Baroque heritage that Goya quickly forsook. Nevertheless, formalist analysis shows that he isolated particular Baroque details, with results that reflect the disintegration of its binding faith. As Theodor Hetzer has pointed out, "something gigantic, uncanny, incalculable" imbues commonplace scenes so that "they no longer form part of a self-contained order" (Licht, 109). Spanish traditionalism preserved the ideological order by placing its gridwork of names and values on a social reality that, like a compressed chaos, would otherwise escape intelligibility and control. The system collapses wherever the grid of belief is removed.

Some form of belief is demanded for all intellectual world views, not only authoritarian systems. The Enlightenment being no exception, its ideology needed to counteract the subversive hints given out by a disjoining imagination such as Goya's. Thus the Encyclopedists developed protective rhetorical strategies while natural scientists, paradoxically, specified technical examples that acknowledge chinks in the armor. The presumed cohesive totality broke down not only in living systems but also in the inorganic ones, as we shall now see. The breakdown occurred, in fact, in the cognitive operations that talked about both kinds of systems.

The idea of encyclopedic knowledge rests on two incompatible tropes. One is a biological metaphor that portrays the disciplines as a tree of words rooted in its axioms. The second metaphor is topological, and it locates each discipline in a space of "field" limited by the adjacent fields. The irksome difficulty of overcoming these separations breeds terms like "overlapping" and "interface," metaphors that merely exacerbate the discontinuity.[4] Thus the systematic unity pursued by the *Encyclopédie* falls afoul of its dichotomous fallacy. Rather than a branching tree structure, encyclopedic order follows the order of syllogistic reasoning. And by this model Jean Starobinski approaches the notion of overlying grids that impose order on a chaotic reality. He echoes Foucault by asking whether the logical model is rather a layer glued artificially over raw anarchic phenomena. He finds the result to be a lamination that passes for homogeneity when actually the overlay is a plywood discourse that conceals its discontinuity with respect to the real heterogeneous netherworld that escapes ordering. The model became an artifice for the Encyclopedists, whose ruse is exposed by such articles as "Stocking," analyzed by Jacques Proust (1977).

Such artifices as "layering" and "overlapping" serve to disguise discontinuity but do not conceal from view the artificer's awareness of their need. Buffon was dedicated to generational and species continuity, but he balked nonetheless at detailed taxonomies. To gather under the same category "the most distant genres, such as putting the bat and the man together into one class, and the elephant and the scaley lizard into the other" is, he insisted, an act of folly (Varloot, 208). Bats and human beings are mammals, as Buffon knew, but their resemblances do not warrant a complex classification system that contrives their proximity vis-à-vis the elephant and the lizard. A more intuitive view of the problem was Goya's blending device. How to classify the indeterminate flying shapes behind the bat, when they can

4. This point is shown in detail by Jean Starobinski in "Remarques sur l'Encyclopédie," *Revue de Métaphysique et de la morale* 75 (1970): 284–91.

be bats or owls or hybrids of both? The blending was Goya's way of exposing Buffon's rational categories of difference and identity. Their futility appears radical when imagination uses dreaming to configure reality. In the pre-rational reality of unclassified forms, the One and the Many seem to be interchangeable. The metamorphic principle available to Buffon also applies to a protean and polymorphic process, where similitude rather than identity is the chief truth.

Nor is the biomorphic world the only realm that requires devices for continuity. The physical cosmos also demands its portion in the universal continuity. But this demand is not satisifed by an external metaphor like the Chain of Being. Even though the human organism is included within the chain, it fits there as one more object. The knowing mind needs also to be included, yet it remains discontinuous from the whole. It is the mind that connects the store of existing things to the abstract system that organizes them. But the latter two realms are not as yet shown to be connected to the mind's own cognitive apparatus.

The desired unification met an obstacle that mathematician Pierre-Louis Maupertuis portrayed as a philosophical debate between monism and dualism. Was it possible for human knowledge to pass from theology to philosophy when these disciplines oversee separate jurisdictional districts? It was true that "the Supreme Being sees the chain that unites these" fields, said Maupertuis, but the chain is beyond human comprehension (*Oeuvres*, 2:168–69). He added that some modern philosophers believed that "Nature does not ever operate by leaps," and this belief permitted them to make "the totality of matter a single block, a single piece, a continuity, without any interruption among their parts" (2:174). However, he was not convinced that the universe is the cohesive totality that Diderot designated by referring to *le tout*. Maupertuis was on his guard, because Diderot had criticized, although also admired, the bold but obscure concept of attractive force, with its corollary ideas of sentient molecules. The mathematician replied that voids also exist in Nature, as evidenced by stellar bodies dispersed in space. But even if voids did not exist, space would always separate the constituents of a material body and thus create discontinuity.

The disagreement between Maupertuis and Diderot is important more for its terms of definition than for its subject. The terms focused on joinings and intervening spaces. Observers were free to decide whether to stress one term or another, whether to focus on links or on separations, on identical traits or on different traits. The choice of perspective necessarily configures data in a manner compatible with the choice; otherwise it would destroy the perspective. Maupertuis demonstrated the dilemma by suggesting that the parts of a diamond are closer together than parts of flimsier bodies, but that they are not any more continuous. We are convinced that the individual body, the diamond, is distinct from another such body. The conviction depends on the chosen perspective of identities. Yet the diamond's identity disintegrates when its constituent parts are themselves regarded as distinct bodies separated by space and hence acquiring other individual identities. The diamond is both continuous in its own identity and discontinuous in being constructed by other identities. Thus Maupertuis could assert that from a certain perspective the universe itself can never comprise a true continuity. The very constituents of material bodies are individually distinct parts, each always being itself and therefore not being something other, regardless of how intimately these constituents join to form the whole that satisfies our belief in its identity.

Where then is continuity grounded if not in the believing mind alone? The connective power behind these constitutive acts resides with the subject, not the object. And this power is the credent imagination. Its function is so basic that Condillac activated it in his statue before full sensory reception is achieved. The statue is only partially humanized and enjoys nothing but the sense of smell when it dreams for the first time. Condillac's point is that imagination retrieves ideas acquired through sensory experience and stored in memory. It then reassembles these ideas by a connecting mechanism that is the same in waking states and in dreams. The statue "does not know any difference at all between imagining vividly and having sensations, and it cannot distinguish dreaming from being awake" (*Traité des sensations*, 1:81). It must believe in their concordance. Condillac's discussion in this passage is dominated by the terms "liaison," "suite of ideas," "chains," and "chainlets" or connections formed by "rings" and links. His continuist ideal quells the suspicion that recombined associations might break away from their origins. Their clear-cut lineage descends from the subject's material needs, and the associations signify only the latter. The terminology contrasts notably with the ambiguous use of terms by Diderot.

Connection was, for Diderot, an essential requisite of mind and Nature, if Chaos is to be denied. He cited a "law of continuity" operating in conditions and substances that are "sensible, living, and organized."[5] The "liaison and consequence" of our reasonings are as necessary for under-

5. *Éléments de physiologie*, vol. 9 of *Oeuvres complètes*, ed. J. Assézat and M. Tourneux (Paris: Garnier Frères, 1875–77), 370.

standing as "the chaining, the liaison of effects, causes, objects, and their qualities" are necessary for Nature (*Éléments*, 9:372). But unlike Condillac, Diderot ignored imagination when discussing intellective mechanisms. He asked, "How can a liaison insert itself between so many disparate sensations, ideas, and sounds so as not to form a chaos of sensations, ideas, and sounds all isolated and disparate but rather a series that we call reasonable, sensible, or connected?" (9:372). The question applies to the faculty of understanding. The reply was that "in Nature there are liaisons between objects and between the parts of an object. This liaison is necessary. It entails a liaison or a necessary succession of sounds corresponding to the necessary succession of things perceived, felt, seen, smelled, or touched." First we see the tree in its parts, one after another, and then we see it in the ensemble that we name "tree," And then,

> As soon as the word "tree" is invented, other signs that are invented link together and are ordered. A suite of sensations, ideas, and words [are] tied together consecutively. Thence is born the faculty of judgment, reason, and speech, although we cannot be occupied by two things at the same time. (9:372)

The passage is relevant again in later chapters, where Diderot's metaphor for the flawed integrity of the cognitive act is "tiny nights" that disrupt the continuous image of a tree. Indeed, Diderot proceeds now to remark that having overly precise ideas about each part of the whole is to have "very precise" ideas about the entirety. An "insurmountable barrier" separates eyesight, imagination, and mind or "spirit." Few of us will have clear notions of the whole, while most others will lack clear notions of the value of the parts, adds Diderot slyly. More aphoristically, "judgment distinguishes among ideas, while genius draws them together" (9:373). There is no plainer instance of the disintegrating potential in eighteenth-century thought than Diderot's. He is not the irrationalist that Goya, from certain interpretive angles, appears to be. But Diderot embarrasses the analytical rationalism upheld by Condillac's model of linear and combinative associations.

While Condillac's metaphor of continuity illustrates his statue's dream, the metaphor also proves to be hazardous. He is bound to acknowledge the disruptive factor that determines dream content, a mechanism that retires in waking thought. But Condillac glosses over disruption by inserting it into the reordering process:

> Many rings in the chain will thus be intercepted, and the order of ideas in sleep cannot be the same as in wakefulness. [Imagination] will only arouse those ideas over which it conserves some power, and it will as often contribute to the statue's unhappiness as to its happiness. (*Traité des sensations*, 1:80–81)

This interceptive factor is assimilated to the linear mechanism and causes the branching phenomena of dream association. Condillac reaffirms the notion of linearity while repeating the feature of interception: "Here then is the dream state: it does not differ from that of waking except that ideas are not kept in the same order, and pleasure is not always the law regulating the imagination. Every dream thus supposes some intercepted ideas on which the mental faculties can no longer act" (1:81).

This network conformed to the century's ideal, but it could not explain what Goya represented in *Capricho 43* or its earlier sketches, *Sepias One* and *Two*. Their discontinuous bats and owls represent branches that stem from separate trunks. Or, to follow Condillac's metaphor, the idea of owls are one linear series that is intercepted by the transverse idea of bats. The newly initiated series interrupts the original one, leaving the latter dehisced at the intercepted "ring." None of the rational metaphors mentioned so far satisfies Goya's dream of Reason. As d'Alembert's metaphor warned, any encyclopedic "tree" that attempted to portray the mind's discontinuities would be "disfigured," and the mathematician shied away from claims for linear continuity in the *Preliminary Discourse*. Similarly, in physiology, a network of fibers branching by continuous venation only permits nodular connections to a vanishing point, as shown by medullary dissolution. So too for Condillac's chain, described in this detailed picture:

> As the chain extends, it subdivides into different chainlets, so that the farther one goes from the first ring, the more these chainlets multiply. A fundamental idea is tied to two or three others, each of the latter to as many or more, and so on. The different chains or chainlets that I suppose to be above each fundamental idea would be tied by the suite of fundamental ideas, and by some rings that would likely be common to many of them, since the same objects and thus the same ideas are often related to different needs. Thus our entire knowledge forms one and the same and single chain, whose chainlets would be joined to certain rings, [only] to be separated from others. (*Traité des sensations*, 1:47)

Discontinuity now shifts to the "different needs" that share the "same ideas." The continuous network seems to link an object and its fundamental idea to a particular need. However, needs are different from one another. Therefore each need is linked to its fundamental idea, each with a series of rings comprising its chainlet. Condillac asserts that several needs are often related to the same idea, so that a particular ring in one chainlet can also serve another chainlet attached to a different need. The contradiction is plain enough, and no diagram can correct it. The ring common to two or more chainlets occurs at a fork or nodule that begins the subdivision ("as the chain extends, it subdivides into different chainlets"). If a succeeding chainlet links with a need, it can do so only by reascending the original chain. It cannot continue along to link with a different need, because any need is linked to its own fundamental idea, which in turn is tied to its own chainlets. The ties between fundamental ideas are due to common chainlets, but these cannot be the ones tied to different needs. They would be chainlets linking different ideas, which themselves were tied to different needs.

Any effort to diagram Condillac's scheme must end in a labyrinth of paths cut off from one another, as when the interceptive factor functions in dreaming. The analysis just concluded reveals the subdividing mechanism of waking life to be nearly as interrupted in its linearity as the branching phenomena mentioned before in dream association. Nevertheless, the ring-and-chainlet model is the core of Condillac's psychology. This is why he must maintain the conformity of waking and dream linkages. His rule permits simplicity for a model that may not tolerate disjunction between the organism's external "needs" and the internal mechanisms that meet such needs. Here the imagination plays its combinatory role. The "happiness" and "pleasure" spoken of earlier stem from needs thus fulfilled. Condillac admits that during dreams "pleasure is not always the law regulating the imagination." But, he argues, while imagination does not always keep ideas in the same order, its connecting mechanism remains unchanged. The conformity restores linearity to Condillac's model while also exonerating imagination from responsibility for the disorderly run of ideas during dreams. Nevertheless, the model does not remove the discontinuity itself.

Paradoxes of Cognitive Disconnection

Goya was a closer observer of dreaming than Condillac; his three versions of dreamwork both confirmed and denied the threat of discontinuity. *Capricho 43*, together with its forerunners *Sepia One* and *Sepia Two*, shared an oneiric element that was continuous among them: above the dreamer there is at least one bat in flight. In *Capricho 43*, indeterminate flying creatures also have owlish traits yet look like bats. A viewer who ignores their differences and combines their similarities can believe they are bats: their identity is that of a generic bat. But a viewer who isolates the features of one flying creature in order to distinguish it from the others may believe instead that they are a motley assortment. This circumstance corresponds to that of Maupertuis's diamond, which alters its identity as the perspective changes and affects the observer's belief.

Capricho 43 and *Sepia Two* expose the connecting role of "belief" in another way. They deploy multiple indeterminate images of the bat and the owl, images that in waking experience collapse into a single allegorical image believed to be stable. Both *Capricho 43* and *Sepia Two* also demonstrate the temporal condition of dreaming: we experience images in a sequence of different split seconds, which are depicted in the placement of the same object on different points in space, but with altered features. Goya seems thus to illustrate the mercurial grounds of reality and the beliefs we may hold concerning it. The ambivalence is expressed by Diderot in the paradoxical terms of a polarity: "the wise man is nothing but a composition of the stupidest molecules" (9:375).

This aphorism depicts the iconic axis of uncertainty among Goya's bats. One pole is the "wise" conglomerate, but this higher coordination continues down until it disintegrates into the "stupidest" particles of Chaos. At this opposite pole are meaningless but living molecules whose stupidity Diderot calls "blind" and "mad." Their disconnected state is a total freedom, with scant indication that they can bundle together coherently. Wisdom, of course, is the coordinated work of the senses and the rational imagination. Its "molecular" beginning is the nerve tip, frayed into discontinuous endings. It is here that a given sense can begin the bundling process that contributes to forming a language. Diderot's aphorism therefore also depicts another iconic polarity in *Sepia One*, where the dreamer's mind radiates beams that end in a riot of disconnected elements. His dream disintegrates into molecular parts that are discontinuous among themselves and converge back via the rays to a coordinating origin in the brain.

If Diderot's organic whole is a sane, intelligible arrangement of particles, *Sepia One* is a mad fragmentation of free elements. Faces, wings, and hooves float in meaningless adjacency, like molecular fiber-ends trailing off into individual autonomies. *Sepia One* does not achieve the orderly spread of images, as does *Sepia Two*, where imagination exercises the regulatory control mentioned by Condillac. *Sepia One* corresponds rather to the "blind" freedom of molecules that, each one sensible, remain stupidly uncommunicative with one another. This total freedom is the disconnected condition of the senses. On the subject of sensory freedom, Diderot observed that "if there is liberty, it is in the ignorant man." But freedom to the point of sensory disconnection is also a madness, as Diderot suggested: "the man reduced to a single sense would be mad." The madness, then, is incomprehension, an ignorance about how elements connect, a figurative blindness. The subject would live in discontinuity where "nothing is left but sensibility, a blind quality, in the living molecule. There is nothing so mad as this" (9:375). Madness is a state of disconnection. Such is the condition of each sense freed from other senses or, in Condillac's terms, chainlets disconnected from one another and from imagination's combinatory power. The rift extends from the cognitive mechanism itself to the knowledge it produces.

Goya paralleled Diderot in the awareness of this rift. Just as the disparate fragments of *Sepia One* have their unknown link in the dreamer's mind, so too the mysterious liaison of ideas and senses must exist but escapes linear description. Goya trains the dream-rays so that they converge on the head. Diderot requires a similar liaison in Nature "between objects and between the parts of an object." But in the same breath he mentions three types of liaison: between parts and a whole, between several wholes, and between the whole and our perception of it. These coordinations remain concealed from view, as do the dream-rays' luminous point of convergence, obscured by the dark head of the dreamer. Goya will seek coordination in a "Universal Language," while Diderot wavers in keeping with the aphorism of the wise man polarized against his disconnected molecularization.

I have already foreshadowed Diderot's inclination toward discontinuity in his remark about perception and the "hole" in the door. In another notable figure of speech that becomes relevant in Chapter 5 he observes: "It seems that we spend our days by little days and little nights" (9:344). The same fragmentation prevents the wise man from uniting disparate sensory molecules into a rational judgment, only now the impediment is the temporal succession of several kinds of perceptions. Diderot argues that when we feel, we do not think, and that when thinking, we do not feel. He asks whether we think when strongly affected by music or painting. His question has a negative reply predetermined by two previous questions: "Do we think when ejaculating? Do we think when tickled?" (9:356). At all levels of experience, a temporal discontinuity opens that demands connection at a higher neurophysiological level: "Violent emotions shake the origins of the [nerve] bundle, but each filament oscillates separately" (9:356). A unique and isolated sensation cannot generate reasoned judgment because judgment coordinates more than one term. It intervenes on behalf of coexistence but also on behalf of simultaneity.

Sensations, feelings, ideas—all must exist in some temporal span. This duration, a day divided into little days and little nights, is what Goya depicts as space in *Sepia Two*. The image is apprehended in a microinstant of day and persists through the "little night" that follows and that precedes the next microinstant. Back and forth between these time frames, the successive images are inexplicably linked as the "dark" intervals between them dissolve. The process is so rapid that we believe a single experience has resulted.

Such is the coordination depicted in *Capricho 43*, although not in *Sepia One*. *Sepia Two* takes up the theme of continuity, or "Universal Language," suggested by its title. A perceived object affords several near-simultaneous experiences. For instance, Diderot presents the paradox of a tree whose parts are scanned rapidly in successive instants so as to coordinate a whole (9:343). But more rationally he also says: "Because every sensation is a composite, it supposes the judgment or assertion of many qualities experienced at the same time" (9:358). The composite is what the wise man achieves at the rational pole of Diderot's paradox. He sees a wall, says "wall," and during the utterance he sees the wall's whiteness and adds the word "white." Because "sensations have duration, they coexist. Animals feel this coexistence. To feel two coexistent beings is to judge. Hence judgment is formed" (9:358). The continuity is rational nevertheless, or, as Hume would say, there is the *belief* that continuity is rational, since Reason joins together the segments of duration. But the joint itself, much like a seam, is a disruption between day and night that is different from the intervening, gradual transition of natural twilight. Truly seamless continuity is obtained by the cohesive power of a "Universal Language" beyond Reason and waking experience itself.

This Universal Language involves the faculty of imagination. Of course, imagination is also one of the judgmental mechanisms of rational understanding. The difference is in the contrast between *Sepia Two* and *Sepia One*. In *Sepia One*, Goya has not yet conceived a principle that might bring cognitive order. This work's chaotic discontinuities correspond to Diderot's statement about the "insurmountable barrier" between imagination, perception, and the rational mind (9:373). Here Diderot is analyzing the combinatory mechanism of understanding, with the image of tree linkages as his example. He suggests the impossibility of both producing a coherent whole and at the same time grasping each part of the whole. This paradox undercuts Condillac's linear model of understanding, as noted before. The same paradox in *Sepia One* produces the trisectional composition that separates the dreamer's head, the floating faces, and the bats. At the greatest barrier of all, the illuminating streaks halt abruptly at the cranial arc that separates the dreamer's imaginational power from the externalized dreamed product. The molecularization of components is fully detailed in this preliminary drawing, and their many implications are discussed in Chapter 4. *Sepia Two* addresses fewer issues, principal among which is the band of light attached to the dreamer's head. It is a feature that corresponds to Diderot's linking function of imagination and becomes pertinent in Chapter 5.

To conclude, the system-building, rational hypothesizing, and confident productivity that marked the Enlightenment's language of empiricism belied a subliminal uneasiness concerning the validity of their perceived continuity. The continuists who used that language either adopted metaphors that unwittingly exposed this uneasiness, or themselves lapsed occasionally in admitting discontinuity. If an artist like Goya glimpsed the Chaos beneath perceived reality enough to depict it visually, the effort was not aimed at negating empirical continuism. Rather, it called into question the orderly circuit of the senses and the verbal language that mediated their signifying process. By invoking a more comprehensive "Universal Language," Goya suggested the prospect of accessing Truth via the unified dream-scanning of discontinuous elements. One such element was the swarm of bats, as the next chapter explains.

2. Metamorphosis of the Bat

> To form monsters and join incongruous shapes and appearances costs
> the imagination no more trouble than to conceive the most natural
> and familiar objects. And while the body is confined to one planet,
> along which it creeps with pain and difficulty, the thought can in an
> instant transport us into the most distant regions of the universe, or
> even beyond the universe into the unbounded Chaos where nature is
> supposed to lie in total confusion. . . . But . . . all this creative power
> of the mind amounts to no more than the faculty of compounding,
> transposing, augmenting, or diminishing the materials afforded us by
> the senses and experience.
> —Hume, *An Inquiry Concerning Human Understanding*

If the traces of discontinuity pervaded eighteenth-century discourse more
than heretofore noted, their correction was recorded less dramatically than
their presence. As a case in point, the above epigraph dwells more on
the Chaos and incongruity of Nature than on the means to dispel them—
namely, the empirical "materials" of the senses. To judge by the proportions of Hume's argument, the description of a deformed perceived reality
overshadows the empirical aspect. Hume also incriminates the very instruments of understanding that collaborate in presenting deformity to the
mind. The imagination takes "no more trouble" to form monsters than
to conceive ordinary objects. If this is the case, one might ask, how can
language describe the true reality of things? Hume did not pose metaphysical questions of this kind, but other contemporaries did so, in terms that
were not only philosophical but also artistic. As Hume suggests, among
his readers were those who posited an "unbounded Chaos where nature is
supposed to lie in total confusion." While such a supposition about Nature
may not have won over the empiricist, the question legitimately intrigued
an artist like Goya. Skeptical philosophy might prefer only to understand
"one planet" and sidestep the question of a verbal language that might
describe the true reality of things. But the artist's visual language could
legitimately hypothesize and explore "the most distant regions of the uni-

verse, or even beyond . . . [to] the unbounded Chaos." Art could do this
because it recognized that "the faculty of compounding, transposing, aug-
menting, or diminishing" did indeed use "materials" that are pliant and can
be configured to languages other than verbal ones.

The uncertainty about resolving discontinuities led Goya to depict the
so-called "Universal Language" that informs the dream-state.[1] Goya envisioned dream language as the regulator of the discontinuities glimpsed
in daytime cognitive normalcy, a regulation achieved by gaining access to
the very "monsters, . . . incongruous shapes and appearances" that Hume
and other empiricists barred from legitimacy in the "one planet" of wake-
ful mortals. The universal dream experience would thus constitute or in-
strumentalize the language of continuity and coherence. However, Goya's
dream also included incoherent monsters, most notably the bats that sweep
over the dreaming Enlightener's head. These monsters appear to be at
cross-purposes with coherence, and the confusion calls into question the
structure of cognition itself. In fact, Goya's inclusion of zoomorphic icons
bears noting not only for the psychology of language but also for the
knowledge claimed by natural history, as the next section shows. As for
the incongruities themselves, if they exist within somebody's dream consciousness, how can this piece of information be mediated by a Universal
Language that is reputedly coherent? The answer is that "coherent" does
not mean "rational" but, rather, "continuous." There is no break between
the dreamer and the dream contents. In the timeless realm of dream, where
sequences replace chronological order, and meaning is independent of
waking chronometry, the only universe is the single continuum of oneiric
consciousness and its contents.

A separate question concerning Goya's zoomorphic incongruities
arises from the nonhuman standpoint. If the monsters coexist with the
sleeping figure in an independent dimension, what is their function? Here
the answer evokes the dilemma, "What is it like to be a bat?" that philosopher Thomas Nagel once asked, taking the bat's standpoint in his book
Mortal Questions. His inference was that states of consciousness are not
really knowable, but only their contents. Language may be capable of communicating facts about this or any living creature, but the mental state itself
remains beyond knowledge. We can know that bats have an ultrasensitive

---

1. "Universal Language" is the title given to *Sepia Two*, the preliminary sketch for "The
Sleep/Dream of Reason Produces Monsters" (*Capricho 43*). For further analysis, see my pre-
ceding volume, *Counter-Rational Reason in the Eighteenth Century* and my article "Goya's
Teratology and the Critique of Reason," *Eighteenth Century Studies* 18 (1984): 35–56.

aural mechanism that allows them to navigate in darkness, but we really cannot know what it is like to perceive as they do the surrounding objects in the form of humanly inaudible sonar information.

Goya invites speculation about the same general issue of an alien phenomenological experience, but this involves a human dream whose contents include bats. Cognitive acquisition, or the knowledge *about*, is one object of Goya's inquiry. But his concern also includes the *language* of consciousness, the eidetic medium of dream cognition that becomes the chief reason why "Universal Language" is the title of *Sepia Two*. The presence of the bats in this work is unusually haunting, and the choice to depict them becomes more intelligible in the light of its iconographical background. Suffice it to say that a wider context of pictorial awareness conditioned the three versions of *Capricho* 43, a context extending to the mythological and emblematic traditions that join with the iconological precedents from which Goya departs. Literary antecedents and concurrent references to bats also belong to Goya's cultural milieu, together with precise scientific data newly compiled for public information.

These factors may pull interpretations in diverse directions. Nevertheless, a Western European concept governs at least intuitively the aspirations of cognitive continuity that are in part represented by the bat's wings. The brief review that follows explains why. The "Flying Man" created by Restif de La Bretonne appears in the illustrations for *La découverte australe* with wings ribbed in the curvature of a bat's wings. Behind the invention of such a character is the preoccupation with discovery itself, not only in terms of geographical or anthropological curiosity, but also with regard to the power to surmount human limitations. Previous to this fiction of 1780, a flying episode is fantasized by Samuel Johnson in the sixth chapter of *Rasselas* (1759). Toward the century's end, Goya's bat motif gains momentum until in 1815 his sketch and engraving of *A Way of Flying: Men with Wings* appears in the *Disparates*. It is noteworthy that the period after 1780 intensifies scientific experiments, with balloon flights undertaken by the Montgolfier brothers.

Judging by their descriptive details, Johnson and Goya shared an understanding of the natural history of chiroptera. They both knew that bats show a pronounced thoracic muscularity and that bat wings are membranous webs. But among nature's winged creatures, the chiropter is also a physiological spectacle for the utopian mind bent on the possibility of human flight. Thus Rasselas listens as the craftsman skilled in mechanical arts informs him that he has "considered the structure of all volant animals, and find[s] the folding continuity of the bat's wings most easily accommodated to the human form" (chap. 6). This will be his model. The experiment fails, however, because a precise observation of Nature does not ensure the scientific adaptation of Nature to human desires. Goya satirized scientific aspiration more strongly when he depicted flying men attached by cords to batlike wings, their heads helmeted with birds' heads as they glide in weird serenity. Both the literary and the graphic versions reproduce the age-old, unfulfilled wish, reflected in the intuited myth of Icarus. But considered as fantasies emerging from the Enlightenment, the intended flights also represent the philosopher's zenith of abstract contemplation, the hoped-for "vantage point," mentioned by d'Alembert in the *Preliminary Discourse*, "high above this vast labyrinth, whence he can perceive the principal sciences and the arts simultaneously" as a "world map" sketched from too great a height for local detail. These are anticipations of scientific optimism, the dream of Reason that Johnson punctures and that seems incongruous when achieved in Goya's fantasies.

Such philosophical aeronautics also imply concepts of time that complement the "futuristic" notion of fiction described by Paul Alkon. While an imaginary voyage like *Rasselas* permits a quality of timelessness to shade the entire narrative, the episode of the bat-wing experiment is timeless only in the utopic sense. The mechanical experiment itself, by its failure, points to further efforts and so to a future time that can be conceived of in mortal terms. The Johnsonian dream of Reason pierces the membrane of atemporality by anticipating, implicitly, a future stage of technical progress that counteracts the "boundless futurity" of imagination mentioned in chapter 44 of *Rasselas*. In contrast, Goya's concept of time reverts to a mythical paradigm beyond the reach of chronometry. The Goyesque mortal succeeds in flying, like Icarus, but the event occurs outside time and points nowhere but to its impossibility in the world of past and present. Goya's vision is fantastic, executable only in the imagination, and thus it canot be applied to the natural world even in the adaptable future.

In short, Nature serves Johnson and Goya differently in furnishing the bat as a model for transcending their present-day human achievements. Notwithstanding the fantasizing power of *Rasselas*, the atemporal scenes invite comparison with a time-bound Europe as yet unfulfilled in its rational expectations. Goya, on the other hand, conceives the dream under the aegis of Saturn, whom he later paints devouring his child. The god of Time exists outside time, just as the dream of aeronautic metamorphosis is an eternal dream of humankind, a fantasy of physiological transformation raised to the dimension of archetype and hence as little related to the natural world as dream is to waking reality.

These intimations of mythic deities suggest a symbolism for the bats that haunts Goya's fantasy world. Just as Saturn, the Titan father-god, precedes the Olympian family that includes Athena-Minerva, so too is the bat a pre-rational creature whose successor is the owl. The bat is a taxonomical monstrosity of bird and mammal. It symbolizes the morphological Chaos whose counterpart in the moral order is the child-eating Saturn. This monstrous old order is replaced by the new gods of Reason and of classifiable forms. And this wisdom is personified in Minerva and symbolized by her owl. By reverting to the old order of Saturnine bats, Goya's vision of flying produces an absurd and destructive state of being that no reasonable mind would desire. It is a dream rendered nostalgic for the anarchy of Unreason, a dream conceivable only by a Reason that has lost consciousness, and that in sleep has lost the ability to preserve the hierarchies of species, concepts, and actions. This reversion, and its consequent turmoil, reappear fully symbolized in *Capricho 43*, where the bats swarm uncontrollably in a sphere higher than the plane occupied by the ineffectual owls of Minerva.

The Natural Order

The diverse discontinuities already outlined would be regulated if not removed by the cognition sought through dream. What the Universal Language attempted to regularize within consciousness, natural history attempted to do externally. Again, the bat illustrated the fault-line of continuity. The standard model for natural order was of course the chain or scale of being adapted by eighteenth-century natural historians who described material continuity. The graduated "ladder" from rocks and minerals to quadrupeds and anthropological forms appeared to be confirmed in the title of a work by Jean Baptiste Robinet, *Philosophical Considerations on the Natural Gradation of the Forms of Being* (1768). When Robinet's ladder reached the level occupied by birds, however, he turned momentarily to a style more suited to that of a melancholy poet or a landscape painter. He asked, "What is this hideous little flying creature that, toward evening, comes out from under the roof of this half-ruined castle? It dares not show itself by day. Is it ashamed of its deformity?" (*Considérations*, 89). The speculative observation ended here, but the colorful language gave evidence of a psychologizing curiosity beneath the practical naturalist's fascination with the bat. Robinet then moved on to adopt the illustrator's manner of seeing:

> Its body is covered with fur like a quadruped. I thought it had wings, yet I perceived only monstrously lengthened bones joined by a naked membrane that, by attaching itself to the body, covered legs and tail. It has no nose: its eyes are sunken into the hollows of its ears. Its muzzle is prodigiously cleaved, and its head covered over with four earflaps. (89)

The sketch might have inspired the excellent illustrators of Buffon's *Natural History*, but other details were nonpictorial, such as the bat's awkward flying pattern and its piercing shriek. The incongruous composite awakened suspicion that the natural scale of graduated existence may be violated. As Robinet wondered, "Is this monster a disfigured bird, or an unformed quadruped?" The latter was unlikely, he conjectured, since the bat had but two feet; nor "is it any more a bird than a flying fish. It has nothing in common with birds except flying. Its internal bodily conformation, lungs, and other viscera declare the quadruped. It even has particular connections with the human species: the male genitals hang down separately, which is peculiar only to the monkey and man; the viviparous female has two mammary glands on the chest for suckling its young" (90). Monstrosity thus consisted of a hybrid condition, a single identity draped over two rungs on the scale of differences. The bat was, and yet it was not. By being itself it was at once something else: either a bird or a mammal, if not both.

The bat's resistance to classification was one of several challenges to the growing science of taxonomy. In this instance, identity was little more than a neither/nor condition. In the face of numerous descriptive signs, the bat defied identification for taxonomical purposes. It had no fixed place in the "Great Chain of Being," and indeed the hierarchical structure was dislocated by this monster's unstable role. The outcome seems to bear out the thesis by Michel Foucault regarding the episteme of resemblances before the Enlightenment.[2] Although empirical knowledge in Robinet's era

---

2. In *The Order of Things*, Foucault addresses the altered representation of reality in the eighteenth century by describing the earlier breakdown of Classical philosophy, as exemplified by *Don Quixote*. Here, orderly signification yields to ambiguity as resemblance dissolves under the digressions of the imagination. In the Enlightenment that follows, by contrast, taxonomy emphasizes differences and identities, and the standard for signs becomes rigorous: signs free themselves of simple resemblance to things and become coextensive with representation itself. There is no equivocating in the identity of things, such as occurred in Don Quixote's dilemma over appearances and reality.

had overthrown the classified order of reality based on differentiations and associations, the anomalous bat forced taxonomy to lapse from precision into the older perplexity of resemblances. Other kinds of evidence are also apparent. The aforementioned generic comparisons with quadrupeds, bipeds, and anthropoids were broken down in dictionaries into entries for specific animals. Early in the century, the Spanish *Diccionario de Autoridades* (1726–37) defined the bat as "a bird very similar to the mouse," whose different species in the diverse provinces reveal that "some have the head of a mouse, and others that of a dog." In the same definition, its size is compared with that of a dove, whereas in the *Dictionnaire des arts et des sciences* (1732) one enormous bat reported in the Indies is as big as a crow (1:209). Much later, the *Encyclopédie* rejected the common classification as a bird on the grounds of flight, because squirrels also fly. Rather, some kinds of bats are rats, others in America are so large they are called "flying cat and dog," and while the snouts of some resemble a dog's or a cat's, others are like a calf's (3:261).

Comparison requires a step into absence. Comparison evokes the missing analogical term that suitably describes the present object. The result makes chiropteran discourse in eighteenth-century learned texts a variegated narrative rather than a uniformly straightforward empirical exposition, as we will see in Buffon's many pages on bat lore. and in the disorderly nature of information in the *Encyclopédie*. Comparisons with absent terms were not improved on by direct observation. for conflicting details blurred identity. The Encyclopedist allowed the bat four legs; the Spanish lexicographer gave it two; the French lexicographer omitted this detail altogether while noting the bat's teeth. All accounts agreed on the featherless wings and membranous pelt. But whether the bat had two ears or four, whether they were longer than a donkey's, and whether it had a tail, remained a matter for debate, thus reinforcing the imprecision already established by the comparisons with other animal snouts.

Etymology was another factor that contributed to uncertainty. The Spanish dictionary listed "murciélago" with two orthographic variants— "murcequillo," "murciégalo"—the latter of which remitted to the idea of being blind (*ciego*). However, none of the lexical sources indicated knowledge of ocular and aural systems. On the other hand, the words "chauvesouris" and "murciélago" gave prominence to the etymon for "mouse," and by extension, to darkness, secrecy, and scavaging food habits. This area is unequivocal enough for the French and Spanish sources to concur in the mammary nourishment of the young and the hooked claws enabling attachment to ceilings and walls. But only the Spanish dictionary retained the notion that bats drink the lamp oil in churches. The factual matter, as phrased by the *Encyclopédie*, was that bats favored fat, lard, and other greases, a preference somewhat distinct from their devouring of insects and, in the distant Americas, even dogs or cats. The latter dimension receives girth from a Spanish reference to victims as large as cattle and human beings. Inevitably, the question of vampirism arises at this point, although neither source mentioned it.

References elsewhere to vampire bats will be considered, but the material under review can be summarized by stressing the mystery that arises paradoxically from increasing detail. Whereas the *Encyclopédie* aims for clarity if not system, its articles follow an order of discussion that depends on the power of logical categories to impose their shaping effect on a malleable subject. In the case of bats, the subject is a basically hybrid and perhaps monstrous entity that corresponds to a multiform body of descriptive facts. The resulting article fulfilled its purpose of supplying information, but its discourse shows an order of its own, in three paragraphs of average length and one paragraph of more than double their size. I have not studied the discursive order of other entries on natural history or zoology in order to judge whether a general pattern exists. What is clear in the case of the entry on bats is its opening refutation of generic misconceptions. The first paragraph establishes that the bat is not a bird, giving anatomical evidence to prove this. The second, lengthy paragraph continues with anatomy but defers the descriptive terms of wings and feet, presented initially, until the latter half of the paragraph. Its priority is to take up sizes, colors, and head resemblances, together with comparisons with other animals. An air of remoteness surrounds discussion here and subsequently, owing to allusions that situate the examples in Egypt and the New World.

With this orientation, the third paragraph begins with the "dark and subterranean places, the caverns, the holes, etc. where they remain hidden during the day and during the entire winter." After mention of habitat there is reference to feeding, dominated by the idea of ferocity, and the passage ends with an allusion to the bat attacking human faces and carrying off a nose or an ear. In the final paragraph this horror seems nullified by the bats' nursing capacity, but in fact the mammary reference is metonymous with the thrice-mentioned word "membrane," and this evokes once again the entire incongruity of featherless wings.

The surreptitiousness and malignancy of bats would seem obvious from this account, and yet the article provides no lexical strategy for value judgment. The only hint of a tonal register occurs in the opening refutation of the aviary classification. I do not want to survey the entire factual literature on this subject—a different pattern might emerge in eighteenth-century British scientific sources—but only suggest the wealth of data about a creature whose iconic mystery in Goya can now be understood to symbolize an uncertainty of greater magnitude in the real world of information. The general atmosphere of knowledge about bats gives the unavoidable impression of intuiting some secret evil. This impression allows the attribution of vampirism to be easily accepted in both name and practice. Linnaeus first gave the name "vampire" to the *roussette* variety of bat, according to Buffon. This quadruped is the size of a large chicken and sucks the blood of humans and animals. Buffon cites the "hideous aspect" of its doglike muzzle, its crooked nose, and its general facial deformity in the *Histoire naturelle* (10:55–94).[3]

The stunning illustrations in Buffon's volumes show these animals at rest with forelegs doubled back and therefore without any visible wingspread (Fig. 5). A likeness of the wings imagined by Goya, Restif de La Bretonne, and Johnson appears only in the engraving for "la grande chauve-souris fer-de-lance de la Guyanne," whose upper lip has a salient membrane in the form of an iron lance-tip (*Histoire naturelle*, 13:292). A disparity of visual and verbal depictions thus deflates the menacing aura carried by the name and factual knowledge of the bat's traits. It would seem that the sinister aspect of chiropteran vampirism in Europe belongs to the late-eighteenth century, or so word-usage alone suggests. The entry for "Vampire" in the *Encyclopédie* condemns Dom Augustin's influence for the belief in "supposed demons who draw blood from living bodies during the night" (*Encyclopédie*, 16:828). Calmet's book ran to a third edition by 1751, bearing the global yet geographically anchored title of a document: *Dissertation on the Apparitions of Angels, Demons, and Spirits, and on the Ghouls and Vampires of Hungary, Bohemia, Moravia, and Silesia*. The Encyclopedist does not mention that bats may be vampires in the demonic sense intended here.

3. Buffon also gives the four-legged *chien-volant* the name "vampire," locating its habitat in Mexico and then in Trinidad in the 1789 *Supplément* to *Histoire naturelle des oiseaux* (Paris: Imprimerie royale, 1749–67). Buffon adduces evidence of the creature's monstrous size, a fact cited in Jumilla's *Histoire naturelle de l'Orinoque* (Avignon, 1758) and corroborated by La Condamine. In the latter's expedition, according to Buffon, navigator-astronomers Jorge Juan and Antonio de Ulloa attest to the creature's blood-sucking trait. Buffon repeats the point in the *Supplément* to the *Histoire naturelle*, adding that the drainage proceeds painlessly until the victim is dead (13:291).

Figure 5. "La grande chauve-souris fer-de-lance de la Guyanne" (The Great Bat of Guyane). Georges-Louis Leclerc de Buffon, *Histoire naturelle (Supplément)*. vol. 7, no. 74. 1789. Courtesy of the Bibliothèque Nationale, Paris.

Both the bat of natural history, whether vampire or not, and the super-natural apparition called "vampire" in Calmet's usage, converge in Goya's general iconology. This conflation of science and superstition appears visually in Goya's sepia drawing called "Dream: A Witch Giving Lessons." The witch's wings are naturalistically batlike, but they serve as a demonological aid to levitation. A sketch for the *Disasters of War* symbolizes political blood-sucking by a monster with the same wings (Lafuente, 109–11). In contrast, the bats in *Capricho 43* barely lend themselves to a vampirical interpretation. The information provided by natural philosophers like Buffon supports the argument for a cognitive interpretation of this etching—that is, the bat's morphological ambiguity upsets the paradigm of continuity and its taxonomical groundwork. The disruption typifies the condition of monstrosity, which may be defined as a state of being alien to the natural order and a discontinuity eminently represented by Goya's swooping bats.[4] As Buffon remarked, "the real characters and the visible nuances of Nature's ambiguity [appear] between these flying quadrupeds and birds" (*Histoire naturelle*, 13:228). The ambiguity duplicated itself in the cognitive realm despite the Enlighteners' best efforts. The discursive order of empirical and factual texts just cited varies considerably in conceptual sequential emphasis. As a result, a transference occurs whereby the morphological discontinuity of Nature as constituted in the bat carries over into the symbolic order intended to represent them both.

The Symbolic Order

Nature's ambiguity carried Buffon beyond the scientific plane of reference and into a mythological mode of thought. The "winged quadrupeds, which are a kind of monsters," reminded him of how the Ancients perceived reality. He conjectured, "it is plausible that their imagination designed the Harpies after these bizarre models of Nature. Their wings, teeth, talons, cruelty, voracity, filthiness, all the malformed attributes, all the harmful faculties of the harpies rather conform to our *rousettes*" (*Histoire naturelle*, 10:61). Buffon then reverted to natural history by speculating on the bat's

---

4. The concept of monstrosity has been studied elsewhere. See Patrick Tort, *L'ordre et les monstres. Le débat sur l'origine des déviations anatomiques au XVIII* siècle (Paris: Le Sycamore, 1980); Emita B. Hill, "The Role of 'le monstre' in Diderot's Thought," *Studies on Voltaire and the Eighteenth Century* 77 (1972): 149–261; and María del Carmen Iglesias, "Los monstruos y el origen de la vida en la Francia del siglo XVIII," in *Homenaje a Julio Caro Baroja*, ed. Antonio Carreira et al. (Zaragoza: Pórtico Librerías, 1978), 617–30.

suction mechanism, perhaps lingual, that enables it to suck without pain, since their large, strong teeth would awaken even a soundly sleeping man, let alone the light-sleeping animals that are their prey. In this double perspective, an eighteenth-century man of science preserved the memory of more ancient traditions.

Buffon's dual fascination with myth and anatomy underscores the powerful, diversified semantics inspired by the bat. The creature's universality took the extreme mythic form of a bat-type personage who symbolizes the ubiquitous, creative life-death force of the cosmos.[5] Closer to Goya, the bats represented "the infernal deities of harassing dreams," according to Pierre Chompré's dictionary of fable at that time (López-Rey, 1:76). And closer still to historical reality, it was but a few steps from chthonic figures associated with deities to Goya's world of popular superstition. Not only were bats popularly believed to play a part in "the whirlabouts peculiar to the witches' malefic arts," but in López-Rey's circumscribing assessment the bats could also symbolize lewdness. A case in point is the gigantic bat in *Sepia Two*, "counterpoised to a bulky owl [and] displaying its lurid breast and belly in a show of obscenity" (1:77).

These diverse ontic and axiological roles—the owl or bat as malevolent agent, vital energy, psychic force, and magic power—suggest the underlying structure of an archetypal matrix. This structure is a generative state, the source and site of all possible beings, forms, and values. The aforementioned naturalists could describe this primordial truth only gropingly, whereas the artist resorted to symbolic allusion. The bat's symbolic role, in fact, extended from Renaissance Neoplatonism to its eighteenth-century Hermetic vestiges, and it is undoubtedly the origin of Goya's iconology of "Universal Language." The bat dominates the dream scenes of *Sepia Two* and *Capricho 43* in order to pose the problem of consciousness that Chapter 1 outlined as the problem of overcoming cosmic discontinuity. The "secret process" of neurophysiology cited by Cabanis had eluded empirical understanding, while the discontinuous aethereal densities of the medullary substance mentioned by Hartley placed limits on that understanding. What was needed was a step that transcended the sensory circuit. This step was depicted in Le Cat's allegorical frontispiece, where the senses are cir-

---

5. Perhaps the most universal of such mythic forms is the Mayan "house of the bats," where Death/Killer Bat, Cama Zuts, decapitates a hunter-hero. In the same saga, a man with bat's wings emerges from the underworld to instruct priests about fire rituals. Jack Himelblau, "Tohil in the Popol Vuh of the Maya Quiche: Role Versus Implied Identity," *Journal of Latin American Lore* 12 (1986): 8.

cumvented by the Minervan deity, who intervenes to connect the palpable world directly to the Absolute.

This need already had been understood by Giordano Bruno two centuries earlier. Bruno's cosmology portrayed the bat imagistically by the immense black wings of Nox.[6] Nox was the *materia prima*, and succeeded Chaos and Abyss in the order of creation. The bat's black wings symbolized the primordial shape in the universe and the generating power behind all morphologies. For Goya's dreamer to return beneath those wings, in the presence of Minerva's owls, was to be immersed in the Universal Language, the key to unifying what the senses could not. In Bruno's words, "By the *Ladder of Minerva* we rise from the first to the last, collect the eternal species in the internal sense, order intellectual operations into a whole."[7] If the huge bat in *Sepia Two* represented the Spanish world of superstition, as López-Rey argued persuasively, the bat's iconological avatar Nox haunted the eighteenth-century vestiges of Neoplatonism. Bruno conceived of thirty statues for his cosmological scheme, Nox being the first principle that can be figured after the formless Chaos and Abyss. The bat's monstrous metamorphic power recalled the essence of the life principle, or Logos. This essence was the object pursued by the Hermetic-Cabalist tradition, whose memory systems turned into magical systems. For Bruno, primordial nature was a *chaos* of elements and numbers, yet not without order or sense when "magic memory draws them out of chaos" (Yates, *Art of Memory*, 217). Subsequently, the "Universal Language" depicted in *Sepia Two* would invoke the combinatory power sought by Hermetic philosophers and their vulgarizing successors who practiced alchemy and witchcraft. Insofar as the bat also represented what Chompré called the "infernal deities of harassing dreams," oneiric language also held the key to making the universal processes of metamorphosis intelligible. This aspect is discussed in Chapter 4.

As the symbol of Nox, the bat also was a metonym for the progeny of mythological Night. According to Hesiod and Virgil, the daughter of Chaos gave birth to the Fates, Death, Sleep, Dream, Care, Discord, and Fraud. This gamut ran from ontic to moral conditions and offers interpreters latitude to separate referential layers of the chiropteran motif. For instance, an illustration for Caylus's *Memoir on Painting* portrayed a bat

6. See Frances A. Yates, *Giordano Bruno and the Hermetic Tradition*, London: Routledge and Kegan Paul, 1964), 309.

7. Quoted in Frances A. Yates, *The Art of Memory* (London: Routledge & Kegan Paul, 1966), 290.

Figure 6. Untitled. (The Bat in the Salon.) Illustration for Comte de Caylus, *Mémoire sur la peinture*. 1755. Courtesy of the Bibliothèque Nationale, Paris.

flying above a woman and her suitor, who together play a comic drama of inconstancy and passion (Fig. 6). A comparable scene of gallantry is illustrated by a devil peering incongruously down from an oval transom window overhead (Bénard, 183). The moral is that harmless irrationality, of coqueterie in one case and of private malice in the other, can turn malignant when it overtakes society as a whole. Thus a winged vampire feeding on a prone female in Goya's *Disasters of War 72* is thought to allegorize the repressive Spanish government of Fernando VII (Lafuente, 169). Another category served by bat imagery is individual human conduct. Johann Kaspar Lavater's essays on physiognomy cite the light-shunning bat for its symbolic expression of ignoble passion (López-Rey, 1:76). Literary examples can also be cited but are reserved for a later context.

Undoubtedly an iconographic history of the bat would confirm the panorama just suggested, including both the natural order and the mystical dimension.[8] These are often contradictory traits: man elevated from low to exalted state, and man with an evil heart; repose and tranquility, yet fleeing from light like someone hiding in fear of disclosure. A Renaissance allegory of Night by Cornelis De Vos—*La partie du Jour*—is less equivocal. It shows a bat flying amid the vapor of a dreaming giant while two owls look on (Fig. 7). A telluric knowledge functions here without benefit of heaven's sunlight, and for emphasis a rodent in the foreground contrasts with torch-bearing human figures near a temple in the background. This knowledge sets in contrast the two owls, whose different visages indicate separate species, and who survey the vaporous dreamer and his ghastly associate.

The joint appearance of bat and owls from the sixteenth and seventeenth centuries to Goya's day suggests a stereotype for nocturnal scenes (Fig. 8). However, the concurrent allegorical lexicon allows multiple significations in the same icon. Thus the aesthetic requirements of atmosphere and feeling were balanced against the symbolic intimations of irrational truths as yet unknown. De Vos's striking composition implicates the bat in a statement about dream and telluric knowledge. Yet the bat also represented ignorance, another trait cited by Valeriano. Thus its immersion in the dreamer's vapory consciousness arguably contaminates the latter's cog-

8. Natural history was not neglected by painters. The color study of two bats by Hans Holbein in 1519, housed in the Brussels Maison d'Erasme, brings a still-life realism into the present context. However, Valeriano Bolzani lists the "many mystical significations" of the bat's "monstrous" figure in the same century (*Hieroglyphice* . . . [Venice: G. de Franceschi, 1602], 1:453).

Nox vbi per medium tenebras deffuderit orbem,
Corporibus fessis est tribuenda quies :
Non scelus aut vetitum quicquam committere faxit
Craftina ne reddat crimina nota dies.

Figure 7. "Nox" (Night). Cornelis De Vos. *La partie du Jour*. Courtesy of the Bibliothèque Nationale, Paris.

nitive integrity relative to the wide-eyed alertness of two owls perched at his side and above him. A comparable sign of irrationality appears in Alciati, where the emblem provides a physiological contradiction.[9] The bat has "diverse understandings," for it declares one thing to this individual and something else to another. Changeability seems to mark the bat's nature. The pictorial counterpart shows its flight above the clouds and near a crescent moon.

However, a negative meaning does not necessarily apply to *Sepia Two*, where bat and owl are counterpoised in a dominant-inferior relationship. The objective remains one of exploring Universal Language. This presum-

9. In Alciati, the bat is "the bird that flies at dusk has the mouse's body and the wings of a bird." Bernadino Daza Pinciano, *Los emblemas de Alciato: Traducidos en rhimas españolas, Añadidos de figuras y de nuevos emblemas en la tercera parte de la obra* (Lyon: G. Rovillo, 1549), 248.

Figure 8. Untitled. (Night Scene with Hovering Owl.) Illustration for Nicolas Edmé Restif de la Bretonne, *Le paysan perverti*, vol. 4, 1776. Courtesy of the Bibliothèque Nationale, Paris.

ably means the dream, which holds the key to understanding all things, including the polysemia of bats. The rich chiropteran semantics available in Goya's iconological tradition are again exhibited by Valeriano's allegorical contradictions. He sketched four bats in pairs, each pair lined up mouth to mouth and attached thereby. Valeriano observed that the chain represents not just mutual duty but also humankind elevated from a low state to an exalted one. The idea of linkage itself also inheres in the curious arrangement of attached mouths. This suggestion of fusion and continuity relates to De Vos's bat enswirled in the dreamer's symbolic vapor. Valeriano recorded the further symbolism of nourishment and abundant milk, suggested by the bat's breasts. He compares them to Diana's multiple breasts, in her aspect of Cybele, and here we cannot overstate the noticeable breasts of the bat in *Sepia Two*. But instead of second-order fertility, Goya's symbolism of abundance refers to generative powers and to the endless capacity for metamorphosis that is endowed in *materia prima*.

Here then is the point of contact between the polysemic symbol and *Sepia Two*. Just as archetypal symbolism evoked the originary matrix of reality, so the Universal Language of dream searched it out. They both supposed that the matrix ensured the continuity of matter by virtue of being a common source and substance. On this stands the ideal of synthesis held by nonmaterialist natural philosophers, an ideal Goya examined critically. Any such unitarian extension was compromised by the differences that characterize all reality. Matter constantly alters, and living species undergo transformation. This mutability and discontinuity was symbolized by the bat. Its polyvalence exposed the dilemma of any language or system that attempts to bring all things into cohesion, a dilemma that also lurked behind scientific efforts in Goya's time. When Buffon concluded that classification was too complicated to be useful, his context was indeed universal: the "animals common to two continents." He added, "it is only ridiculous to devise classes in which to gather the most distant types (*genres*), as for instance to put together in one class man and bat, and in another class elephant and scaly lizard" [*Histoire naturelle*, 1984, 208]. The effort was "ridiculous" and "absurd" because classes are too narrow to encompass the space between types. In today's terms, species are close enough to be assigned a single genus but each is remote enough from the other to claim a separate classification as a species. Similarly, individuals in one species are not so close that they lose their differences by sharing a single identity.

These taxonomic fissures lay bare the polysemic and polymorphic capacity of living matter, a capacity usually concealed in language by rational categories. Despite the convention of categories, the evidence in these first chapters makes it appealing to entertain the Foucauldian notion that beneath the grid of language lies Chaos. If the bat is the symbol of that teeming matter, the general metaphor for the reality of an unclassified Chaos would be the abyss. Such was the use of this trope made by the poet Juan Meléndez Valdés in 1795, when he praised Buffon's efforts to put order into the universe and "its dark abyss." But the poet expressed more confidence in continuities, the "admirable chain," than did the scientist: "Buffon, tell me which fate you assign in the animal scale for each being, which order for matter, which path runs from the disgusting bat to the orangutan and to neighboring man" (*Obras*, 2:1050). Buffon himself placed notions of "scale" and "path" under skeptical consideration, as the discussions of evolution in Chapters 4 and 5 suggest. The shadow of discontinuity persists so long as identity and difference particularize matter by discrete entities. But at the source or matrix heaves the Chaos of matter. Here the abyss of irrationality and morphological confusion exceeds the ordering power of language. The hybrid, unclassifiable bat assumes a symbolic role in this regard.

Goya's squadron of bats grew more pronounced in the progression from *Sepia One* and *Sepia Two* to *Capricho 43*. In terms of numbers, the squadron asserts its domination of the dream situation. But its qualitative meaning remains unchanged by number. Indeed, its numbers denote the same anarchy embodied by the bat's anatomy, which exhibits the primordial anarchy of form. This material primality is a chief message of dreaming as Goya depicts it. Whereas ordinary dreams unfold in time, the "dream of Reason" stands in an indivisible instant of imagery. The scene therefore encompasses present and past in a single vision. The bats rise up from a previous place that is no longer glimpsed but inferred symbolically by their horrible morphology. Their present horror is precisely what they carried with them from the originary abyss. Again the Hermetic-Cabalist quest for universal truth shows its ancient imprint, and again empirical science hovers over the discontinuity of scientific matter and the *materia prima* of spiritual doctrine.

3. The Idea of Chaos

One can compare the universe to certain works of a sublime obscurity whose authors occasionally bend down within reach of their reader, seeking to persuade him that he understands nearly all. We are indeed fortunate if we do not lose the true route when we enter this labyrinth! Otherwise the flashes of light which should direct us along the way would often serve only to lead us further from it.

—d'Alembert, *Preliminary Discourse*

the boundless chaos of a living speech

—Johnson, "Preface" to the *Dictionary*

Alike in ignorance, his reason such,
Whether he thinks too little or too much:
Chaos of thought and passion, all confused.

—Pope, *Essay on Man*, 2

As the preceding chapter indicated, eighteenth-century natural philosophy and art had important intimations of reality's disjunctions which ordinary language could not master. The epigraphs to this chapter provide literary evidence that evokes a similar inkling of a "Chaos," or at best of a "labyrinth" that challenges Reason, language, and taxonomy. The preceding chapter also showed how an awareness of primary matter took its metonym in the bat by being coextensive with black-winged Nox. The idea of *materia prima* underpinned eighteenth-century efforts to represent empirical reality. But primary matter resisted classification because it undergoes perpetual metamorphosis, and this metamorphic property too was illustrated in the natural and symbolic orders just discussed. Further evidence of this disordering factor exists in the literary realm, but it may be deferred to other contexts. The germane point is that even if reality's lurking disorder was only dimly suspected in the eighteenth century, its consequences were disturbing enough to make at least one principle unacceptable to all thinkers, whether scientific or spiritual. That principle was the relativism of values. It is true that cultural relativism came to be nurtured by the doctrine of the plurality of worlds and other new heterodoxies, but the prospect of intellectual and social anarchy remained abhorrent. Historical laws and the rules of both Reason and human nature were taken to be intelligible and constant, not relative, regardless of their different circumstances among eras and societies.[1]

At the same time, Reason could not alter the irrational underside of its flawed nature.[2] Many forms of discourse intuited this flaw, and a different kind of evidence appeared from another source not discussed thus far, a preoccupation with the concept of Chaos. The idea of Chaos was posited either as the foundation on which the material universe arose, or, as d'Alembert's words in the epigraph suggest, as the abyss into which the individual's mental universe might collapse. The preoccupation with cosmological Chaos, on the one hand, and cognitive Chaos, on the other, was symptomatic of the deep unease regarding discontinuity in the eighteenth century.

Chaos in Cosmological Thought

As the absolute form of discontinuity, Chaos was regarded as the originary condition of physical Nature. It lurked behind explanatory systems that were unable to account for each and every link among events and phenomena. It also became the metaphor for cognitive confusion in systems where, as Buffon remarked, "the author has fallen into darkness and chaos." The subject of Chaos holds capital importance for the eighteenth century. Theologians and natural philosophers alike formulated the idea of a primordial Chaos as a gauge for the history of the world. Their discussions, whether pietistic, historical, or scientific, all measured the span of worldly time. In this view, the non-biblical history of the earth and its nations reckons millions of years since the creation of the universe, instead of the several thousand since Genesis. Accordingly, Buffon came up with the phrase "dark abyss" of time immemorial to denote what lies between

1. For further discussion, see Peter Gay, *The Enlightenment, an Interpretation*, vol. 2: *The Sciences of Freedom* (1969; reprint, New York: Norton, 1977), 292, 320, 382.

2. The idea of an aberrant Reason is discussed in Volume 1 of this work, *Counter-Rational Reason in the Eighteenth Century*, which argues that Reason's identity took two forms. In the Christian Enlightenment, whose dualism allowed for a spiritual realm beyond the material realm, Reason's destabilizing potential was limited to mild forms, like duplicity and caprice. In contrast, aberrant Reason loomed more broadly and elusively among secularized and atheist thinkers in the form of an intuition, namely, the structural discontinuity in the universe.

the origins of the world and the present, a phrase that became part of the title of Paolo Rossi's book, *The Dark Abyss of Time*. As Rossi suggests, there is a considerable difference between inhabiting a globe shaped by God's benevolent hand and, in contradistinction, being alert to the mutability of the forms of life and the succession of worlds hidden behind the present shape of Nature.

This historical formulation is not to be confused with another formulation based on mythography. The myth of a foundational Chaos exerted a metaphorical power for thinkers who tried to account for causal energies. As a supernatural factor, it functioned in creation myths either as an effaced foundation or as an imprinting agent, or finally as *materia prima*. An eighteenth-century mythographer like Nicolas Bergier understood Chaos to mean a void or nothingness *prior* to matter. The absence of things characterizes Chaos, a point on which Lucretius is cited for support. However, Bergier was aware of the Mosaic account of earthly beginnings when he pointed out that the biblical "tohu vavohu" means a formless void, a phrase describing an earth *already created materially*.

Whether Chaos exists prior to matter or is the condition of originary matter had no little philosophical importance in the eighteenth century. A preexisting Chaos puts a cosmological stamp on material substance, because the latter originates from a primal condition independent of the Deity. But the Mosaic account ensures God's preeminence prior to matter and prior to matter's formless or chaotic condition. On the other hand, virtually all pagan myths of Creation suggest that in the very beginning there was Chaos alone. From Chaos arose the Goddess of All Things, named Eurynome by the Pelasgian myth. The well-known Olympian myth of origins affirms that Mother Earth arose from Chaos to bear her son Uranus. Another version current in the eighteenth century came down from Hesiod and was cited by Bergier in his four-volume *Origin of the Gods of Paganism* of 1767. In Hesiod's *Theogony*, "Chaos was before all things, then the Earth." The causal chain interested Bergier, and he recited the cosmic genealogy of forces begotten in the beginning: that from Chaos were born Erebus and Night, who begot Day and Light (*L'origine*, 3:33–34).

Concern for these remote beginnings today might seem marginal for an empirical eighteenth century that is more attentive to immediate causes than to unprovable primeval ones. Nor could theology feel challenged by the pre-Creation question, inasmuch as myths had long been assimilated to Christianity by allegorical means. Yet the quest for origins compelled more than antiquarian and idly speculative minds. The very concept of

Nature was ultimately at stake. When Leibniz negated Chaos as a factor in the history of the universe, he argued that disorder is the product of human limitations not God's limitations. This was more than a metaphysical axiom. It also safeguarded confidence in scientific methods. Leibniz dismissed the speculative problem of a transition from original Chaos to the organized world by simply denying that there ever was a Chaos. But his explanation was couched in the terms of pragmatic observation: "the apparent Chaos is but a sort of distance: as in a pond full of fish, or better, as in an army viewed from afar, from where it is impossible to distinguish the order observed there" (apud Rossi, 54).

Nevertheless, the idea of Chaos continued to be selected for consideration as late as 1795 in James Hutton's *Theory of the Earth*. Hutton's Newtonian position argued for an orderly structure: "Chaos and confusion are not to be introduced into the order of nature, because certain things appear to our partial views as being in some disorder" (apud Rossi, 115). This insistence, coming so late in the century, suggests not simply that thought systems abhorred discontinuity, but also that the abhorrence responded to a subliminal awareness of Chaos lingering in a wider sector. This dimension opened parallel to new geographical explorations that, together with expanded travel in general, fed modern geological research and was fueled by it in turn. Irregularity and disorder sensibly affected voyagers who beheld mountains, grottos, spectacular rock formations, and the remains of ancient civilizations, all beheld with fascination.[3] Scientifically speaking, the landscape also gave evidence of natural upheavals and great deluges that explained geophysical puzzles as well as the biblical Flood. Consequently British thinkers from Robert Hooke to Thomas Burnet approached the observable world as a post-catastrophic Nature, a Nature in which the order of proportion is absent. The discovery of time in Nature, as Rossi points out, subverted the traditional image of the perfection of the universe. The discovery was "a sort of new chaos."

The postcatastrophic awareness related first to religious thought because of its impact on faith. The order and beauty inhering in the world, and reflecting God's greatness, are retrojected in time. The backward shift does not alter respect for Divinity, yet the shift does unsettle the secure sense of time and permanence from a mortal standpoint (Rossi, 36). This temporal indeterminacy also became relevant because of its inference about

3. The widespread appeal of geographical disorder has been documented graphically by Jean Stafford, *Voyage into Substance: Art, Nature, and the Illustrated Travel Account, 1760–1840* (Cambridge, Mass. and London: MIT Press, 1984).

the chaotic essence of history. This notion can be summed up in the image of Nature as a vast wreckage made of broken materials and paralleled in art by Hubert Robert's obsession with monumental relics. The eighteenth-century interest in ruins has of course been the subject of many studies, but in the current context it may be regarded as symptomizing the long-term issue of Chaos.

Ruins are the signs of creative energy later dispersed. The absorbing interest in ruins betrays a concern that is manifested more plainly in scientific discussions of Chaos in the natural world. These discussions centered on the theme of material causality, the reverse analog for the decaying process reflected in Robert's pictured monuments. As mentioned earlier, the mythographer differed from the theologically oriented historical naturalist, who situated the Deity in advance of Chaos. However, the texts Rossi studies indicate a common preoccupation that has gone unnoticed. Their common theme assigned to Chaos an essential structural role in the universal order.

The theory of the earth advanced by Thomas Burnet and the Mosaic cosmogony together hold that Chaos made up the material substratum of the physical world. The world originated out of Chaos, defined by Burnet as "the matter of the Earth and Heavens, without form or order; reduced into a fluid mass, wherein are the materials and ingredients of all bodies, but mingled in confusion one with another" (apud Rossi, 40, 34). All this is transformed by the Divine word into the terrestrial earth. Burnet's explanation conferred certainty on the causal unity of matter and Logos, both of which are instrumentalized within a Divine origin.

However, certainty was dislodged by attention to originary causes and to the scientific measurement of time. Thus Newton's letter to Burnet maintained its piety while refining the concept of material Chaos. Newton referred to a Chaos common to planets and sun but separated by God into fragments. The solar chaos acted even before assuming a compact, well-defined form. This chaotic subset, projected onto the chaos of each planet, created the Mosaic evening and morning of first day. However, Newton believed it was "unphilosophical" to seek any origin beyond God.

Despite this exchange, recorded by Rossi, Burnet's discussion of a structurally material Chaos remained closer to mythical explanations than to scientific ones. God transformed Chaos into a fluid mass, mixed together in confusion. He gradually organized it into a gigantic body of "egglike structure" whose "yolk" was the central fire. Around it lay a great liquid mass, "the *great Abyss*," or the sea, subterraneous waters hidden in the bowels of the earth (Rossi, 34, 41–42). The elements in this description coincided with images in Athanasius Kircher's geophysics, with its central volcanic fires. Echoes of the Ancient Philosophy may also be heard, and they carried over into the discourse of French vitalists like Raymond Vieussens, who found organic links between living beings and the lowest mineral forms, right down to the originary fires of the universe.

This network of details aside, the concept of Chaos was implicated in the operations of matter and logos. In Le Cat's treatise on sensations, for example, the motor fluid is the "minister" of the Divine Being's universal spirit. By means of this "spirit," "He disentangled the Chaos, gave life to His works" (xxxi, 2). This "spirit," termed "logos" by other thinkers, is a cognitive immanence. Here the claim made by Le Cat followed naturally: the purpose of studying physiology is to understand the link between the Deity's unifying spirit and the human operations of body and mind. A cardinal factor in the cognitive process is the motor fluid that transmits aether, a quintessential element that is discussed in Chapter 9. The Quintessence is derived from Chaos, according to Hermetic lore.

Le Cat's linkage of the nervous system to a logos-dispelling Chaos is noteworthy. The notion resonates allusively to certain vestigial ideas of the Ancient Theology. The Quintessence or "Fifth nature is the life and the movement of every growing thing, retaining within itself the celestial virtues, named Green Lion, Chaos, Hyle" (Grosparmy, in Valois's *Cinque Livres*, 74). While it is unnecessary to identify Le Cat's physiology with any of the several branches of Hermeticism, we are well reminded by numerous scholars that the Hermetic tradition survived vigorously into the eighteenth century. Indeed, the *Liber chaos*, a tractate of 44 pages by Raymond Lully, was published in 1722 by the Mainz publisher Häffner. References to alchemist authors abounded in scientific literature, much of their knowledge remaining viable despite the discredit that had fallen on the idea of a philosopher's stone. And Giordano Bruno's *Torch of the Thirty Statues* named Chaos as one of the three "infigurables" that pre-dated the formed statues (Yates, *Bruno*, 309).

The implications of connecting a primal Chaos with occult forms of knowledge will become apparent. The subject enjoyed enough currency that the *Encyclopédie* devoted more than three columns to its entry on Chaos. The article begins with the definition given by the Ancient Philosophers, that Chaos is "a confused mixture of particles of all kinds, without form or regularity, which they suppose to have essential movement," and from which the universe was created (3:157b). A similarity to Burnet's materialist conception, at odds with the assumption of an empty vortex, can be detected. In addition, the Encyclopedist is cool to enthusiasm over the concept of vortices from any quarter, ancient or modern. He detects a common origin in this concept. All nations seem to have "conserved the memory of a state of darkness and confusion prior to the arrangement of the world." Throughout time, the idea of Chaos had been disfigured by ignorance and by poetic imagination, according to the Encyclopedist. As a result, his chief concern was to maintain piety in the scientific questions of first creation, matter, and movement. Therefore the article defends Mosaic physics and its assertion that God created Chaos before separating its diverse parts. This is not to say that the article omits a historical survey of the idea of Chaos, only that it claims that the idea invited chimerical thinking when detached from the Scriptures.

Chaos in Cognitive Thought

The preceding survey centered on the cosmological principle of Chaos in order to show its Hermetic-vitalist basis and its link to such concepts as energy and neurophysiological processes. There was also a microcosmic aspect of the principle of Chaos that subsisted within the larger system. This was a cognitive counterpart taking the form of a metaphor. The mental processes were portrayed as a chaotic wellspring when abandoned to the imagination. La Mettrie, for instance, observed in a context of volatile effacements and replacements:

> Such is the chaos and continual, rapid succession of our ideas. They chase after one another, so that if the imagination does not employ, so to speak, a part of its muscles to be in balance with the brain's cords, to hold on for a time to a fleeting object and keep itself from falling upon another, which it has not yet the time to contemplate, it will never be worthy of the name of judgment.[4]

The cosmic or comprehensive dimension of reality, and the psychological or individual dimension of reality, fixed the two pole of Chaos. Between them was not only La Mettrie's metaphor but also the metaphor employed by Condillac for the mind's violent swirl of "bizarre" images in its phase prior to rational thought. The word "vortices" (*tourbillons*) ordinarily refers to the eddying vacuums of outer space, but Condillac bor-

---

4. Julien Offray de La Mettrie. *L'homme machine*, ed. Paul-Laurent Assoun (Paris: Denoël-Gonthier, 1981), 117.

rows it in the *Traité des animaux* to describe the "animal" sensations that end in a "chaos" of images. Condillac speculates that each physical need corresponds to a mental center around which movement agitates toward the circumference, and that each "engulfs" or swallows the other, growing more violent and disordered in turn. The metaphor that most interiorized the idea of Chaos, however, was Diderot's use of this word to indicate the absence of any liaison (*Éléments de physiologie*, 9:372). His use of "Chaos" rests on a limited and linear image of discontinuity rather than on an amorphous chaotic mass. Yet the term sharply focuses the legitimate site of the problem at hand, which is neither Heaven nor Nature but Mind itself. It is the multitude of sensations that demands coherence.

Throughout the eighteenth century, then, diverse books alluding to the idea of Chaos engaged in three kinds of discussion: historical, mythical, and scientific. The categories shared a materialist vision that featured the role of motion. In the previous history of Chaos, its least tangible form was given by Bruno, who portrayed this idea as pure space that cannot be imagined. It is one of three "infigurables" existing before the thirty statues were created. But like a Kantian a priori, it must exist in order for its progeny, *materia prima*, to unfold itself. The succession is not mediative but genealogical, however. Chaos breeds Orcus as its son, an Abyss of infinite appetite that seeks the father's amplitude. Its daughter is Nox, the primary matter that is depicted as an old woman clothed in black, with immense black wings (Yates, *Bruno*, 309).

These imagistic attributes supplied the tangible quality that might have been missing in Bruno's Chaotic abstraction. Comparable images appeared in the poetry of Goya's day, as well as in his aforementioned oneiric symbolism of bats and related broad-winged creatures. Most eighteenth-century readers doubtless knew of Bruno only indirectly, if at all. But the metaphorical associations with Chaos had affinities both with Hermeticism and with Hesiod's *Theogony*, and the latter work enjoyed numerous editions in English (1728, 1795) and in French (1767, 1774, 1785), aside from citations by mythographers like Nicolas Bergier. Other sources among the century's prodigious Classical information should not be discounted, including Pindar's Olympian odes and the *Deorum origine* by Apollodorus of Athens, whose last French edition was in 1675. Finally, an epigonic essay in 1809 titled *On Chaos and the Manner of Its Representation* by A. L. Millin provided the iconographical history as well as cosmogony of the concept, observing that many poets and mythologers speak of it but that no monument, ancient or modern, has represented it.

The preceding references do not aim to establish a chronicle of influences or sources, but simply to suggest a historical field of conceptual forces. Certain ideas were taken as common property by diverse models throughout the same period, and from period to period down through the generations. This pattern of conservation included specific notions of Chaos and aether that, each in its domain, elicited similar nuances in otherwise different systems of thought. As indicated earlier, the history of the idea of Chaos was implicated in most theories of matter and motion. How this link affected scientific discussion, particularly Newtonian cosmology, can be illustrated by recourse to the Lullian doctrine. Again, the point will not be to argue that the alchemist Newton derived his ideas about Chaos from the Hermeticist Lully, any more than he did from Mosaic physics. Rather, the point is that scientists inadvertently exposed how intractable discontinuity was as a rogue factor in an otherwise systematized universe, one where matter and spirit were unified, and, microcosmically, where mental processes were continuous with physiological ones.

Before proceeding, I should add that my suggestion follows a methodological premise that scholars increasingly resort to in eighteenth-century studies. The period was characterized by multiple laminations of ideas that now deter research from privileging any single superimposition, including the empirico-rationalist layer of thought. In the specific example of Chaos, the historical laminations of this notion are mythic, occult, and pseudoscientific. Therefore when these discourses perpetuated certain features of Chaos they highlighted its capacity to deflect the rational intent of the cosmologies that assimilate it in the eighteenth century. This grid of shared properties marking any concept, a grid that frames both contemporary and diachronic levels, permits such concepts to be viewed, if not as the "conceptual strudel" in Eric Rothstein's epistemological analogy, then as a *millefeuille* field of forces acting vertically and laterally on one another.

In brief, the grid of discourses containing the idea of Chaos ran from Ancient Philosophy to Newtonian physics. The Hermeticists believed that the creation of the world proceeded from "a mass called Chaos, which by divine will was divided into three parts," including a "Quintessence," and whose matter was universally metamorphic.[5] In Newtonian discus-

---

5. See Nicolas Valois. *Les cinque livres, ou La clef du secret des secrets*, preceded by Nicolas Grosparmy, *Le trésor des trésors*, ed. Jean Roger, (Paris: Retz, Biblioteca Hermetica, 1975), 73. The "third part" of Chaos, being less pure, produced "the Quintessence in a mass called the confused mass," from which the four elements came. The identical origin can be found in Lully's late medieval *Liber chaos*, reprinted in 1722. The "essence" of Chaos is quadripartite and participates in the universal transmutation of form and matter. Lully attributes to Chaos both motion and grades and species of plants, animals, and metals ("De Motu Chaos" and "De

sions, Chaos entered to cast the shadow of discontinuity via the problem of gravity. As Alexandre Koyré has shown, gravity alone cannot explain the origin of planetary motion, nor can gravity explain how the infinite universe and its structure relate to gravity's action. Because, for Newton, matter existed in its essential condition of reciprocal attraction, the atoms of Chaos could never have been convened to form the present system. The assumption, of course, was that God created Chaos and thus existed prior to it. And while Newton declined to speculate with Burnet about a first cause—before the original Chaos broke into smaller ones—the issue of matter and motion remained crucial. Koyré explains that if Chaos were infinite, then diffused matter would convene under gravity into an infinite number of great masses at huge distances from one another, like stars and planets. But then it would be impossible for circular revolutions to be attained (Koyré, 186–88).

Newton's struggle to maintain a continuous system in spite of all had two dimensions. Explanation must eliminate discontinuities in time by showing causal succession from the very first moment, and explanation must supply syntagmatic continuity within the system. Thus, gravity operated explicably from the Beginning through the purposeful action of an intelligent and divine Agent. And it operated at the level of minute particles as well as cosmic distances. But in the speculative vein stressed by Rossi and described earlier, Newton was stymied by the final rift in the regress outlined in his letter to Burnet, where he referred to a Chaos shared interplanetarily but divided into fragments by a divine cause. At some frontier, the natural system ceased to exist. It became necessary to graft on the outermost limit a supernatural system that was discontinuous with it.

The awareness of discontinuity was arguably nothing but a constituent of the awareness of scientific limitations, and therefore not a special source of anxiety. In reply, one may cite G. Tonelli's evidence of Leibniz's centrality for the eighteenth century's "law of continuity."[6] If one does not adhere to this argument, then one can cite a comparable precept of continuity in biology, documented by Francesca Rigotti.[7] In either case, the observer will confirm an internally unruffled "paradigm" of continuity

---

tribus Gradibus chaos"). Naturally, Lully's Christian God created Chaos, but Lully focuses on its actions and its relation to man through material generation and decay.

6. G. Tonelli, "The Law of Continuity in the Eighteenth Century," *Studies on Voltaire and the Eighteenth Century* 128 (1963): 1621ff.

7. Francesca Rigotti, "Biology and Society in the Age of Enlightenment," *Journal of the History of Ideas* 47 (1986): 216.

in Nature under attack by a minority of skeptics like Voltaire and Samuel Johnson (Rigotti, 232). The field of biology is the most incisive example, because it embraces the problem of cognition. Rigotti finds in biology two strands of the law of continuity, both deriving from Leibniz's concern to explain and eliminate from the universe every possible source of disorder and imperfection (216). One camp consisted of the preformationists, who argued for a successive unfolding of predetermined order. The other camp comprised the advocates of the Chain of Being, among whom were Jacques Delille, De Beaurieu, and Delisle de Sales. The two camps were allies as far as the skeptics were concerned, for whom the disputed issue involved the theory of a continuum, advanced by Bourguet, Plouquet, Charles Bonnet, Kästner, and Jean Baptiste Robinet.

Discontinuity in its specific entailment will be the subject of later chapters in this volume. What the preceding theory exposes is the confidence of continuist thinkers. Their rational order rested on the placid assumption of an uninterrupted chain of entities whose junctures were "filled" by links. When scrutinized, however, the junctures between entities often reveal not links but empty spaces. Compensations or insertions must therefore be supplied, and they were of two kinds. One of these preserved the scientific temperament through a tentatively rational skepticism even while conceding the limitations of empiricism. The second interstitial "filler" drew on imagistic and ultimately mythic evocations.

As an example of the empirical replacement of linkage, Buffon's change of heart is instructive. He abandoned his earlier confidence in the possibility of a cohesive science, believing first in relativity and then in nothing. Jacques Roger has described this shift explicitly. No longer finding the means to discover order in a mutable universe, Buffon contributed to the relativism of his period. No rigorous linkage of phenomena was plausible except in metaphysical terms, but a metaphysical principle of linkage would be plainly deficient in methods for isolating individual links (Roger, 756). Because Buffon realized that everything acts on everything else, and that first causes are unknowable, an agnostic shadow fell between the unexplained junctures.

As in other contemporary discussions, Buffon illustrated the dilemma by way of the biblical catastrophe. He made vivid use of Chaos in real and metaphorical senses. How, he asked, can the scientist imagine that

> in the midst of the confusion of a comet's tail with the great abyss, in the midst of the ruins of the terrestrial orb, and in those terrible moments when not

only were the earth's elements confounded but when new elements arrived again from heaven and hell to augment the chaos, how then imagine that the ark floated tranquilly with its numerous cargoes on the crest of the billows? (*Histoire naturelle*, ed. Varloot, 169)

The methodological difficulty emerged in Buffon's response to one author who strained after natural explanations for Noah's survival. It is futile to impute physical causes to an Almighty Will, for "one falls necessarily into darkness and Chaos." Buffon reverses the methodological coin of Newton's caution against "unscientific" speculation about supernatural causes. Nevertheless, his literal and figurative evocations maintain the awareness of Chaos as something more than an academic topic.

A second kind of compensatory "filler" preserved the spectral ancestor of Chaos that, paradoxically, needed to be dispelled. As noted, the spectre haunts natural events by invoking the unintelligible primal cause, and it haunts physical entities by exposing a chaotic array of partial linkages. But forms themselves are also affected by the absence of links. Above all, the formlessness of Chaos struck deep irrational chords. This was particularly true, not surprisingly, in poetry. Here the awareness of Chaos hovered over intelligent understanding rather than over material Nature. The leaps and swerves of the orderly mind produced gaps that constitute another species of discontinuity, and this came to be represented figuratively by the physical Chaos discussed by scientists.

The metaphorical cognizance of Reason's breakdown is best remembered in Alexander Pope's *Dunciad*. Here the "controlling metaphor of Chaos and Old Night," as Jean Hagstrum observes, took the "crawling, damp, embryonic inchoateness" of Unreason and thrusted its unperishing reality on the reader (Hagstrum, 234). Much has been written about this mock epic that needs no rehearsal. Transcending its satire, the *Dunciad* has come recently to be regarded for its powerful theme of metamorphosis. The unceasing and often unpredictable changes of form comprise a major feature of discontinuity and its irrational aura. What Max Byrd calls the "fantasias of 'chaotic unreality,'" elaborating on a phrase by W. K. Wimsatt, are the violations of boundaries that the epoch fell prone to despite its strong sense of classification (Byrd, 448).

In addition, Pope's kingdom of the Dull can be rescaled to more realistic proportions. The lines describing the triumph of Chaos and the enslavement of science are richly symbolic for the period, rather than satirically rhetorical. The dense verses surely resisted overinterpretation by any contemporary reader balanced on the social tripod of rational science, religious piety, and blind superstition. These verses depict the moment when reasonable intelligence is devastated by the Dog-Star that

> Smote ev'ry Brain, and wither'd ev'ry Bay;
> Sick was the Sun, the Owl forsook his bow'r,
> The moon-struck Prophet felt the madding hour:
> Then rose the Seed of Chaos and of Night,
> To blot out Order, and extinguish Light. (4:10–14)

An audience dwelling in a conservatively rational milieu must have noticed the allusive pause after each ravaged dominion ruled by intelligence. The words "Brain," "Sun," "Owl," and "Prophet" reach a connotative density that could not fail to confer their special hues on the threatened concept of intelligence. These verbal keys borrow terms from the physiology of thought, the symbolism of light, the Minervan owl of wisdom, and the certainty of religious revelation.

What is allusive for audiences oriented rationally, piously, or conservatively held yet greater meaning for a Catholic audience forming the readership of a Spanish poet like Diego González. Here the "Seed of Chaos" means the interposition of infinite space, a gap prohibiting linkage of any kind between one dominion and another. Once again, the context is Creation. In Pope, existence reverts to the originary condition of Chaos that first served as the raw material for subsequent intelligible forms. In González, the intelligible dominions have already been created. However, a new Chaos emerges to separate them. The event in its most radical mode is the separation of matter and spirit. González takes his example from the moment after Adam's creation when, endowed with life, Adam embodies a metaphorical Chaos:

> The noble being [is] composed of matter and spirit, parts of such rare and opposite conditions that no gradation leads from one to the other, nor can there be any, or any order, proportion, or analogy; for an infinite chaos intervenes between one and the other, more untraversable than vast space. (Polt, 113)

The space is metaphorical insofar as body and mind are concerned. It becomes quite a powerful metaphor when "matter" and "spirit" are construed in the cognitive terms of things and their abstract representations.

Space then is an "infinite Chaos" in two related conceptions. There is a chaotic void or scattering of material objects disconnected from the ideas representing them. In reality, concrete forms are themselves materially discontinuous among one another. This fact is made vivid by contrast with the amorphous but continuous mass of the original Chaos. But on another plane, ideas form a chaotic scattering of abstractions. Groups of ideas may cluster more "closely" or coherently as classifications, but the latter spread disconnectedly in their sum total.

Ultimately, it is possible to apply this spatial metaphor to the subject-object relationship and thus to cognition itself. Exactly what occupies the space between the object and its idea? The transformations of the physical into the mental are endless, as well as disconnected from one mind to another. Pope's anxiety over metamorphosis suggests his intuitive recognition that orderly mental categories do not banish the chaotic physical forces underpinning Nature. González piously recognizes that no gradation can join spirit to matter. The different readerships of these two poets do not negate the shared response to discontinuity. Pope and González tacitly invoke the split between the thing and its immaterial idea. The juncture between thing and idea involved poorly answered questions of physiological and psychological processes.

While these questions will be addressed in succeeding chapters, their import is already clear. The same preoccupation brings together cognition, the problem of discontinuity, and the theme of Chaos. From their convergence, a physiology of Chaos may be inferred. Chaos entails primal substance, the stuff of the universe before God or Nature shapes it into matter and mind. Order is a mental construct in its own right, what González would derive from "spirit." Between this order and Pope's symbolic dominions of Brain, Sun, Owl, and Prophet there intervenes a process whose factors bear denominations that differ by cognitive orientation. Implicated in the process are fibers, crystals, vibrations, and aether, the emphasis varying with the specialized observer: brain physiologist, pious natural philosopher, or freely imaginative intuitionist.

The placing of imagination as a centerpiece of cognitive psychology was of course a major achievement of the eighteenth century. The achievement had one facet that relates to the metaphor of Chaos. In Kant, the empirical imagination acted "to solidify the chaos into an image, to *stop* it, by creating an orderly series which the mind can contemplate" (Warnock, 140). This insight was not a sudden discovery but belonged to a longer history of speculation about image-making.

The continual motion of successive ideas in our minds is a "Chaos" produced by the imagination, as La Mettrie noted in a passage cited earlier. "See this bird on the branch," he said:

> it seems ready to fly away. Imagination is the same. Always carried away by the stirring of blood and spirits. One wave makes a trace, effaced by the one that follows it. The mind runs after it, often in vain, and must wait to regret what it was not quick enough to grasp and fix. Thus the imagination, a veritable image of time, destroys and renews itself ceaselessly. (*L'homme machine*, ed. Assoun, 117)

The "spirits" were the same as Le Cat's "motor fluid," both being constituted by aether. This same aether was the quintessential substance derived from Chaos in Hermetic cosmology. In eighteenth-century neurophysiology, aether also mediated the neural messages transformed by imagination and reason into judgments. "Spirits," "wave," "trace"—La Mettrie's failure to choose a term of untainted semantics is remarkable. In this way, the stuff of unintelligible disorder in the cosmos became the agent of orderly knowledge in the human microcosmos. That is, explanations for mental operations used metaphors that were filtered through the conceptual cross-combinations that run through the history of ideas. This point is elaborated in Chapter 9.

The role of imagination in La Mettrie needs to be understood from the standpoint of cognitive mechanisms rather than artistic production. The "pleasures" and "dangers" of imagination comprise a debate in the eighteenth century that would be less confused if the two distinct areas of cognition and artistic creativity were kept separate. La Mettrie complains that too little judgment and too much imagination allow the latter to be "too abandoned to itself, almost always as if occupied in looking at itself in the mirror of its sensations" (117). The complaint involves the discontinuity of successive "traces or images" that are not properly held together so as to examine attentively their resemblance or truth. Attention is the "key or mother of sciences." When attention is not engaged, "the liveliness of the springs of imagination" is such that objects cannot be scanned. The consequences are adverse to intellectual enterprises, although the aesthetic results may be defensible in another branch of endeavor.

The Abyss and the Labyrinth

The fact that discontinuity persisted as a motivating stimulus was an irrational feature of the eighteenth century. This companion to the awareness of Chaos was a common theme throughout the century. It was also a vestige of intellectual history. Although the enduring preoccupation with Chaos survived from earlier periods only to be assimilated to rational explanation, it was not forgotten. The assimilation process itself betrayed a discomfort with the systems devised to eliminate it. Here the contrast between Newton and Leibniz has been instructive. For Leibniz, the world's perpetual motion was proof of a perfection requiring no supernatural intervention. But for Newton, in Alexandre Koyré's phrase, the world was a clock running down and requiring constant renewal by God. The disquieting feature of Chaos was its infinite locus and the seeming void in which matter subsists. Space loses its substantive character. The stuff constituting the world became increasingly the void of the Atomists. Traditional ontology, the idea of Being itself, lost ground.

This gradual sense of loss appeared under a corollary metaphor. Within the generality of Chaos, an "abyss" would seem to be a precise spatial configuration. Yet an abyss is just as infinite and confounding. The tower and abyss of later centuries studied at length by Erich Kahler has accustomed scholars to associate this metaphor with the Romantic movement. But the word "abyss" enjoyed a long philological history prior to this. The pertinent phase began with empirical philosophy and the need, expressed by Hume, to fathom the "immense abysses" (*Inquiry*, 83). Just before the empirical phase was post-Renaissance astronomy, which persisted alongside Newtonianism thanks to the Catholic followers of Kircher, who believed in "abysses" between suns, the space that Kepler fills with stars (Tuzet, 55–61, 226–29).

The so-called Catholic Enlightenment is therefore an appropriate context in which to note that empirical science spanned the metaphorical abyss, notably in Spain.[8] Respect for Buffon's exploration of the universe moved the poet Juan Meléndez Valdés to invoke him for having "delved into the dark abyss to raise somewhat the universe's veil" (*Obras*, 2:1050). The "veil of nature" was arguably a commonplace trope, one used even by Étienne

---

8. I distinguish between the secular Enlightenment, whose empirical and materialist phalanxes set aside dualist problems, such as spirit and matter or God and vital force, and the frankly Christian orientation, whose conservative form in Spain has been called the "Catholic Enlightenment" by Joël Saugnieux. See Volume 1, *Counter-Rational Reason*.

Gamaches in his treatise on astronomy of 1740. However, the Spaniard Meléndez was not such a materialist that he excluded transcendental causes. His poem attributes to Buffon a cosmic scheme that provides for an orderly chain of beings, including a scale of animals from "the disgustingly ugly bat to the man-related monkey." The poet dispels the Goyesque dream of terrifying bats, now replaced by a reassuring universal order, which nonetheless retains "somewhat" the ancient and inscrutable abyss fathomed only by God.

The contrast between Goya's irrational knowing and the authentic science praised by Meléndez occurred in 1795, the same period that gestated "The Sleep/Dream of Reason Produces Monsters." At stake was the nature of knowledge, both its source and its accuracy. The fact that Meléndez elsewhere resorted to such images as "the deep abyss of nothingness" and "the blind labyrinth of the human breast" suggests an unease behind the poem about Buffon. In these images, the intimations of slipped moorings appear in terms of sensory perception. Space and visibility dissolve before the poet, leading his judgments to embrace negation. The abyss could be conceived as an unfettering of the mind from categories bound to Reason. To this extent, the references return us to the previous discussion of Chaos and the birdlike cognitive mechanisms described by La Mettrie. In a poem where cognition and aether are linked, Martin de Bussy mentioned the abyss as a precondition for intuiting the kind of knowledge manifested through dreams. More of this in Chapter 9.

Thus an inward dimension expanded for the first time in the eighteenth century. An abyss within the mind transected Buffon's "dark abyss" of immemorial time. Just as the newly revised cosmic history unfolded its temporal and spatial "new" Chaos to human consciousness, so did its psychological equivalent designate remoteness and confusion or mystery. This inner space of consciousness was memory, what Charles-Louis Richard called the waking condition where successive perceptions push down earlier ones until they reach the "abyss of the past" (9). As with the cognitive process figured as Chaos, once again the physiology of thinking took a metaphor suited to the insecurities that accompany the loss of familiar and fixed boundaries. The brain itself was represented as a labyrinth. Evidence for this figurative anatomy of mind will come in the next chapter. The point here is the discovery of the need itself for such figuration.

The figurative abyss stemmed from the emotional unease exhibited in the case of Meléndez and others like him. Undeniably the metaphor will serve later to express Romantic feelings, but in the present context the source of perturbation was intellectual. An interesting point of bifurcation from the Goyesque crisis of Reason's monster-producing dream, is "the spectre Spleen" conceived by William Haley. In *The Triumph of Temper*, this phantom rises from the monstrous abyss, and the verses are accompanied by a ghoulish engraving of Demogorgon's Hall (12–13). The idea of "spleen" in this detailed scene takes distance from the conventional poses of splenetic melancholia and their associations with the anatomical seat of the passions. The abyss is a less common image among Spanish poets, but it is more explicitly didactic. It serves as a political lesson for José Marchena's epistle on liberty to Lanz: "Into the abyss of tyranny / Doth licence hurl the people" (Cueto, ed., *Poetas*, 67:623). Both Marchena and poet Alfonso Verdugo associate it with moral retribution wreaked by the monsters that rise up from the "cavernous blind abyss" (67:135).

Nevertheless, the eighteenth-century abyss is associated as much with philosophical quest as with moral values. Voltaire admires Pope because "he carries the flame into the abyss of Being" (*Oeuvres*, 9:442). Voltaire adds a note on Locke's modest aims in acquiring knowledge, to the effect that the intellectual faculty cannot "fathom this abyss" of the nature of matter (9:455). In his *Discourse in Verse on Man*, Voltaire urges Helvétius to practice moderation when using Reason as his guide: "At the edge of the infinite your course should stop; / there the abyss commences: it must be respected" (9:401). Diderot meditates more profoundly than Voltaire, whose characteristic skepticism resists unverifiable explanations in the experiential world. When Diderot ponders the ruins of a painting by Robert, he imagines life itself to be an abyss. But these reflections in the *Salon* of 1767 concern the inward experience of time and human destiny.

While Diderot's complexity in this *Salon* invites many approaches, one interpretation is irresistible. His lyrical response to the marble tomb, crumbling into dust, homes in on the abyss as a symbol of discontinuity. The world is old, he realizes with Buffon, and he walks "between two eternities." The experienced moment, or life itself, is a hiatus between the past and the eternity of death still to come. Wherever Diderot glances in Robert's painting, things and people announce their end. Everything from the ruined colonnade to the vast gallery and the broken vault is annihilated except Time itself. Diderot's existence compared with the boulders and forests is not merely a measure of ephemeral individuality. It also emblemizes a collective experience: "a torrent sweeps the nations one upon the other down to the bottom of a common abyss; I myself, alone, try to stop short along the edge and pass back through the flood streaming by me on each side!" (*Oeuvres*, 11:229–30). The lyricism, although meditative, remains within the analytical spirit of other texts commented on earlier. The mortal body is not simply flesh, but is a "weak tissue of fibers" next to the more durable bronze that obeys a separate, "general law" of metals.

The descriptors "tissue of fibers" and "general law" serve the specific function of organizing knowledge. Such descriptors turn against themselves by instilling new doubts about making connections between threads, either filling gaps properly among categories, or else smoothing the transitions from one to the other. Diderot speaks of time and decay, whereas the naturalist Buffon speaks of the "thread" of life and old age. However, Buffon bases his figurative analysis on the labyrinth rather than on the abyss. The thread of life weaves through this "labyrinth" only to be severed in old age. But is not this also true, he asks, even in day-to-day life, where

> this feeling of existence is destroyed by sleep? Each night we cease to be, and consequently we may not regard life as an uninterrupted succession of felt existences. It is not a continuous web; it is a thread divided by knots or rather by cuts that all together belong to death. Each one reminds us of the final cut of the scissor, each one portrays to us what it is to cease to be. (Varloot, 107)

Like art critic Diderot, the natural philosopher infers from immediately coherent data a deeply subjective conviction of indwelling schism.

Whether it is Voltaire looking incomprehendingly into the philosophical abyss, or Diderot contemplating the existential abyss, they find their understanding impeded by an inability to cross from one realm over to another. As for Buffon, his implied labyrinth elsewhere appears as an explicit metaphor that expresses this disorientation. Voltaire hears the voice of virtue asking to be shown what Alexander Pope claimed to exist: "This order so hidden from so many diverse beings." But Voltaire says the task is beyond him. He listens to a description of his own life's work: "Your grand study is man, and with the thread / of reason you search the precinct of this labyrinth" (*Oeuvres*, 9:415). But Voltaire asks whether it is demonstrated that he has reasoned his way out of the human labyrinth, and if so, the demonstrated wider "precinct" obviously has suffered its own cleavage. When asked to show "this invisible chain / of the world of spirits and the sensible world," Voltaire prefers to cite his duty to keep silent about the issue.

The discontinuity between sensible and abstract realms entails other complex issues, like the physiology of perception that occupies the next chapters. The emphasis here is that skepticism adopts a particular trope that entangles the rational discourse at the same time that it describes the entangled process itself. The Spanish poets who provide the context for Goya's final annihilating vision confirm the entanglement. Juan Pablo Forner declares that "Nature closes the path sought by dark Reason" and that while "experience penetrates and disentangles / the blind labyrinth of things," not even "the light of a thousand laborious vigils" can pierce the shadows of eternal darkness (*Discursos*, 37). So much for the inaugural poem of Forner's *Philosophical Discourses*, devoted promisingly to "the science of man." His second discourse on "the diverse inclinations of Reason" indicts "the sophistic error with which [man] reasons / . . . in its blind and confused labyrinth (Cueto, 63:371). The poem *On Egoism* by Tomás Iriarte in 1776 asks helplessly, "But in this difficult labyrinth / of opposing reflections / that so confound human instinct, / is there no Daedalian thread to guide us?" (Cueto, 63:41).

Rather than being isolated but symptomatic usages, these examples belong to a far-reaching stratum of associations that can be traced to bifurcating traditions of several centuries. An entire corpus existed in seventeenth-century Hermetic works all over Europe, comprising poems printed on the page in the form of labyrinths. One eighteenth-century carry-over in France is a typographical maze of print in French and German appearing in 1758 under the title *Labirinthe spirituelle*, containing bilingual biblical texts laid out in square shapes with four centers.[9] In seventeenth-century Spain, the mystical graphs, circles, and floral alphabets in the *Laberinto* of Juan Caramuel are an immediate example of irrational paths to knowledge. However, those open paths were considered to give access to a cognitive medium that differed from stymied empirical Reason. The Jesuit Juan Nieremberg in 1645 devoted a chapter titled "The World Is a Poetic Labyrinth" that described Porphyrus's panegyric to Emperor Constantine. This consisted of seventeen labyrinths in which verses are crisscrossed diagonally and vertically so that the same letters spell different verses expressing a myriad of sentiments.

Joining the later seventeenth-century Spanish undercurrent is the polymathic author Athanasius Kircher. This Jesuit's peripheral influence on the prestigious eighteenth-century essayist Feijoo would filter into the variegated subculture of Goya's Spain. Kircher's anthropology and quasi-

9. Janet Bord and Jean-Clarence Lambert, *Mazes and Labyrinths of the World* (London: Latimer New Dimensions, 1976), 117.

occult natural philosophy included many scientific descriptions, as well as engraved illustrations of subterranean mineral labyrinths and volcanic fires said to nourish the earth's living surface. Comparably, the French eighteenth-century natural philosopher Delisle de Sales believed that electricity reigns in labyrinthine, vaulted caverns in the same way that fire is trapped beneath the earth (Tuzet, 340–44). Here the context is aether's role in overcoming continuity, as Chapter 9 will discuss. A distinction must be made, however. The cabalistic journey into alphabets and graphic signs was more supernaturally oriented than the emerging geophysical sciences. But both modes adopted the labyrinth in the eighteenth century. The entry for "Labyrinthe" in the *Encyclopédie* consists of a comprehensive summary that joins Antiquity to recent geological and archeological studies. Notably mentioned in this entry are the bats inhabiting the labyrinth at Crete, described by Tournefort in 1702. And bats are what might be called a Goyesque curiosity in a report for the *Mémoires* of the Academy of Sciences, a society otherwise interested in the site's underground tunnels and chambers. A different sort of compilation by Dom Pernety's *Dictionnaire* carries forward to the eighteenth-century the Hermetic interpretations of the labyrinth in the Middle Ages, making it symbolize the idea of putrefying matter (Van Lennep, *Alchimie*, 158). Thus in Alchemist and Encyclopedist circles alike, both the irrational and the rational associations of labyrinths are preserved intact.

Yet another crosscurrent plays an important role. Whereas the *Encyclopédie* emphasizes the infinite routes and detours in the mythic labyrinths of Antiquity, the tradition of emblem literature transforms the visual effect of mazes into intellectual and moral meaning. The book of emblems by Francis Quarles, reprinted often between 1635 and 1777, calls the World "a lab'rinth, whose anfractious ways / Are all composed of rubs, and crook'd meanders." Although based on Psalm 119:5, the text displays its imagistic sense by adding: "This gyring lab'rinth is betrenched about / On either hand, with streams of sulphrous fire." The picture shows a man trapped at the center of a deep labyrinth, gazing out to a distant watch-tower crested with an angel holding a lighted torch for ships seen far from shore (Fig. 9). The spatial and indeed architectural quality of the scene will become relevant in a moment.

In the Quarles emblem, the certainty of knowledge is assured by a divine lantern, allowing mortal steps to be directed by the "Great God, that art the flowing spring of light." The same certainty controls the Porphyrian mazes mentioned earlier, where language in its infinite potential

Figure 9. Francis Quarles. "Labyrinth." *Emblems Divine and Moral*. 1635. Courtesy of the Bibliothèque Nationale, Paris.

for expression nevertheless allows its twenty-six letters to shape baffling configurations that eventually submit to human powers of understanding. These linguistic and graphic efforts belong to yet another undercurrent of semiological preoccupations with aphoristic gnomoglyphica, as Mario Praz has called them, together with hieroglyphs, ideograms, and related scriptorial signs. These ancient inscriptional codes were believed to reflect, in Madeleine David's argument, the common wellspring of language. Needless to say, the Universal Language invoked by Goya's dream was the final gesture of this belief.[10]

The Quarles emblem is Goya's ancestral antithesis. Goya's *Capricho* emblemizes the dream of Reason in its dual condition: the darkness of sleep, and the state of disconnection from the fibers of neural physiology.[11] In Quarles, the prayer for a cognitive thread leading out of the labyrinth is a prayer for eyesight and light: "Enrich mine eyes with thy refulgent ray." The visual faculty permits reception of the figurative light of understanding. A contrary medium, the dream, enables Goya's sleeper to gain comparable "insight" without the light of Reason. In Quarles, the light that unifies human and divine realms overcomes two kinds of disjunction, first with regard to the discontinuous paths in life's labyrinth, and second with regard to matter and spirit. The unifying knowledge in Goya, such as it is, challenges the metaphor of light, eyesight, and languages of the rational Logos.

It may now be clear that the discontinuity between light and darkness, between eyesight and dream, and between Reason and imagination,

10. The move from Goya's "Universal Language" (*Sepia Two*) to "The Sleep/Dream of Reason Produces Monsters" (*Capricho 43*) is described in my previous volume, *Counter-Rational Reason in the Eighteenth Century*. It argues that the dream in *Sepia Two* does not allude to Reason but only to the primary reality symbolized by the bat. Reason appears in *Capricho 43* in the form of Minerva's owls, discontinuous from the bat. In both works, imagination controls the dream process, but only in *Capricho 43* does the relation of imagination to Reason become a problem. This complication offers different possibilities when we attempt to interpret Goya's meaning. As for imagination disunited from Reason, its power of making free combinations was widely acknowledged and has been described by several scholars who cite numerous authors, including Addison, La Mettrie, Johnson, and Condillac. See, further, James Engell, *The Creative Imagination* (Cambridge, Mass.: Harvard University Press, 1981), 36; and Jacques Marx, "Le concept d'imagination au XVIIIᵉ siècle," *Thèmes et figures du siècle de lumières: Mélanges offerts à Roland Mortier*, ed. Raymond Trousson (Geneva: Droz, 1980), 147–59.

11. The physiology of dreaming is described by the same textile imagery used widely for nerve anatomy and perception; the latter is shown in Chapters 4, 5 and 6. In the dream process, the soul loses "the thread that guided it when awake; if [the thread] remains in pieces, they are retied to a tissue formed by the imagination on the same canvass." Abbé Jérôme Richard, *La théorie des songes* (Paris: Chez les frères Estienne, 1766), 84.

is the governing issue behind the lesser discontinuities of the emblematic labyrinth. The Quarles emblem presumably unifies the visual image and the abstract word within a higher synthesis. But the success of this union depends on the presumed continuity between Reason and imagination.[12] Quarles has no doubt about an unflawed continuity. But rational idea and mental image were not so easily linked in the eighteenth century. There was a fault-line that transected the conversion-process of images and concepts. A striking example is Diderot's vivid sketch of imagination in *Éléments de physiologie*, where the imagination is defined through the device of allegorical children and adults in emblem literature: "The imagination is the image of childhood that is attracted to everything without any rule" (*Oeuvres*, 9:365). To comprehend this idea requires visualizing the helter-skelter flurry of a child among desirable objects. Our comprehension of Diderot's remark is nonsensory, although the mediating image of comprehension cannot be said to be abstract.

Image-making includes figurative images as well those perceived by the senses. Figuration, interestingly enough, also acquired a labyrinthine character when writers described it. Diderot gives imagination an architectural metaphor in order to stress the retentive power of its unending vistas, which perpetually sidetrack us: "The man of imagination strolls inside his head like a curious visitor to a palace, where his steps are detoured at each moment by interesting objects; he goes on, he comes back, he never leaves" (9:365). The spatial basis for this deviant course without exit is the straight path of Reason. How, asks Diderot, can imagination "derange the regulated march of reason"? His reply is that the erratic path is occasioned by reviving the sounds and features previously encountered in Nature.

Other figurative images, as distinct from sensory ones, filled the iconology of the period. In Gravelot's book of emblems, *Sagesse* or Wisdom (Fig. 10) walks in a labyrinth. The emblem for *Le Penser* is a tangled yarn of twine viewed by the Thinker (Fig. 11), while *Science* is the least thwarted

12. It is always the imagination in conjunction with Reason (variously named "judgment" or "understanding," or *raisonnement*) that anchors reliable, empirical intelligibility. The numerous eighteenth-century examples include La Mettrie, for whom imagination was "inseparable from judgement" as it "embraces through reasoning" all things (John Falvey, "The Aesthetics of La Mettrie," *Studies on Voltaire and the Eighteenth Century* 87 [1972]: 397–479, esp. 427 and 430). Hume attributes to the imagination a power of conceiving and supposing beyond mere combining or associating (Jan Wilbanks, *Hume's Theory of Imagination* [The Hague: Martinus Nijhoff, 1968], 77–78, 82–83). Finally, Reynolds balks at the supremacy of imagination over Reason, the position taken by Blake when seeking a new spiritual cognition. Ernest Lee Tuveson, *The Imagination as a Means of Grace: Locke and the Aesthetics of Romanticism* (Berkeley and Los Angeles: University of California Press, 1960), 138–39.

SAGESSE

Figure 10. Hubert François Gravelot. "Sagesse" (Wisdom). *Iconologie*, vol. 4, p. 65. 1791. Courtesy of the Bibliothèque Nationale, Paris.

LE PENSER

C.N. Cochin del.   C.L. Lingée Sculp.

Figure 11. Hubert François Gravelot. "Le Penser" (Thought). *Iconolo-gie*, vol. 4, no. 17. 1791. Courtesy of the Bibliothèque Nationale, Paris.

by entanglement, with its orderly garland and chain (Fig. 12). What is labyrinthine in these contexts can be mastered by an unarmed Minerva in her
secluded sanctuary. The temple of Minerva, with its ready access for enlightened celebrants, is a frequent motif in Spanish authors and artists at
this time.[13] The goddess in this conception is a Minerva whose external
dress lacks extensive armaments. This uncomplicated Minerva, when not
presiding over artistic women, is otherwise located in her divine temple or
in the libraries of mortals, which are the orderly sanctuaries built on the
crypts of retrievable wisdom.

But a more dramatic architecture emblemized Minerva's binary nature. The continuity of cognitive faculties and their resulting knowledge
was affirmed by some authors and doubted by others. Thus an engraving
that depicts the Chain of Reason as a series of steps leading up through
smoke and clouds to a man at the summit illustrates the work of continua-
tionist Charles Bonnet (Mazzolini and Roe, 67). In contrast, a "forest cut
through with avenues" represents the crisscrossing information that fills
dreams (*Encyclopédie* 15:355b). The binary relation between freedom and
death is celebrated by the "sacred labyrinth" envisaged in the anonymous
Songe patriotique of 1790. The narrator of this essay-dream visits the site of
the fallen Bastille, where a future temple erected to Liberty by the architect
Belfond will require underground foundations for its labyrinth of massive,
angular surfaced vestibules, terraces, halls, and inner porticoes that extend
in infinite directions and offer countless perspectives. Beneath this maze,
which nonetheless is regularized by a pyramidal shape, there will be deep
vaults to house defunct future deputies (*Songe*, 47). The irrational context
of a labyrinthine temple contrasts with the classically designed temples of
Minerva envisioned for Rome and Naples during the mid-century decades
(Moli, 350–55).

Parallel to these evocations was the taste for labyrinths in eighteenth-
century gardens. The hedge-maze in the Villa Pisana, south of Venice,
enclosed a dominating statue of Minerva that crowned the central ob-
servatory. The maze attracted 200,000 tourists to its 6,400 square meters
(Bord and Lambert, 133). A late seventeenth-century labyrinth at Versailles
was destroyed in 1755 but enjoyed renown together with another labyrinth
at Choisy-le-Roi. In England, Batty Lanley's *New Principles of Gardening*
(1728) joined the reprints of sixteenth-century gardening books to stimu-

---

13. See my article "El templo de Minerva en la España del XVIII," *Hispanic Review* 59
(1991): 1–23.

Figure 12. Hubert François Gravelot. "Science" (Knowledge). *Iconologie*, vol. 4, p. 79. 1791. Courtesy of the Bibliothèque Nationale, Paris.

late construction of turfmazes, shrub and bush mazes, simulated ancient earthworks, and Roman mosaics. The Hellenist Jackson Knight found significance in the idea of the labyrinth, calling it the microcosm of the earth and the macrocosm of the human body.

This landscaping fashion transcended its visual spectacle and occupied a conceptual dimension that falls outside the scope of this book. The concept was associated first with the quest for knowledge and ultimately with the life cycle itself. The theme of death inspired the "sacred labyrinth" in the Parisian temple of Liberty just mentioned, and this very theme attached itself to the life-cycle issue by entering a mythic dimension through the notion of the body returning to the Earth-mother, possibly with a subsequent rebirth. The same mythic aura hovered more rationally through knowledge of Antiquity: the Minotaur at Cnossus signifying the sacrifice to a king as sun-god. From this standpoint, Theseus conquering the bull represented the human aspiration to light symbolic of knowledge. These intimations go beyond the present subject, except to suggest that scholars remain without a more relevant philosophical explanation for the phenomenon of labyrinths in the eighteenth century.

Such an explanation may inhere in the idea of picturesque beauty then in vogue. Without digressing into a subject that enjoys ample commentary by scholars, it is important to contrast the picturesque to the labyrinth motif. A picturesquely cultivated landscape where Nature is allowed to grow wild will develop at worst into a contained, well-placed bramble. The gardener never permits Nature to sprawl into the hopeless entanglement of a labyrinth. Indeed, a "natural" labyrinth cannot be placed within the scheme of controlled freedom and naturalness. The ideal or natural labyrinth inspires the design of ancient earthworks in Crete and Egypt, where the uncovered ruins display an archetypal idea of what a labyrinth should be and signify. What it signifies has little to do with the picturesque wildness that expresses the self-emancipatory yearning of a human nature constricted by too symmetrical a Neoclassical Nature. Not that natural labyrinths imitate, or that they exist in Nature as such, but this is precisely the point. The picturesque beauty sought through the naturally unkempt areas of an otherwise well-kept garden differs in purpose from the abstract idea of a labyrinth transplanted to a garden. Labyrinths represent the shape and extent of what Nature would become if it ran wild in its fully fecund immensity. The monstrous result would baffle human efforts to master or chart it. But a garden maze is an exhilarating transfer of that unrealized possibility to a human scale, a transfer that affirms the triumph over the unfathomable.

Undoubtedly the literary and landscaping manifestations just reviewed demonstrate confidence in the human capacity for overcoming complexity and mastering the entire "precinct" that tripped Voltaire's Reason into admissions of discontinuity. A characteristic self-assurance underlies the formal modesty that begins Bonnet's essay on the faculties of the soul. He announces that his project consists of meditating, decomposing, anatomizing, hypothesizing, and finding links for the principles of the soul. Any psychologist embarked on an analytical explanation of the nature of the faculties must consider the risks, he implies. And so he adds in the edition of 1782, "Perhaps I'll plunge myself into a Labyrinth more tortuous than Daedalus's; but I won't fear getting lost because the thread that I shall use will lead me easily to my point of departure" (*Oeuvres*, 13:3). Bonnet is a confident explorer of "the South Sea territories of the metaphysical world." If he does not find what he seeks he may discover new, unexpected truths, and in any event his wish is that other voyagers will follow and explore beyond his discoveries.

This modest self-assurance is Cartesian in character and can be traced to the contrast made by Descartes of method to labyrinth (*Oeuvres*, 52). The "horizontal" progress or linearity of method conquers the complexities of the intellectual labyrinth. More sensitive to how elusive the conquest is, Diderot uses words like "extravagance" and "bizarre" for the peculiar chains of conjectures and resemblances devised by thought processes. This has been pointed out by Pierre Saint Amand in a study of Diderot aptly titled *The Labyrinth of Relationship*. Diderot was not so optimistic as Bonnet about mapping the entire labyrinth, but Saint Amand contends that Diderot freed the process of analogical relations from any "fear of the multiple" or the labyrinthine. To a degree, Diderot opposed the multiple, as did Condillac and d'Alembert. Saint Amand argues nevertheless that for Diderot the universe was a complex chain of transformations or labyrinths within labyrinths, whose dynamic may be plotted on the axis order-disorder-paradox. The universe as labyrinth was a saturation or fullness, the overall Structure that was constantly displacing particular circumstances and also, inevitably, particular texts (Saint Amand, 56ff.).

The scientific community did not remain immune from the dynamic of intellectual doubt. I have been suggesting that the very presence of themes like Chaos or abysses attest to the assimilation of an unexorcised dilemma. Acknowledgment came from the bosom of Encyclopedism, when d'Alembert's *Preliminary Discourse* cautioned that the encyclopedic tree cannot precisely represent the branches of knowledge because the general system of arts and sciences "is a sort of labyrinth, a tortuous road which the intellect enters without quite knowing what direction to take" (46). The encyclopedic tree grows as far as it can, meets obstacles, must withdraw, and "plunges on to a new route" only to retrace or jump over once again. D'Alembert, who has come to personify the ideals of an Enlightenment that privileges Reason, nonetheless retreated from its linearity by admitting the "discontinuity of these operations." In an overdetermined choice of words, he concludes that "however philosophic this *disorder* may be on the part of the soul, an encyclopedic tree which attempted to portray it would be *disfigured*, indeed utterly destroyed" (emphasis added).

It is noteworthy that specialized studies of the mathematician d'Alembert repeatedly comment on his admission of discontinuity or systemic impasses. Paolo Casini has pointed out that he never accepted the notion of "inserting the idea of succession within the definition of Nature." D'Alembert used metaphors after 1759 that tended to the irrational by displaying either ambiguities or dichotomies of matter and spirit, and other lacunae that struck Diderot's attention. Consequently, the d'Alembert viewed by Diderot in the latter's *D'Alembert's Dream* took positions that were "prolongations" of his own doubts concerning such questions as the thinking stone, the passage from stone to humus, humus to plant, and plant to animal kingdoms, questions that resist any model of rational continuity (Casini, 22–24).

To examine the books of physiology and medicine in the eighteenth century is to find their authors reaching for the metaphor of labyrinth as an expression of mystery. The glandular system in human bodies perplexed Le Cat, who remarked that "the entire industry of Anatomy has been unable to discover the slightest trace of the platoon of vessels that is imagined to be there, as if, I say, a substance so compact, so solid, a labyrinth so impenetrable could allow to pass a matter as gross as this grease" (*Sensations*, 135). Here the passage from glands to nerves appears blocked, the solid mass standing opaque before the microscope like a compacted labyrinth whose walls and intervening spaces have collapsed. The anatomist Vieussens studied the internal ear, its standard name being "labyrinth," where cavities contain the air needed to receive the acoustic impressions from external objects. The semi-circular canals grow narrower in extension, the bony layers are spiral, the "pit" is a semi-oval canal, all is conch-shaped and designed to conceal and protect "the soft nerve of the Ear that is hidden there," delicately susceptible to harmful impressions (*Traité nouveau*, 68–69). The description highlights the idea of a remote sanctuary.

Most significant perhaps is the dependency of cognition itself on a labyrinthine structure. When memory tries to retrieve a word or an image,

> we may almost feel, how some of the Spirits flying through all the *Mazes* and *Meanders* rommage the whole Substance of that medullary Labyrinth, whilst others ferret through the inmost Recesses of it with so much Eagerness & Labour, that . . . they often bewilder themselves in their Search, till at last they light by chance on the Image that contains what they look'd for.

This highly figurative passage appears in Bernard Mandeville's *Treatise of the Hypochondriack and Hysterick Passions* of 1711, whose third edition came out in 1730 (Yolton, *Thinking Matter*, 169). What the century-long debate in neural physiology over "thinking matter" had at stake grows vivid in this revealing passage. Rather than deciding whether spirits or vibrations convey messages to the brain, the issue is the chaotic process itself. Chaos is no longer a cosmological phenomenon external to the mind. The issue must now also be appreciated from the changing perspective of cerebral data that never cease to remain in motion. The ferment of sensory information succeeds in producing a coherent reality despite the ostensibly obstructive cerebral structure. Yet to describe the mechanics of data transmission is not only to marvel over the success human beings experience when they remember or reason. It is also to wonder whether that successful coherence is truthful in spite of the obstructive organic architecture. Not every physiologist wrote as fancifully as Mandeville, but the landscape of cognitive blockage and discontinuity was the backdrop for their debates, as we shall now see.

4. The Cerebral Labyrinth

> The general system of the sciences and the arts is a sort of labyrinth, a
> tortuous road which the intellect enters without quite knowing what
> direction to take. . . . The intelligence studies the first objects that
> present themselves to it. It delves as far as it can into the knowledge
> of these objects, soon meets difficulties that obstruct it, . . . plunges
> on to a new route; now it retraces its footsteps, sometimes crosses the
> first barriers only to meet new ones; and passing rapidly from one ob-
> ject to another, it carries through a sequence of operations on each of
> them at different intervals, as if by jumps. The discontinuity of these
> operations is a necessary effect of the very generation of ideas.
> —d'Alembert, *Preliminary Discourse*

In the epigraph above, metaphorical "barriers" require the intellect to move
"by jumps" through a "labyrinth" of knowledge. D'Alembert's metaphor
situates the mind on "a tortuous road" outside of itself, "retracing" foot-
steps for each "sequence of operations" in order to overcome the "intervals"
between the separate sequences. This image of discontinuity refers to an
external world of objects and discourses. However, it bears an extraordinary resemblance to certain metaphors that described the *internal movements* of mind in eighteenth-century neurophysiology. One theoretician
observed that

> Our brain is, if you will, a forest cut into a thousand lanes: you find yourself
> in one such alley, that is, you are busy with one such sensation, one such act
> of imagination; if you give yourself over . . . willingly when awake or by ne-
> cessity in dreams, from this lane you will enter a second, a third, following the
> way they are traversed, and your route, however irregular it seems, depends
> on the place you started from and the forest's arrangement.[1]

The discontinuous journey is striking in both instances, and similar references to jumping or retracing along furrows abound in such discussions.[2]

1. Jean Henri Samuel Formey, *Essai sur les songes*, in *Mélanges philosophiques*, vol. 1 (Leiden: E. Luzuc fils, 1754), 182. Also in *Encyclopédie*, 15:355b.
2. "The brain is a promenade cut up into a thousand different paths that have but one

More striking yet is that a duplication of the external problem of cognitive discontinuity shows up within the brain process itself. It is as if the stymied quest for an uninterrupted sequence of discovery had been projected on those internal processes that make the discovery: perceiving, thinking, and dreaming. Whether this projection stemmed from deliberate or coincidental factors is beside the point. Eighteenth-century empirical authors resorted to a single figure of speech that portrayed a desired uninterrupted sequence coupled to an existing discontinuous condition. Their rhetorical density suggests a significant preoccupation with contradictory models. Discontinuity extended from the physical brain to the forms of knowledge that it created, and this axis meant that the subject-object relationship was implicated in both directions. I will return to this point shortly.

As for the brain itself, anatomist Marcello Malpighi once remarked that the medulla is a "maze," and he accompanied this metaphor with a more elaborate image of the human head as "the temple or palace of Minerva, goddess of the sciences."[3] The coincidence of these tropes might be unremarkable in poetry, but in eighteenth-century biological science their contradictory sense is worth pondering. The two tropes not only proposed different spatial models of the mind, they also polarized each other's assumptions about how the mind behaves.

By citing Malpighi, my purpose is not to offer a technical history of the brain,[4] but rather to situate the cognitive aspect of biological thought within the general problem of discontinuity. As demonstrated, figurative language imposes itself as a chief criterion for the evidence to be chosen.

---

main avenue, which you must pass through in order to reach the others. However irregular may seem the path chosen afterward, however tortuous the labyrinth you find yourself involved in, it has its beginning at this same avenue" (Abbé Jérôme Richard, *La théorie des songes* [Paris: Les Frères Estienne, 1766], 82–83). "But during sleep all the avenues of the senses are closed, [and] the soul being deprived of commerce with external objects can no longer receive any impression except from the animal spirits that wander haphazardly through the brain's cavities and reopen certain traces" (80). One scientific dictionary had this entry: "The imagination is stirred by the spirits owing to vestigial imprints. . . . The surviving spirits sometimes jump and insinuate themselves into these series of totally disconnected folds or vestiges" (M. D. C. de l'Académie Française, *Le dictionnaire des arts et des sciences* [1688], new ed., 2 vols. [Paris: Rollin Père, 1732], 2:434). The psychologist David Hartley acknowledged "some little impediment and confinement in certain regions [of the brain], on account of some exceedingly small discontinuity, arising from this intervention of the pia mater between certain regions" (*Observations on Man, His Frame, His Duty, and His Expectations*, 2 vols. [London: S. Richardson, 1749], 1:19).

3. Marcello Malpighi. *Discours anatomique sur la structure des viscères, sçavoir du foye, du cerveau, etc.* (Paris: D'Houry, 1683), 83.

4. Such a history would be obliged to examine obscure works dealing with cerebral structure, such as J. J. Hensing's *Cerebri examen chimicum* (Giessen, 1707), which affirms the presence of phosphorus, and G. D. Santorini's *Observationes anatomicae* (Venice, 1724), which contextualizes the brain's anatomy. Regarding Thomas Willis's famous work, see Chapter 7.

Malpighi's contradictory metaphors—the brain as maze or Minerva's palace—reproduce the subject-object relationship mentioned two paragraphs earlier. Cerebral matter itself is convoluted and segmented, but it aspires to an abstract knowledge that Minerva alone can integrate into a continuous sequence. In this dichotomy lies a double dualism. First, the subject's mind stands in cognitive relation to the world as object—an internal/external opposition; and second, the physical brain stands in relation to its disembodied ideas—a matter/spirit opposition. The brain as maze is really a picture of dead ends, either because the blocked animal spirits must retrace their path, or because the wall of one medullary segment stops where the wall of another segment begins. Yet these discontinuities are minor when compared with the deadend where brain matter leaves off and abstract thought begins. For now the traditional mind-body or spirit-matter duality takes a novel turn. No longer is abstract thought an internal event. As d'Alembert's metaphor indicated, abstraction or "spirit" is externalized as shared knowledge, including culture. Insofar as society and culture rest on principles, concepts, and values, they too are immaterial entities. The new discontinuity thus is as much internal matter (brain)/external spirit (culture) as it is internal mind/external matter. As such, the discontinuity is interactive or reversible. Not only is the brain discontinuous with the external world of ideas, but the latter's spirituality is discontinuous with the brain. And yet the overall ideal of eighteenth-century thought was that an uninterrupted continuity integrated these and all other realms, a synthesis that, if not yet discovered or understood, belonged to the Minervan wisdom that most thinkers aspired to.

This then is the landscape of cognitive blockage. The context of discontinuity was nothing less than the problem of knowledge and cognition addressed by the entire century. It was the context of culture at large. In Enlightenment discourse, the brain was both an organ and a trope for observers across a broad spectrum: anatomists, natural philosophers, writers, and artists. My assumption is that the "figurative" aspects of biological and evolutionary science filtered into the general cultural discourse, and conversely. As such they were factors absorbed in the consciousness of an iconoclast artist like Goya or polymathic geniuses like Diderot. What these creators expressed are tokens of the context just alluded to. Goya's achievement by making the act of dreaming eidetic was to extend the landscape by universalizing the medullary labyrinth.[5] He conceived the brain as the locus

5. I shall argue that Goya exposed the continuity of Chaos, which extended from Nature to the mind and back again—that is, through its Universal Language his dream captured a

of a dreamwork whose Universal Language exposed chaotic Nature's continuity with mind. This binding energy and related factors are examined at the end of this chapter and in Chapter 7.

Readers who have come this far may well need to identify themselves with one of two groups at the end of this chapter. The intellectual historians who seek a rapid narrative may want to move briskly through the scientific details in succeeding chapters that justify my arguments, and proceed to Chapters 8 and 9. However, the historians of biological science, as well as cross-disciplinary scholars interested in the theory of "thinking matter" as developed by John Yolton, will find useful the precise information supplied in the next chapters.

My subject calls for a three-pronged strategy centered on the philosophical concern for continuity, and advancing on one flank by using evidence from works on psychology and physiology, and on the other flank by interpreting the irrational concept of cognition in Goya. The points on the axis of continuity-discontinuity remain to be plotted in the next pages. Its relevance to themes such as Chaos and labyrinths was discussed in the previous chapter, but these themes also impinge on organic models for anatomy, larger biological systems, and human thought itself. Such models embrace what may be called "continuism," the ideal of continuity defined through linear and sequential notions of linkages. But this unifying quality is ultimately defective before the multiform and disjunctive condition of Nature. The contradiction emerges in metaphors used by Diderot and Buffon for cognitive activity, to be examined in the middle sections of this chapter. In turn, Goya responds radically to his perception of discontinuity, making it an emblem for the mind in *Sepia One*. This complex drawing, an early version of *Capricho 43*, has never been subjected to a detailed interpretation. It is analyzed as a meditation on cerebral structure at the end of this chapter.

The Axis of Continuity and Discontinuity

Among scholars of all periods there exists an undeclared consensus that recognizes the discontinuous nature of reality: a discontinuity among organic

---

reality defined by the chaotic aspects of Nature. Whereas natural philosophers acknowledged discontinuity by depicting both Nature's harmonies and its Chaos, they did so in a language whose metaphors themselves expressed discontinuity. Goya, in contrast, made continuity manifest through a language that exposed all of reality to be metamorphic.

forms, between matter and spirit, and within the historical process. The consensus usually remains undeclared because most scholars emphasize continuity instead. They regard the process of material and intellectual transformation as a transitional process, one of change rather than of rift. Consequently scholars imply an evolutionary series of alterations whereby the latest form is intelligible by causal relation to its predecessor. The idea of metamorphosis comes under a similar focus of understanding. A material form gradually emerges continuously from its predecessor so that, in Newton's words, "any body can be transformed into another, and all the intermediate degrees of qualities can be induced in it" (Dobbs, 232).

This notion of continuity is familiar to all students of the eighteenth century. The diverse models designed to certify this notion (e.g., Chain of Being, *emboîtement*, etc.) have long since been described, although the fact of such diversity is less remarked on. Still less noticed are the components of the continuist ideal, especially the concepts of "beings" and "forms." Once these concepts are analyzed as they were understood at the time, the scaffolding of continuity begins to disassemble. What stands revealed are the scaffold and the agent of its fracture in coexistence. Perhaps the best demonstration of this self-subversion is to take an author who is least identified with systematic thinking, who nonetheless certifies the notion of continuity at an inaugural point and who in the same work finally devises a profoundly suggestive counter-model.

Denis Diderot begins his *Elements of Physiology* with the problem of classifying "beings" or "entities" (*Êtres*). His subject-matter will involve the parts of the organic body—that is, a living form composed of smaller living forms. The relation among forms inevitably presents a problem. Not only is one organism diversely structured in its parts, but its comprehensive form differs from the comprehensive forms belonging to other categories. Nevertheless, Diderot affirms that forms are organized into categories so that their relationships may become intelligible to the human mind. The "place" of one form relative to another is the touchstone for classifying entities more intelligibly. When understood as a system of taxonomical relationships, these entities are said to comprise a single "chain." Therefore, Diderot warns,

> One should not believe that the chain of beings is interrupted by the diversity of forms; the form is often just a misleading mask and the link that seems to be missing may exist in a known being that has not yet, in the progress made by comparative anatomy, been assigned its true place. (9:253)

The "chain of beings" remains an undisputed premise in this text by Diderot. If a gap in the chain appears, it does not negate the existence of an unbroken linkage. Rather, the missing link is a naked form awaiting assignment to its proper place or category. In the realm of natural being, beyond verbal classifications, the forms themselves are held to be continuous. But discontinuous forms are seemingly present through the veil of language because they wear the "mask" of a category that disconforms with an adjoining category whose form is correctly placed. The discontinuity of forms is illusory owing to their insertion, "out of order," into mistaken categories. Expressed differently, the missing link is an undiscovered category that will unmask the form placed improperly elsewhere. What Diderot leaves unsaid is that form and "place" are not identical but that an unnatural taxonomic language attempts to make them so.

Subtle problems arise to challenge this idea of continuity. If forms wear deceptive "masks" when imperfectly classified, what does this say about the transformative effect of verbal signs on the "place" or "presence" of natural forms? Under such metamorphic conditions, when, if ever, are things actually "present" to the knower? We shall see that Diderot addresses these issues elsewhere, as does Goya. But in this instance Diderot accepts the premise of a continuous chain of beings and even dismisses the illusory discontinuity by recourse to the distinction between continuous naked forms and those masked by another form mistakenly imposed by its identifying category.

Diderot contradicts these affirmations in a profoundly original section of the *Elements of Physiology*.[6] Examining the cognitive moment prior to language and its appearances, he observes the apparent continuity known through the senses. This analysis exposes the fact that discontinuity is not only the antithesis of continuity but is indeed its necessary constituent. The inescapable liaison becomes clear on contemplating the perception of daylight and the certainty that a day lasts as long or as continuously as there is daylight. In truth, day does not follow night in one continuous stretch but is broken up by eye-blinkings into tinier events that admit and shut out light. We spend our days by tiny days and tiny nights, muses Diderot by way of marveling at the disconnected relations among perceptions and objects. Each time we blink it is night, he observes. If we do not notice

6. The notes that comprise Diderot's *Éléments de physiologie* are not methodical. For a discussion of how to approach them, see Geoffrey Bremner, "Les 'Éléments de la physiologie' et le sens de la vie," in *Diderot: Les dernières années, 1770–84*, ed. Peter France and Anthony Strugnell (Edinburgh: Edinburgh University Press, 1985), 81–91.

the interruption, it is because we are not paying attention. The physical explanation may be that the impression of light lasts beyond the eyelid's shutting, but Diderot's point lies elsewhere. The perceiver is under the illusion of continuity.

The argument does not stop here. We cannot think, see, hear, taste, smell, or touch at the same time, according to Diderot in this pensive text. Specifically, "all sorts of impressions are made, but we are never at more than one of them" (*Éléments*, 9:344). And therefore more generally, the mind "is in the midst of these sensations like a guest at a raucous table chatting with his neighbor: he does not hear the others." Careful Diderot specialists point out that many statements in the *Elements of Physiology* are notes jotted down from Diderot's readings, not necessarily his own beliefs. In this instance, few doubts are possible. The test for authenticity is, first, expressive style, here unique enough to be Diderot's, and second, the repetition elsewhere of the same thought. In this respect, the entire problem of continuity seems to govern Diderot's notebook from its taxonomical inception.

The interdependence of continuity and discontinuity stands exposed by Diderot's radical step from an encompassing framework to the constituent sensory acts required for that framework. As soon as his analysis moves from integrating entities systemically to examining the perception of a single entity, the continuity of relationships breaks down. Diderot's arguments are not important because they contradict each other. The point, rather, is that his preoccupation with continuity bore the seeds of its negation as well as its validity, and that the negation found grounds for its revalidation in other thinkers, as we shall see after the next example.[7]

The ideal mechanist continuity was perhaps most lucidly portrayed in Hume's *Dialogues Concerning Natural Religion*, when Cleanthes is made to declare that the world is

> nothing but one great machine, subdivided into an infinite number of lesser machines, which again admit of subdivisions to a degree beyond what human senses and faculties can trace and explain. All various machines, and even their most minute parts, are adjusted to each other with an accuracy which ravishes into admiration all men who have ever contemplated them. (17)

7. It is true that Diderot's awareness of continuity entailed "beings," while his awareness of discontinuity entails "events." But on the plane of an integrative framework, events are simply the succession of things; one event is the succession of the particular thing in a series of tinier perceptual units.

This modular conception is sensorially concrete, taking into account sub-microscopic atoms linked to larger entities and so on up the perceivable scale of phenomena and interplanetary events. It makes specific Leibniz's grand scheme of a material "plenum" with no discrete "intervals." However, and this is crucial, the scheme falls into the age-old dilemma of the One and the Many. If the originary oneness persists, how can it also be many other things?

Aside from this problem, the mechanist model just cited also omits proof of how the parts "are adjusted to each other." What design or condition determines an adjustment of parts that ensures that they fit into an uninterrupted continuity? The model just mentioned derives partly from the Newtonian clock, which is a dynamic conception of universal motion. Presumably the connecting parts are continuous by virtue of figurative gears enabling either smaller wheels to engage larger ones, or coiled springs to expand and contract so as to set other parts into motion. A quite different conception of meshed parts permitted nonmechanists a new emphasis. Now a graduated scale was conceived on which each component was a transition from its adjacent smaller neighbor toward a larger one on the other side. Here the idea of transition implied a different kind of motion from that of the mechanist scheme. Organic components became conceivable, thus introducing notions of temporal connections of an evolutionary and metamorphic kind.

Rather than parts shaped metaphorically like Newtonian gears, the shape of ringlike links maintains the continuity between transitional elements. Many proponents of this model are known, including Charles Bonnet, who used two quite different images for the same idea: the scale or ladder of beings (*L'échelle des Êtres*) and the chain (*Chaîne*) made up of links (*chaînons*). Buffon's image of steps leading up into the misty pinnacle, mentioned in Chapter 1, indicates the paradox of these metaphors. A static quality emerges. The image suggests an orderly ranking that fits each element into its appropriate place. Continuity consists of the sheer orderliness of the elements by their size, their morphological complexity, and their logically adjoined categories of classification. The paradox is that a temporal progression of forms is intended despite the stasis. The ladder that ascends in space is the externalized version of a preformationist encasement in time, where each stage of a living form is enclosed in its successor, ready to emerge at a later phase. Bonnet faced yet another paradox. He was obliged to reconcile prodigious variety with nuanced similarity. The beings that constitute the scale submit to a graduated regimen of differences that do not obliterate sameness: "Everything therefore is *graduated*, or *nuanced* in Nature: there is no Being that does not have others *above* it or *below* it, which resemble it by some *characters*, and which *differ* from it by others" (*Essai de psychologie*, 366).

By contrast, the image of tiny ring-like links interchained among one another was perhaps the most perfect model. It permitted living organisms to be imaged by analogy with the preformationist theory of organic boxes within boxes. Bonnet recognized nonetheless the difficulty that "we perceive them only as badly linked, *interrupted*, and in an *Order* that differs, no doubt, a good deal from the *natural Order*" (365). His denial of discontinuity resembles Diderot's, but whereas Diderot blamed taxonomy and hence language itself for obscuring the true totality of connectedness, Bonnet declared that the totality escapes our notice due to "the weakness of our *eyesight*, the imperfection of our *Instruments*." He was comfortable with this explanation so long as mediatory roles remained unexamined. But the flaw in the continuist ideal was glaring enough for him to summarize three factors in continuity that seem to have broken down.

Before reviewing these factors, it is important to notice that the missing element in both the mechanical and the organic models was a pervasive unifying agent. Diderot's assumption that objects were universally connected but perceived disconnectedly placed the blame on language, not on any subject/object disjunction. That is, in the terms of Goya's Universal Language, if the cognitive medium itself were continuous with mind and matter, all would be continuous.[8] Nothing so pervasive characterized either Hume's or Bonnet's model. What was needed was a different unifying agent, one that overcame the conditions that disrupted continuity. That agent subsisted in the very source that gave rise to the Universal Language, as we shall see in a moment.

8. The Universal Language would be part and parcel of reality, united with external objects as well as with the subject's mind. This was impossible with verbal language, but the language of dream plausibly would be at once the medium and the phenomena made manifest by it; its vocabulary would be images that also constituted the reality external to them. This interpretation follows the empirical skepticism that holds that representations or ideas are the reality, and that things in themselves external to perception are at best unknowable. Because dream images are like waking ideas in that they flow from the pathways traced by animal spirits, they "float" coterminously with the objects they represent. Unlike words and distinct national tongues, which are the required vehicles of waking ideas, the dream language is universal, made of the same stuff in all minds and pervading all represented phenomena. In my next volume, *The Universal Dream Language of Minerva*, I shall show how his interpretation diverges from customary approaches to universal language studied by other scholars, most recently by Robert Markley, *Fallen Languages: Crises of Representation in Newtonian England, 1660–1740* (Ithaca, N.Y. and London: Cornell University Press, 1993).

The three factors in continuity were: a connectedness among entities, an uninterrupted communication from one "end" to the other, and an ordered relationship. These conditions are more easily met in a mechanist scheme of moving parts in a clockwork universe than in the same universe also populated by living organisms. This more complex universe is biophysical and demands an explanation for the transitional connections between inert beings and living beings, between mineral, plant, and animal substances, particularly when sensory capacity permits some living entities to think and exercise the imagination. An extreme example of such a connection might be the relationship between the astronomical sun and the human idea. The "connection" in fact is plausible. Within the scope of models for continuous matter, the literal connection between the astrophysical world and the organic one did indeed find a model that unified the mechanist description in Hume with Bonnet's chain of beings.

The unifying factor in this conception was aether. In the physical chemistry described by Étienne Gamaches, the Cartesian vortex is accommodated to Newtonian physics. The result is to allow the macrocosm and the microcosm to be joined by a single substance. Gamaches's scheme allows the addition of smaller and smaller post-Cartesian vortices encased in one another. However, a problem of motion and connectability arises from

> the tiny vortices whose discovery is owed to modern physicists. . . . One feels that one cannot fill the Universe with vortices encased (*entasés*) in one another, without being obliged to recognize that aether is nothing other than an assemblage of tiny vortices composed of an infinite number of tinier ones, which themselves are enclosed in yet tinier ones and so on infinitely, so that one cannot assign any limits to the divisibility of matter, and the least atom is immense within its kind. (*Astronomie physique*, xxi)

The model rests on an image of encasement closely akin to Bonnet's organic model, allowing mechanical motion in space to share the same process as organic development in time. But Gamaches's model needed also to explain what occupies the "space" between vortices. Bonnet furnished the explanation by relying on the complementary model of ringlike links. Gamaches remains within the same model by using the "fluide intermédiaire," or what Descartes called the "matière subtile," that fills the pores between the particles of Newtonian aether.

Of course one must ask, Isn't the aether discontinuous by virtue of the intermediary fluid? Put another way, what explains the "connection" between these fluids? The problem becomes insoluble. The discontinuity is resituated to the sub-atomic level of aether and inter-aethereal fluid, a problem of atomic chemistry or of logic whose infinite regress cannot ever offer a solution. However, the problem has another formulation. Because the aether penetrates everything in the universe, is not "everything" to be understood as one continuous and undifferentiated mass of aether? The answer is bipartite. It is yes in the fundamental sense of the "One and the Many" constituting the structural rhythm of cosmic creation and differentiation. This half-answer satisfies hypotheses as different as the separation of the unity God-Chaos into the polymorphous universe, or, in contrasting modern terms, the "big bang" expansion and slow retraction to a single undifferentiated particle. This is the fundamental mystery of science and religion: the persistence in the "many" of an original oneness, the energy resident in the first monomorphic particle or in the divine Creator.

The second half of the answer is that the variety of beings in the universal encasement does not exclude their continuity because the aether is present at every point. Logic here poses the problem of what a "point" actually is and what separates one aethereal point or particle from another. But aside from this irreducible problem, such points, particles, and vortices require individuation. Being separate from one another, their condition is often spatially mobile and temporally mutable. In order to empower this flexibility, "the fluid that flows between the pores of the aethereal matter is simply a mass of tiny vortices of another order than those of aether, but elastic like them" (Gamaches, xxv–vi). From the standpoint of encasement theory, a continuous flux throughout the universe is maintained. The "tiny vortices of aethereal matter" change incessantly in position as they circulate. The same dynamic ensures continuity from the standpoint of organic matter. Gamaches is not a physiologist, however, and does not elaborate this further aspect of aether theory.

The flaw in Gamaches's model is evident from today's critical perspective. He resorts to a diploid structure of matter in order to maintain the idea of continuity. He preserves the Cartesian "subtle matter" in a minor presence to serve the all-important aether, whose differentiation must be explained. Aside from this function the subtle matter has no interest, and indeed it has no individuating capacity to make it significant: "this fluid is to aethereal matter what aethereal matter is to sensible bodies, and so just as aether does not oppose the movement of these bodies in any way, so too the subtle matter does not present any obstacle to the movements of the particles of aether" (Gamaches, xxvii). In short, the focus is on the content rather than on the vehicle, on the aethereal marrow, so to speak, that fills space and the entities in space rather than on the empowering vehicle that permits individuation.

In this way, the illusion of continuity was upheld. Yet the sleight of hand was no more dishonest than the overlooked discontinuity between Bonnet's scale of beings and his chain of links. The scale or ladder is similarly a formal vehicle that "holds" the connected beings on its rungs. What makes Gamaches important is that he furnishes a sophisticated feature. The material contact between beings is also explained. Their literal connection derives from the aethereal contents of the minute vortices. This refinement is merely supposed, as we have seen, but it permits the satisfied declaration that "the hypothesis of tiny vortices is fully justified by the light it sheds on the most secret processes of Nature" (Gamaches, xxxvi). These secrets reside in the organic realm, and in particular within the crevices separating mind and matter.

The flaws just outlined in the various representative models of continuity should not encourage a mistaken conclusion. It was not the case that nonbiological inquiry removed the issue of discontinuity. The proof is that the mathematician d'Alembert portrayed the physics of his day as lacking clear linkages between most of the observable truths. Isolated and "floating" truths, disconnected from one another, are anomalies that defy integration in a continuous network of understanding. The difficulty was noticed by d'Alembert in the area of mechanico-vital causality, where individual events may be understood, but not their connection.[9]

Discontinuous Organic Models in Buffon

The scope and varieties of the discontinuist preoccupation have been underestimated, if noticed at all, by scholars. While the ideal of continuism

9. One dramatic instance of unexplained linkages in the human body is the relation between voice, facial hair, and genitals, a relation certified by the effects of castration. Citing this reference in *Essai sur les éléments de la philosophie*, François Duchesneau showed that the absence of links is clearest in physiological explanations made by analogy with Newtonian physics. The action of gravity on capillary movement remained hypothetical, while other conjectures made by reductionist iatromechanism exposed lacunae that the empirical linkages favored by d'Alembert often failed to remove. D'Alembert was obliged to accept "an open inductive state" for the less formalizable aspects of physics, despite the possible inconsistency resulting from empirical observation and established systems. His examples included apparent plant sensitivity, asexual reproduction in animal organisms, and regeneration of members. François Duchesneau, *La physiologie des lumières: Empirisme, modèles et théories* (The Hague: Martinus Nijhoff, 1982), 86–87.

has long been recognized, the subtle ways in which its metaphors announce its inconsistencies remain neglected. The major metaphors devised by Buffon and Diderot belong to this category. They are especially informative because they are linear models, thus offering a rather different conception of continuity than the models discussed earlier. More significant, they bring two independent realms into association if not continuity: external Nature and internal cognitive processes. These separate realms otherwise represent the ultimate dualist rift even when continuity might be demonstrated within each of them. The linear models offered by Buffon and Diderot also invite analysis that goes to the heart of the opposition between rational language and the Universal Language discussed in the preceding chapter—that is, they address the problem of access to true knowledge. If the linear ray of light is a visual metaphor for rational understanding and connectedness, then palpable mass is an alternative tactile metaphor for insight and connectedness. Acts of transmission through material contact become the functional equivalent of the pervasive aether that Gamaches identified to be the agent of continuity, as mentioned earlier in this chapter.

It goes without saying that the linear trope is eminently suitable to express the ideal of continuity. The straight line furnishes a clear metaphor for any gesture that involves reaching goals or connecting entities. The model suits human thinking most of all. The mind seeks the shortest route to an intellectual conclusion by taking an undeviant, straight-edged path of thoughts. We reach out directly to "grasp" an idea. Even associationist thought seeks its narrative line. So too in human actions. An unobstructed progression is the optimal standard for a series of gestures designed to complete a project. A direct path safeguards the standard, and Buffon is emphatic about its linearity when he describes fallible efforts: "how many reflections and combinations are necessary in order to avoid those oblique lines, false routes, deadends, and remote lanes!" (*Histoire naturelle*, ed. Varloot, 213).

The straight-line metaphor combines several features that permit its application both to Nature and also to human thought. The linearity as an uninterrupted progression in space not only represents the way of Reason, it entails consecutivity in time. These same traits can designate a rational Nature whose constituent elements Buffon will classify. As a natural historian, Buffon must account for the continuity of Nature's work or progress. The connections between species and forms will be as closely linear as those in human genealogy. Yet Buffon's linear sensibility reveals ambivalence. He grants to human thought a rectilinear capability because it is patterned on

Nature's own operations. But he also declares that while man follows the straight line of mental clarity to reach a given point, "if he wishes to grasp another point he can only reach it by another line. The warp (*trame*) of his ideas is of a single thin thread extending lengthwise without any other dimensions. Nature, by contrast, never takes a step that goes only in one direction."

The different linearities prompt a remarkable description of Nature's crablike motion. Buffon conjures up a quadrilaterally moving creature of the sort envisioned by Ezekiel, one that ascends, goes down, and retreats all at once while it advances.[10] In Buffon's words, as Nature is "marching forward, she spreads to the sides and rises up; she traverses and fills three dimensions at the same time. While man can attain one point, she reaches solidity, encompasses volume, and penetrates mass in all of their parts" (214). The sensibility of Nature is simultaneous, immediate, and not limited by human Reason to what it "sees," whether the sighted object is something aligned with the mental eye or is the goal reached by traversing space. In contrast to the linear medium of light rays, Nature's medium is quadrilineal, combining volume with time. Hers might be said to be a blind sensibility, overcoming the visual separations of space by being immediately "there," simultaneously occupying all spatial directions.

It will be recalled that Touch in the allegorical frontispiece for Le Cat's treatise on the senses was able to communicate directly with Minervan truth, circumventing the clockwise path. Appositely in Buffon's portrait of Nature's blind sensibility, the truth of her totality offers access without linear mediacy. The metaphor of Truth as a light ray is overthrown. Unlike the eye distanced from the image, or the subject distanced from its object, Nature touches all things in the direct contact of her total embrace. Buffon himself alludes to this metaphorically tactile difference. He compares sculpture with Nature's grasp and her total penetration of material substance. What do "our Phidiases do when they give shape to crude matter?" he asks. The answer tempts comparison with the mythic blind sculptors mentioned by Diderot in the *Letter on the Blind*. In that mythic society, the tactile knowledge furnished by blindness causes space to collapse. An unmediated stereognosis replaces the rational knowledge obtained through

10. See Knight on the vision of Ezekiel: God equals eagle, bull, lion, "the emblems of the Aethereal Spirit, the Creative and Destructive Powers." Knight's study of the Priapus cult exposes the Orphic meaning: "the generative power of light"; fire as active power of creation and generation; "the Aetherial spirit, or active productive Power"—whose symbol is the bull. Richard Payne Knight, *An Account of the Remains of the Worship of Priapus Lately Existing at Isernia* (London: T. Spillsbury, 1786), 116–17, 142, 146–48.

linear "contact" of eye and illuminated object. Buffon's ordinary sculptor is limited by eyesight and Reason, thus merely rendering his art as an exact surface rather than by the stereognostic knowledge through touch of masses in depth. His

> genius marches straight along as many lines as there are features in the figure, and the least deviation deforms it. This marble, so perfect that it seems to breathe, is thus only a multitude of points reached by the artist with painful and successive [advances]. . . . Nature on the other hand knows how to brew and to stir right down to the bottom. She produces these forms by nearly instantaneous acts, developing and extending them in three dimensions at the same time. As her movements reach the surface, the penetrating forces that animate her operate on the inside. Each molecule is penetrated, and the tiniest atom is forced to obey once Nature wishes to use it. She works in all directions, forward, backward, above, below, to the left, to the right, on all sides all at once. As a result she embraces not only the surface but also the entire volume, mass, and solidity in all their parts. (214)

Behind these contrasting portraits of human limitation and encompassing Nature is a half-formulated judgment. Acts of knowing can only be described by metaphor. Buffon intuitively questions his century's grand metaphor, which organizes knowledge under the principle of continuity. The same metaphor describes the universe, Nature, and the operations of the human mind. It seems to describe even the structure of knowledge: a continuous line from one category to another, straight in its restricted context although perhaps circular in its encyclopedic totality. At all events, knowledge is figured by a linear, here-to-there metaphor, first as a subject-object relationship, and then as a consecution of sense impressions, ideas, and reasonings that lead from one topic to another.

But what of Nature? Buffon understands that Nature presents a challenge to current assumptions of cognitive coherence, so he proceeds indirectly, defining our apprehension of continuity by the primary metaphor that confirms it. This metaphor is eyesight, with its spatial and lineal character. Buffon further opposes Nature's "blind" multidimensionality to the sighted sculptor's "straight" march along "successive" surfaces without the slightest "deviation." By this opposition, the grand rational metaphor of the age comes under a shadow. Nature's crab-like motion produces unorthodox linearities that cannot be reduced to the linear continuities of Reason. Thus Buffon issues a cautionary exclamation about avoiding "those oblique lines, false routes" cited earlier. He has observed the misguided "combinations" that twist Nature into false systems. By his own analysis, he realizes that the necessary combination would require another mode of "continuity."

The metaphor for this alternative mode is furnished by Diderot in the famous spider-brain image mentioned by Mademoiselle de l'Espinasse in *D'Alembert's Dream*. Here the separation of Nature's and the mind's motions in Buffon is overcome and synthesized. If the linear sensibility is a systematic progression in space that represents the way of Reason, then the arachnoid sensibility is the weaving and plying of connective fibers that hold the lines of thought together in a continuous network. The spider at the center of its web, like the Intelligence at the center of the universe, is immediately and simultaneously in contact with everything. The spider is Nature herself, cast in the image of Minerva's counterpart. The microcosmic counterpart is the linear "warp" of human ideas, supplemented by other ideas about Nature that take nonlinear directions. The arachnoid sensibility supplements "the single thin thread extending lengthwise without any other dimension," cited earlier by Buffon.

Buffon's implicit criticism of reigning metaphors is clear from his own supply of metaphors. Diderot's spiderweb image exists concomitantly with Buffon's, and both expose a groundswell of questions preoccupied with discontinuity. Does not the network model produce knots and blocked messageways, much like the labyrinth that is the model's mythic prototype? Arachne's punishment, after all, was not just to be an insect weaver but also to hang as a trapped body at the tapestry's labyrinthine center. And how else are all things in Nature's scheme actually connected? Rational threads are insufficient, causing Buffon to work with supplementary threads across the linear warp. He dismisses the cumbersome classifications of Linnaeus and devises other classes based on a binary system of resemblances and differences. The result is an imperfect continuity that approximates Nature's. But discontinuity menaces from within like some unspecified "monster" that Goya's "dream" of Reason materializes through the bat that represents just that metamorphic energy of Nature, as noted in a previous chapter.

A vast spread of species confronts Buffon's search for continuity. He admits that "our nomenclature is presented by a meshwork of figures whereby some are attached by the feet, others by the teeth, by the horns, by the fur, and by other relations still smaller." At the point where the scale marks apes and humans, the relations are of course much larger. Overall, the linking scheme depends on the word *lacis*, an entangled network whose patternless windings become visually bizarre in Buffon's account of knots and crossings. These attachments and points in common do provide a continuous system. They fail to provide room for major anomalies. The scheme also abandons the criterion of difference, a standard that Foucault insisted was the eighteenth-century measure of identity, as opposed to earlier Classical standard of resemblances.[11] Be this as it may, Buffon classifies the organic world by odd convergences such as teeth and fur. The logic of species distribution still awaits a "Universal Language" to overcome the disconformities.

Buffon cannot describe Nature's continuity without separating her constituent entities, which are ordered by connective frames or categories that ramify like a webwork. To omit this ordering would leave a model of Nature as an amorphous, monstrous agglomeration. At the same time, the webwork does not have a single, unmediated, controlling center. It consists of Buffon's language, which is rooted in the metaphor of eyesight and light, of Reason and space. It is a language, therefore, that generates a mediating distance. Yet Nature stands in its tactile immediacy, as Buffon himself attests. Nature's all-embracing "sculpture" can be known only through another dimension of language. But Buffon's categories do not eliminate their spatial premise. He mentions, notwithstanding Foucault, "this grand tableau of resemblances in which the living universe presents itself as if it comprised a single family" (Varloot, 218). His pictorial figure conceives of groupings within a single scene, called the "tableau." Here it may be asked what links the individual groupings as a single "family." Is not the tableau more a network with several centers, each organized around a group of individuals? Such groupings are like juxtaposed scenes that leave interstices between them. The tableau itself remains discontinuous until such time as its groupings rearrange themselves so as to dissolve the intervening spaces and regroup the scenes around a single center.

The discontinuity is apparent to Buffon himself. His unifying scheme for morphology requires a framing device from group to group. The scheme obliges him to turn away from resemblances and to consider just the opposite. He looks at differences, "where each species claims an isolated place and should have its own separate portrait." And when this is done, several major exceptions among the species intrude, including the elephant, the rhinoceros, the hippopotamus, the tiger, and the lion. Buffon perfunctorily notes the repeated hiatus and passes on to the "graduated similitudes" of all other groups and species.

11. See above, Chapter 2, note 2.

The preceding discussion has addressed Buffon's classification of living species in their synchronic, morphological state. It has not implied any failure to appreciate the difficulties of continuity-theory. Buffon's concerns obviously included the successive generations of species, but this evolutionary sphere succumbs to the same problems of continuity, now involving organic transformations of matter that bear separate study. Nonetheless, Buffon's synchronic terms for classifying Nature eventually meet a grave obstacle to achieving a graduated continuity.

Buffon's very first *Discourse* declares: "Nature marches by unknown gradations, and therefore she cannot completely hold herself to these divisions since she often passes from one species to another . . . by imperceptible nuances" (167). This text is as much an admission of taxonomical discontinuity as it is a testimony for natural gradation. It invites us to survey the different entities that compose the universe and to discover "with astonishment that one can descend by almost insensible degrees from the most perfect creature to the most formless matter, from the best organized animal to the crudest mineral" (166). The statement appears to confirm the Great Chain of Being. Nevertheless, this is no mechanistic chain, but a vitalistic universe in flux, if not in metamorphosis. Buffon no longer merely observes the live, linear tableau; he wants also to watch its temporal progress through generational change. Even more, the mutability reconfigures the concept of matter and removes the terms of discussion from taxonomic synchrony to generational diachrony.

By considering generational change, Buffon must also acknowledge the impossibility of a "general system." He concedes the impossibility even for a single branch of natural history, to say nothing of its entirety. A systemized scheme of classes and subdivisions results in an "arbitrary order," he admits. This judgment reflects severe caution, the result of inserting "the crudest mineral" into the discussion. Now the obstacle to continuity is posed on the sweeping scale of matter pure and simple, instead of living matter that is classifiable under the animal kingdom. When organized, living beings and their categories are considered in their mutual relationships, their complexity warrants organic metaphors like the spiderweb or the "family" picture, which carry unifying explanations. But these are synchronic metaphors. They require a diachronic concept in order to account for generational change. It is here that matter, plain and simple, becomes a factor. The origin of life, and the essential relationship of living matter to inert matter, are issues that concern Buffon.

The reason Buffon's shift from organic matter to just plain matter is important involves pervasiveness, that necessary factor for continuity, plus the energy presumably inherent in matter. The biophysical universe coheres, when contemplated as a totality, because the same raw material constitutes each and every being contained within it. The gradation among these beings follows "imperceptible nuances" owing to "median species" and "bipartitioned objects" (*espèces moyennes, objets mipartis*) that escape human classification. The resulting apparent discontinuity is an obstacle that may be overcome by other concepts such as molds, generative matter, and vital force. These concepts pierce the secret of matter, linking all entities without interruption, and they are dealt with in later chapters. Buffon's response both to gaps between species and to evolutionary gaps within a single species is to reaffirm confidence in the unity of matter. He cannot accept the principle of "degeneration" whereby a new type emerges from a species just because, say, certain equine features are transformed for the worse into asinine ones. Anomalies like the donkey have an evolutionary explanation—of this Buffon is certain. But the notion of "family" must not be wrenched in order to conform to a continuity that is more rational than it is materially evident.

Consequently Buffon prefers to tolerate discontinuities of "intervals" between degrees of nuanced transformation rather than to force an implausible theory. This tolerance exacts a price, however. The honest observer must concede that "the higher the species, the fewer their numbers and the more the intervals that exist between nuances to separate them" (195). The lower species display narrower gaps and closer calibration by virtue of their numbers, a fact that seduces Reason into a flawed classification: "We must not forget that these *families* are our work, that we have devised them only for our mental comfort, that if we cannot understand the real continuity of all beings it is our fault and not Nature's" (195).

Faced with this inadequacy, Buffon withdraws to the manageable continuities that belong indisputably within single species and their evolving generations. His voluminous study is organized on the principle of the unbroken line that inheres only in the succession of individuals capable of mixing and breeding new generations. His last word on the subject in 1770 was to substitute the metaphor of "thread" for the original "straight line." By that time, much literature on brain structure and nerve anatomy had influenced general discourse, as we shall see. Buffon's occasion was the study of birds, which obliged him to note certain resemblances, such as those that exist between an ostrich and a camel, despite the separation of orders. The result exposed the "Chain of Being" for the metaphor that it was. Once again Nature is an "immense tableau," this time where

> each order of being is represented by a chain that sustains a continuous set (*suite*) of rather kindred objects, similar enough for their differences to be difficult to grasp. This chain is not a simple thread that merely extends in length. It is a large warp or rather a sheaf (*faisceau*) which, from interval to interval, projects side branches that join the sheaves of another order. And it is especially at the two ends that these sheafs wrinkle and ramify so as to reach the others. (236)

One "extreme end of the chain," in the order of quadrupeds, rises toward the order of birds by way of the bat varieties, while at the other extreme the chain descends to the order of whales. The middle finds a "branch" extending from ape to man, while another point "shoots a double and triple branch" toward the various reptiles (236).

The metaphor of a tree makes these allusions deceptive. Their true meaning grows clear against the richer image of the "sheaf" or "bundle." A reference like "the lower end of the sheaf divides into two branches" makes sense only if we consider Buffon's original notion of the "chain." Faced with resemblances and deviations within a species, Buffon must arrange their order while also accounting for the occasional homologies in other species. The most useful model is the linear pattern of "a large warp or rather a sheaf." This bundle of parallel threads is like the warp quoted earlier, but it offers the advantage of an additional dimension in the form of ramifications whose only imagery relates to a tree. Thus Buffon mixes metaphors by speaking, in one instance, of "the other branches that escape their order or main sheaf." The word "trunk" never appears because it connotes an immobile structure. It does not permit the flexible weavings that follow Nature's multidimensional course when parallel threads or lateral offshoots ply and cross over into the fabric of another loom or warp. The pervasive imagery of the "fiber" takes its cognitive justification here and is discussed in Chapter 6.

The linearity of the "chain of beings" yields to the sinuosity of the spiderweb and sheaf or bundle. The shift marks the new insight that continuity in Nature is more than a rational "here to there" sequence. It also marks the awareness that cognitive acts need powerful intuitive metaphors in order to "grasp" reality in its complexity. The linear metaphor reappeared when Buffon referred to "the ladder of time" in a late essay on the epochs of Nature, published in 1778. However, this ladder or chain is a trope for the evolutionary and metamorphic complexity just alluded to. Buffon is quite distant from mechanistic and deistic world views in his conception of organic matter and its differentiation into living forms that alter through time. He resists the most speculative models of biomorphic development, such as germ theory. But he does not abandon his own metaphor of proto-typical "molds" that shape transformative matter. In short, Buffon's evolutionary preoccupation confronts his taxonomical rationality. There is a contest between his linear and arachnoid sensibilities.

This synthesizing contest turns on the notion of matter, the "common property of animal and plant, this power to produce its likeness, this chain of successive existences of individuals that constitutes the real existence of the species" (173). The statement has a vitalist tone and amplitude that show Buffon's respect for the properties of living matter that persist temporally in differentiated entities. One such property is the prodigious fertility of matter, although it is "a rather ordinary magnificence for Nature." Another aspect is matter's commonality, its ubiquitous generating inherence in lower and higher organisms, in polyps and in poets alike. This second aspect is important because it brings the text into the framework of writings by Robinet, Needham, Bonnet, and Diderot, whose fascination with the polyp was the gateway to wider issues of neural and cerebral activity. These issues raise the question of how intelligence is to be defined, and whether it determines the concept of knowledge. Such issues are implicit in Buffon's remark about the reproductive power of matter to "assemble in one being an infinite number of similar organic beings, and compose its substance in such a way as to allow each part to contain a germ of the same kind [as that being] and thus be able to become a whole that is similar to the one containing the part" (173).

How this substance is composed and where it ceases to be life-bearing and organic were enigmas left to contemporaries more skilled with the microscope. One of them, John Needham, collaborated with Buffon and drew on his prestige for accrediting experiments in regeneration. Such enigmas chip away the ideal of continuity and carve into its pedestal of flawed models an awareness of discontinuity. Buffon's shifting use of models is perhaps the most impressive example, given his scientific stature. Nowhere is this more plain than in the way his metaphors contour the idea of matter in its fundamental implications.

As mentioned, he applied the chain to taxonomical relations. But these abstractions did not fulfill the materially figured connectedness of even a metaphorical chain. If living entities are joined to one another as individual links, the image of a chain must be modified. Such a modification is achieved by metaphors of a spiderweb or a warp of threads and fibers. These images present individual beings as forming a chain of connecting cells that make a fiber. Many such fibers or threads touch or cross and form a continuous web. As groupings or sheafs, their offshoots weave into neighboring sheafs and extend the material continuity. The only unexplained factor is perhaps the unbroken contact from one generation to the next. Yet temporal continuity in a material sense can also be represented by a chain. Here the linkage among entities follows from reproduction and differentiation. The generative process consists of material transmission. Transmitted matter remains matter, and only its changing forms signify differences in time and in individuality.

From this standpoint, Buffon's organic models shifted emphasis away from abstract continuity and its static resemblances. Continuity was the tangible process of transmission and transformation. It entailed the generative property of matter. Through reproduction, the continuity of evolution could be touched materially. Its connecting thread was the very substance carried forward during the physical metamorphosis of a living component of a being at moment A into the living component of another being at a later moment B.

The Brain as Labyrinth

Organic metaphors can be analyzed to a misleading extreme of literalness, but their limitations need to be exposed in order to reveal the equally misleading impression that their premises are invariably sound. Beneath the premises of organic metaphors often lie fantasies that sustain half-understood insights that remain rationally unutterable. One such metaphor is Diderot's spider-like brain that is in tangible contact with all things in its universal web. The figure gives persuasive evidence of connectedness. It carries the assumption that the parts of knowledge are linked and therefore unified within a continuous system. This assumption reflects a major ambition that remained unfulfilled in the eighteenth century. The ambition of continuism itself bears scrutiny. It was premised on certain beliefs about intelligence and about the brain, an organ that itself continued to be less than fully understood at the time. The brain served as a metaphor for continuity, which was assumed to be tangibly knowable. Alexander Pope remarked in his *Essay on Man* that "the scale of sensual, mental powers ascends," and adds, "the spider's touch, so exquisitely fine! / Feels in each thread, and lives along the line" (1:207–18). Yet an organism capable of "feeling" or grasping all within its network leaves unanswered questions about its processes. Is the network continuous within itself right up to its comprehending brain center? Or is it a labyrinth filled with pathways and barriers? Is the spider-brain actually a knot in the network, attaching the incommunicable threads by their ends at different points of its circular wall?

When Diderot proposed the spiderweb image in *D'Alembert's Dream*, he preceded it with the image of "meninges." In this conception, three membranes envelop the universe in the same way that the brain and spinal cord are enveloped by the arachnoid, the dura mater, and the pia mater. Inevitably the reader is led to recall Newton's remark that God needs no organs, because His body is space. Diderot's meninges simply metaphorize the Supreme Intelligence, which functions through the aether. Several ramifications about aether's association with intelligence will become clearer in later chapters. The immediate point is the suspicion that a pervasive unifying agent can achieve continuity at all levels of reality: within the subject's internal world and within the external macrocosmos, while healing the dualist split between both.

The spiderweb labyrinth and the human brain thus participate in becoming the two halves of a single metaphor, both for cognition and for reality itself. Their convoluted landscapes give them imagistic power as analogs of inextricable circumstances that lose the thinker in their winding connectedness. Broadly focused, the same confounding power fills the archetypal labyrinth that traps the Minotaur in an endless library of information. Narrowly focused, the labyrinth is homologous with the brain's gyri, which conceal the enigmatic physiology of cognition. The maze baffles mythic explorers awaiting the Theseus who can enter and return from the sinuous journey via the thread provided by a Minerva-inspired Ariadne. What baffled latter-day explorers was the maze of human knowledge that needs a mapped route. The map surfaces at the level of language, which d'Alembert conjectured to be both a tree and a labyrinth. At the level of physical matter, neuroanatomists described the threadwork of nerves up to the cerebral lobes and their cavernous interiors. Nevertheless philosophers remained mystified by the unmapped seat of intelligence itself.

These parallels entail both Encyclopedic knowledge and cognitive process, but they are not the vistas that open experientially on the spectacle of natural and human history. The latter vistas are everyday cognitive experiences known to everyone when attention is not coerced by the metaphors and models of scientific discourse. They are vistas open to visual inspection and spontaneous speech, unbound by the formal rules of procedure and language. This nontechnical, everyday dimension has its own discourse, examples of which are found in art, literature, history, and philosophy. Among these examples are the illustrations for Buffon's *Histoire naturelle* and Goya's introspective art.

A glance at *Capricho 43* makes vivid the experiential knowledge just described. Here the idea of discontinuity, if allowed its way, can provoke practical questions at every turn. Does the picture bear any resemblance to the text that explicates it ("The Sleep/Dream of Reason Produces Monsters")? If so, in what way are images congruent with words? Then there is the problem of how the viewer begins to describe or interpret the scene. Should we speak first of the owls, as conventionally symbolic of Minervan wisdom and, by extension, of the brain? If so, what rational connection can these owls have with the bats? Or should we begin with the bats, a possible symbol of monstrosity? If so, how do we bridge their discontinuity with the feline or the sleeping figure? Perhaps the starting point should be the sleeper. His connection with the cat (assuming it is a cat and not a lynx) is domestic ownership.[12] This feline pet might lead to the owls by way of some informal linkage in animal folklore, but in fact no connecting chain exists here either: each living species occupies a plane of its own. Taxonomical planes may also be called the parallel threads in Buffon's warp, but these are discontinuous unless some offshoot of a sheaf can be shown to cross over. And last, if the linkage of bat and owl were made, the incongruous result would relate Minervan wisdom to a sinister or monstrous icon.

Unable to discover an organizing center for interpreting *Capricho 43*, we glimpse the intellectual disorder whose external form is visual discontinuity. The disorientation subsides on turning to Goya's earlier version, *Sepia One* (Fig. 13). This preliminary pen-and-sepia sketch makes a clear spatial separation between the dream and waking reality. It also excludes the verbal language of *Capricho 43*. The sleeper slumps over his work table in the rational world, a scene of oblivion. The dream space above him exhibits its own consciousness through the awakened state of the many

12. Several art historians consider the feline in *Capricho 43* to be a lynx. See George Levitine, "Some Emblematic Sources of Goya," *Journal of the Warburg and Courtauld Institutes* 22 (1959): 121; and Fölke Nordstrom, *Goya, Saturn, and Melancholy: Studies in the Art of Goya* (Stockholm: Almqvist and Wiksell, 1962), 100.

Figure 13. Francisco de Goya. *Sepia One*. "Sueño" (Dream). Courtesy of the Museo del Prado, Madrid.

human faces peering out with diverse expressions. But the disembodied faces fill only one sector of the dream, which is diffused with light against an eerie shadowed sector, where bats spread their lobated wings.

It is readily surmisable in *Sepia One* that the sleeper's brain generates the creatures populating his dream. The lower region of the scene demarcates an arc that curves down from the sleeper's head, shoulder, and hip toward the chair's back and the cat. The upper chamber curves its lobular bottom around the arc of head and waist. *Sepia One* seems to be organized bicamerally.

Lest I write too hastily about the drawing's spatial composition in the terms of a bicameral brain, this analogy should follow the sober text of a respected anatomist. Current notions of the brain as a convoluted maze are reinforced by the many flexures of its arteries and smaller vessels with their inosculating branches. In Goya's day vivid writing in another style characterized the chapter on brain anatomy in the book by the noted physician Albrecht von Haller, *First Lines of Physiology*. Haller described the ashgrey color of the corpora striata, with its palmated streaks and lesser medullary specks. In this area, each band of white matter joining the parts of the brain sends out a hemispherical "mamillary" protuberance. Into the cavities descend striated bodies that

> terminate outwards by a sort of convex sulcated end, imprinted by the gyri of the brain; and terminated by a foot, having as it were four furrows, whence the name of *hippocampus*, which externally are covered by exceedingly thin medullary plates, but are inwardly of a cortical substance. At the beginning of the division of the foot of the hippocampus, the taenia ends in two white striae, a long and a short one, inserted into this foot and into the brain. . . . A like protuberance is continued in the posterior horn of the ventricle, crooked inwards at its extremity like the claw of a bird. (*Physiology*, 1:201)

Here Haller's imagistic language adds that the medullary portion, "painted with transverse and palmated streaks, is called the *psalterium* or harp."

Returning now to *Sepia One* we note the light and dark areas of the dream sphere. The whitish human segment and the blackish-grey animal segment are distinctly separate. The cleft is not merely due to the one-sided luminosity, or the rigorously segregated living species. The cleft also rises from the source of the lighted dream segment. The source radiates a fanlike sheaf of straight lines streaking from the dreamer's head. These rays or striae diminish from left to center as they approach the point of greatest brilliance. The brightest shaft is the unstreaked column of faces that suggests an identification of the dreamer's head with his oneiric heads as they are variously dreamed. The striation continues to the right and completes its path, the circumference of human consciousness. The striae never invade the zone of darkness, which is condensed by the closely grooved hatching that replaces them.

There is a cleft in the dream chamber, and it suggests that the sleeper's brain does not generate the entire dream content. An independent energy emanates from the wing-borne bats and from the powerful horse that bears down on the scene from above. Although a human energy may have conjured the oneiric faces floating in light, quite another life force resides in the bats' mammary glands and in the horse's front hooves. Once these divisions are understood for what they mean, the composition appears to display a trifoliated or trilobated structure. The surface furrows and streaks form a random nervation. The lateral lobes dramatize their chiaroscuro around the bat, where the surrounding sulcated surface throws in relief the bat's dark protuberances. The black right wing of the dominant bat pulls these surfaces toward itself like a magnetic center. Given these observations, it is no interpretive risk to link *Sepia One* and *Capricho 43*. They both portray states of subjective or irrational reality generated by indeterminate sources of primal energy.

The extraordinary ease with which *Sepia One* lends itself to an interpretation that reproduces the brain's role in the cognitive puzzle bears witness to the extent that discontinuity preoccupied the eighteenth century. The parallel with neuroanatomy reinforces the role of metaphorical expression in both natural philosophy and art. More about this will become relevant in Chapters 6 and 7. Its importance here is the structural coherence that permits interpretation without self-contradictory questions of the kind posed earlier for *Capricho 43*. The relation of *Sepia One* to *Capricho 43* is analogous to the relation between organized knowledge and discontinuous experience. *Sepia One* invites mention and eventual discussion of the brain by virtue of its pictorial anecdote and spatial construction. The sketch is fantastical, but its irrationality lends itself to analysis. As such, *Sepia One* also emblemizes confidence in the brain's power to break free of cognitive labyrinths.

In contrast, *Capricho 43* emblemizes the discontinuous spectacle of experiential knowledge. The implausible but not chaotic scene permits comparison with *Sepia One*. Both scenes depict dreams, but both also depict objects related to drawing and etching. These depictions refer to the world external to art more than they address the dream world within it. The pencil, the burin, and the engraver's bench are emblems of everyday reality.

They evoke the immediate environment of a productive artist: among the dreamed faces, one might easily be Francisco de Goya himself. This referential immediacy to a historical milieu permits more general evocations appropriate to a paradigmatic work of art. One such evocation might be to a personage comparable to Goya who could experience eighteenth-century life as a creator of ideas or images. Granted this general case, the sleeping figure could represent any kind of engraver. He might do illustrations for literary works or, just as likely, etch plates for books about science and mechanics. Finally, he could be a medical illustrator, someone associated perhaps with a disciple of Haller, the dean of anatomy and physiology in the Enlightenment. Whichever interpretation we choose, it historicizes and corroborates the cognitive problem posed by the organic metaphors examined previously.

From this "external" standpoint, another kind of labyrinth coils around the problem of knowledge, specifically, the problem of meaning in *Sepia One* and *Capricho 43*. Such an effort ties interpretation to historical circumstances. Goya's nervous disorder in the 1790s brought him into the frequent company of medical men, particularly his friend and host Martín Zapater. If the artist had wanted to depict any of these physicians in a state of dreaming, no better fantasy than *Sepia One* could have been contrived. The device of composing the dream space by analogy with brain anatomy would be an ingenious private joke. Nevertheless, to take up this interpretive thread would again mean to reenter the maze of questions and possible hypotheses. What can the dreamed faces signify? Their diverse expressions are ironic, serious, and grimacing. Their combined ambiguity undermines the "real life" seriousness of the dreamer and his work, whether he is the artist's scientist-friend or Goya himself.

According to some art historians, a self-caricaturing gesture is Goya's intention in *Sepia One*. If this interpretation is extended to a man of science, then the brain conceit becomes more than a structural device. It can also be viewed as tracing an intellectual geography where theories of nerve and brain activity are regarded ironically, with irony being the form taken by skepticism during a caricaturizing dream. Nevertheless, *Sepia One* is, after all, the sketched prelude to "The Sleep/Dream of Reason Produces Monsters." It shares with the etched finale an interest in image-making, in thought mechanisms, and in what might be called neural "energy," concerns also shared by psychologists in the same period. Goya's biographical relevance to these concerns lies in the intimations of uncertainty about continuism already documented in scientific writing and reflected artistically in the distorted forms of the dream-world.

Whether Goya's works are interpreted along the aforementioned historical lines or as a hermetic iconology, they lead to the issue of how the eighteenth century understood the physiology of dreaming and neural energy. The theme of energy is tied to the pictorial evidence of *Sepia One*. The agent responsible for producing the faces in the striated dream-space is the brain of the sleeping figure. Who or what is responsible for producing the crosshatched, dark animal zone is less evident. The difference between these zones may be understood by the notion of "sources." The brain's own activity readily accounts for the dreamed faces. But if the scene's striated zone originates in the sleeper's dream, another energy seems to condense the monstrous images in the crosshatched sector. This blackish-grey animal sector is discontinuous with the human faces, and is also divided within itself. Relationships break down in ways that parallel real-world discontinuities. For instance, can there be any relation that links a bat's wing to a horse's hoof? Function aside, they are morphologically dissimilar, so that the question becomes relevant insofar as taxonomy is placed against the background of natural history. Buffon's classifications of natural forms permitted, incongruously enough, the biomorphic proximity of an ostrich and a camel. But the question about incongruous relationships, when posed against the background of Goya's nerve illness, calls attention to certain obscurities facing medical research.

The cleft in taxonomy that allows juxtaposing a bat's wing and a horse's hoof parallels the cleft in the pictured dream chamber. This rift, when considered by Buffon, hinders a definition of living matter that seeks to forge a perfect chain of beings. In a parallel dimension, a division between a "normal" dream of droll faces and a "monstrous" dream of beasts, when considered by Goya, entails the theme of connecting forces or energies. When the brain dreams, it generates a labyrinth of juxtapositions. Goya glimpses into the primal abyss of metamorphic matter, where shapes resist classification and subsist in the guise of an originary reality. The idea of such a substratum has been entertained from the Romantic age to this day. [13]

The "primal humus" and the memory it nourishes are two factors considered in the neurophysiology of Goya's day. For "humus" we might read any of several substances named by eighteenth-century biologists to explain vital energy: the life-giving "nervous sap" that vitalizes both the

---

13. As Hermann Broch in this century phrased it in *The Death of Virgil* (San Francisco: Northern Lights, 1983, p. 66), such energy is "the primal humus of being, the groundwork of cognition and recognition which nourishes memory and to which memory returns."

medulla and the plant-seed, mentioned by Le Cat; or the "aether" mentioned by Newton; or the "vital force" mentioned by so many of their contemporaries. As for "memory," it is an unanchored faculty. Without memory, knowledge would be a deposit of unlinked experiences and references. But, as Condillac suggests at the outset of his treatise on the senses, our knowledge cannot be traced to its foundations because memory cannot recollect the moment when learning began. Original ignorance is an abyss that can be connected to nothing but the paradoxical first ground it rests on.

It remains then to locate the center that organizes subsequent cumulative knowledge. Condillac allows for two selves that require a coordinating link: the feeling self and the reflexive self. While the partnership avoids both labyrinth and abyss, it is a disjuncture nonetheless. Furthermore, the partnership of selves is not described by brain physiology and anatomy. For assistance we must return to Haller, who recognizes that duality will not account for cognitive complexity.

Haller explains that during a solitary instant of perception "five different beings are joined together: the body which we perceive; the affection of the organ of the sensory by that body; the affection of the brain arising from the percussion of that sensory; the change produced in the mind; and lastly, the mind's consciousness and perception of the sensation" (*Physiology*, 2:33). The unstated assumption is that a joining actually occurs. It is not clear whether Haller means an actual fusion or a series of events at a speed whose intervals are measurable only by microchronometer. In any event, he vaguely locates the resolving coordination in the maze of brain nerves.

This center, called the "common sensory" or "sensorium," is an elusive entity that supposes juncture and continuity. Throughout Haller's text, this supposition holds until he confesses ignorance at a crucial moment. His terminology is linear and dendriform, running counter to the metaphorical maze. Haller images the cerebellum as a network, its smaller lobules sending out their medulla, "which is, by degrees, so collected together in rays or branches, meeting in one trunk, that the whole resembles the figure of little trees" (1:204). The medulla terminates in three parts, either sending striae and fibers transversely, or ascending to intermix confusedly with other fibers. Yet the unbroken continuity proceeds thereafter. The pons extends from the cerebellum, and then the medulla oblongata descends in a conical shape as the nerves pass out from the medulla of the cerebrum and cerebellum to the region where sensory nerves are identifiable.

The dendriform images used by Haller aim at denoting direction and connection, but they also belong to the larger imagery of fibers, as the next two chapters show. Despite this stylistic strategy, however, the seamless design is challenged at both ends of the network. In order to appreciate this impasse, the anatomical details must be described. At the neural end, the nerve fibers are continuous with the brain fibers, but the nerves themselves divide into branches like blood vessels. As they recede from the brain, they grow softer and less bulky until their extremities end in pulp, as also happens in the optic nerve. The point of dissolution is no more determinable than the connection between the last fibrous atom and the first nonfibrous one. Haller declares that the brain extends the reticulated path of nerve fibers, which never break off by their division into smaller threads, and that these "only recede from each other by an opening of the cellular substance that ties them together" (1:213). Actually the "tying" is more of a floating together in a viscous medium. Haller has in effect replaced the notion of continuous contact with the notion of a mediatory substance that supplies the connection. This medium leads us back again to the theme of energy and life force.

At the other end of the network, the cerebral parts suggest vivid metaphors of connectedness. The dura mater has an inner plate that is continuous with the small nerves and blood vessels of the outer plate; one of its sectors disperses "shiny fibers in the shape of branches and palm twigs." The brain's next covering is like a spiderweb, and indeed is picturesquely called the "arachnoid"; its thin, tender membrane is pellucid like water. The innermost covering, or pia mater, invests the surface of the cerebrum and the spinal marrow, which send vessels into the pia mater "in regular order, like little roots." Here Haller enters another labyrinth, "betwixt every furrow and fissure" of cerebrum and cerebellum.

Now the interruption has to do not only with anatomy but with mentality. It occurs within the mechanism of thinking, where Haller suggests a broken physical contact at the sensorial end and at the cerebral end. No longer a continuous fiber, "the tender pulp of the nerve" is what is struck or impressed by external objects and what "conveys, by the nervous spirits, some change to that part of the brain where the impressed fibers of the nerve first arise from the arteries. We know nothing more than that new thoughts are thus excited in the mind" (2:32). The supposition of a "joining together" of the five perceptual and mental acts now unravels. Thought occurs enigmatically in the unnamed "that part" of the brain where "some change" enables nerve impulses to become new thoughts by leaping across the gap from "brain" to "mind."

Similarly, in external sensation, there is no literal joining but a mediated union that seems to govern the point of contact between nerve fiber and impression. The mediating agent is the "tender pulp of the nerve," which consists again of threads, this time riddled with "openings" in the cellular substance that "ties them together." The permeability of the pulp is underscored in Haller's graphic description of tactile nerve fibers.

Unintended by the scientist, the microcosmic dualism of mind and body intruded its philosophical controversy into an empirical context. Fittingly, Haller used the sense of touch to illustrate connectedness, although not privileging it as did Buffon and Diderot in the earlier examples. Touch originates in the cutaneous papillae of the skin, a "cellular network whose fibers and plates are closely compacted and interwoven together in an intricate manner, which renders it porous" (1:244). The microscopic eye dims as it attempts to observe these round papillae "seated in cavities of the cuticle and receiving nerves very difficultly seen" (1:245). Not specified is what manner of path the neural message travels. Haller thus misses the issue of discontinuity, which here concerns porousness; his imagery is limited to the rootlike ramifications that dissolve into cellular substance. But the question is about the minuscule gaps spaced along the fibrous track. The issue is perhaps philosophical, but it is no less anatomical. The dendriform or spiderweb model of linear continuity is replaced in the porous medium by a continuous chain. However, this model also breaks down. Ordinarily, a series of interlacing links form a continuous chain because each link touches another at every point. Less perfectly, but still continuous, the beads of a necklace are said to be "attached" to each other by a string, although it is the string that holds them together. Finally, if the string is removed and the beads are left to float in a "cellular substance," the continuity dissolves. The last circumstance is what marks Haller's description of tactile sensation.

The discussion of discontinuity may appear to risk exaggeration into an infinite regress. But the philosophical issue of dualism does not vanish on this account, particularly since communication and contact engage anatomists intensely in the debate over vibrations and fluids. All such means and mediators of continuity from external world to internal perception hang suspended in the enigmatic fissure between matter and mind.

As an anatomist, Haller is also philosophically conscientious. Take the color red, he suggests. What does the *idea* of redness have in common with a slightly refrangible ray, separated from the seven portions of the whole ray? There is no connection, Haller replies, except what is supplied by "that part" of the brain called the mind, of which we know nothing. Haller states: "Thought is not the express image of the object, by which the sentient nerve is affected." The explanation leaves "thought" undefined. No medullary part, not even when shaped like "the claw of a bird," can grasp the thought of redness after receiving the red sensation from the nerve forkings. Enlighteners like Haller, Diderot, and Hume, uneasy about this problem, conflated three separate issues. The first, as indicated, was the conversion of a sense datum into a thought. The second concerned the factor of transferal within the concept of continuity. However, eighteenth-century science had not yet become aware of synapses (another metaphor), the space between cells at which impulses pass from one neuron to another.

The third issue regarding disembodied "thought" addressed the separation of brain from mind, nerve from brain, and sensation from nerve ending. It concerned the organizing center of knowledge and the energy that fuels cognition. Here Haller uses the phrase "indissoluble connection" to mean subject-object connectedness, but it acquires a new guise in the concept of *correspondence*. This seems to mean that two things that "correspond" are like two planes running parallel to each other, much like the parallel planes of animal species seen classified by Buffon (owls and bats may be in some way similar when viewed alongside a sleeping human being, but the three species are discontinuous). Haller is aware that redness has nothing in common with a refracted ray of a certain length, but the prospect of discontinuity is inelegant. The concept of correspondence provides the missing continuity between abstraction and sensation, or mind and matter. The means is a central intelligence linked to a "sensory" in the brain:

> It is established as a perpetual law by the Creator, that certain changes, made first in the nerve, and then in the common sensory, shall produce certain new corresponding thoughts in the mind, which have an indissoluble connection with each other; so that, although what we perceive in the world be arbitrary, yet that it is real, and not false, appears plainly from the perpetual agreement of similar thoughts arising from similar affections of the sensitive nerves, in all persons at the same time, from one object, in one person at different times. (2:33)

Several items are to be noticed here. The "certain changes" cannot be specified. The "corresponding thoughts" are of another ilk from the sensory perceptions they succeed. The similarity of "similar thoughts arising from similar affections" does not add up to the closed space of sameness. Semblance is not identity, and it is identicality that the notion of correspondence aspires to and falls short of.

Haller wrote within the Newtonian tradition of a regularity through-out the universe whose source may be called, by convenience, God or a supreme Intelligence. It will become important to discover in later chapters of this volume the "connection" between this Absolute Sensory and the individual mortal one. In the current discussion, we may note that the Haller-Cullen school had a French follower in Daniel Delaroche, who spoke of a "vital principle" instead of a "Creator." And instead of Haller's "mind," Delaroche spoke of "*âme*" or "soul," (assuming that he would have said "*esprit*" for "mind"). The "soul" is intimately attached to the nervous system, so that the "movements excited in the soul exert an influence on the body and vice versa" (*Analyse*, 1:44–53). Despite these differences in wording, and despite the more general incompatibility of materialist and spiritualist psychologies, Delaroche claims that every observer agrees on the existence of "an immaterial and thinking substance" (1:44). What he calls the "sensorium" is the cognate of Haller's "sensory"—the part of the brain where the soul, which by being immaterial cannot be said to reside in a material place, "coordinates" the movements of the nervous system.

This excursion into the language of neuroanatomy shows why the prevalent concern with discontinuity could not remain a purely scientific one. As soon as the concept of a "sensorium" was admitted (actually perpetuated from ancient times), the wider philosophical problem raised its head. The variant sensoria demonstrated the choice for anyone who was interested in the concept of mind during the eighteenth century. One could follow the materialist thread from nerve fiber to brain fiber, as it trailed off to be lost in the viscous medium where the sensorium was somewhere to be located, or one could accept the spiritualist continuum of energy from the Divine to the human intelligence. Supposing, however, one were also interested in the nature of dreams, as in Goya's case. Then the sensorium would be an idle factor apart from a few realistic images retrieved from memory. The sensorium would not explain the discontinuous phenomena depicted in *Capricho 43*. Quite the contrary, the coordinating center of understanding would be a mystery regardless what concept of mind were believed. In the etching, the disparate species resist connection, while in *Sepia One* there is no manner of relating the bat to the human faces. Even a focus on the single squadron of bats in *Capricho 43* highlights their amorphous manner of trailing off like so many indecipherable nerve ends floating in the "cellular substance."

The source of Goya's dream remains the unknown center of the labyrinth, whether cerebral or cosmic. The bats are the metaphor for binding energy thus far understood fragmentarily. Their chaotic flutter on the horizon is a broken chain with gaping synapses that leave the individual neurons ungrounded in the Absolute. If the bats are primal, metamorphic matter, their external origin will be understood by a different language from the verbal one of Buffon's taxonomy. But if they are monsters, their creator is the dreamer abandoned by Reason. In this case, the swooping black immanence makes its temple within the cerebral labyrinth.

The Blind Minotaur

The metaphorical labyrinth brain was at the root of diverse images for discontinuous neural structure and process, but its inner sanctum in the sensorium did nothing to resolve the discontinuity. A solution was at hand in the role played by aether in its pervasive, tactile mediacy. The evidence for aether's role will be apparent in Chapter 7. I use it here to consider a more immediate issue that also concerns the sense of touch. This issue is the cognitive act and whether its most apt metaphor is rational light and the visual sense, or metamorphic matter and the tactile sense symbolized by Goya's bat. I shall aproach this issue indirectly by way of another sensory organ in its historical setting.

The physiological labyrinth actually begins in the internal ear, before being extended to the brain. From the three semicircular canals to the winding cochlea, intelligible language begins to be shaped. The English poet Jago extolled "sage philosophy" for explaining "how various streams of undulating air, / Through the ear's winding labyrinth convey'd, / Cause all the vast variety of sounds" (Nicolson, *Newton Demands the Muse*, 91). The poet's confidence in what I have called "continuism" aligned him with the scientific reasoners, remote from those who, like Goya's dreamer, "on instinct live, not knowing how they live: / While reason sleeps, or waking stoops to sense."

The Goyesque perspective was more adventurous in conceiving new hypotheses about reality, but it also originated in experience. Goya devised his vision of dormant Reason during a lengthy nervous disorder that ended in deafness. While no detailed account of the severe ordeal comes down to us, the modern playwright Antonio Buero Vallejo has portrayed his deafness as an insulation against brusque intervals of roaring sound. Through the maddening gaps in silence rushed the unmodulated sounds that eventually inspired the famous artistic nightmare. In this view, Goya's ears and brain could not control or "make sense of" the world's linguistic raw material. His external reality seemed irrational, and hence unabidingly monstrous. We may imagine, as the playwright does, the artist staggering in pain about the studio, his body convulsing in protest against the insufferable noise of verbal language.

The symptoms just described confirm one hypothesis among Goya specialists, that his disease was Ménière's syndrome "in its worst form," as Philip Hofer puts it. Inside Goya's ear, the cochlea swelled abnormally with serous fluid and water, inducing vertigo and apopleptic movements. The intervals of relief from auricular torment were also those of creativity. But the passage from painful noise to soundless images was a labyrinthine time frame, with Goya as a minotaur puzzling out the endless cycle.

The mythic Minotaur is symbolically blind. The myth contains a fable about the Enlightenment, as I shall suggest. Eyesight is of no use to the Minotaur in the blind alleys that trap him. He must "feel his way" through the passageways, without Theseus's thread of contact between the exit and his hooves. The minotauran Goya is trapped in a cyclical time frame of proportional magnitude. Deaf instead of blind, he struggles to understand the map—both its center, whence the piercing roar originates, and its exit, where silence will reward a journey.

Goya's labyrinth begins in the cochlea, the relay of acoustic intelligence but now the excruciating origin of incomprehensible sounds. It swells until its sonic universe is commensurate with the adjacent brain. The sensations and resulting vertigo are experiences Goya must understand in order to bear and later pictorialize them. His mind also swells with the effort. Each physical paroxysm twists his thoughts another notch until the mind, a chamber of insensate noises, relieves its burden by expelling the turmoil into another space. Here, noise and pain take the shape of monsters. Goya's cognitive act is made instinctually rather than by reasoning.

The fable for the Enlightenment begins in myth and ends in brain anatomy. The Minotaur is the instinctual knower who dwells in discontinuity at the innermost core of reality. Theseus enters and returns from the labyrinth without ever knowing what the beast knows—and what Goya intuits through dream. The conventional approach to the myth takes the perspective of an intruder who enters the labyrinth equipped with a device for coming out again. Theseus's endeavor requires three assumptions: that an exit exists, that the exit is also the entrance, and that Ariadne's external authority can provide another outsider with knowledge of the maze by means of a system: the thread that is a ready-made method.

But what knowledge does the labyrinth hold? What does its map look like? The answer depends on whether its significance is viewed cosmically or microcosmically. In the brain-as-labyrinth metaphor, the physiologists who approach the brain adopt the perspective of nerve ends receiving external sense data. The "thread" to the interior is the sensory path of impressions traveling along neural fibers to the sensorium. The coordinating center of thought, the sensorium, is never the starting point of anatomical description, simply because its location and nature are unknown. The scientific Theseus is a rationalist who accepts a preconceived method, penetrates most regions of the brain, and returns safely. He never reaches the inner network of endlessly forking fibers that dissolve into nerve solution at their terminal points. Concealed there in the cerebral fluid is the unvisited seat of intelligence.

The perspective of the randomly wandering Minotaur is seldom considered. From this standpoint, the labyrinth teaches cosmic rather than microcosmic knowledge. To possess it, one must begin at the center, controlled by God or some universal intelligence like Diderot's spider brain. It is doubtful that even the Minotaur knows the complete map, for he is found at a place still accessible by a continuous external thread. The problem is to grasp the thread at the other end, at the seat of the unifying intelligence.

By the same token, the Minotaur may be regarded as knowing more than Daedalus from the perspective of the brain-as-labyrinth metaphor. The mental labyrinth is darkness itself, where the sense of touch rather than sight affords a cognitive margin of safety. The rationalist "sees" with his systematizing thread only to the extent that the device helps to find his way out. The thread does not enable him to see *into* the labyrinth, much less to see its center. On the return journey, he glimpses light at the tunnel's end. Thus what the rationalist knows is partial and only known by a preexisting method not of his own fabrication. What the sightless Minotaur knows is discovered in the contact of its body against the wall, head-on against the dead end. Its knowledge in blindness is a superior empiricism in recognizing that there exists no system for organizing the universe of thought. It knows, without preconception, that if one begins in the middle of things, in the confusion of a living reality, then all solutions are partial. There is no exit, only "falsifiable" leads.

Modern science begins in the eighteenth century with the defense of the experimental method. The blind Minotaur may therefore not appear to be an apt symbol despite this fable. At least Theseus emerged successfully with practical results, if only through a partial journey. This measured feat is arguably what characterizes modern science. On the other hand, is there a superior truth that can be attributed to the Minotaur?

This truth is mythic, like Goya's. It acknowledges the fundamental irrationality of the universe, beginning at the sector that employs Reason and where history records terror and holocaust despite scientific achievement. This truth remains unchanged in the eternal march of events. *Capricho 43* suggests such a universe, engendered in the bicameral brain depicted by *Sepia One* and trailing indeterminately into an infinity of soaring bats. Goya's universe, to borrow another phrase from Hermann Broch, is a "phantasmagoria of timelessness . . . shot up from the chaotic humus of the nocturnal unnamed" (*Death of Virgil,* 43).

An intuitive vision such as Goya's is sometimes explicated profitably through the language of a later, equally intuitive genius. This is certainly the case for one of Broch's hypnagogic meditations in the profound fiction, *The Death of Virgil.* Here Broch matches Goya by suggesting that the true reality may best be grasped by dropping the thread of rational systems and entering the labyrinth of time—that is, transcending structured categories and surrendering to the free combinations of mind and nature, space and time. In surrender there is access to the immemorial wisdom, sought by ancients and moderns alike and indecipherable by ordinary language. (For this reason, the Virgil of Broch's novel refuses to release his imperfect epic poem.) Visual images such as Goya's manage to convey some of this wisdom. But even *Capricho 43* is limited to intuiting the tangled knowledge of organic convergences, the crenated plane of future and past time where all life forms entwine with all natural substances. Broch's Virgil glimpses this plane of "time-crests and time-hollows" in his dying hours. He sees the cosmic labyrinth embracing the above and the below, the animal, the mineral, and the vegetal, a "flood of naked creaturekind extending over the breathing earth, extending forth under the breathing heaven with its constant changing from day to night, enclosed by the immutable shores of the millenniums, the naked herd-stream of life broadly advancing, filtering up from the humus of existence, constantly filtering back into it, the inevitable togetherness of all that has been created" (*Death of Virgil,* 42).

To summarize: the cosmos itself is an organic labyrinth where the "humus" of Being rests in the earth. The cosmos is also a brain, and the brain a cosmos, both encompassing a labyrinth of ventricles and nerve paths. But where is the seat of Intelligence? The brain is commensurate with the "filtering" convergences enclosed by the cosmos. Therefore the seat of Intelligence depends on more than the primal humus and its energy. Because Goya's era sets materialist philosophy against Christian thought, the organizing Intelligence is a mystery whose nature must embrace both the clockwork structure and the Great Chain of Being. Continuity is the master assumption for materialism and theocentrism alike. The perfect continuum interfolds natural and supernatural processes, an originary cognitive event that finite minds seek to recreate.

But in the labyrinth the cavernous darkness is impenetrable and makes the sense of touch a unique authority. In the passageways, progress is a thread of light, and we may refer figuratively to the use of eyesight. The light would be characterized in two different ways in Goya's time: a Christian believer would call it God's love, whereas a skeptic like Hume would associate it with the faculties of Reason united with imagination. Goya distills both metaphors into the enigma of "the sleep/dream of Reason." Richly nuanced, the enigma lifts one of its veils when recast in the words of one long, motif-laden passage by Broch (66). In this passage, the idea of dreaming grows from primal humus and gives finitude and temporal shape to timeless transcendence. There is the idea of monstrosity that procreates in the night and then devours, like the god or monster-father Saturn depicted elsewhere by Goya. There is also the "eye of night" that paradoxically sees without light and is the antithesis of the blinding void. Finally, there is the gesture of sinking into the soil, a gesture not of conventional death but of love and human birth. Conversely, death is represented by eyesight, an irony that negates the rational emblem of optimistic eighteenth-century cognition.

Broch's "eye of night" text is today's version of the earlier grand themes that inhere in the brain-labyrinth metaphor. These themes are cosmic discontinuity and the Chaos of reality. Even the cycles of time produce an illusory continuity. As *Capricho 43* shows, there is neither day nor night. Diderot's eye-blinking paradox confirms this discontinuity by another means. Broch's vision goes further. It hints at the metamorphic nature of reality emerging from the cleavage between daylight's temporal changes and the timelessness of unchanging night. There is no connection between the sterile movement of the days that empty into death and the fertile rhythm of nocturnal creating and devouring. The eye-pit, with its capacity to see without light, is a fertile abyss, a "lightning-cleft of nothingness." Between its renewing and its obliterating powers is a cleavage.

Some of these apparent obscurities will clear up in the discussions of metamorphosis in subsequent chapters. The point now is that Broch clarifies the Goyesque intuition about the ground-soil from which dreams and life arise. Here the theme of material Chaos reenters, as in Chapter 3. Broch mentions "the primal source of the unformed and invisible, which always lay in wait to break out into storm and destruction." This primal source is the womb of all reality, and yet its living spawn is destruction. The Chaos may be interpreted politically at a historical level, but it subsists more deeply. It is the ruin inherent in all constructive energy, the Chaos of a self-violating law of creation. What confirms its chaotic nature is the paradox of its own constancy, "which always lay in wait" to act chaotically. Beings and forms are engendered, they later meet "storm and destruction," and the prevailing circumstance remains the disruptive continuity of their perpetual undoing.

5. The Discontinuous Spiderweb

Far as creation's ample range extends,
The scale of sensual, mental powers ascends:

. . . .

The spider's touch, so exquisitely fine!
Feels in each thread, and lives along the line.
—Pope, *Essay on Man*

The eighteenth-century problem of knowledge implicates another mythic being besides the labyrinth-bound Minotaur described in the previous chapter. Minerva's arch-rival, the maid Arachne, haunts the story of the spider and the silkworm in the book of fables by J. J. Boisard. In this version, the talented Arachne is already transformed in punishment for boasting that she could weave as well as the goddess. The arachnoid complains of the admiration heaped on "the miserable silkworm's thread, a thousand times grosser" than her own beautiful threadwork, which unjustly is swept away by the broom each day (*Fables*, 58). The mild silkworm replies by admitting that the spider indeed weaves a nearly divine tapestry, but that neither her knowledge to do this nor the result has any useful purpose. This pragmatic lesson deemphasizes the Minervan ideal of a contemplative knowledge or creativity as described in Chapters 1 and 2.

In point of fact, however, the common spider spins its web for a very practical purpose, that of obtaining food. This stratagem makes her knowledge a snare, and it is treated as a treacherous feature in another imaginative context, also unsympathetic, this time in the book of icons by Jean Boudard. Here the spider is shown weaving in order to trap its prey, thus becoming a perfect emblem for Wickedness. Its web is spun with threads that leave no gap in continuity through which the victim might escape.

There is much suggestive symbolism in Boisard's literary fable of 1773 and Boudard's visual icon of 1759. They reflected different facets of the spider's condition, yet prompted the same reaction: a facile contempt for the qualities of divine beauty mixed with dangerous cunning. Yet these qualities are the very ones associated with Minerva's arts, mixing the pragmatic, daylight knowledge of the Enlightenment with the shadowy areas of a cognition as yet half-understood. The spider embodies a twofold earthly disposition toward a higher sphere filled with peril and plenitude. It stands for continuity by aspiring to attach itself to the external world. First, the mortal Arachne's aspiration trespasses on the absolute knowledge of an art that only Minerva may fully possess. Arachne dares to extend the weaver's skill so that it becomes continuous with the goddess's artistic perfection. Second, the elegant weaver as the cunning insect sets an uninterrupted network that traps and incorporates the victim into its unified system. Her threads are spun out from her insides, and they annex an external victim. Together, the spinning subject, the web, and the clasped object form a continuity of tactile attachments from the inner world to the outer one. The importance of touch and tactile knowledge in overcoming the discontinuities of dualism has already been noted in the preceding chapters.

Diderot's Spider Brain

The images just cited had a near counterpart in Diderot's evocation of a spider brain at the center of the universe. This well-known metaphor occurred in the rational dialogue that complements the delirious monologue that is *D'Alembert's Dream*, a defiant format for the Encyclopedic age. The dialogue turned on an implicit definition of continuity: that an unbroken network unites the knowing subject with every other object in the universe. The spiderweb is a system of fibers, some might say infused with a "vital force," that symbolizes the connectedness of rational knowledge with the absolute.

Behind this image is a hypothesis about "the general and universal order," stated by the dreaming d'Alembert as the fact that "everything is tied in nature and that it is impossible for any gap to exist in the chain" (1966: 181). This condition, among its other results, binds the knowing or feeling subject to the known or felt object. Despite this intuition, its validity is debated. The skeptic is Dr. Bordeu, who is not fully satisfied by the fact that each person believes him- or herself to be an integrated whole composed of connected parts. Bordeu describes the enigma of the knowing self. That I am myself, is clear,

> but the reason for the fact isn't by any means [clear], especially if you adopt the hypothesis that there is only one kind of matter, and that man, and animal life in general, is formed simply by juxtaposition of several sensitive molecules.

Now each sensitive molecule had its own identity before the juxtaposition, but how has it lost it, and how have all these losses added up to the conscious individuality of the whole? (178)

The answer supplied by Bordeu's interlocutor is an important example of tactile knowledge, the optimal form of cognitive continuity between subject and object: "I imagine that contact alone would be enough . . . When I put my hand on my thigh, I can feel perfectly well at first that my hand is not my thigh, but after some time, when each is at the same temperature, I can't tell which is which, where one begins and the other ends, and they are as one." There appears to be no difference between these sensations per se and the consciousness of them. But the doctor is unconvinced because there always remains one detached position in the mind that acts as the observing subject, discontinuous from the body as object.

In this debate, Dr. Bordeu faces Mademoiselle de l'Espinasse, who proposes that he imagine a spider at the center of its web: disturb one of the filaments and the insect responds alertly. The threads are attached to the spider's insides and form a "sensitive part" of the subject. Dr. Bordeu grasps the implication, and he depicts the entire body as a network: "The threads are everywhere; there is not a single point on the surface of your body that is not the terminus of one of them, and the spider lurks in a part of your brain I have already mentioned, the meninges, which can scarcely be touched without reducing the whole organism [*machine*] to unconsciousness" (183). The metaphor seems apt in connecting the brain to its nervous system, but the continuity between the two proves to be paradoxical.

The spider brain is identified with a specific focal point, the meninges, whose delicacy cautions respect. But why should these membranes be singled out as the hub of all continuities? The answer is that the purpose of the three meninges—dura mater, pia mater, and arachnoid—is to envelop the brain and spinal cord. They function as protectors by the device of separation, an essential feature since they can scarcely be touched "without reducing the whole organism to unconsciousness" (*Éléments*, 9:183). Diderot seems aware of how crucial this separating function is in the cognitive network: "The meninges are always affected in madness, apoplexy, delirium, drunkenness" (9:319). Yet the subject's entire communicative web is said to converge at this point, where "the spider has her niche."

The metaphor of connectedness thus becomes double-edged. Continuity is defined by a neurocerebral system coordinated precisely at the points of separation in the meninges. Meningeal discontinuity safeguards mental coherence. Conversely, to meddle with these membranes is to provoke some form of incoherence. The type of interference implied by Diderot can be learned by his interest in nerve interfusion. This phenomenon, called anastomosis, affects the intercommunicating network: the union of fiber branchings will scramble a system where each spider-leg is a nerve thread that transmits its own signal code ("Each sense has its language"). Thus Diderot not only links delirium to vexed meninges, he also observes that "if there is some anastomosis between the nerves, there will be no order within the brain. The animal will go mad" (9:320). Continuity must depend on discontinuity in order to prevent Unreason. A threadwork of wrongly connected neural branches will produce an anastomotic derangement. Taken on the analogy with the Minervan ideal of continuity, the human who achieved knowledge through complete nerve interfusion would, like Arachne, be in mortal peril.

The spider metaphor does more than depict the intercommunicating subject-object dimension. The same brain and nerve system may be projected macrocosmically and infused with a material cognitive "energy" that unites all things. Mademoiselle de l'Espinasse expresses just this idea. She challenges Dr. Bordeu to deny "that the whole world hasn't its meninges, or that there isn't a big or little spider living in some corner of space with threads extending everywhere" (*D'Alembert's Dream*, 184). In effect, the doctor denies nothing. Their discussion moves to the nature of fibers and filaments, the scientific background for which is examined in the next chapter. The importance of fibers may be appreciated here in a philosophical framework. References to fibrous matter appeared everywhere in eighteenth-century biological discourse in a proportion that indicated concern over how to universalize the continuity of cognitive relationships. Fibers direct the intellectual energy or "life force" that brings all things into palpable connection. Macrocosmically, the fibroid web with its metaphorical spider represents the Deity or absolute Mind that gives the Chain of Being its order.

The reverse concern over discontinuity was just as powerful. But now the micro-macrocosmic connectedness failed for want of a tie to the realm of abstractions. Just as troubling was the realization that a single perception of an object was composed of discrete sensory data that required a connection. Again, the opposite seemed true when Diderot claimed that the web-bound spider will react to the vibration of a single thread when it is irritated by a speck of matter. That is, the spider brain commands total knowledge because, as in the universe, everything in the system eventually touches everything else. But was this precisely the case, given the uncertainty about where the mind forges the final link in understanding? Not really. There remained the paradox of continuity and separation in the meninges, which was still not solved. Quite the opposite. A pragmatic treatise on nervous ailments by Daniel Delaroche betrayed a weakness in just this area. His imprecise terms for describing vibratory transmission prompt our skepticism. The "movements" initiated by the brain "extend with the same facility to the bodily extremes" as in the reverse direction (*Analyse*, 1:41). The speed of this "extension" turns out to be infinite. Delaroche equates this speed with the signal transmission from nerve ending to brain. The stimulus by "external bodies touching the nerve endings is communicated in an instantaneous manner along these nerves and will excite sensation in the brain."

Clearly "instantaneous" communication is incompatible with the idea of impulses that "extend" and travel "along" the nerve fibers, as Hume also noticed. The simultaneous register of external object on perceiving subject is impossible. But if an interval occurs during the transfer, another interval presumably occurs between the mentally perceived object and its conversion into an abstract idea. At this point an insuperable difficulty arises. There exists no material filament known to tie the physical and abstract events into the larger web of continuities. The solution offered by Hume is of no help to rationalists or materialists. It is "belief," says Hume, that bridges the mysterious gap, an irrational act that splices the sensory sequence into its intellectual counterpart. The notion of continuity remains an article of faith that demands revision as each facet of the spider model is put to the test.

One such test is set down in Diderot's *Elements of Physiology*. Each filament leg of the spider has its own language, just as each human sensory organ does. Diderot will experiment with one of these languages and demonstrate that it is impossible to unify even a single cognitive experience. The object before his eyes is a tree. But in order "to have this exact notion of the parts and of the whole, the imagination must paint the entirety in our understanding and we must experience this event [*sensation*] as if the tree were present" (9:343). In truth, two disconnected stages compile this knowledge, and neither of them is a simple entity. Rather, the first stage is a series of joinings whereby

> the eyespan embraces one part [of the tree]. If the eye does not repeat experience, it will not know the tree. If the part sighted in the experience of

one eyespan is not tied to its predecessor, in such a way that the part we see is joined to the part we have just seen, we may multiply these experiences all we wish and scan the whole tree, but unless these experiences are tied to each other we will have no precise notion of the tree. (9:343, 373)

The same requirement applies to the second stage, which converts sensation into idea. If we

examine carefully what happens in the understanding when we wish to perceive the entire tree, we proceed within ourselves as externally: by more or less extended spans that overlap successively with each other and which we scan with extreme speed, a speed so great that we are persuaded that we see internally the entire tree at once, just as we are persuaded that we saw the entirety outside ourselves all at once, which is untrue in both cases. (9:343)

In short, Diderot's cognition must begin with "seeing an object and attaching a sound to it, the sound 'tree,' and then utter and understand the word 'tree.'"

This analysis breaks down the integrity of the cognitive act, a grave enough result. Even more, the overlapping spans do not alter the fact that the primary reality consists of discontinuously perceptible elements in series. If attention is drawn microscopically to the corpuscles that compose each entity, the cohesion cannot be verified. We ignore these facts for the sake of sanity and intelligibility. Only Goya was willing to contemplate the chaotic entirety without the filtering effect of Reason. He converted Diderot's "raucous table," cited in Chapter 4, into the table where the reasoner sleeps, crowded with symbolic monsters, a chaos knowable only through the extrasensory medium of dreams. Diderot, more rationally, limits himself to recording discontinuity as it relates to mental experience. His response is appropriate to the tone of the *Elements of Physiology*, which in the section quoted is less metaphorical than elsewhere. Nevertheless, the images chosen here strike smartly because they challenge the chief sensory language of Reason: eyesight.

Each time we shut our eyelids it is nighttime, observes Diderot in a passage already cited in Chapter 1. The explanation of course is that "the impression of light we receive lasts longer than the duration of the eyeblink, and so there is no cessation of light" (9:344). Consequently, what we call "day" is really broken up into "little days and nights," although we perceive that fact only when we pay attention. Diderot's point is that our perceptual mechanisms are discontinuous, and the simultaneity we assume to be occurring while we think does not take place at any level of consciousness. Quite plainly, "we cannot think, see, hear, taste, smell, or touch at the same time. We can be at only one of these things at a time. We cease to see when we listen, and so on for the other sensations. We believe the contrary, but experience disabuses us at once." The same idea is repeated emphatically elsewhere—in a reference to the homeostatic body that concentrates awareness at only one place—"Man is always at the place of sensation: he is but an eye when he sees . . . He is but a tiny part of the finger when he touches" (9:312).

Diderot's analytical minutiae erode belief in a unified, synthesizing perception. They disturb the privileged surface of Lockean psychology and its sequel in Condillac. The prevailing associationist orthodoxy still had no rival at this time. Its limitations remained unexposed by nineteenth-century phenomenology and neuropsychology. Diderot's incidental ana-lyses were the first inkling that the perceptual act is already eminently fractional when measured by a single unit of duration. We can only per-form one act at a time, and we stop seeing when we hear, stop hearing when we touch. High-velocity intervals of sensory vacuum punctuate the perception by an individual sense. Therefore it is impossible to create an integrated perception in a single sensory impact. All the more so when intervals separate the several acts of seeing, touching, and hearing an ob-ject. Discontinuity marks both individual perception and the coordination of many perceptions.

By exposing discontinuity, Diderot jostles several comfortable no-tions. Our belief in the coordinating capacity of mind is firm, but we mis-takenly hold this coordination to be simultaneous when actually it is serial. Furthermore, while the conscious mind organizes the field of reality that it surveys, it does so with much less control than we would like to believe. In a century that took light for its emblem, Diderot's choice of light is an ironic example to choose for demonstrating these deceptions.

So moved is Diderot by the singlemindedness of consciousness that he scores its discontinuity with the extreme example of a philosopher who walks the streets at midday sunken in mental darkness: "for him who thinks deeply, it is night in the noonday streets, a deep night" (9:344). With the mind concentrating inwardly on thought, the body's automatic reflexes take control of environmental circumstances. We walk without stumbling over objects, and we halt or turn when obstacles so require. But this mod-ern explanation takes a different form in Diderot: "The eye leads us. We are the blind man, the eye is the dog that conducts us, and if the eye were not really an animal alert to the diversity of sensations, how would it lead us? The fact is that the eye is an animal within an animal, exercising very well its functions all alone" (9:345).

Is this account to be interpreted as extolling the virtues of eyesight or exposing its limitations? Whatever the answer, the fact remains that the seemingly coordinated mind compartmentalizes its activity. Consciousness is partly unconscious, even in the waking daylight. This can only mean that the objects in perceivable reality stand all around us partially shielded from our knowledge. If the contents of this "knowledge" inform our awareness, another knowledge seems also to exist, in this case in a sightless cognitive mode. We know things unconsciously—that is, blindly—and perform accordingly, like Diderot's philosopher in the night of the noon day. The "unseen" obstacle avoided by the absorbed stroller is known by another means that is discontinuous with the mind's conscious activity. The day and night modes of cognition await a connection that neural fibers seem to be excused from performing.

The Symbolism of Cognitive Acts

We have seen that the spider-brain metaphor served the multiple purpose of affirming a universal subject-object continuity while also exposing the fractional nature of perception. The paradox raised the issue of how material fibers could transmit unifying signals for sense data yet also link them to immaterial ideas. One explanation relied on the eighteenth-century assumption that a vital energy or invisible yet material "force" maintained cosmic connectedness. However, the arcane basis for this assumption weakened its scientific credibility and pointed to another source in the aethereal matter of fibers and, primarily, of the Neoplatonic Minerva, as will be suggested later.

It remains to show that the fabled spider also inspires two other symbolic meanings in the age of Goya and Diderot. She is a failed aspirant to absolute knowledge, and she enacts the role of a unifier of object and subject. These roles coincide in conferring on the spiderweb a forbidden status. The power to unify knowledge seems not destined for mortals, at least not in the eyes of the moralist. Such power does, however, fit rationalist and continuist ideals. It appeals equally to the occultist, who will note that the spiderweb materializes out of the invisible. The threads issue from the spider's inwardness, conceptualized as an abstraction, and these threads become the "simple fibers" that biologist Le Cat defined as "the basic unit of solids." The origin is a proto-fibroid mystery, enshrouding the pre-rational domain so attractive to Goya's analysis of reality beyond the senses. It is significant that Le Cat's discussion of fibers appeared in his treatise on sensations, discussed in Chapter 1.

It is useful to interject *Capricho 43* into the spiderweb symbolism because the sleep/dream of Reason begins in the brain's fibral mechanism but ends with a supernaturalist disclosure. Goya carries the physiology of dreams beyond its sensorial mechanisms in order to intimate the instinctual knowledge that skirts the rim of primal reality. Along this cognitive rim, the subject-object "connection" is supra-rational, to the extent that metaphors like Diderot's spider-brain are devised to describe it. The fact that brain matter is capable of transcending itself magnifies interest in nerve fibers, whose material composition is less certain than their anatomical description.

Because the fibrous neural matter is so problematic, Le Cat scrutinizes the nature of the simplest substances and hits upon the spider. When illustrating the primal states of solids, fluids, and gases, Le Cat's example of fluids is the spider's "glue" (*Traité . . . des nerfs*, 41). This observation further empowers the spiderweb as a cognitive metaphor. Spiderweb filaments do not constitute matter in the same way that the spider's material body is matter. Regardless of their organic origin, the threads pertain to the arachnoid subject only when they are still an excreted fluid—that is, before solidifying into threads. Thereafter, the threads extend beyond the bodily self and, although joined to the subject body, they belong to the external world of objects. The poet Alexander Pope expresses the cognitive result in the famous couplet cited in this chapter's epigraph: "The spider's touch, so exquisitely fine! / Feels in each thread, and lives along the line."

The "glue" mentioned by Le Cat is one of several eighteenth-century models that explain fibers and primary matter. As mentioned, spider's glue holds special interest for the spiderweb metaphor because Le Cat cites it in his treatise on sensations. The glue is made filamentous by exposure to the air. The glutinous corpuscles float separately in the liquid, which evaporates when externalized by the body. No longer part of the subject, the corpuscles are compressed by the air and become solid fiber. The same process affects animal fibers, as Le Cat is quick to note. A literal connectedness bolsters the figurative continuity from sentient subject to external object.

The physiological symbolism of the spider also fascinates the mathematician Maupertuis, who draws the following cosmological metaphor: "Everything is tied together in Nature. The Universe is held by the spider's thread in the same way as that force which pushes or draws the planets toward the sun" (*Oeuvres*, 1:50). The comparison of gravitational force to the tangible arachnoid connectivity is a bold stroke for a systematizing materialist like Maupertuis, who proposes to philosophize imaginatively. He actually posits a nervous system for the cosmos, and identifies gravity as the constituting factor in the neural impulse. He chooses a spiderweb for his model because its threads are associated with "contractile force," a term Diderot used. Among the continuist doctrines popular at this time is that of an indefinable energy that permeates the universe and creates a continuous gradation responsible for uniting mineral, plant, and animal forms. This doctrine finds adherents in more or less committed degrees, luring Maupertuis into a figurative cosmology that calls this "force" an invisible fiber. The mysterious strength in living matter puzzles Maupertuis less than it does Diderot, who illustrates it not only by spider threads but also by silk filaments and wood fibers, as we shall note. All such networks materialize the unseen force. It is a life-giving energy in its terrestrial activity, and in its absolute scope binds the universe together. An invisible force, it exerts a cosmic pull as might the fibers of Mademoiselle de l'Espinasse's spider at the center of its own enmeshed universe.

To say that a force "permeates" the cosmos means that no place or point can exist where such force is not present. This blanket force ensures that both continuity and gradation mean connectedness. A cosmic "pull" is possible because invisible threads actually attach the material elements that otherwise could not be continuous with one another. As in a chain, the linked elements do in fact touch, but the continuity is not the same as contiguity. Mere juxtaposition is the state that describes a series of discontinuous elements, as Le Cat demonstrates with his glutinous corpuscles. Only when the spider's glue evaporates can these particles touch one another and form a continuous thread. This distinction is stressed by Diderot, who in *D'Alembert's Dream* supplies Bordeu with a remarkable answer to Mademoiselle de l'Espinasse. The lady speculates that if everything in the cosmos were interconnected, and if she extended a rod from Earth to the star Sirius, then it would be possible to hear everything in space, however faintly. Bordeu responds that between the star and herself "there are only contiguous bodies, and not continuous ones, as there *should* be" (emphasis added).

This dialogue clarifies the reason that sensory vibrations are an appealing explanation for the general theory of cognition at this time. Being able to know the external world, and to "hear everything" in the universe, would depend on a state of connections rather than on a state of contiguity. Material continuity must link the subject and perceived objects in an unbroken relationship. This requisite favors a vibrationist and even a tactile theory of cognition. Vibrations from the object transmit their impact to the subject through a series of collisions in the manner of moving billiard balls touching one another and thus relaying part of their momentum or energy. The vibrating matter—aether, as suggested later in Chapter 8—by being interposed between object and subject, thus preserves the transfer of contacts. The collisions finally reach their destination in the subject, thus completing the connection. Therein lies the continuity.

Fiber threads are a model illustration of this process of individual cognition, but the model also serves the macrocosmic context whose center is the spider brain. The designs by Maupertuis and Diderot affirm the belief that intelligence inheres everywhere in the Universe. The thread is invisible, but this does not diminish the tangibility of material energy or "force." Human eyesight is what proves limiting, despite the use of microscopes, a deficiency conceded by the scientists themselves. Where difficulties arise in this model, the cause lies in the controversial hypothesis of vibrationism itself. As noted in Chapter 1, Hume wondered about the bridge between material sensation and intellectual abstraction, which seemed to be a gap rather than a joining (*Human Understanding*, 84–85). And Goya's irrationalist vision suggests that dreaming provides access to knowledge of a certain kind without benefit of sensory fibers or even of the material presence of objects.

Despite these difficulties, the fibrous network is confirmed in its metaphorical value through discussions of cosmology and individual psychology. Goya exceeds Diderot by his extrasensory oneiric cognition. But *Capricho 43* induces a mental state that belongs to the paradigm of exalted states that even Diderot can accommodate to moments of "high truth." Diderot speaks of an idiot suffering the hysteria of a fever, calling his eloquence a genuine mark of understanding. And then:

> The fever falls, the hysteria ceases, and stupidity revives. Now you can conceive the nature of the soft cheese that fills the cavity of your skull and mine. It is the body of a spider, all of whose nerve threads are the legs or web. Each sense has its language. [The spider] itself has no language of his own; it does not see at all, it does not hear at all, it does not even feel. But it is an excellent intermediary. If I had the time, I would provide this entire system with more plausibility and clarity. (*Salon de 1767*, 11:146)

The brain subordinates its role to independent signal tracks. Furthermore, one fiber can transmit a complete code of signals. Each nerve thread is a spider-leg endowed with its own "language," a figurative way of depicting each of the five senses. Each is intelligible in its independent state. Like the polyp that can only touch and feel, a particular sense can by itself facilitate reception or "understanding" of messages from environment to percipient. While the brain may coordinate these separate languages and so form human language, the concept of language per se is already fulfilled at the less developed neurological stage. Only the rational element is absent. This idea will play a key role in the discussion of tactile cognition at the end of this book.

The spiderweb therefore constitutes an absolute system of unified knowledge, metaphorically speaking. It embodies a universe of intelligence where all entities are interconnected. The metaphor expresses a synthesizing ideal of the Enlightenment. The moralist standpoint in Boisard's fable shows that the ambition to pursue the ideal is punished by Minerva when anyone attempts to weave a grand continuum, as did Arachne. Thus the real theme of this metaphor is how to unite the Many into the One. But its counter-theme is the folly of Reason in cherishing such an ambition. The counterpoint brings its own theme, which is discontinuity, a condition that Goya's irrational dream contemplates and perhaps overcomes.

The Discontinuous Nerve Bundle

Another way to examine cognitive discontinuity is to ask which is the daytime knowledge and which is the dream. This question emerges from *Capricho 43*. Does the sleeper "see" during his dream what the feline behind him sees with open eyes? When he awakens, what will he see? These are the extreme limits of Goya's epistemological problem. More mundanely, the distinction between the two forms of sight follows Diderot's paradox of the absorbed philosopher walking in the "night" of midday. But now it is a question of viewing objects in front of the subject and behind him. The subject's back is turned, and he knows the objects in front of him while being unaware of what is behind him. He turns around, only to lose the first event in order to view a second event that he can never affirm to be identical to what was occurring behind his back in the previous moment. Turning again toward the original event, he must overcome the discontinuity between the second event and the one he views again. But this time he has also lost the continuity between his earlier viewing and the one now repeated. There is no fusion or unity, only seriality. Perceptual flashes occur in separate durations, and these acts are linked by intervals of nonperception. What we call continuity is a carry-over, like the after-image of light or of form during eye blinks. The perceptual durations overlap, thanks to memory aided by belief. We see an object, remember it, and on turning back to see it again we believe it is the same object seen before.

This kind of overlapping earned a different metaphor in the eighteenth century. No sensation can be simple or momentary, observed Diderot in his notes on fibers. Rather, the sensation fills a duration of instants that are bundled together in a "sheaf" (*Éléments*, 9:313). A more complex bundling was described by Haller, its function being to serve "during the time of our perceptions." Here the discontinuous effect is more noticeable because the components lack homogeneity:

> Five different beings are joined together: the body which we perceive; the affection of the organ of the sensory by that body; the affection of the brain arising from the percussion of that sensory; the change produced in the mind; and lastly, the mind's consciousness and perception of the sensation. (*First Lines*, 2:33).

We only realize that these events are discontinuous when we direct attention consciously to their several junctures. The perceptual sheaf or bundle is separable into its component events by consciousness.

These accounts of cognitive discontinuity were self-denying. While calling attention to interrupted acts of perception they emphasized connected organic parts. Explanations moved from abstract to material planes and back again. But a smooth joining of the dualities—both private and cosmic dualities—defied logic. Only Hume overcame the impasse by invoking an enigmatic "force" identified with the imagination.

Hume explains what fuses the perceptual bundle into its seeming cognitive unity. The unifying agent is belief. The application of belief enlists the imagination to sustain a series of discrete images. The result is a constancy in our impressions that we call continuity. Hume points out that when we have constantly similar impressions of the sun or sea,

> The imagination is apt to disregard the gaps in our perception, and regard our successive perceptions not merely as similar to each other, but as strictly identical. If our different impressions are very like one another, then the imagi-

nation passes very easily from one to another, . . . so easily that it may feel as though there were only one *identical* object present to the mind. The imagination, that is, confuses similarity with identity, and thus the fiction arises that there *is* an identical object, the sun, when all we actually have is a number of very similar perceptions of light, heat and so on. (apud Warnock, 24)

Such is the power of imagination. This faculty has inspired many serious books to date. I cite it here for its relevance to the force necessary for overcoming discontinuity. Hume expresses this force in many ways in *A Treatise of Human Nature*: as a "feeling," as "vivacity," as "superior force." The vagueness of terms in his otherwise rational discourse exposes the inadequacies in biological research at the time. Hume refers to the "quality" of present ideas. He says that the ideas to which we assent are those that we connect to real perceptions that have the same quality as present ideas, "call it *firmness*, or *solidity*, or *force*, or *vivacity*, with which the mind reflects upon" them (*Treatise*, 1:106). Hume translates this quality into "*belief*." His most striking example is the familiar one of standing firm in a belief despite an impeccable argument to the contrary.

How can the mind retain a measure of assurance about any topic when contrary thoughts and sensations assault the judgment and imagination? How is it that the mind is not reduced to total uncertainty? Hume's answer is that all our reasonings derive from custom and experience, and that "belief is more properly an act of the sensitive than of the cogitative part of our natures" (*Treatise*, 1:183). Given a proposed issue, we feel stronger conceptions on one side than on the other, and the strong conception forms our first decision. New probabilities modify this, but after the first and second decisions "the action of the mind becomes forced and unnatural, and the ideas faint and obscure." New data and ideas influence the imagination less vigorously, and the principles of cause and effect no longer sway the process of our "natural conception" of ideas" (1:185).

Diderot's and Haller's fiber metaphors, and Hume's theory of belief, are not separated by a material-mental divide. Rather, Hume affirms a material pattern for the mental process, a process grounded in "natural" conditions of body and brain. Although he is speaking of the mind, he proposes that its beliefs rise out of "sensitive" and affective sources rather than from rational or "cogitative" acts. Beliefs are the cornerstone of his skeptical analysis, and so these materialist attributions are noteworthy. The sensory and affective sides of psychology are dominant in Hume. He speaks of "sensation" experienced less and more strongly by the imagination, more feebly in proportion to commonly held judgments and opinions. First and second decisions do not succumb to new opinions because "the posture of the mind is uneasy; and the *spirits* being diverted from their natural course are not governed in their movements by the same laws, at least not to the same degree, as when they *flow* in their usual *channel*" (*Treatise*, 1:185, emphasis added).

These references to spirituous activity implicate Hume in a vitalist position, odd as this may appear, inasmuch as the vitalists, in various ways, conjectured animating mainsprings in the universe. That Hume was a philosopher while the biologist Jean Baptiste Robinet, let us say, was a vitalist does not make them incompatible thinkers when the premise is "spirits." Indeed, Hume's devotion to intellectual analysis salutes the natural world by drawing analogies between the two. If one goal of scientific knowledge is to discover the concealed "power or force which actuates the whole machine," one goal of philosophical understanding is to trace "the secret springs and principles that actuate" the operations of the human mind. Just as the external, actuating force "never discovers itself in any of the sensible qualities of body," so too in the thought process "nature throws a bar to all our inquiries concerning causes and reduces us to an acknowledgment of our ignorance" (*Human Understanding*, 24, 73–75). The "concealed power or necessary connection" is an ambiguity in Nature that has an ambiguous parallel in the human mind.

This admission of limits to understanding was no conventional acknowledgment. It belonged to a surprisingly widespread if half-conscious insistence on discontinuity both in nerve bundles and in perceptions, a repeated insistence made during the very effort of describing a continuous system. No better illustration of these deficiencies is available than Hume's discussions of power and will. His reliance on physiology is as strong as are his admission of its dead ends. He has no doubt that without the animal spirits flowing naturally "in their usual channel" the link between body and mind would dissolve. And yet he pleads ignorance of precisely what this link consists of. Hume analyzes the physiology of psychological events. We are conscious of an internal power because we feel that the simple command of our will directs the mental faculties and moves the parts of our body. An act of volition produces motion in the limbs and also raises new ideas in the imagination. From these experiences we acquire the notion of power or energy, and we attribute other mortals with the same power. We do not know, however—adds Hume—the means by which this energy or will operates on that limb, nor do we know the mystery of the union of mind with body, much less how spiritual substance influences grosser matter. When we turn to the volitional power itself, we cannot be conscious of it. We know of its existence only by past exertion or the experience of one event following another. Proof of the will's mystery is the lesson of anatomy itself. The motion of a limb teaches us that

> the immediate object of power in voluntary motion is not the member itself which is moved, but certain muscles and nerves and animal spirits, and, perhaps, something still more minute and more unknown, through which the motion is successively propagated ere it reach the member itself whose motion is the immediate object of volition. (77–78)

Hume takes for granted the nerve fluid that is much discussed among physiologists, but he approaches the fluid's submicroscopic features at a point of abstraction, where anatomists terminate their descriptions. The continuity between neural impulse, will, and abstract thought remains an enigma. At the same time, as invisible as the animal spirits may be, they are too crude a substance to be identified with the "force" that connects physical impulse and mental thought. Hume then wonders if perhaps "something still more minute and more unknown" is the power in question. He can find no "more certain proof [than] that the power by which this whole operation is performed . . . is to the last degree mysterious and unintelligible" (78). The mind wills a certain event in the beginning, but at once "another event, unknown to ourselves and totally different from the one intended, is produced." The neural mechanism is activated, and "this event produces another, equally unknown, till, at last, through a long succession the desired event is produced" in the form of a motor response (78).

The direction of Hume's analysis moves implicitly toward the energy or "power" that we saw invoked earlier in the macrocosmic sphere. Without imputing any metaphysical intentions to Hume, it is noteworthy that his remarks add one more increment to other thinkers' diverse remarks about neurophysiology and universal continuity that converge on an arcane theory of cognition. The unnamed power of cohesion is vaguely related to spirituous matter, also identifiable with aether, which will be evident at the end of this volume.

Hume's explicit concern with the ways that nerves act on the body was also addressed by Haller's physiology. But as for animal spirits, Haller did not believe in a crude model of nerves as hollow tubes. He suggests that perhaps a subtle fluid in some special way "flows," either in the form of electricity or as magnetic fluids (*First Lines*, 1:221–22). A disciple of Haller, the physiologist Samuel Tissot, discusses the theories that might account for the cohesion of matter to spirit. The four possibilities were animal spirits, nerve fluids, electricity, and aether. But what precisely was the agent that travels to make the connection of nerves to brain? Diderot too is puzzled on this point, because the effect of "force" is instantaneous. If there is any truth to fluid theory, it obviously has not yet accounted for the slowness of the flow, which is too slow for any simultaneous concurrence of sensation and expression (*Éléments*, 9:321). Only Condillac seems unconcerned with these issues. In a discussion of dream images and hallucinations, he offers an indifferent opinion as to whether they emerge by fiber vibration or by animal spirits (*Origine*, 42).

The divergent opinions about the concealed processes of transmitting neural signals formed part of the debate between vibrationists and fluid-ists. This aspect of Hume's Western European milieu entails the role of aether, examined in Chapter 9. If any consensus existed, it was the tendency toward characterizing some kind of energy flow in cognition. After mid-century, opinion was summarized in the *Encyclopédie* article "Fiber," which cites the force of Newtonian attraction to explain the cohesion of solids and fluids (therefore also the cohesiveness of the molecular composition of nerve fibers). In later decades, Daniel Delaroche and Pierre Cabanis co-incide by eliminating some of the previous alternatives. Delaroche calls the principle of cohesion in nerves a "vital force" or a "vital principle," gener-ated when the contact of atoms binds fibers through Newtonian attraction. But Cabanis feels moved by this cohesive energy, "this very tendency, so blind in appearance," to ask what force holds things together (*Rapports*, 394). He claims not to know whether the cause is gravitation or "sensi-bility." Either choice affiliates him with Hume's Newtonian perplexity. As for the nervous system as a whole, its diverse parts communicate with each other in a manner related to electrical currents, as Volta's experiments were beginning to suggest (414). Delaroche, on the other hand, follows Newton by applying the aether theory to the fluids in the nerve fiber and the medul-lary substance. Indeed, Delaroche names aether the principle of electricity as well as of heat, chemical reaction, and sonar conduction. Aether is the universal fluid that causes light to reflect and refract, and this combination of properties allows the spirituous matter to send sensory impressions to the brain (*Analyse*, 1:292–3).

In short, an elusive consensus emerged to compensate for the failure to explain the mysterious continuity between body and mind. The idea of soul was replaced by the idea of effluvial spirits, or force, or aether. Without such notions, an intolerable discontinuity would have overshadowed the ostensible "progress" being made in the physiology of psychological processes. But in fact, advances in anatomy and physiology did not shed light on the most crucial area of consciousness. The references to "force," "vivacity," and "spirits" were necessary, but they remained unsatisfactory descriptions. They jeopardized the materialist enterprise of explaining cognition without a supernatural context. This fact is understandably overlooked in the history of science because such references are a revolving door into an unscientific dimension. The references marked a boundary line without dimension, leaving little room for research. Nevertheless, these same arcane terms, embedded as they were in scientific discourse, never lost their currency. They remained the signs of philosophical centrality in an age of nascent scientific materialism. The history of ideas has yet to recognize their pervasiveness, notwithstanding their vagueness. They may in fact have been the signs of a vigorous natural philosophy unwilling to surrender the theory of cognition to scientific disciplines cut off from universalities.

The idea of perfect continuity allowed the physical universe to join with living forms of cognition. The idea of continuity—a bundle, a network, a force—was a trope for the organic unification of reality at any magnitude of form or event. Because matter was considered unified in a continuist scheme, cognition itself became a trope for that organicity. Only living matter can think and feel, although all forms of matter are connected with and through thinking and feeling. As Condillac said for the field of knowledge, the liaison of ideas "is found in the same combination that applies to the very generation of things" (*Origine*, 42). By "things," Condillac does not refer to any form of matter, although this eventually becomes a problem for consideration. His liaison of ideas takes place on the same effluvial site where other generative impulses arise—whether neural signals that connect volition to muscle, or molecular recombinations that restore severed parts in nerveless organisms. Fundamental matter is found where the spider's fluid crystallizes into fiber, and where fibrous crystals soften into humus. But this place is also where the conditions of vital energy and the origin of life begin to emerge.

These unknown fermentations also implicated the problem of cognitive processes. How cognition and generation can occupy the same biological space and address the same sensory problems is discussed in Chapter 8, regarding polyps. However, the material conditions of vital energy and the origin of life relate to human understanding, and on this point David Hume and Hartley are explicit. The Newtonian Hartley believed that the flow of aether vitalizes the medullary substance. The subtle and "elastic" fluid diffuses through the "pores" of gross matter and through the "open spaces" of finer substances (*Observations*, 1:23–24). The texture of the medullary substance is so uniform, and its vessels are so minute and regular, that no interval or vacuity can disturb or interrupt the vibrations of the aether. The continuity between external and internal spheres is preserved by the uninterrupted diffusion of energy. While this standard summary of Hartley suffices for the present, it is fraught with problems, which are discussed in Chapter 9.

Alongside Hartley's blunt account of uninterrupted signal transmission, Hume's position seems respectfully laconic. Just as we are ignorant of the force or energy by which bodies operate on each other, so it is equally incomprehensible to Hume that a mental energy, even the Supreme Mind, can operate either on bodies or on itself (*Human Understanding*, 83). His acknowledgment of energy is clear, as are the terms "power" and "force." Only the explanation is missing. Activity in the human mind is due to "some instinct or mechanical tendency which may be infallible in its operations" (68). Rational structures stand aside, as do the physiological mechanisms commonly cited in this regard.

Hume did more than announce his skeptical suspension of understanding. He also confers a name on the mental process that pulsates with the rhythm that regulates the external world and its own constituent objects: "an instinct which carries forward the thought in a correspondent course to that which [Nature] has established among external objects." Human subjectivity feeds on a natural source, "though we are ignorant of those powers and forces on which this regular course and succession of objects totally depends." The pattern cannot be any more primordial for human beings than for other living forms: "As nature has taught us the use of our limbs without giving us the knowledge of the muscles and nerves by which they are actuated, so has she implanted in us an instinct" (68).

Organic Energy

Hume's instinct, Diderot's spider brain, and Goya's irrational dream were clues to the energy that holds the key to the universals of meaning in all matter. But their continuist metaphors did not conceal the space inevitably left by a missing link. We saw earlier how the mathematician d'Alembert cautioned that discontinuities must be expected in knowledge. It bears re-marking that his mathematical counterpart, Maupertuis, was just as alert to the problem. Preoccupied with discontinuity, Maupertuis called the unit of organic life "attraction" or "memory" or "instinct" (*Oeuvres*, 2:168–76 and passim). Whether attraction and memory could inhere in the tiniest parts of matter was debatable, and Diderot objected that they could not. But Maupertuis pursued the idea that the universe is an organic whole. He was unequivocal about the generative and cohesive energy in particular bodies. However, this belief was allowed to become a local question alongside the general problem of discontinuity in the universe.

Maupertuis's concept of organic power or memory was an irrational hint within a larger, more quantifiable apparatus. He did not stress the Lockean association of memory and imagination, but his appeal to a primordial condition had the merit of flirting, however briefly, with frankly organicist conceptions. This organic energy need not be juxtaposed to the unconscious energy that in the Goyesque conception enables dream to represent truths that are unformulatable in the ordinary languages of perception and verbal abstraction. Yet that power is instinctual enough to be involuntary, as memory and imagination often are. If it seems disparate to frame the mathematician and the artist within the same organicist context, other thinkers may figure as middle terms between the two extremes. Indeed, when Mary Warnock describes the faculty of imagination, she considers its treatment by thinkers from Hume to Kant. She calls the imagination "a power in the human mind which is at work in our everyday perception of the world" (*Imagination*, 196). Here the imagination is no longer synonymous with memory, but the "power" of imagination is operable on objects either absent or present. Moreover, it is independent of Reason by virtue of its involuntary impulsion on our thoughts. In this nonrational capacity, imagination's instinctual mechanism can compel the representation of things as freely as Goya's dreamwork, although with greater coherence. The issue here is not so much the cognitive function of the imagination per se, which has been studied amply from many standpoints. Rather, for the present context of the enigmatic "glue" that joins mental and material spheres, the issue is the materialist basis of the imaginational mechanism. The composition of mental processes begins with the nature of neural matter, both the fibral vehicle and its spirituous contents. Theories about these functional materials submitted to the same eighteenth-century dualist pattern as the mental experiences produced by those functions. The next chapter shows why.

6. Theories of Vital Force, Matter, and Fiber

I ask [the atheist] . . . whether the rotting of a turnip, the generation of an animal, and the structure of human thought, be not energies that probably bear some remote analogy to each other. It is impossible he can deny it. —Hume, *Dialogues Concerning Natural Religion*

Therefore there is no difference between a *spiritual substance* and a *material substance* other than what can be made between the modifications or ways of being of a given substance. . . . What is material can imperceptibly become spiritual.

—La Mettrie, *Histoire naturelle de l'âme*

See through this air, this ocean, and this earth,
All matter quick, and bursting into birth.
Above, how high, progressive life may go!
Around, how wide! how deep extend below!
Vast chain of being! —Pope, *Essay on Man*

The early chapters of this volume have referred to the ideal of continuism by way of its nemesis discontinuity and set forth the concepts and metaphors behind the subliminal uneasiness over discontinuity that, I argued, the continuists felt subliminally. While the discussions were accessible to readers of all scholarly disciplines, portions of the two preceding chapters grew more intense in their technical discussion of the biology that underlay the concepts and metaphors. The discussions that follow in this and the next chapters, prior to the final ones, examine more closely the materialist and vitalist theories that are susceptible to the discontinuist preoccupation. Although the exposition may give the false impression of being designed primarily for medical historians and for historians of science, the purpose is quite the opposite. The general reader can credit the arguments that build toward the last chapter only if they are based on evidence that will satisfy specialists. At the same time, historians of biology will be challenged by a newly visible pattern that emerges when outdated scientific thought is treated under the focus of an unresolved, century-long preoccupation rather than within a hard-core chronology of contrary theories.

Not all aspects of the discontinuist preoccupation were articulated by any one thinker. The inklings of a universal agent binding cognitive process to cosmic matter and absolute Intelligence were embedded piecemeal in the discourses of diverse authors. The three quotations at the beginning of this chapter attest to the dissimilar vocations of those authors, to whom the painter Goya can be added.

The "energies" Hume mentions in the first epigraph correspond to the enigmatic "powers and forces" he and others associated with the imagination and universal forces mentioned in the preceding chapter. Now Hume extends the cohesive force from mind to all physical matter, whether decaying or generative. In the third epigraph, Pope hails "matter" more assertively by evoking the Chain of Being: here matter is the cohesive factor that links all mental and physical objects in the universe. In the second epigraph, lest these claims of unity prompt a dualist to protest by reminding us that thoughts and things belong to separate realms, La Mettrie invokes "substance" as the common ingredient of spirit and matter. Each thinker in his own way offered a component part of the puzzled aspiration to continuity that prevailed in Western Europe. What the Spanish artist fantasized enigmatically, the English poet proclaimed, the French scientist rationalized, and the Scottish philosopher debated. They shared an intuited sense of puzzlement or wonder mixed with both assertion and denial that a single "thread" connected the subject-object dichotomy at all levels of reality, from the body-spirit suture at the neural-signaling level that in turn ensures unbroken intelligibility at the level of knowledge, to the planetary level of connectedness among material beings that extends into the cosmic Chain of Being, that finally connects to the Absolute or the One, an ultimate Spirit that circles back to the individual level of spirit or mind and body.

The grand unifying vision immortalized by Pope and advocated by continuist thinkers was embraced less enthusiastically by Buffon, Goya, Diderot, and others who wrestled with its paradoxes. Their hesitations will be better appreciated in the light of their ideas about the nature of matter. Goya's "dream of Reason" is by no means an unlikely context for discussing the concept of matter.[1] The status of material and phantasmal forms in *Ca-*

---

1. Barbara Stafford has argued that artists and theorists aspired not only to encompass materiality but also to "visualize" and "visibilize the invisible." Stafford, "Conjecturing the Unseen in Late Eighteenth-Century Art," *Zeitschrift für Kunstgeschichte* 48, 2 (1985):341.

pricho 43 is ambiguous, and it challenges empirical explanations of perception. How material entities constitute a mental image and how imaginary beings appear to have concrete existence are problems that place barriers to understanding *Capricho 43*. In earlier chapters, there were glimpses of the bats' metamorphic power. Their seeming palpability underscores the mystery of how mental phenomena seem material or, conversely, immaterial and yet "real." The existence of imaginary entities defies the materialist explanation of cognitive events. Consequently, the meaning presumed for such terms as "reality" and "materiality" dissolves under the imprecise notion of what matter actually is.

The elusive nature of matter has led research into the cultural environment in Spain and beyond. Spain was not devoid of pseudo-scientific ideas of the kind that nurtured the superstitious affinities of Goya's patrons.[2] The Spanish alchemist Diego de Torres Villarroel, a precursor of Goya who cultivated the genre of literary dreams, wrote a book on the philosopher's stone that fostered the animist belief that mineral forms are alive and that decoctions and elixirs of quicksilver manifest life in "the spirit of metals" (*Suma medicina*, 190–98). Their local environment must be exchanged for a Western European one when the essence of matter is at issue. Fundamental questions about matter can be formulated in similar ways even though diverse communities pursued the answers with dissimilar methods. In Western Europe, empirical and hermetic sciences coexisted, as scholars continue to point out. The continuity of old ideas after 1700 can be observed through English poetry, both in its "physico-theology" and in Christopher Smart's satires of diverse scientific endeavors (Jones, 76–77). Samuel Johnson preferred to believe in the alchemist quest for transmuting base metal into gold as late as 1775, according to Boswell (McClelland, 66).

The empirical approach to the specific nature of matter stopped short of the philosophical implications that concerned scientists like Buffon, Needham, and Robinet. Concrete shapes are intelligible for what they represent. So too are their relationships to one another. However, the concrete shapes in themselves—their cohesion, their plasticity, their very existence—all have material causes that began to draw empirical and speculative attention only in the eighteenth century. Biology and natural philosophy advanced toward ever more fundamental components of reality; concurrently, the question of what matter is and does claimed increasing attention.

2. See Chapter 9 on "irrational science" in Volume 1, *Counter-Rational Reason in the Eighteenth Century*.

Theories of Matter

One scientific question prompted by *Capricho 43* and pursued experimentally by alchemists and biologists alike was the genesis of material beings. A common formulation of this question was, How can an inert seed, dry as a grain of sand, come alive and sprout fibers? A pebble in the road and the stone of a peach appear equally mineral in their constitution, and yet only the peach stone can generate life. The mystery involved the self-organizing capacity of matter, and the fact of its existence everywhere along the ladder or Chain of Being, fascinated eighteenth-century thinkers who could imagine a continuous interlinkage of lower rungs to higher rungs. In this relational perspective, the factor to consider was not so much how the processes of germination and generation worked as what were the qualities of matter that permitted it to achieve organic status. What agency, in other words, created or promoted the sentient and self-generating traits of matter?

The question inevitably became philosophical and turned on the definition of intelligence in matter, although obviously not in any teleological or self-conscious sense of the word "intelligence." In mechanical theories of matter as well as in vitalist theories, the problem eventually came down to simple forms of matter that were governed or characterized by motion or energy, usually termed "force." In this respect we are well reminded by La Mettrie's theory of matter and "substance" that not even a philosophical mechanist could be satisfied with a conventional notion of matter's passive-mechanical properties.

The essence of matter in La Mettrie, as Aram Vartanian points out, is a "motor force" that enables matter in its passive extension (shape, size) to assume active forms (motion). This idea was prepared for by Newtonian attractionist physics, on the one hand, and Lockean philosophy, on the other. Both approaches narrowed the Cartesian properties of matter and soul (*res extensa/res cogitans*) so that "matter might well have properties seemingly incompatible with its essence."[3] Thus La Mettrie is caught in a circular argument and needs the concept of a "force motrice" to break it, as Vartanian shows. This concept belongs to La Mettrie's metaphysical *Histoire de l'âme* rather than to the more empirical *L'homme machine*. Nevertheless, it is precisely the activity of mind or soul that lent a compelling

---

3. Aram Vartanian, *La Mettrie's "L'homme machine": A Study in the Origins of an Idea* (Princeton, N.J.: Princeton University Press, 1960), 42, 66.

interest to matter for all natural philosophers. It thus appears significant that La Mettrie was vague on the essential difference between raw and sentient matter in the context of motor force. The material substance (*substance des corps*) that possesses motor force carries a name similar to the substantial forms (*formes substantielles*) that enable matter in organized beings to *feel*. Certain substantial forms constitute the organism's "life principle" and thereby its vegetative or sensitive soul, according to Vartanian. We are therefore beyond the domain of raw matter. Buffon, in fact, will abandon the term "raw" matter for "dead" matter. On the other hand, the life principle receives the name "vital force" in the physiologies proposed by other naturalists. The common denominator of *force* in both "motor" and "vital" forms of matter remained a mystery. The difficulty fell beyond La Mettrie's purpose in writing, at any rate.

What stirred a special curiosity about the composition of matter was the concurrent research into fibers. The standard description of matter as presented by historians of science does not take fiber or material substance per se as a point of departure. Rather, historians contrast mechanist and vitalist physiologies with respect to such concepts as force, generation, and sensibility. The present chapter differs in approach by concentrating on the way matter focuses these concepts. It emphasizes the concurrence of variant ideas about force, generation, and sensibility, independent of their diverse historical development, in order to search out the Enlightenment's undeclared position regarding the unity and continuity of generative and thinking matter. This approach will be easier to understand if preceded by a review of the standard categories in themselves.

A first observation is that mechanism and vitalism are the classic opposing schools for explaining reproduction, growth, and related physiological functions. A corresponding opposition of materialism and spiritualism does not follow so neatly, however. A mechanist view that does not distinguish a clock from a dog can explain vital processes either dualistically, by means of an immaterial soul, or materialistically, by citing a material "force" between particles, such as cohesion or expansion, that is innate or internal to matter (omitting spiritualist monism for purposes of simplification). While Newton denied such innate force, Leibniz embraced the *vis viva*, a power that later more advanced mechanics termed "energy." The concept of force has several names for the function it fulfills. The eminent mechanist and rational physiologist Friedrich Hoffmann called it the *anima sensitiva* that distinguishes organic forms from nonliving matter. The greatly influential chemist and physiologist George Stahl,

a critic of mechanism, called it a "force substantielle motrice" an immaterial agent operating beyond the organic structure that is in fact an extension of the soul (Duchesneau, *Physiologie*, 47, 24–25, 478). Stahl's vitalist
or animist view took a materialist form in the Montpellier school, where
Théophile de Bordeu adhered to a belief in a universal property of sensibility, as distinct from the immortal soul. The same force in living matter
took the name *vis essentialis* in the work of Caspar Wolff, a follower of Stahl
and Leibniz (Duchesneau, 313–14). Finally, the organic "inner mold" of
Buffon's theory exhibited "an active, penetrating force analogous to the
forces of chemistry and magnetism," although the human soul existed as
a different entity (*Histoire naturelle*, ed. Varloot, 24, 216, 220). The historian Thomas Hankins has explained why the materialist heirs of mechanist
physiology failed to account for the properties of life. These eighteenth-
century materialists revived the Stoic pneuma, which was "the breath of
the cosmos, the activating principle responsible for all change and all life."
Instead of explaining natural phenomena by the organization of matter,
they "made matter active by giving it the properties of life. In essence, they
distributed the soul throughout matter in order to get rid of it" (Hankins,
36, 125, 127, 134). The activating principle took the name "energies" when
Hume ascribed it equally to rotting turnips and human thought, as quoted
in the epigraph to this chapter. In sum, if any linkage existed of inert
matter, vital substance, and intelligent or "thinking" matter, the common
element was transcendent. It could partake of Divine Intelligence as well
as inorganic stuff.

A second observation regarding the nature of matter concerns generation, or the continuity of force in time. Again Wolff commands attention
for advocating the epigenetic theory, which holds that matter is essentially
active in the Aristotelian fashion of an embryo beginning as homogeneous
mass and forming organs one after another. Replacing epigenesis, however,
was preformation, a theory whose revival after its seventeenth-century
eclipse carried dualist baggage, as Chapter 8 indicates. This camp included
Charles Bonnet, Lazzaro Spallanzani, and Albrecht von Haller, converted
from epigenesis. However, generation as exhibited in the freshwater hydra
or polyp argued in favor of materialism and atheism for La Mettrie and
Diderot, insofar as the soul appeared to be distributed throughout matter
(Hankins, 134, 141–45).

A third and final observation about the properties of matter concerns
sensibility. The vitalist Bordeu believed sensibility to be a universal property of matter, and irritability only a special case of it. In contrast, the

physiologist Haller's experiments with nerve tissue purported to show that sensibility involved messages to the brain whereas irritability was a distinct property of the muscle. The debated issue here concerned the importance of functional differentiation. Was it of any consequence as far as the life principle and the nature of matter are concerned that one kind of tissue contracts and the other conveys messages? The answer depends on whether one believes that matter requires a soul in order to be alive. According to Hankins, materialist Diderot preferred vitalist Bordeu to Haller, at least in *D'Alembert's Dream*. For the vitalist "there was no difference between the organic and the inorganic except in the degree of organization. His whole world was dynamic. The universe was a great animal, and it was also one enormous elastic body conserving *vis viva*. There was no real difference in his philosophy between the dynamic and the vital, no difference between physics and physiology" (Hankins, 127). This conception of matter supposes that the difference between motion, self-organization, and neural message is only a question of degree. It remains to consider how "thinking matter" fits into this gradation, as Chapter 8 attempts to do. However, the physiologist who believed in the soul's immortality, as Haller did, preferred to confine the explanation of vitality to observing the organization of matter and its functions, rather than invoking an abstract vital force, as Bordeu did. The latter explanation would amount to calling the soul by another name: the pneuma that activates matter by its infusion throughout the universe. In one respect, the constant factor in all cases is the continuity maintained from microcosm to macrocosm: a Divine or universal force that is present in every existing thing.

The relation of fibers to the life principle dominated most physiological studies. Haller expounded the fiber's more particular role as the foundation of all biological functions. Its relation to vitality was especially prominent in the research of John Needham, who observed that the substance resulting from his crushed-seed mixtures produced what he called "filaments." These linear materialities ramified and seemed to be on the verge of pullulating with life. Needham's chief goal was to find the key to life's generative principle. But in this pursuit his filaments whetted a second interest. The material contents of the filamentous substance suggested a theory of natural gradations in the universe, a scale beginning with mineral states and extending to plants and then to animal states. It was a scheme that links the realms of inorganic and organic matter within a continuous chain. The linking vehicle was conjectured to be Nature's "vital" principle, what Needham termed a "vegetative force."

It would of course appear that inert minerals were incapable of vegetating and springing to life. One question, however, suggested an alternative truth. What if all material forms were found to share the same primal composition or, more mysterious, if they were infused with a single force that emanates from a farther source? Needham sought to answer this question by analyzing inert matter placed under conditions that favor metamorphosis. And while he stopped short of advocating an unbroken calibration from stone to tree to higher life-forms, as Robinet did, his brews and powdered amalgams persuaded him that a single generative principle animates them all.

One group of Needham's experiments supported a self-activist concept of matter after microscopic separation of elements. He placed wheat in a marble mortar, added water after pounding the wheat, and allowed the mass to evaporate into a gelatinous substance. Observed under a microscope, the mass seemed to "consist of innumerable filaments"; thereafter the substance

> was in its highest point of exaltation, just breaking, as I might say, into life. These filaments would swell from an interior force so active, and so productive, that even before they resolved into or shed any moving globules, they were perfect zoophytes teeming with life, and self-moving. (*Observations*, 31)

Confirmation of this spontaneous generation was Needham's primary objective. He indicated in passing how the composition of matter can explain the graduated continuity of material beings from the largest to the smallest. The secret lay in the filament, which embodies the connective substance that was everywhere present.

Each filament is infused with a life-teeming content, reports Needham. At no microscopic point does the animal or vegetable matter lack this vitality. Yet even this lowest class of minute matter can be broken down still further without eliminating the vital substance. On reaching the vanishing point under the most powerful lens, "we are yet at an immense remove from the Universal source, notwithstanding that some of them are small beyond conception, and no less simple in their motions" (43). Needham hints at molecular units so simply organized as to be "mere machines, without any true spontaneity." At the submicroscopic level, the bodies might easily be mineral granules, because their motion is mechanical. Yet the vital substance exists here as well, affirmed by Needham as the factionally minute end of the "vast gradation" that stretches from the most compounded to the most simple of entities. At the latter end, the moving atoms seem to reach an "oscillatory balance" at the point of invisibility under the most powerful magnifiers.

The belief in graduated continuity placed Needham closer to Robinet than to his occasional collaborator Buffon. Certainly his association with Buffon did not ensure his duplicating the latter's concept of matter. Indeed, he parted company with the materialist theory of organic particles because it replaced the soul with self-active matter (Roe, "Needham," 161). Buffon denied the false analogies used by naturalists who compared plants with animals and who thought they had observed minerals in a vegetating state. The naturalists reasoned fallaciously that because blood circulates so does sap, and that the "petrifying sap" of stone formations once flowed in a similar way (Varloot, 43). Buffon could demonstrate on his side that certain geological specimens were actually composed of the shells and other remains of once-living creatures. He was unwilling to partition Nature into segments that remain unconnected at their base. In fact, he believed in a common "interior mold" that directed the organic molecules to their proper place. He also contended, despite the mold theory, that the common denominator escaped current simplifications.

Even though Buffon examined living forms at their macroscopic level, he contributed to submicroscopy by advancing an important concept of matter. The conventional distinction regarding organic matter entails the opposition of "organized" matter to "raw" matter. Buffon contended that the geological evidence shows raw matter often to be simply dead matter. With this argument he revised the accepted distinction by naming the two groups "living matter" and "dead matter" (178). Armed with this concept, Buffon could apply certain principles to microscopic nature as well as to the visible world. Thus he asserted that there really exists in Nature "an infinity of tiny organized beings, similar in their entirety to the large organized beings that figure in the world." Moreover, these small organized beings in turn are composed of living organic parts that are the common constituents of animals and plants alike. As for these organic parts, they "are primitive and incorruptible parts" that cannot be further reduced, so that "the assemblage of these parts form to our eyes organized beings" (175). The workings of all metamorphoses are explained in this way, and foremost among them is living reproduction. This is Buffon's real interest, permitting geology to slip away unexamined. By eliminating the idea of "raw matter" and substituting "dead matter," he begged the question of inert "incorruptible parts." All is a question of organization and "change of form" that operates so as to generate living beings, the point of Buffon's research.

Nonetheless, the common base, always transformable, is neither organic nor inorganic but simply "dead" matter. The question is whether "dead" is equivalent to "inert." If so, organic and mineral beings would enter the same pyramidal structure. Buffon did not go this far, except to draw an analogy of the kind that at times he admonishes in more adventuresome naturalists. Just as "millions of tiny salt cubes need to collect in order to form one perceptible grain of sea salt, so too millions of organic parts resembling the whole are needed in order to form a single germ contained in an individual elm tree or polyp." His point refers to how life reproduces itself, but the premise refers to how matter is constituted. And consequently, "just as we must separate, crush, and dissolve a cube of sea salt in order to perceive the tiny cubes composing it through crystallization, so too we must separate the parts of an elm tree or a polyp in order to recognize the tiny elm trees or tiny polyps that through vegetation or development are contained in those parts" (175). Whatever Buffon might intend here for the theory of generation, his theory of matter rejects "raw" in favor of "dead." Whether all "dead" particles are transformable under the right combinatory circumstances is neither negated nor affirmed. The analogy invites speculation in this vein. Buffon himself stated that Nature consists of living organic parts "whose substance is the same as that of organized being, just as there is an infinity of *raw* particles similar to the *raw* bodies we know" (emphasis added). Because Buffon prefers the term "dead" to "raw" a few pages later, as just shown, we are left to wonder if the "interior mold" of Nature might not be found at a primal generative base of all substance.

The pattern in these seemingly rival theories has to do with the mystery of universal energy as manifested in matter. All the theorists and researchers speculated on primary matter either in its fibrous form or as an organic vitality. In both cases some communicating force was said to generate activity at a given level of spontaneity or animation. Viewed in their entirety, the partial speculations each contributed to a comprehensive vision of an inexplicable all-embracing continuity. While some thinkers preserved the idea of a soul, others renamed the soul a "self-active" matter or a force distributed throughout all matter. Their school of thought was inconsequential—mechanist, vitalist, animist, theist—but their abiding focus on an overarching factor enabled them to share a concept of transcendent continuity throughout the universe of matter and spirit (or its equivalent name). Finally, the research on fibers and generation converged on the key function of sensibility. Sensible matter pointed in both directions of the scale of continuous beings: downward toward the indifferent point where the organic and the inorganic are identical except for organization, and upward toward the realm of eternal forms. In short, the focus on sensible matter brought regeneration and cognition into the same continuum as "raw" matter. More profoundly, it gave a temporal dimension to the entire scale that communicated with the Absolute.

Conventional notions of primary matter in the eighteenth century were far from codified by any one author. One approach studied the tiniest substances constituting nerve fibers. This perspective incorporated concepts from the Ancient Philosophy such as "igneous matter." The approach could be harmonized with Newtonian concepts such as the aether. The subject of aether will occupy Chapter 9, but its place in the stages of developing thought is pertinent here. Needham fitted his concept of "vitality" or "expansive force" within the genealogy of terms appropriate to the discussion, beginning with Newton. The basic unit of matter in Needham's theory is the filament. He devises a new class of organisms called "vital beings" whose vitality consists of "a very subtle and very active spirit, acting in a brute matter." This text and the following ones are also cited by the historian Shirley Roe in connection with the "expansive force" that informs matter. Needham says that it is "very attenuated, very exalted, ethereal according to Newton, electrical according to present ideas, very elastic by its intimate nature" (Roe, "Needham," 162, 166).

In another approach, fibrous composition also reveals an infinite number of minute plates or scales that are disposed in various directions, according to the physiologist Haller, who notes a difference between the solid portion with its interceptive small cells, on the one hand, and the watery part, on the other. But these observations open no secret doors. If nerve matter were of the same composition as cosmic matter, the revelation would indeed sustain an organicist universe. Aspects of Claude-Nicolas Le Cat's research tended in this very direction.

Part of Le Cat's system distinguishes between the dense "motor" and "animo-vegetal" fluids that circulate outside the filamentous network and the refined "sensitive fluid" that mixes with the organs of feeling. All these substances intermingle in the biosphere in graduated proportion so as to form "an ensemble, a single machine whose wheels are meshed in one another." But the model is not as mechanical as it appears. The composition of all earthly animal life is an "intussusception" (*engraînure*) that

results in a "communication with the fluids of the universe." The graduated intermeshing involves progressively more rarefied liquids that slip into
each other. The rarefied universal matter is inspired through air or else absorbed by some other transpiratory means at the contact point of nerve
ending and external environment (Le Cat, *Traité de . . . la nature*, xxxiii,
xli–ii).

Neither Needham nor Le Cat extended his ideas to the mineral realm,
as we shall find Robinet doing. They both affirm that connective matter
exists and is shared at the living microscopic level and at the levels of environment and cosmos. Needham's "vegetative force" is present in every
filament and microscopical point, ready to be released by decomposition
(Roe, "Needham," 162). Le Cat affirms that one and the same fluid process exists for the geological macrocosm as for the human microcosm. He
dramatically selects the most volatile trope imaginable in order to compare
the earth with the human organism. In the central depths of the globe,
he wrote, natural fires stoke rich mines, which, joined to the sun's heat,
produces vegetation and the life principle for animals. The same process
that is responsible for thunder and volcanoes, for example, also explains
malignant fevers. Conversely, these pathological or geophysical calamities
are so primal in their structural relation to the foundations supporting
each type that they generate good as well as harmful results. Thus, "Etna
vomits flaming terror and lava, and Sicily recovers its tranquillity. In this
other Vesuvius that is our little world, a burning and contagious fever or a
fiery delirium announces an approaching death. From the very heart of this
terrible furnace there leaps a critical and salutary eruption that expels the
lethal germ and cures the sick patient" (Le Cat, *Traité de . . . la nature*, lxxi).

Le Cat's metaphor offers a unifying vision that is unsupported by
anatomical or other evidence. But he is a serious physiologist in all other
respects, and his notion of animal spirit is credited elsewhere as well. In a
more rigorous medical anatomy, Jacques-Benigne Winslow reported that
animal spirit resists current dissecting methods aimed at determining its
contents. Whether it is a serous fluid or a derivative of chyle or blood, the
substance eludes isolation from the cerebral grey matter. But Winslow does
not deny the substance itself in the editions of 1732, 1752, and 1766. In contrast, the psychologist David Hartley reaches a Newtonian position regarding light and aether through a synthesizing effort that carries him beyond
anatomy. Hartley's vibrationist position approaches Le Cat's imaginative
analogies in one important respect. Hartley repeats the accepted fact that
aether communicates its impulses to the optic nerve and vice versa, and

claims the same communication by epidermal friction as well as taste, smell, and sound. The external, inert object acts on the aether by attraction or by impulse, and the aether in turn affects the nerves. What is more, the nerves can and do affect the aether in this reciprocal relationship (*Observations*, 1:21–2).

Thinkers like Le Cat, Winslow, and Hartley speculated on matter by focusing on neurophysiological process rather than on the broader nature of matter in the general scale of beings. As a result, they differed from the naturalists cited earlier in their attention to rarefied and invisible spirituous matter, however named. In turn, spirits were involved in the cognitive process. But if the intelligent matter in cognition also ran throughout the continuum, its metamorphic quality was implicit. Although not all beings in the universal chain displayed intelligence or even sensibility, the implication was that the "aether," "expansive force," "active spirit," "soul," or whatever it was called, underwent metamorphosis right up to the Absolute Being or the One. Again, if the interlinking continuum were indeed the true underlying reality that Goya intuited in his Universal Language, then his monstrous bat was in fact the appropriate symbol of primal energy or metamorphic matter. Furthermore, since the continuum was constituted by metamorphic matter, the true underlying reality was also a Chaos. Finally, the rarefied matter extended to the Supreme Being, whose cognitive power alone could fathom that Chaos. Did the "Dream of Reason" therefore mean that access to true knowledge of reality must come through the spirituous process of dreaming that Goya called the Universal Language, another term for the continuous aethereal matter?

Material Continuism

The views cited thus far were relevant to the nature of matter and its transactional properties as exhibited in "living" and "dead" substances. None of the surveyed naturalists advanced a uniform principle of generation for the mineral realm together with animal and plant realms. But several others evinced what might be called "material continuism," the continuity affirmed on the basis of a theory of matter. One sweeping hypothesis was advocated by Jean Baptiste Robinet, who had the same synthesizing flair as Hartley while also venturing further. Robinet construed the uniformity of generation to mean that stones too have a "vegetative principle" and that the "germs" of metals are a liquid matter that penetrates the pores of the entity until it petrifies.

Robinet desired to unify the universe, but he was not religiously inspired. On the contrary, the moral consequence of his pan-germination was that whatever exists is neither evil nor good. Light and darkness conserve a perfect balance in the Infinite. This scheme originates in a metaphor of gradation rather than in a Newtonian model of harmonious parts. Robinet's universe consists not of well-fitted modular clock units but rather of a substantive continuity derived from the essence of matter. Within each mineral lies an "attracting spirit" that manifests the "principle of affinity" characteristic of the earth as a whole. No other explanation accounts for phenomena such as crystallization and, more astonishing, the internal formations that resemble plant and animal structures. Just as natural earth fire is Le Cat's analog of organic volatility, so too does underground fermentation excited by the earth's "central fires" anchor Robinet's notion of uniform generation. His petrography abandons geology for biology and draws on the theory of germinal seeds in plant and animal organisms. It is no coincidence, in Robinet's opinion, that shells, bones, bark, and reticular tissue in plants as well as in animal fibers all exhibit a marked mineral texture. There exist mineral germs that are nourished and grow just like fiber and vein textures, he maintains. Going further, he finds elementary matter to consist of a "mineral sap" of "crystalline" nature that can harden into vitrified or laminated solids. In the same way that plant seeds require a sun-warmed soil to germinate, the earth's thermal centers work to compose lithic and metallic substances (*De la nature*, 1:286ff).

The philosophical materialism of Robinet's theory should be emphasized. It differs from Hartley's materialist synthesis by confining his hypothesis to the planetary biosphere, without considering the Newtonian, cosmic dimensions of aether and light. Consequently, the fundamental unit of matter that Robinet calls "attracting spirit" or "sap" exists to the same degree of primality as aether. His concept of matter also borrows the authority of Buffon's distinction between living and dead matter: that "all matter is organic, living, and animal. An inorganic, dead, inanimate matter is a chimera, an impossibility" (*Considérations*, 8). This leaves no doubt that his intention was more than a mere analogy between fiber and rock. There exists a "natural gradation of the forms of being," and this means all beings or material entities that comprise the natural world. In lower beings such as minerals and plants, we do not suspect that anything more than matter exists, and we explain an entire form or phenomenon by its material composition. But Robinet claims that we pay excessive attention to the visible assemblage of phenomena. We ignore how "there must necessarily exist an invisible world that is the foundation of the visible world, and one to which we must restore everything that is real and substantial in Nature" (10).

In this thesis, pan-germination plays a role. Its uniform operation confirms the universal plasticity of matter, which is to say that matter has a capacity to be shaped repeatedly into new forms. For this reason, Robinet recognized that the study of polyps is so crucial. Their regenerative plastic force reflects their material constitution, the "organic" or "living" molecules that reproduce pandemically and undergo metamorphosis. When Robinet dismisses Buffon's "dead matter" as nothing more than "living matter" under another form, he is carrying the notion of plasticity to its logical conclusion. Conscious of this liberty, he interpreted Buffon's "inner mold" theory so as to include under germinating forms certain stone textures, sand granules, and saline particles, as well as biological forms. The "inner mold" of Buffon should not be taken literally, he says, nor should it be limited to superficial oppositions of live and dead matter. On the contrary, the "organic molecule" is a trope: "It is an image, if you will, which [Buffon] uses to aid the imagination of people who need sensible representations, but it is an image so imperfect" that Robinet must elaborate its wider implications (*De la nature*, 1:228). And here he launches into examples like polyps and crayfish.

The "organic molecule" carried Robinet away from the Leibnizian Chain of Being, which was conceived for the purpose of ordering the universe. The model implicit in both Robinet and Le Cat revised the metaphorical chain by introducing another kind of connectedness, an inward-outward continuity that eventually involved the "presence" of an object to the mind. In contrast to the external conception of continuism, the focus on matter ultimately related to the organism's internal mechanisms in relation to the surrounding world. Here the pathway to a continuous network begins by way of fiber anatomy and then neurophysiology itself, and then leads outward to the immediate environment and beyond.

The plastic and regenerative constitution of matter entails sensitivity, or at least the potential for it. This was the case for Robinet's dismissal of "dead, inanimate matter" as a "chimera," although Needham did not go so far. At bottom this meant that if organic matter is self-active, as Buffon and Needham contended, it can at any morphological stage "know" its material needs and survive accordingly. Buffon's concept of "general force" differed from "impulsion," vegetative force, and other contemporary accounts, but these all served in some way as Nature's "universal agent," capable of intelligent if not conscious activity.[4] Whether "knowledge" is the appropriate term is debatable. At the simplest level of the polyp, matter's self-organizational ability would be tantamount to a *functional* cognitive activity, albeit nonconscious, as Chapter 8 proposes. In this perspective, Robinet's material continuism permitted a physio-psychologist like Pierre Cabanis to bring into rhythm the physical and moral springs of human conduct. But simpler life forms also "know" how to survive and reproduce. Theirs is a cognitive behavior that redefines the concept of knowledge and the nature of intelligence, not necessarily a conscious attribute.

Cabanis, too, ground an almond into powder and allowed its muci-laginous contents to decompose. But instead of halting before his micro-scopic observation of swirling animalcules, he explained how inert matter passes from the vegetative state into life, and from life into death. It is in this biomorphic perspective of capabilities for generating and surviving organically that we must understand Cabanis's treatment of substance in 1802. Like his predecessors, he believed in the continuity of matter, men-tioning the intervals that separate the different realms of animal, plant, and mineral state. They all cling to a "multitude of intermediate echelons that bring the most distant existences close together" (*Rapports*, 383). But also like his predecessors, Cabanis believed in "a secret force" that is primal sub-stance. This force informs psychological and mineral orders no less than plant and animal kingdoms.

Without a "continuist" theory of matter, Cabanis could not advance his search for the physical circumstances of irrational mental states. Work-ing in the same time frame as the painter Goya, he shared the same curi-osity about the origins of bizarre ideas and their manifestations in di-verse states of mind. Cabanis wanted to explain materialistically all related states of abnormal exaltation: "delirium, dementia, maniacal transport, furor, disorderly imaginings, catalepsies, ecstasies." Again like Goya, he dismissed imaginary causes adduced by superstitious spiritualism. But as a biologist as well as a moral psychologist, Cabanis inserted mental phe-nomena into the uninterrupted material continuity of self-transforming

---

4. Le Cat hinted at the connection between this energy and a knowing universal or di-vine spirit when he referred to "the impulsion of an aethereal medium that is spread through the universe and that penetrates the pores of gross bodies" (*Traité des sensations*, 1:lx). For a general discussion of the theories of energy in reference to regeneration, see Shirley A. Roe, "John Turberville Needham and the Generation of Living Organisms," *Isis* 74 (1983): 159–84, esp. 162–68.

substance. Whereas Goya's irrationalism could not conceive that any order rules the monstrous metamorphoses of reality, Cabanis found an orderly path through the changing social reality of thought and body.

Evidence of the orderly path resides in the so-called physical "laws" Cabanis cited as proof that all transformations belong to the "eternal movement" of matter. Transformations and gradations in Cabanis's case are limited to material ones, but the transformation of sense data into more abstract cognitive signals will become equally important later in this chapter. The process of change extends in a "rising chain" of organized live matter that "by degrees" again descends through human and lower animal life, and downward still toward the state of absolute death. Cabanis echoes earlier versions of this process: organic matter decomposes, gases escape to prompt vegetation, and mineral composites like bones or shells accumulate, are pulverized, and fertilize the earth. But he also approaches Robinet's theory of material gradations, seeing "similarities" rather than drawing analogies as Buffon does.[5]

Cabanis moved quickly to reassert his main idea of unbroken rational continuities. Now under focus was the transitional region "between the vegetal system and the animal system," where the "zoophytes" and polyps are situated. The assumption was that matter decays and develops because of an inherent tendency for graduated sensitivity. The fibroid-structured mineral veins, the "irritable" primitive plants, the "stupid mollusks," and the ascending generations of self-organizing animal intelligence are all compelled by the same "secret force."

The persistent belief that matter is continuous by virtue of an omnipresent component sustained itself by the vitalist physiology described earlier. As Hankins notes (125), even Haller preferred not to delve into the nature of vitality even though he could not accept mechanist accounts. While physiologists themselves may have avoided drawing philosophical conclusions from their experiments, this does not negate the inferences contained therein. Diderot, for instance, intuited the sameness of vital matter regardless of function. Contractile nerve tissue and sensory nerve tissue both held for him the same secret of life: its vitality, its organizational ability, and its generative power. It is significant that Diderot paid more attention to sensible matter, where the secret involved the continuity of

---

5. For example, Cabanis contended that "the successive vegetation of some mineral veins and their finger-like branchings seem like . . . the convergences of the most imperfect plants, in some way, at least in their manner of growth." This organic image holds anatomical implications that pass without comment. P. J. G. Cabanis, *Rapports du physique et du moral de l'homme*, vol. 2 (Paris: Crapelet, 1802), 384.

matter and its unfailing power to behave intelligently—that is, according to rational laws; this power was displayed most notably in the primal form of sensory-cognitive nerve gluten.

The enigma of matter rested not so much in life in itself as in the non-conscious intelligence that makes life possible. Life depends on the organizing capacity of matter, a capacity that turns molecules into "intelligent" organisms.[6] Diderot intuited the truth of linking self-active matter with elementary cognitive processes in the *Elements of Physiology*. The significance of this link in pointing toward a universal cognitive principle cannot be exaggerated. Diderot's most important remarks about matter occurred in the context of sensory ability and fiber composition. He centered his remarks around the idea of "gluten" as the essential substance in fibers that creates "a continuous whole." But continuity in this case was an ideal that must find support in the pillars of sensory fiber and coordination. The mere constituency of gluten yielded no useful material clue: "Analysis of gluten: earth, water, and oil; but combined and by this combination forming a whole that is neither water, nor earth, nor oil, nor anything that can be broken down by analysis" (*Éléments*, 9:278). It was "the whole" that escaped capture, and this concept overshadowed the scientific constituents when competing for Diderot's attention.

Diderot's only recourse in order to assert continuity was abstract reasoning, which he pursued until he could assert an empirical belief or "hope." His reasoning began with two alternatives. Gluten, which

> unites the molecules of the fiber, is either sensible or is not. If it is sensible, the molecule is a continuous sensible whole. If it is not, the fiber is reduced to a thread composed of sensible molecules separated by as many interposing inert molecules. This would no longer be a sensible whole. I hope that fiber is more plausibly flesh joined to flesh, forming a continuous whole somewhat homogeneous and alive. (9:278)

The enigma of vitality was not resolved, only transferred to the enigma of continuity. Diderot needed to analyze the material unit-substance of a "continuous whole" in order to explain sensory coordination. But unable to determine that material basis, he shifted to "flesh," a higher level of coordinated living matter that was equally baffling but more obviously "a sensible whole." The same water, earth, and oil that forms gluten also

6. The validity of defining intelligence in this way, and the "language" thus entailed, are both matters that will be discussed in my next volume, *The Universal Dream Language of Minerva*.

forms flesh, says Diderot, "and this kind of flesh thus coordinated forms fiber, and fiber is organized fiber as a result" (9:278).

Scholars agree, as Otis Fellows has pointed out, that Diderot's philosophy combines "naturalistic humanism" and "vitalized materialism." This philosophy is confirmed by the *Elements of Physiology* to the extent that its schematic notes on brain and nerve anatomy occasionally flash synthesizing hints of neural hypothesis that apply to human beings. In one such intuitive flash, Diderot's immediate context is brain secretion, even though his notes belong to the section on muscles. And here he brings the material gradations of Robinet close to the properties of muscle nerve. His problem is to explain the "reasons for the contractile force of the nerve: silk threads, spider threads, the swelling fibers of white wood, the ligneous fibers of plants" (9:323). Along the entire sweep of filamentous matter, "dead" or "alive" in Buffon's terms, a principle of *force* informs the organized molecules.

This remarkable conjunction of resemblances follows a passage where Diderot subjects himself to a peculiar catechism. Whatever earlier assertions he has made concerning brain secretion and nerve fluid are now challenged by irresolute responses to settled questions: "Is the brain a secreting organ? That may be. Do we find the nerve trunks to contain the same medullary substance impregnated with lymph? I wish so." The same text names the medullary "lymph" to be the nutriment of all nerve filaments, as well as being "the principle of their growth . . . of their force, of their weakness." But is it also the immediate cause of their sensibility and very life? This is what Diderot cannot bring himself to declare resolutely.

This vacillation alongside the unreconciled concepts of energy cited earlier circumscribes the space of an absent factor. At the nonteleological core of intelligent life there existed something material, but exactly what this substance was escaped definition. This enigma was the meeting point of diverse theories of matter, all of which lacked an explanation for the connective metamorphic unit that might be intelligent matter in one form, regenerative force in another form, and Divine substance in yet another: in short, an ever-present and linking transformative element or power that a visionary like Goya would call the "Universal Language." The spidery fibers Diderot cited could be found in inert or "dead" matter as well as in human neurophysiology.[7] Here Diderot puzzles over the elastic and vi-

---

7. Even the fluidist theory that Diderot seemed to share with the earlier physiologist Raymond Vieussens was compromised by the question. On the one hand, a severed nerve does not contract. Instead, the separate ends "lengthen and grow limp, allowing the medulla

brative quality of nerve fibers that "are not stretched out either to their origin or to their termination." Suddenly Diderot inserts the term "electric matter," and writes that "it is not retained by the nerves since it is communicated, it penetrates the animal and distributes its force as much to the flesh as to the fat and the nerves" (9:317). But his notes do not amplify the subject, so the theory of universal aether cannot explain the puzzle but remains a remote factor in his neurophysiology.

These disruptive concepts betray dissatisfaction with existing doctrines of matter and its nonteleological intelligence. Indeed, Diderot's deeper probe indicates that the debate between fluidists and vibrationists—whether the neural signal vibrated along solid nerves or flowed as spirituous matter in hollow nerves—ultimately addressed an idle question. The fibrous structure itself bears little consequence, whatever it is, since the enigmatic "energy" transcends it. In a revealing detail, Diderot begins his section on nerves by declaring, "the origin of the animal force is in the soft pulp" of the cervelet, from which stem the nerves in a constant state of excessive irritability (9:318). That he does not here distinguish irritability from sensibility will become clear in a moment, when he alludes to the sensorium. Stress falls on "animal force," without clues to secondary issues like its manufacture, its mode of conveyance, and its relation to the external environment. He is struck by the spectacular effect of the animal force in the strictly biological context of dismembered bodily parts. Seeking the simplest examples so as to reach a first principle, he adopts a minimalist view of vital matter by saying that it takes "very little to form the common sensorium." He then leaps with this principle to the opposite extreme by applying it to aberrations in the complex human brain.

This leap is logical, assuming the same animal force both in the tiniest magnitude and in complex neuro-cerebral structures. It is therefore no surprise that Diderot's vitalized materialism turns from its humanistic origins and seeks the basic unit of organized sensibility in simple matter. And he finds it in the worm—in fact, he regards the simple fiber itself, without cavity, to be a "worm." Moreover, the worm-fiber represents for him a model of prototypical coordinating intelligence. The model also addresses the enigma of what constitutes a material "whole." Nothing in this regard is revealed by the composition of gluten, analyzed at the outset. But Dide-

---

to escape in tubercule form" (*Éléments de physiologie*, 9:317). Here Diderot apparently follows Vieussens's description of the directions of fluid flow. On the other hand, if the fiber is hollow and limp, where does the fluid obtain "its celerity and its terrible energy"? He asks, "What is it that pushes it with such violence inside a sluggish canal?"

rot cannot admit that gluten is not sensible. To admit this would reduce the fiber to a thread of alternately live and inert molecules, as we saw. As he is stymied by this empirical blind alley, he turns in another direction. But the changing course is no repudiation of the possibility that matter develops and decays by an inherent capacity for graduated sensory capacity.

Diderot proceeds then to examine the totality that escapes analysis. As he says, "the nerve forms a whole, a complete animal with soft [medullary] substance" (9:278). He also knows that this substance cannot "separate or break, any more than a pricked worm can." The fact was that worms, just like polyps, could be severed and still preserve not only life but their regenerating properties. The study of such basic neural units, therefore, would plausibly disclose the key to the most primitive signals by which sentient organic matter brings order into its condition. Since the study involved organisms at their lowest organized level, the glutenous nature of fiber molecules remained in the background. The foreground focused on the simplest of vital activities, which is instinctive and pre-visual, but no less sensible or sensorial. Sensibility was understood as a coordinated ability on the part of matter to function successfully, which is to say by implementing a rudimentary, prototypal knowledge, nonrational and unconscious to be sure, but nonetheless effective. From this standpoint, matter had at its disposition a uniformly operating or "universal" language that is fitted to sensibility—to the transaction between self and environment. And with this concept, larger issues about intelligence and cognition may be framed.

Fiber Anatomy and Neural Signaling

The basic unit of sensibility is the fiber, just as it is the basic unit of the spiderweb universe described earlier. The fiber is also the basic unit of cognition. Indeed, "the fiber is to physiology what the line is to mathematics," writes Diderot (11:276) echoing Haller. The terms "fiber," "thread," and "fibrilla" are leitmotivs in the annotated compendium of extracts from eighteenth-century books on biology that is Diderot's *Elements of Physiology*.[8] "Fiber" and "chain" are both metaphors for the uninterrupted bond

---

8. The lack of method in *Éléments de la physiologie* has been described by Geoffrey Bremner. Diderot writes on a scientific text, sometimes paraphrasing it and sometimes just supplying his own commentary. See Bremner, "Les 'Éléments de la physiologie' et le sens de la vie," in *Diderot: Les dernières années, 1770–1784*, ed. Peter France and Anthony Strugnell (Edinburgh: Edinburgh University Press, 1985), 81–91.

among things from the microscopic to the cosmic ends of the universe. But the fiber reference also cuts the bond where it seems to be the strongest, at the seat of the intelligence that is responsible for making connections.

Today's stale images for thought processes were, in the Enlightenment, fresh coinages stamped in especially figurative terms. When Hume wanted to express skepticism about the truth of speculation he said, "though the chain of arguments" is logical, "we are got into fairyland long ere we have reached the last steps of our theory" (*Inquiry*, 83). And when the same Hume disputed our faith in cause-and-effect reasoning he said, "if you insist that the inference is made by a chain of reasoning, I desire you to produce that reasoning" (48). It is curious that the intelligent thought process is represented here by a continuist trope that Hume challenges nonetheless, thus undermining confidence in that very process. The trope has always reflected, however, an ideal to strive after. As today we might speak of the "strands" of thought "woven" together in discourse, Hume also refers to "the thread of discourse" or "the internal fabric, the operations of the understanding" (*Inquiry*, 19, 31). Buffon cites the "warp" of ideas as "a single thin thread extending lengthwise" (Varloot, 214).

The eighteenth-century idea of connection had its physiological basis in the nervous system. The organism connects its parts with a network of motor and sensory threads that coordinate the whole. The organism is unified: a tiny universe of living parts. Yet its unity is contradicted by the nerve endings of those sensory threads. These filamentous endings do not connect with anything, but instead float in the medullary substance and dissolve into viscosity, as Diderot indicates in the next section. Where the liquid mass again solidifies, it is called "brain." Between medulla and nerve, an unnamed space demarcates the missing link in an otherwise accountable internal unity. The question then arises, If the material continuity between fiber and fluid seems to dissolve, how can a continuous path exist? And even discounting this space, yet another sort of gap exists between the sensory impression in the material brain and the idea or mental perception of that same event. And again a question intrudes itself. In an unbroken universe of links in a chain, how can the external object be present to the mind? How can a continuous material path be traced from sensation to abstract sign?

When the problem of fibroid discontinuity was first formulated, its bluntly biological thrust seemed to have no satisfactory answer. Just the opposite situation applies to fibroid constructions in the manufacturing world. Enlighteners displayed a general fascination with the regularity of weaves and other fibrous structures.[9] This fascination can be observed in numerous articles in the *Encyclopédie* that are devoted to thread and its textile products. The entries on cloth, cotton, and fur, as well as on brocade, damask, satin, velvet, and *double fond* often appear with detailed diagrams that illustrate the microscopic level of unit structure. The entire eleventh volume of diagrams is devoted to weaving. The Encyclopedists' zeal for descriptive completeness is unmatched in these entries when compared with entries for other raw materials and their products.

The textile model carried over into nerve anatomy. Le Cat's treatise on sensation includes diagrams of fiber weaves in animal muscle. The muscle fiber is composed of "organic fibers," which in turn are composed of filamentous "simple fibers." These silklike basic threads are shown as being united in parallel lines and then rolled into the cylindrical form of an organic fiber. Many such organic fibers make up the muscle fiber, and Le Cat illustrates the structure with sketches of right-angle crossings, circular and longitudinal weaves, and other layered or interlaced arrangements reminiscent of the *Encyclopédie*'s articles. Under the microscope the organic fiber appears hollow, a fact disputed by anatomists allied with the theory of vibrations. But Le Cat reports the existence of a "canal" shaped by the fibrous cylinder itself (*Traité* 44). The difference of opinion had no bearing on the anatomists' shared belief in an uninterrupted nervous system. Yet their need either for canals or for solid fibral continuity indicates the importance of a model that maintains an open path from the organism's external surface to its innermost regulatory seat of vitality. The details of the debate complicated an otherwise simple philosophical problem. If primary matter constitutes nerve matter, and if they both belong to an unobstructed chain of material particles reaching from the external world into the organism's autoregulatory center, what is the material nature of the "message" along that path, whether at the level of self-organization, of sensibility, or of abstract cognition? In elementary terms, what is the signaling agency or "language" of life?

The immediate sphere of Le Cat's discussion is the muscle fiber. However, impulses communicated from brain to muscle are only one aspect of the larger network of intelligible signals throughout the nervous system. This includes the sensory communication between the organism and the

9. Jacques Proust has studied the importance of textiles as a "language" in Diderot's article on the stocking. Proust, "L'article 'Bas' de Diderot," in *Langue et langages de Leibniz à l'Encyclopédie*, ed. Michèle Duchet and Michèle Jalley (Paris: Union Générale d'Éditions, 1977), 245–78.

external environment, a communication described by the textile metaphor of a spiderweb. The network of signals is the first code of vital reception and response. The code must be mastered or "understood" by any organism, muscular or otherwise, that functions, survives, and reproduces itself. It is a physiological language, to be sure, but no less a language than the one referred to by modern microbiologists as the "genetic code." The manner of its communication at a more sophisticated level becomes an important issue for philosophical as well as biological reasons. If there is no "direct" contact between the external object and the knowing subject, then the sensory fibers provide merely a representation of material reality. This possibility is what makes the anatomy of fibers so important. Fibrous structure determines the conveyance of signals, and the nature of these signals may be deduced by that structure. If we believe Le Cat and the fluidists, sensory communication depends on the distension and contraction of the nerves, according to how swollen or depleted their ducts may be. The process is likened to the hydraulics of fountains and canals, except that the fluxion is gauged in terms of oscillation and vibration instead of quantity (*Traité*, 49).

To accept this account also means supposing a prior model of fluid substances whose composition had a debated premise. The problem with these fluids was that they represent coarse liquid states in which the more refined "animal spirit" travels. And in turn, the "animal spirit" is host to a more rarefied and mysterious "universal spirit," which may be a fluid of sorts and not at all an abstraction. Le Cat's concerns are "motor fluid" and "sensitive fluid." This distinction permits him to identify the substance he believes carries feelings through the body. But the notion of canal fluxion seems to remove importance from the fibroid cylinder-like structure of the network. The neural contents of fluxion form the foundation of a communications theory that would appear to be opposed to vibration theory (184–85). Nevertheless, the experimental evidence for Le Cat's argument resembles those of the vivisectionist Cheselden. The most serious evidence of both observers is the textile base of the nerve fiber itself. Le Cat identifies this base with the fluff and oil that constitutes cloth. The same ingredients make paper, which is pressed into a fibrous solid after the fluff is milled with water and its "gruel" or "nutritive sap" has jelled and dried (44). Paper, cloth, and nerve matter are reducible to fiber within a general concept of organic matter. Nutritive sap is the associative bond that inserts elementary nerve matter into the polyfaceted universe of connecting and communicating substances.

The parallel fibers so often cited and diagramed at this time presupposed an acceptance of pattern and orderly connection. This acceptance was the sequel to the fibrillary theory associated with Haller's work on irritability. Haller believed that the fiber was the substratum of all vital functions.[10] This governing concept was both structural and signal-oriented. It was a cue for Haller's contemporaries to maintain beliefs about epistemological continuity that are the equivalent of earlier vitalist cosmologies, such as the *Archè* of Van Helmont.[11] Because Haller was perhaps the most respected physiologist in Western Europe, he lends respectability to peripheral speculations based on experiments that coincided with or follow his governing concepts. Thus Le Cat's interest in nutritive sap in conjunction with fibroid matter gains significance. Haller describes fibroid composition of gluten and earth from several standpoints. The fiber's submicroscopic structure consists of earth, water, oil, air, and iron. Analysis by decomposition reveals elastic, separable filaments. In short, the fiber is a multiple and polymorphous substance (Duchesnau, *Physiologie*, 130–33).

The polymorphic vitality of fibers supposes a quality not easily reconciled with orderly connection. The fully connected track, remember, was assumed to exist but was not observed empirically. And so anatomical discussion ended in submicroscopic speculation, without which the premise of continuity would collapse. When Charles Bonnet defends the fiber's integral significance for the concept of life, he makes the germ its basic unit within a mathematical conception of organic infrastructure: "The germ is, so to speak, composed of a series of points that in succession form lines. These lines prolong themselves, multiply, and produce surfaces" (*Considérations*, 2:296). Similarly, the vibrationists cited by Haller (Giacinto B. Fabri, Gottfried Bidloo, George Cowper, George Cheyne, Thomas Morgan) all ignore cellular anatomy in their model of communicating fibers because nerves lack tonic or tension. Theories to correct this oversight are cited by Duchesnau.[12]

10. Haller's synthesizing concept corresponds to Baglivi's study of organogenesis in the fetus, where blood solidification initiates a process of increasing complexity until the fiber is formed. François Duchesnau points out the common ground between these ideas and quotes directly from Haller: "The fiber is for the physiologist what the line is for the geometrician: the means for knowing where all figures originate." Duchesnau, *La physiologie des lumières: Empirisme, modèles, et théories* (The Hague: Martinus Nijhoff, 1982), 120–21, 130.

11. A Neoplatonist outlook underpins the medical writings of Jean-Baptiste van Helmont. See, further, D. P. Walker, *The Ancient Theology: Studies in Christian Platonism from the Fifteenth to the Eighteenth Century* (London: G. Duckworth, 1972), 258 and passim. See also Lester S. King, *The Road to Medical Enlightenment, 1650–1695* (London: Macdonald; New York, American Elsevier, 1970).

12. These corrections include Hartley's aethereal oscillations. Also mentioned is Nicholas Robinson's *New System of the Spleen, Vapours, and Hypochondriack Melancholy* (1729). Here

Insight into the status of conventional eighteenth-century anatomy will be gained by examining one widely consulted specialist who over the decades revised his opinions, and also by examining the *Encyclopédie*'s effort to convey a consensual summary to its readers. Both these epitomizing or consensual examples suggest that the ideal of connectedness and continuity rested with the fiber under inconclusive circumstances. The uncertainty is significant because the preoccupation with fibers just outlined does not seem to have sufficed, even though the model affirmed such continuity. The two examples that follow are revealing in this light. Despite their cautious path among competing theories, a careful reading indicates a shift away from fibers themselves and a subtle highlighting of the matter implicated in the signaling process itself. This nuance prepares us for later chapters, which emphasize aethereal matter as a constant among diverse theories.

Fiber anatomy endured longest in the version of William Cheselden, whose fourth edition of *The Anatomy of the Human Body* was published in 1730, was later revised, and reached a ninth edition in 1768. Cheselden frankly confesses ignorance in the details of the debate between vibrationists (proponents of solid nerve fibers) and fluidists (proponents of nerve fluid). His confessions, together with revisions of the *Anatomy*, reinforce the confidence in his probity inspired by those efforts. Like Winslow before him and Delaroche later, he tries to follow nerve fibers to their end, having noted their parallelism. The threads all

> pass in as direct courses to the places they serve, as is possible, never separate nor joining with one another but at very acute angles, unless where they unite in those knots which are ganglions, the use of which I do not pretend to know: they make what appears to be a communication of most of the nerves on the same side, but never join the nerves on the opposite side. (*Anatomy*, 4th ed., 247)

This discontinuity in the entire system is insignificant, however, alongside the continuity on the same side of the circuit that seems plausible although beyond microscopic verification. On the one hand, the nerves seem to be

> a bundle of straight fibers not communicating with each other: and I am inclined to think that even the minutest nerve, terminating in any part, is a distinct cord from its origin in the brain or spinal marrow; or else do not see how they could produce distinct sensations in every part; and the distinct points

---

the elementary fibers are said to have oscillatory machines ("machinulae papilares") that effect rapid transmission of vibrations to the soul; but this model clearly abandons the fiber model's linear conception of connections established by conventional anatomists.

of sensation throughout the body are so numerous, that the whole body of nerves (which taken together would not make a cord of an inch diameter) must be divided into such a number, to afford one for every part that has a distinct sensation, that surely such a nerve would be too small to be seen by the best microscope. (246–47)

There is no reference to the mechanism that unifies the disparate sensations, or to the effect of nerve bundles, a concept Diderot used with little profit. The impasse causes Cheselden to shift the terms of emphasis. Rather than pursuing the question of signal combination and conversion, he addresses the transmission of signals. He repeats elsewhere the commentary of earlier authorities who have examined the tiniest fibrils and reported "many small distinct threads running parallel, without any cavity observable in them" (226).

The absence of a cavity does not persuade Cheselden to be an assertive vibrationist. The sensory role of nerves is indisputable, "but how they convey those sensations to the brain is a matter of great dispute" (247). The qualification "great" is amplified in later editions of the *Anatomy*. Early editions note the most general opinion, to the effect that nerves are "tubes to contain animal spirits, by whose motions these sensations are conveyed: and diligent inquiry has been made to discover their cavities, but hitherto in vain." There is small cause for expecting canals to exist and still less for belief in nerve fluid at all. Cheselden conjectures further that "if each nerve is distinct from its origin, as I have endeavoured to show, and too small to be the object of the best microscope, I do not see how such cavities are like to be discovered." In the face of such evidence, we might wonder in retrospect why fluidism gained adherents among some experimental biologists and was not rejected by Diderot. The empirical caution in the case of Cheselden prompts him to add a qualification in spite of all: "Nevertheless, nerves may be tubes, and possibly a fluid, whose cohesion is very little, and whose parts, no finer than light, may move freely in them" (247–48). In a significant shift, the 1760 edition states more directly, "However, I *think* the nerves may be tubes and *that* the fluid, whose cohesion is very little" (236–37, emphasis added).

What justifies Cheselden's more decisive later position seems to be the strong focus on the fluid. This focus lessens concern for the fibroid nature of the nerve. The fact that the nerve ending is not tied as a fiber to the cerebral medulla ceases to be a problem. And while it is impossible to know where such fibers lead, greater importance is attributed to animal spirits. Even the separation of fibers loses its urgency because their dissolution in the common medullary pool can be said to unite them by a different medium. Cheselden does not amplify his image of fluid "no finer than light," and still less does he identify it with aether. But he could not fail to be aware of the Newtonian theorists around him, and the encouragement his newly modified stance might lend by its comparison to light. In contrast to Hartley, however, he is too scientific an anatomist to declare for an unverifiable neural pathway facilitating an aethereal substance. The significance of the aethereal component becomes apparent in Chapter 9.

Summarizing his view of the physiological debate, Cheselden displays Olympian sagacity, but also small appetite for philosophical implications:

> Those who deny animal spirits in the nerves suppose that the sensation is conveyed by a vibration. To which it is objected that they are slack, moist, and surrounded with soft parts, and are therefore unfit for vibrations, as indeed they are for such as are made on the strings of a musical instrument; but the minutest vibrations, such as they cannot be without, may for aught we know, be as sufficient for this end, as the impulse of light upon the retina is for the sense of seeing. So that perhaps sensations may be conveyed either, or both ways. However, it being usually taken for granted, that it must be one of these ways at least, the advocates for each have rather endeavored to support their opinion by arguments against the probability of the other, than by reasons for their own. (248)

In a similar composite vein, the *Encyclopédie* attains stature for impartiality in a consensus article on "Nerve." It avoids partisanship by such phrases as "some physicists call" the nervous sap animal spirits, or "it is probable that" medullary fibers connect the solid parts of the brain to the nerves. But these qualifications reflect deep differences of opinion among competing theories. When the article states that "perhaps there is no portion of the spinal medulla" lacking connective fiber, the "perhaps" is less a cautious reservation made from the standpoint of one assured school of thought, and reflects rather more a hesitancy in striking a balance among competing schools. The fixation on connectedness stands out all the more. As a result, a bias favoring the canal structure of fibers appears couched in the same qualified phrasing. This cautious bias lends support to belief in the continuity of the entire system, whereby it is "the medullary substance that spreads throughout the extent of the nerve tubes and that is undoubtedly emitted by the brain. But is it enclosed in the tiny vessels along the nerve, or is it contained in the nerve cells? This is what cannot be determined" (*Encyclopédie*, 11:100). The interim doubt does not make the fluidist model itself less prominent in the article.

Considerably more hesitation marks the *Encyclopédie*'s article on "fiber" despite its exhaustive information. As a paradoxical result, what might be termed "blind" microscopes shroud the neural object in darker veils notwithstanding their aid to discovery. The microscope is unequivocal in the fact that fibers are of two general types, simple and compound. The simple fiber is defined as a filament whose physical composition is an assemblage of elementary particles distributed in "linear" fashion. (The difference in the terms "fiber" and "filament" will be more relevant in the next section.) The microscope also clarifies the structure of the still more minute fibrilla but cannot do the same for its material composition. This uncertainty stems from the inadequacy of current instruments, declares the Encyclopedist. Fibrillas are "transverse fillets that tie the cylindrical muscular fibers." To the naked eye, the fibers of the animal body contain bundles of more slender fibers that, viewed under the microscope, "present a prodigious number of small fillets enclosed in a common envelope, and so on continuously. We do not know where this progression stops" (6:675). The Encyclopedist concludes that conjecture alone governs discussion of fibers and their composition.

These terms of analysis enter the crucial but nebulous terrain of "vital force" and the nature of matter. Each "elementary part" of the fiber, taken alone, is said to be formed by a particle of matter united permanently and immutably. No natural agent can sunder the bond. The article ventures further, and takes up atoms. The contact of atoms produces cohesion, whether manifested in solidity or fluidity, and the cohesion is due either to chemical attraction or to a "Newtonian" attraction, if not to one of the vegetal affinities. The *Encyclopédie* ends this section of the article with a molecular approach to discussion of solids and fluids. However, it stops short of questions about vital force discussed earlier, questions that divide mechanists and vitalists of both materialist and spiritualist persuasion.

The attempt to name what exactly binds the universe into one continuous linkage thus moved from a discussion of matter in general to a focus on the prototypal form of matter: the fiber. But even here, what seems to have held the secret was not so much fibrous matter itself as the force conveyed through matter, particularly in the neural network and cerebral processes. As to the nature of this force, its transmissibility was a controlling factor, which is why the controversy over hollow or solid nerves attained the vehemence that it displayed. Nevertheless, if the controversy itself proved to be irrelevant, as I suggest, the reason was that the transmissible element could be conveyed without regard to the density of the neural fibers themselves, as will be shown.

Signal Transmission and Conversion

The recurrent vocabulary of fabrics, fibers, and threads belonged to a lexical family whose variety in eighteenth-century usage emerged most forcefully in Diderot's *Elements of Physiology*. The complexity of fibers is summed up by Diderot in one charged sentence: "The fiber is composed of other fibers, without limit" (*Éléments*, 9:277). For Diderot, two kinds of fibers exist, the "muscular" and the nerve of "organic" fiber. Both kinds combine into thicker neural units: "A bundle of organic fibers or a muscular fiber make the elements of the nerve. The nerves make the elements of the muscle" (9:279).

No little confusion surrounds these and further references. It will be helpful at this point to glance at the lexical paradigm that made the fiber the dominant model for connectedness in eighteenth-century discourse. The *bundle* (*faisceau*) comprised a *sheaf* (*trousseau*) of parallel *fibers* (*fibres*) that may be regarded as uniting separable *threads* (*fils*). The thread in turn consisted of finer *strands* (*brins*), a distinction based on the silkworm model where, as the *Encyclopédie* notes in the entry "Silk," as many as twenty-five cocoon strands make up a single thread (15:271). Anatomy goes beyond the silkworm, however. The strand was less thin than the *filament*, the hair-fine fiber whose yet more slender form was the *fibrilla* (*fibrille*), which was cell-slim and bore the diameter of an invisible celium.

This progressive diminution to the microscopic level was not a gradation adhered to strictly. Some authors also spoke of *tufts* (*houpes*) made either of strands or of threads. But the main fibrous unifier was the *bundle*, and this enveloping form became a metaphor in its own right when Diderot needs to express the tying-together of sensation and thought: "No sensation is simple or momentaneous. It is, if I may so express it, a bundle" (*Éléments*, 9:313). Even a single sensory event must exist in time and have a duration. One sense datum extends in time like a bundle of smaller sensations. From this bundle, says Diderot, are born thought and judgment.

These straightforward terms did not eliminate the disparity of their dual reference to observable anatomy and the presumed continuous network of communications both internal to the organism and reciprocally with the external environment. First, regarding the continuous material anatomy, Diderot reports that "each fiber is a bundle of fibrillas many thousands of times thinner than the finest hair" (9:279). He also declares the reverse: "Fibrillas are composed of fibers" (9:278). The contradiction was resolved by the concept of "bundle," which applies to both muscle and nerve fibers. It applies no less to sense data and ideas, as will be seen shortly.

Material bundles are of two types, muscular and sensory, and each type determines the relation between fiber and fibrilla.[13] Even so, Diderot blurs the obvious muscle-sensory organ distinction at the level of the simple fiber, and with suggestive implications. Although his notes on physiology in this compendium are unsystematic, an observable pattern emerges in regard to the indiscriminate primacy of the primitive fiber. At its most tenuous extremity begins the mystery of continuity and signal communication. Furthermore, just when fibrous materiality is least material, the crucial processes of sensation, cognition, and organized vitality seem most salient. Diderot's ruminations arrive in a roundabout way at the inference that all of life's organic mystery is subsumed in the "fiber worm," a reductive model in which even cognition may be studied.

Diderot's fiber may be understood to "unbundle" or unsheaf itself endlessly, like so many layers of an elongated onion. But he leaves us wondering whether these bundles may be unraveled and removed until nothing is left. Such a construction would account for the discontinuity that occurs when the delicate filamentous endings grow increasingly insubstantial as they trail off into the medullary substance. Conversely, the fibers combine and thicken in their extension leading away from the brain and toward the body's external surface. In this direction, their structure is determinate: "In each visible fiber one finds a series of meshes ["fillets"] that unite with other meshes, which, twisted at their ends, form a heavier fiber" (9:324). But at the medullary end, the tiny white fibrillas float in their own substance, no longer separated by sheaves (9:278, 316).

Yet even here the need for an explanation based on connectedness

13. For muscles, "the bundle of fibrillas make the fiber, the bundle of fibers make the muscle" (*Éléments de physiologie* 9:324). But a simple or "organic" fiber is composed "of other fibers, without limit." The fiber is itself a fibrilla, and the distinction depends on the manner of bundling and the thinness of the particular thread. Both kinds of bundles tie together fibers of different diameters. Thus "each fiber is a bundle of fibrillas," but each fibrilla is a slender fiber that in turn may sheaf together yet more filamentous threads. It is not absurd, therefore, to assert that "fibrillas are composed of fibers," because fibroid structure is by nature an "endless division" and "without limit." Each fibrilla is a fiber at once bundled by a fiber wider than itself and bundling fibrillas narrow than itself.

perpetuated the fiber model. The cerebral medulla "is fibrous or made of parallel meshes engendering the nervous fiber" (9:315). The nerve endings unravel into branching networks or "meshes" distributed in parallel fashion at this section of the brain, where structure is better defined than in the cerebellum. In this sector, the communication system appears clear. The nerves are, "properly speaking, a continuation of the same [medullary] substance, but they are fibrous, but [*sic*] they are made by fibers, separated by an envelope that stems from the pia mater" (9:316). The nerves appear in "medullary sheaves ["trousseaux"], very soft at their origin, composed of small packets of distinct lace meshes, straight and parallel, and united into a more solid bunch by the pia mater" (9:315). This aspect of brain anatomy is a concern of the next chapter.

Diderot's anatomically frustrating descriptions highlighted a philosopher's grasp of an essential model, the orderly network that links the external world to the mind. At the epidermal end of the network, the sensory terminal is a mesh of filamentous branchings that make contact with the object. The same meshlike structure characterizes the network in the muscles. At the other end, "the nerves form with the brain a whole resembling a plant bulb and its filamentous roots" (9:313). The details offered here, however, did not clarify the problem of continuity within the network. Indeed, the brain anatomy expounded by Winslow remained indecisive on this debated point, as the next chapter shows. Diderot's philosophical orientation allowed him to dispense with physiological minutiae that are of prime concern to empirical scientists. But his omissions unveiled the filamentous metaphor that elsewhere inspired his master image of the universe as a spider brain.

The foregoing details display contradictory metaphors owing to incompatible transmission vehicles: the parallel arrangement of bundled fibers in a lacework mesh conflicts with the bulbous, free-floating medullary arrangement of unbundled fibrillas. Where do the latter end, and where does some other structure pick up the nerve signal? Diderot offers an overall formula that summarizes the communications system: "All parts of the body communicate with the brain and among themselves through the nerves" (9:279–80). The connection presumably includes the parts of the brain with each other. He confirms this by an analogy: "The cerebrum is the filter and the cerebellum the reservoir of the nervous fluid" (9:279). These regions are linked by a fluid, which also transmits the signal. But if that is the case, then the nerve must be hollow. And Diderot asserts precisely this in his shorthand style: "A bundle of simple fibers forming a hollow canal, called fibrillas or organic fibers" (9:279). This explains the mechanism that conveys fluid, but leaves the actual convection process unaccounted for. The theory of fibrous vibration is not dismissed, nor can it be because no such canal exists in the smallest fiber unit. There is rather "the simple fiber without a cavity" in the medullary substance, the whitish filaments that are "the origin of the nerve fiber" (9:278).

In fact, these directly incompatible details opened the door to other puzzles about the fibrous system and the deeper mystery of living matter, all of which caused Diderot to back away in doubt. He interrogates himself in a series of factual statements phrased as questions:

> Is the brain a secreting organ? That may be. Do we find the nerve trunks filled with the same medullary substance infused with lymph? That is my wish. Does this subtle lymph seep in from the tiniest nerve branchings? Correct. . . . Therefore it is the immediate cause of their sensibility, their life, their movement. I wouldn't be able to know how to admit this. (9:323)

The conclusion is equivocal because "the fiber is contractile even in a dead animal" (9:321). This is not a non sequitur. Irritability was mechanical for Haller but vital for Bordeu, a special case of sensibility. In this debate, Diderot inclines toward the tensile strength of fibers, here apparently death-defying compared with the "subtle lymph." His remarks proceed sequentially to note how robust the nerve is even when the fibrillas are very weak. By illustration, he jots down "reasons for the contractile force of the nerve: silk threads, spider threads, the swelling fibers of white wood, the ligneous fibers of plants, although soft" (9:323). The role of polymorphous fibers gains renewed prominence, by contrast to the unknown nature of nerve fluids and the alternately hollow or solid fibrous units.

Diderot persists. If the uniform nerve fluid produces sensation, how can he account for the variety of sensations? "I cannot conceive it." One the other hand, "everything is explained by considering the fiber as a worm, and each organ as an animal" (9:320). In other words, by breaking down organic life into ever tinier parts, we reach that much closer to the secret of vital signs that persist after death, as in the case of contractile fibers. And if contraction is merely mechanical and not vital, what of regeneration? Here we draw closer to the secret of the vitality displayed after dismemberment and regeneration, as in worms. The frequent study of polyps at this time is related to this fascination with neural amputations.

Yet a more important feature of minimal fiber study eclipsed fluidist theory. Fibers were known to be aligned in separate and parallel tracks, except where they dissolved into medullary substance. The five sensory fibers were also separate, as were their signal tracks and traces. These discontinuities were coordinated by the common sensorium in higher organisms. However, the fundamental question was how to define living matter at its most elementary level of vital signals. If life-signals can exist at the level of a single fiber-worm, then a single sense that is tracked by a single fiber can suffice by itself to comprise a vital system of signals. While unremarkable for lowly organisms, this fact eventually colors our understanding of the debate about which of the human senses, touch or sight, was the primary one. This debate was at the back of Diderot's mind when he created the myth of a tactile society in the *Letter on the Blind*.[14]

The temptation to reduce nerve communication to a fiber worm model also reflected on the inability to verify a continuous signal circuit in complex organisms. It was an admission, at the least, that the wished-for connections between organs, between nerves and brain, and between the parts of the brain still eluded laboratory explanations. This elusiveness persisted despite the microscope's ability to analyze the simplest fibroid composition. As Diderot notes, "the fiber is reduced to a thread composed of sensible molecules separated by as many inert molecules interposed [therein]" (9:278). And despite an elaborate vocabulary of terms for such fibers, the molecular thread just mentioned remains the only unit that sheds light on the life principle. Diderot says for the third time, "The formation of fiber is nothing but the formation of a worm" (9:278), and a fourth time, "The simple fiber is without any cavity. I regard it as an animal, a worm." But on this occasion he appends a special coda: "It is this being that the animal, composed by it, nourishes. It is the principle of the entire machine" (9:279).

This principle interested Diderot for its activity in sense perception and ultimately in the thinking process. As noted, one sensory event extends in time and constitutes a bundle of smaller sensations. It follows that a

14. Diderot raises issues of language and cognition that have their source in the preoccupation with living fiber discussed here. Speculating on how sensitive a knowledge might be attained by an entire people living in blindness from birth, he writes: "a society of blind people could have sculptors and draw the same advantages as us, that of perpetuating the memory of fine actions and people who are dear to them. I have indeed no doubt that the feeling they would experience by touching the statues would be greatly more vivid than that which we have by seeing them." *Lettre sur les aveugles, Lettre sur le sourds et muets*, ed. Yvon Belaval and Robert Niklaus, in *Oeuvres complètes*, vol. 4: *Le nouveau Socrate, Idées 2* (Paris: Hermann, 1978), 46.

bundle of sense data makes an idea and that an idea or thought is a bundle of smaller ideas. The difficulty here will be detected by Hume and posed as a problem of temporal intervals that must somehow be connected, a continuity of inexplicable origin.

The perceptual bundle could not be accounted for when posed as an anatomical problem of fiber bundles. Winslow tries to follow nerve threads through the cerebral substance to their end, but he finds the mass so soft and the filaments so delicate that they break under the lightest touch (*Exposition*, 443–44). Delaroche believes in the straight-line model of connections and accordingly presents the nerves as

> packets of medullary fibers, each enveloped in a particular membrane and in that manner separated from all the others. Thus it is almost impossible for them to be able to communicate any movement reciprocally. As a result, nervous movements can only be propagated along the length of the medullary substance of the same fiber. (*Analyse*, 61–62)

Both Winslow and Delaroche shared the unstated premise of a signal track. The track was needed for tracing the fiber from one end to the other in order to diagram the brain's reception of the stimulus external to it. A similar reason required them to stress separation among individual fibers. If one signal follows a single track, it cannot be confused with other tracings.

It becomes pertinent to note in these discussions that two distinct nerve fiber systems were at work, today rigorously distinguished. The muscle fibers and the sensory fibers were recognized and treated separately in the eighteenth century only to a degree. Beyond that, there was no reply to the question of where the final "bundle" of sensory events is located, or how these events are connected and unified. Microscopic anatomy sufficed to distinguish muscle and sensory fibers but it could not glimpse the level of conversion. Writings on anatomy established that irritability and regeneration, as well as the neural seat of cognition, all depended crucially on the theory of fibers. Yet it is difficult to determine which fiber is the subject of these writings when they address such topics.

Critical definitions are at stake in the absent distinction. If all fibers are nerve fibers, and if some neural signals manifest vitality, how can irritability differ from sensibility or the latter from thought, except in degree? [15]

15. The dualist separation of soul and matter rested on the distinction between sensibility and irritability, a position Haller and Needham, among others, held. This position reserved intellect and related faculties to animals and humans having a soul, while excluding other vital organisms that lacked a "sensitive principle." The doctrine was misappropriated by

In short, how does the signal from brain to muscle differ from the signal from sense organ to brain and from brain to "mind"? Posed in this way, the general problem of vitality has for its particular case the conversion of a neural signal from sensation to perception and then to idea. The importance of fibers becomes philosophical as well as anatomical. The theory of fibers must consider not only the internal material connectedness of brain to muscle but also the relation between external material object and "mind"—that is, between environment and "self." The concerned fiber in the second instance holds the key to the interchange of perception, abstraction, understanding, and language. In the first instance, the conversion of a neural signal into motion is executed by a seemingly different type of fiber insofar as the relation involves muscle and "brain" rather than "mind." Now the relation appears to be purely physical, without abstraction, and not implicated in the external world when such motor responses are autonomous or involuntary. However, some motor fibers are related to the will and hence to "thought" in some level of abstraction or another. Signals are transformed, but in different degrees of response and in more or less abstract "language" codes.

These distinctions, crudely simplified as they may be in the preceding discussion, were not addressed explicitly in the eighteenth century. More is said about them in Chapter 9. But the preoccupation with dismemberment, regeneration, autonomous movement, and, as Chapter 8 shows, polyp behavior, reflects an intuitive acknowledgment of the importance of fiber and fibrous substance beyond its self-evident anatomical and physiological importance. This preoccupation was not negligible. It concerned lower organisms in the same relation to higher ones as today's microbiology concerns viruses relative to human beings. Primitive fiber was no less broadly applicable to the neurophysiology of communicating signals in Diderot's day than today's genetic engineering is to the coded language of life itself. What exactly defines "language" is a separate consideration that must await another context. For the moment it may be noted that when fiber is the subject, Enlightenment authors eventually shifted interest from the nerve's local function to the general idea of connectedness—which is to say, transmission and ultimately communication. An unfathomable point was reached where discussion no longer differentiated between the two systems of sensory and motor fiber.

---

materialists who allowed for both vitality and sensitivity in matter by degrees determined by organization. See Roe, "John Turberville Needham," 168, 175–76.

This is not to suggest that neural signals per se were considered to comprise a code. The issue turned rather on the material nature of fiber as a general concept for neurophysiology. The concept reflected an unexpressed insight into the connection between the two types of nerves by virtue of a common fibrous substance. Conjecture about the nature of this substance extended to the previously discussed vital "force" itself, as well as to the fluid, animal spirits, or aether that might be the medium of such force. The neural fiber was the vehicle of this quintessential vitality. It was the key to meaningful signals that maintain life however concretely or abstractly it was defined: whether contractile after death, regenerative after amputation, reproductive, or sensible and intellectual.

This rendering of signal transmission by the term "language" finds no difference between sensory fiber and motor fiber except in the degree of adaptation and need. Condillac makes "need" the crux of all perceptual combinations in the animal brain (*Traité des sensations*, 146–47). The analogy with combinatory transformations of sense data in the human brain is plain enough. All of "our needs fix onto one another, and we may consider perceptions to be like a set of basic ideas which include all those comprising our knowledge" (Duchet and Jalley, 125). Language is language at any level of fibrous activity as long as the substance of sensory and muscle fibers remains constant. To the extent that neural signals carry information for the organism's survival, at any level of need, it is arguably the case that they constitute a language capable of orchestrating the organism's response according to the need manifested. From the standpoint of vital signaling, it is a useful and only minor hyperbole to call the ability to execute this orchestration an "intelligent" performance.

Among the higher levels of signal transformation are conscious human emotions. In 1749, David Hartley presented a purely materialist basis for sentiments and moral feelings, thus furnishing one of the clearest accounts of the physiology of abstraction. His initial premise is that "all human actions proceed from vibrations in the nerves of the muscles" (*Observations*, 1:503). When nerves vibrate, their medullary particles vibrate in infinitesimal proportion. Because this substance is uniform and continuous, giving rise to nerve fibers of the same substance, it is the immediate instrument of sensibility in its broadest meaning. Hartley deciphers actions so as to show how they correspond to "motives" arising from seven classes of pleasures and pains. He offers evidence that "motives are [the] mechanical causes of actions, as natural phenomena are for the mechanical operation of heat, diet, or medicine" (1:502). Experiences such as gratitude, resentment, compassion, benevolence, love, and hatred constitute sensibility, which is conveyed along the nerves from the brain to the spinal marrow. Hartley concludes that "the moral sense is therefore generated necessarily and mechanically" (1:504).

The actual mechanics of signal transmission seem less urgent at this higher plane of neural transmission. Whether nerve fluid or fiber vibration controls sensation and, at a higher plane, imagination, will be discussed in Chapter 9. The choice is often an indifferent issue to other natural philosophers. For Robinet, it is enough to contend that "everything in the human understanding has its reason for existence in the play of the brain's intellectual fibers" (*De la nature*, 440). Condillac does not care which of the mechanisms explains the origin of human knowledge (*Origine*, 42ff). But an undeclared factor has been insinuated into this plane of fiber activity. Robinet's notion that an "intellectual" class of fibers exists alongside the two types already mentioned demonstrates the sway held by the fiber model. Robinet generalizes in his capacity of a synthesizing author who enjoys no special philosophical ranking but who is an accurate barometer of the scientific climate. He can assert on the face of published evidence that

> everything is explained by fibers. Some are loaded with metaphysics and physics, others with morals, others with pleasure and pain. Their harmony depends on the harmony of the ideas which they alone produce. The more fibers in motions, the more ideas we have. The theory of their decomposition is the same as that of their composition. In the measure that fibers slacken their motion, ideas decompose. If only one fiber stirs, we have but one idea. (*Origine*, 33–34)

Robinet writes in 1761, the apogee of the fiber model's hegemony. His mention of fibral motion betrays a belief in vibrationism, but this tenet is secondary. Two major assumptions take precedence, the first of them being the "loaded" or charged nature of the fibers. The contents of their load differ, some of them physical and others abstract in varying degrees. But the material fibers remain constant in their attributes. Their uniform substance and vibratility throughout the system call attention to Robinet's first assumption about charged fibers. He implies a distinction between the substantive composition of the fiber and the contents transmitted. We are thus turned back to the original questions. What sort of living matter constitutes a neural signal? How is this to be distinguished from the sensory, moral, or metaphysical load carried in the signal? At issue is vital matter itself, still to be defined.

The term "thinking matter" has been elaborated by John Yolton in defense of a materialist philosophy of representational signs. His thesis corrects the established view that psychologists after Locke regarded things "present to the mind" as being represented to the mind just short of material presence. These different views may be related to the challenge of Jacques Derrida's analysis of logocentrism. As is well known, he postulates a continual regression from material presence through the cognition effected by nonphysiological signifiers. These problems will be discussed in the final chapters of this book. It is noteworthy in Robinet's case that he diverges from Derrida's denial that physical reality is wholly present to the mind. Robinet suggests, somewhat clumsily, that a material harmony of fibers corresponds to an influencing harmony of ideas. This is not precisely the same as a material object being "present to mind," but the chains or links invoked by Robinet as well as by Condillac maintain a material continuity. This dependency of body on mind also recalls Hartley's physiological base of moral sentiments. Be this as it may, fibers vibrate in harmony with ideas that have transformed our sense impressions of material things, according to Robinet. The natural order is harmonious, this harmony is perceived and transformed into an intellectual order no less harmonious, and the vibratory mechanism for perception and signal transformation alike is a harmony of fibers.

No doubt Robinet's account might be phrased in reverse, so that the material fiber endings "pick up" the external harmony by physical contact and then convey the sensations to their point of transformation into equally harmonious ideas. In fact, the theory of aether makes room for a tactile account along these lines, as Chapter 9 suggests. The point now is the immediate intellectual "grasp" of physical reality suggested by Robinet. Given the fact that

> everything holds together in the universe, [then] all beings are related and we have ideas of all these relations. In the place of ideas let us put the intellectual fibers. Why would these fibers not have the same relations and the same differences by virtue of their motion as Nature has introduced among all beings? No doubt the same harmony exists among the fiber vibrations that transmit our ideas of things? (*De la nature*, 34–35).

The sheer materialism of this scheme is complete, and the ideal of continuity remains intact. Robinet has no need for the mediatory signs insisted on by Derrida. He assumes an unbroken contact from external reality to abstraction, although he does not explain the physiology of abstraction any more than do contemporaries like Condillac. But his belief in a continuous physical transmission from object to idea is clear. The natural order is linked in all its parts into a harmony; the intellectual order is similarly linked inasmuch as abstract ideas "represent" this arrangement. The representation is actually a presentation, a full presence of the original natural order confirmed by the fibers' activity. Their vibrations link the natural and the intellectual orders by conveying through a matching "harmony" the original external reality. However, it must be repeated that no thinker at this time demonstrates in physiological terms the materiality of abstraction that is here assumed and that is denied by Derrida.

Coda

The interest in fibers unfolds in three categories: (a) the nature of fibral material; (b) the material connectedness of nerve fibers; (c) the fibral conductivity of neural signals. Eighteenth-century authors leave all three categories unresolved. There is no clear logic of inquiry that proceeds in orderly fashion to discuss nerve signals, their transfer by fibers, and the mediatory role of the core fibral substance. But as inquiry edges closer to elementary matter, the preoccupation with network linearity seems less likely to confirm the ideal of connectedness. Again the *Encyclopédie* reveals the characteristic temper of the intellectual world. It lists among the properties of simple fibers their "transparency." The description uses a metaphor belonging to another dimension, external to the perceiving organism. The fiber is said to refract light, a property most evident when the fiber is dried: "it can then produce the effects of a prism, that is, it can break down a ray of light and show the prime colors by separating them" (6:665). By this supra-anatomical leap, the microscopic world suddenly opens on exterior space. The universe of light condenses its volume into a ray and is engulfed by a minute granule of dried fiber. The fibral material refracts this undifferentiated mass of light into meaningful colors.

The implications are left unstated by the Encyclopedist. Is the described event a mechanical one, or does the fiber have a transformative power by virtue of its composition? More than transformative, is the power analytical in its plenary state, when the fiber no longer is a dried, detached speck but a living network imbued with aethereal light? In such a case, it would be continuous with the aether-infused, external world of light. And if so, this might explain the age-old origin of the metaphor "the mind sees the light," although the meaning is that it understands the external world. The material point of contact is a nerve fiber whose composition maintains literal connectivity from outer to inner realms of aether. But if that is the case, what happens in darkness? Is the connection broken? Or does another circuit that dispenses with internal aether reconnect the broken network? Whatever the answers, the brain is an object of study that must be taken into account.

7. The Limitations of Brain Anatomy

> But as it seems impossible to trace out these communications anatomically, on account of the great softness of the brain, we must content ourselves with such conjectures as the phenomena shall suggest, trying them by one another, and admitting for the present those which appear more consistent on the whole, till farther light appears. The same or even a greater obscurity attends all inquiries into the uses of the particular shape and protuberances of the medullary substance of the brain.
> —Hartley, *Observations on Man*

Readers less interested in the technical details of the last two chapters may consider them remote from the discussions of Goya's art, but questions about neurophysiological connections and signaling also arise from the extended artistic terms of Goya's *Sepia One*. The common preoccupation with sensibility on the part of eighteenth-century artists, literary writers, and scientists has long been recognized by scholars. But the ramifications of sensibility were more complex than mere feelings; they also entailed the biological process believed to generate moral experience and determine social behavior, a process understood by most participants in the Enlightenment. A familiar example is the fact that knowledge of sensory phenomena gained by John Locke from his teacher, the brain anatomist Thomas Willis, and disseminated thereafter into the general consciousness was largely responsible for the rise of sensibility in England by way of Richardson's *Clarissa Harlowe* and reaching into France from Diderot's fiction to Sade's.[1] Still more general, the materialist biology underlying moral behavior gathered psychologists, metaphysicians, and physiologists into a common project with artists, illustrators, and literary writers who

---

1. See George S. Rousseau, "Nerves, Spirits, and Fibres: Towards Defining the Origins of Sensibility," in *Studies in the Eighteenth Century 3: Papers Presented at the Third David Nichol Smith Memorial Seminar, Canberra, 1973*, ed. R. F. Brisenden and J. C. Eade (Toronto and Buffalo: University of Toronto Press, 1976), 137–57; reprinted with postscript in *The Blue Guitar* (Messina) 2 (1976): 134. See also the tightly woven visual and scientific documents presented by Barbara Stafford, *Body Criticism: Imaging the Unseen in Enlightenment Art and Medicine* (Cambridge, Mass.: MIT Press, 1990).

struggled to visualize and make expressable the connection between concealed neurophysiology and overt activity. In sum, the hypothesis that the awareness of sensibility had roots in well-publicized scientific details is no longer doubted.

Answers to the aforementioned questions about connections and signaling found their strongest resistance in the anatomical recesses of the brain. How we know what we know, and the status in reality of what we believe we know, were questions never addressed by the anatomical models of order, linkage, and unity. An important failure becomes apparent amid the crisscrossing opinions of various authors. Structure and function were often poorly distinguishable, so that despite their precise descriptions, anatomists neglected the unsolved problems of the actual message-tracing. Whether the brain orchestrated the system, or the unifying agent was a refined, spirituous medullary substance, the account did not change the key issues of the manner of conveying the message and the constituent makeup of transmission. The same enigma resurfaced regarding matter, its connective and transformative nature, and its relation to some primal element such as aether.

For these reasons, the histories of brain anatomy and of cerebral physiology should be kept separate, although no such distinction existed in the eighteenth century. Brain anatomy had a vast literature that by the eighteenth century codified cerebral structure, but the functional roles of the brain remained a topic for much disagreement. A similar confusion typified accounts of the brain's neural interface. While such accounts concurred when pinpointing the fibral network, they also identified various fluids that reputedly unified the sensory-motor system. These fluids were diversely characterized. Often they yielded in importance to the theory of vibrations, as in the much cited case of David Hartley. The fact that Hartley wrote in English does not mean that his assertive continuist position triumphed throughout the British Isles. The history of science was complicated by insular variations in the descendancy of Willis's brain anatomy, which from a historical standpoint needs be compared with those in the Malpighi-Vieussens descendancy on the Continent.[2] The comparative history of anatomy is not this book's concern, nor is a comparative description of brain research in eighteenth-century Western Europe (although no

2. From this standpoint, it should be noted that Winslow's work in French was translated into English in many editions, while Haller-Cullen's heavily technical physiology of 1766 improved the detailed vocabulary of brain research without challenging the prestige of Willis. Haller's work was also translated from German into French.

comprehensive historical chronology has been published despite numerous specialized studies). My purpose is to suggest a Western European perspective in its main theoretical outlines, as they concern governing principles rather than empirically recorded facts. The point is that the relation between psychological processes and brain anatomy emerged very slowly, through overlappings and reversions that permitted sophisticated insights to coexist with naive vestiges of earlier science. Furthermore, Western European notions of neuropsychology continued to fluctuate in an atmosphere of indecisive authority that bore directly on the mind-body problem.

Dissolving the mind-body split presented a challenge to brain research, although the issue was not framed in directly philosophical terms. Here the differences between Willis, Malpighi, and their successors are only of historical interest. More pertinent is the observed dichotomy of brain matter into base and highly refined textures despite divergent observations about their function. The notion that the brain served as the "animal core" of the organism (*noyau animal*) was a conventional truth for the French Academy of Surgeons, as François de La Peyronie claimed in 1743.[3] Belief in this generative principle persisted in mutant form throughout the century, as discussions below of Le Cat, Buffon, and Diderot indicate. However, the generative brain theory bypassed problems of cognitive process that pitted materialism against dualism. Even so, La Peyronie's dissections confirmed the peculiarity that the two chief substances of the brain were transparent and opaque. To have arrived at this conclusion seems important to La Peyronie, for unexplained reasons, but the characteristics of cortical transparency and medullary opaqueness were precisely what other thinkers noted as the stumbling blocks to comprehending the ultimate secrets of material cognition. In the light of this impasse, a heightened relevance surrounds the unreconciled metaphors used in biological discourse to explain the continuity of physical and mental processes. Without an overview of the conceptual interface proposed in following discussion, we do not face

3. La Peyronie stressed not the brain's neuropsychological control center but "the principle of fecundation, of development, of growth" embodied by animal and human brains. He maintained that the cerebral chambers and lobes corresponded to as many partitions in fruit pits and other seeds. This generative theory diverted attention from the more philosophical issues attached to brain anatomy. Even so, his dissections and separations of cortical substance, medulla, pineal gland, corpus callus, optical nerve layers, and other "tubercules" not only reflected standardized anatomy for the century but led him to conclude that the two chief substances of the brain were transparent and opaque. François de la Peyronie, *Mémoires de l'Académie de chirurgie* (Paris, 1743), 4–11, 16.

squarely the inconsistencies that were overshadowed by the unified models devised by the believers in a continuous psycho-physiological system.

Brain Anatomy and the Mind-Body Problem

The "paradigm shift" in late seventeenth-century biology noted by George Rousseau involved Willis's identifying the brain as being the unequivocal seat of the soul. The new certainty, however, did not remove the ongoing problem of the mind-body split, because Willis continued to distinguish between the immaterial rational soul and the animal soul found in beasts and humans alike. Even so, the fact that Willis was the fulcrum of the new orientation adds authority to historian of science Robert Frank's advice that "in any discussion of 'mind and body' in the Enlightenment, Willis should command our attention."[4] The difficulty with this historiographically sound procedure is that after Willis's death in 1675 his books exerted influence primarily on readers trained in his technical background. Consequently, Willis declined into a "relative lack of prominence in nonmedical writings" (Frank, 142). Indeed, except for Diderot, nonmedical authors as a rule failed to deal with neurophysiology of any sort, much less with brain anatomy. The many superficial allusions to nerves, fibers, and animal spirits in literary and speculative works in both Britain and France derive from multiple sources. These latter formed a common currency of beliefs that, after mid-century, incorporated Haller's physiology, its Edinburgh variety, and the Montpellier school into a loosely confederated point of view.

But what carried forward to Goya's age was the common coin of metaphorical subdiscourse embedded in the discourse of cerebral anatomy and physiology. Even granting divergent influences, a communal Western European discourse can be posited because neurophysiologists from Willis to Haller perpetuated tropes that concretized the soul's activities and thus concealed the discontinuity between body and soul. Examples will be more pertinent in Chapter 9, but several of them drawn from Willis's brain anatomy can serve for the moment to indicate the blurred interrelation between anatomical structure and physiological function.

Willis believed in the duality of a rational soul separate from the ani-

---

4. Robert G. Frank Jr., "Thomas Willis and His Circle: Brain and Mind in Seventeenth-Century Medicine," in *The Languages of Psyche: Mind and Body in Enlightenment Thought*, ed. George S. Rousseau, Clark Library Lectures 1985–1986 (Berkley and Los Angeles: University of California Press, 1990), 109.

mal or corporeal soul. Despite their distinction, the animal soul "came to take on a complexity of meaning and function such as to infringe significantly on the autonomy of the rational soul" (Frank, 131). The animal soul consisted of two subordinate entities—the vital soul and the sensitive soul—exercising respectively lower and higher bodily functions. The vital soul was "a kind of 'flame' in the circulating blood," while the sensitive soul was "lodged" in the nervous system and consisted of animal spirits moving in the brain and nerves. In order to link these lower and higher functions, Willis proposed a chemical "alembic" composed of the cerebral and cerebellar cortices that distilled the "particles of animal spirits" from "the most subtle and active spirits of the blood" (Frank, 131–32). The model poses many unresolved questions. First, what does it mean to say that the sensitive soul is "lodged" in the nervous system when its constituent parts also subsist within the blood before reaching the alembic? Second, where is the rational soul situated in relation to the animal spirits whose movements are "guided by will"? Third, what material differences are there between "message," "inward perception," and "consciousness," said to be located in the brain (134, 137)?

Willis's achievement stands measured against the diachrony of the mind-body problem as it concerns the brain. Willis refuted the Galenic belief that sensation, imagination, and memory reside within the cerebral ventricles. As for wider implications, his imagery for spirits that "carve" or "flow" was revisionist insofar that it dramatized the space-specific nature of neural signaling. By locating perception and thought in the brain, Willis linked anatomy and chemistry to a material process that shrank the immaterial dimension allotted to the rational soul (Frank, 138).

Nevertheless, dualism persisted throughout the eighteenth century even among those who embraced the revised neurophysiology. The reason is that the discontinuity of body and mind persisted in the imagery exemplified by Willis's alembic model, which belongs to the class of metaphors that James Bono terms "intrascientific" and "extrascientific."[5] Such metaphors can forge links with other discourses and exchange meanings so as to redirect the implications of key terms. In this sense of a transdiscursive exchange, Willis's images reconstituted the usages of his predecessors and fomented more refined questions beyond medical discourse. Most of this imagery is implicit, and Frank infers analogies to explain Willis's under-

5. See James J. Bono, "Science, Discourse, and Literature: The Role/Rule of Metaphor in Science," in *Literature and Science: Theory and Practice*, ed. Stuart Peterfreund (Boston: Northeastern University Press, 1990), 75, 81.

standing of how neural anatomy interacts with chemical functions. The result reinvokes the mind-body problem, as three examples can illustrate.

Frank uses the analogy of a stream of water flowing through a solid mass of gravel to describe the spirits moving through the solid nerve network. He is cautious enough to state that "Willis himself does not use the image" of percolation, yet he has little doubt that the intent was to account for the passage of spirits through solid but porous matter. But the spirits' function seems to be determined by the immediate structure, a correlation that mechanizes mental operations and removes the volitional and rational faculties to a nonmechanical domain ("correlated these textural differences with differences in function" [Frank, 132]). The rational soul is forgotten, although never denied. Second, Frank paraphrases Willis's account of the peripheral nerves by calling them the "grand highways" that propagate spirits over long distance. Here the image skirts the issue of whether nerves are hollow tubes designed for flow or solid fibers designed for vibrations, and subverts the belief that spirits "carve out" tracts by repeated movements along the same path (Frank 138). Spirituous motion itself comes under an ambiguous control, changing form by a corpuscular chemistry that also receives a "requisite tension" from an unknown will when thinking is involved. Frank explains: "Classes of matter could be seen as having inherent chemical properties and resultant forms of action. Conversely, *when he* [Willis] *needed* his particles to act like so many billiard balls as they transmitted an impulse up or down a nerve, that property of mere mass and incompressibility *was also open to him*" (144, emphasis added). The phrasing "when he needed" and "was open to him" substitutes for the disembodied volition of the human subject whose body is consciously imagining and thinking.

Finally, the analogy of "ripples on a pond" or "wave fronts" to and from the brain portrays the manner in which "messages traveled as propagated percussion waves within the fluid mass of particulate animal spirits." Here the image skirts the issue of what agency makes the messages intelligible, and indeed what exactly imagination is ("an inward perception arose. . . . If the impression was carried farther forward into the corpus callosum, then imagination resulted"). Frank then repeats, "although Willis nowhere explains these mechanisms in a systematic way, they were assumed again and again in his explanations of function and dysfunction" (132–34, 137). It is reasonable to judge from this second qualification that Willis's precocious insight is considerably enhanced by the articulate terminology of today's scientific knowledge. Despite Willis's efforts, the passage from matter to abstraction remained unresolved.

The Medullary Thread

Marcello Malpighi's anatomical discourses were translated into French in 1683, and for the next century a dyadic style of describing brain anatomy took over. Malpighi called the medulla an "incomparable labyrinth," despite the advances in lens-making. The cerebral cavities are, he explains, "diversified by so many turns, folds, and entanglements" that their rare marvels are more than a match for current microscopy (*Discours anatomique*, 83). He borrows the vocabulary of literary myth in order to admit the limits of anatomy. The brain is "the most beautiful part" of the head, and according to the poets the head is "the temple or palace of Minerva," because there the "spirit forms knowledge." But he also separates the loose figurations of poetry from the role of science: "our curiosity brings us to this palace a second time in order to consider this brain and examine its nature."

The examination itself, however, is not free of metaphor or wonderment. Malpighi looks at the medullary substance under a microscope and sees "a sponge" in the ramified fibers (86). The tiny vessels are like "little alembic tubes animated by a ferment" of volatile salts. These natural salts are changed into the "animal spirits" believed to activate the thought process, described as the "marvelous actions of the internal senses" (84–85). The terms of explanation will hardly change in the eighteenth century, except for the sense of wonder. But even after cerebral activity finds a respectable place for the often suspect faculty of imagination, Diderot will liken the effect of a strong imagination to a man caught in a labyrinth: "he strolls within his head as does a curious visitor in a place where his steps are diverted at each instant by interesting objects. He goes off, comes back, but never leaves" (*Éléments de physiologie*, 9:365).

The unsolved problem remained: where in the brain is the imagination located? Indeed, where are the sites of memory, reason, and the sensorium itself? But above all, are the submicroscopic spirits merely invisible, or are they the continuous agents that connect matter and spirit in the brain? Specific areas for imagination and memory are designated by Willis, but the inconsistencies of his mapping are evident even in the meticulously researched summary offered by science historian Frank:

> He believed that the cerebrum and its underlying structures served the voluntary functions, especially those of memory and imagination. Memory, being largely a matter of storage, was the province of the cerebral cortex. The huge, seemingly irregular mass of the cortex in man, with its many gyri and sulci—

the mounds and recesses—was well suited to the capacious memory and free association of images that was characteristic of humans. The cerebellum, in contrast, has an orderly, determinate, and almost clock-like structure which would seem to be designed for some function distinct from that of the cerebrum. This function, he concluded, was the supply and direction of animal spirits for involuntary acts, like heartbeat, respiration, and digestion. (Frank, 135)

This account follows the principle that the brain's sharp spatial differentiation corresponds to its different functions. Nevertheless, the brain's constitutional integrity as a continuous, systemic organ is an unknown quantity that plagues the scheme in two respects. Willis does not specify the chemical functions of spirits as they relate to the fibral matter or medullary substance that informs both brain segments. Without such a relation, the dilemma of substructural continuity and functional discontinuity arises. This dilemma will become clear in Jacques Winslow's later anatomy, discussed below. Nor does Willis's scheme indicate how the animal spirits, specialized for involuntary acts, also carry out rational activities in a separate cerebral segment, as many physiologists claim (see Chapter 9). As Frank explains, the spirituous particles reside in a differentiated neural matrix consisting of distinct types of substance: cortex, medulla, and peripheral nerve fibers. Nevertheless, according to Frank, these same spirits are both freely "particulate" and yet a "fluid mass," a paradoxical condition that goes unchallenged. Furthermore, whereas the spirits "percolate" or "flow" as a "stream," they carry "messages" that "propagate" as "percussion waves" or "intersecting ripples" (133–34). The constituency of these "messages" is nowhere explained.

To recognize these inconsistencies is not to diminish Willis's remarkable scientific precocity, but rather to notice how the unified system-building of science exposes disjunctures among its components despite mechanist metaphors and spatial concepts. Willis himself confesses his self-doubt when speaking of his research into the faculties and organs of the "soul," in that after "the force of Invention [had been] spent . . . I awakened at length sad, as one out of a pleasant dream," realizing that "I had drawn out for my self and auditors a certain Poetical Philosophy and Physick" (apud Frank, 107). The confession adds one further nuance to Goya's title, "The Sleep/Dream of Reason Produces Monsters."

The anatomical map is darkest where motor and cognitive functions need the most light, while morphological attempts evoke their own metaphors. Non-Latin books on physiology and anatomy rarely organized their chapters on the brain by separating morphology, anatomical structure, and function. On the contrary, discussions in French and English treatises proceeded as if the brain were a landscape to be described from left to right and from bottom to top. The metaphorical "labyrinth" applied to the brain contradicts just such an approach. Emphasis on description in its own right fosters this tendency to metaphor. Diderot is the best means of documenting such imprecision, since his *Elements of Physiology* sifts the widest range of technical readings available in his day and represents the understanding of a model Enlightener and rare literary author who can articulate his readings of brain anatomy. Thus, Diderot reports the brain's *structure* in itself to be a soft substance like "a mass of wax, sensible and living," ready for each of the five senses to engrave its own language on it (*Éléments*, 9:369). But when the brain's *function* relates to communication with other bodily parts, he sees its structure as resembling either a "filter" of nervous fluid or a "plant bulb" that has sprouted roots (9:315, 313).

Although Diderot elsewhere conceives the universe as a continuous spider-brain, as noted previously, his metaphorical precision here confounds the continuist ideal. For now the means for imprinting signals on the cerebral "wax" eludes description, just as neither the "filter" of nervous fluid nor the rooted "plant bulb" explains how a continuous flow links the external sensation to the internal sign. A wealth of detail garnered from diverse readings maps the site where neural transmission takes place, and yet cannot corroborate the continuist ideal of an unbroken universal linkage in its most crucial instance: where the external world is present to mind.

The specific sources of Diderot's information, while of interest to Diderot specialists, is beside the point in the Western European context. The mainstream of biologists from Malpighi and Vieussens to Winslow, Haller, and Cullen deposited a common residue of metaphors and functional analogies that blurred the neurophysiological instrumentality beneath the anatomical precision. Diderot's indecisive "filter" or "plant bulb" drew upon these images, in this instance causing the brain to appear to be an odd-looking organ when compared with Willis's description, and without compensating by any decisive account of function. In another functional analogy, Malpighi reported that the brain's lobate partitions evoke the liver's appearance, and the metaphor is justified by the belief in their common secretory role. Winslow repeats the image and function alike, but he gives more prominence to the "inequalities or windings like the circumvolutions of intestines formed by waving streaks or furrows very deep and narrow" (*Exposition*, 617). Written in French and later translated into

English, the "windings" are *anfractuosités* in the original. This word gives the nuance of a sinuous channel, though perhaps not fully enclosed like the intestine. Albrecht von Haller's imagery, endorsed by William Cullen and the Edinburgh school, emphasizes the palmately veined and lobular clefts of the outer structure. The cerebrum is "shaped like a half egg quartered into hemispheres," while the cerebellum also has two lobes, although not as deeply parted, and its wormlike process gives it the name *vermis* (*First Lines*, 1:204). The specificity renders all the more vague Willis's assignment of imagination to an undifferentiated cerebrum.

One source of confusion in the anatomy books is that after figurative language entered legitimately to describe morphology, it then also permitted functional analogy to slip by. As a result, an irrelevant correspondence of structure to function impeded proper framing of general issues. For instance, the sponge metaphor gained precision in the eighteenth century in the wake of Malpighi's influence. Raymond Vieussens described the fibrous inner substance shared by the medulla and its nerve filaments, calling it "a spongy medullary content" in 1715. Vieussens belonged to the party of hydrokinetic theorists who expounded a system of body fluids, including a specialized nerve fluid. The system assigned a replenishing power to the brain and made it a secreting organ like the liver. Malpighi's earlier analogy of brain and liver was now enhanced by the idea of a cerebral supplier of lymphatic fluid called "nervous sap." But the systemic perspective Vieussens adopted overshadowed specific cerebro-neural functions, causing neglect of the possible effects by "nervous sap" on motor messages and sensory reception. The neglect circumvented the larger question of transmission and internal-external linkage. In 1732, the idea of brain secretion was acknowledged by Winslow, who praised Malpighi's comparative anatomy while expressing caution about the accuracy of the secreting function. Consequently the relation between nerve fluid and animal spirits was not formulated as an issue concerning their common role in psychomotor activity. Attention to the tenuous medullary fluid also flagged.

What continued to make the brain an enigmatic maze at this time were the microscopic dead ends and the theoretical problems that followed suit. Ever since Willis's classic anatomies of brain and nerves, which ran to sixteen editions in Latin or English from 1676 to 1720, brain anatomists agreed to distinguish between the portion of the brain known as the medulla oblongata, comprising the nerve sheafs at its base, and the medullary substance believed to be the common constituent of soft brain matter as well as spinal marrow and nerve fibers. But the points of contact between soft brain matter and tiny nerve endings were undetectable by microscope. Malpighi was the first among the moderns to dispute the widely held claim that nerves do not penetrate the medullary substance, but rather emerge from it. The ensuing debate left undefined the site of the sensorium and several other cognitive zones related to volition, motor response, and thought itself. The unresolved primary issue, however, remained the mechanism whereby the nervous system permits transactions between the external environment and the living organism.

The issue must be stated in an environmental way in order to include all levels of reproductive matter and in order to pose the question of the brain's minimal required role in the sensory-motor system, regardless of its morphological complexity. But the issue is also reducible to the debate between proponents of nerve fluid and vibrations. The influential Winslow remained undecided about the claim that nerves emerge from the brain's medullary substance, and this hesitation enlivens the debate. At stake was not simply whether the brain is a secreting organ, like the liver, but also what links the sensory-motor path to higher thought processes. In 1732 Winslow credits the belief that the very finest nerve ends *apparently* change their structure and become minute tufts or brush hairs in the manner of capillary endings. But he also denies that such a structure emerges, thereby avoiding the issue that fluid alone cannot attach nerves to brain. [6]

An opposing and more decisively continuist view emerges in 1749 when the Newtonian naturalist David Hartley upholds the doctrine of vibrations.[7] The point here concerns Hartley's support of a medullary-based, continuous signal system. After Malpighi had earlier described the outer cortex as "a mass of numerous tiny glands heaped up and tied together" from which "emerge the white roots of the nerves" (*Discours*, 91), Hartley extends these origins with respect to the medulla. The nerves arise in the medulla and are made of its white substance (*Observations*, 1:91). This connection permits him to speak of sensibility as being conveyed *from* the brain to the spinal marrow along the nerves. Because the soft pia mater

6. Winslow looks forward to further study that will clarify questions referring back to the hydrokinetic hypothesis, for how can the brain secrete and still retain its ashy color, a trait that cannot result from a mixture of blood, lymph, and cortical grey substance? Jacques-Benigne Winslow, *Exposition anatomique de la structure du corps humain* (Paris: Desprez and Desessartz, 1732), 639.

7. The extended controversy over whether nerves are solid fiber or hollow (porous) tubes is examined in Chapter 9. See also Edwin Clarke, "The Doctrine of the Hollow Nerve in the Seventeenth and Eighteenth Centuries," in *Medicine, Science, and Culture*, ed. L. G. Stevenson and R. P. Multhauf (Baltimore: Penguin, 1968); and Rousseau, "Nerves, Spirits, and Fibres " (note 1 above).

with its blood vessels "enters the interstices of the several folds of the brain, one may suspect that it penetrates not only the cortical substance but also the medullary, along with the several descending orders of vessels" (1:18). With the pia mater distributed in this way, the medullary substance would subdivide into regions of various sizes. Hartley draws an analogy with the cellular membrane of the muscle system and concludes that the "separate portions, fibers, and fibrils" in the medullary substance diminish into a perfectly uniform and continuous texture that permits vibration throughout. The medium for this vibrational network is Newton's aether. Hartley does not abandon the doctrine of glandular secretion that is variously termed "nervous fluid" and "animal spirits," but he accommodates it to the universal concept of aether.

During the middle decades of the eighteenth century, brain theory in France and Germany focused on the medulla, owing to the busy agenda of Claude-Nicolas Le Cat. As a member of all the leading European academies, Le Cat held title to doctor, surgeon, and physiologist. His approach was from the standpoint of the biochemistry of medullary substances, but it obeyed a philosophical vitalism. Le Cat compares the soft matter of the cerebellum with the powder of ground almonds or flower bulbs, two types of reproductive matter used frequently in research on generative processes. Just as the grooved filaments rising from the rain-moistened and earth-warmed powder carry reconstituted sap that will nourish new life, according to beliefs held at the time, so too, contends Le Cat, is the brain's soft marrow the storehouse of a "nerve sap, gelatinous and spirituous," that flows through animal nerves (*Traité de l'existence*, 202). What is more, the brain and nerve bundles comprise the general "roots of animal vegetation." The medulla is the specific origin of seed activity in the way that the chestnut is the fecundating source of the tree. Here the analogy grows strained, but it attempts to unite the mind-brain linkage with the larger linkage of organism with its material environs. The spirituous matter is not identified with aether, however.[8]

What earns Le Cat respect today is his reputation as a frequent lecturer at Berlin's Royal Academy of Sciences, together with the fact that he withheld publication of his research, begun in 1739, until 1765. Le Cat em-

---

8. The seed-husk compares with the dura mater and the pia mater of the brain, here assigned a double role as life principle for the entire machine and also supplier of the substance for membranes, cartilage, muscles, and glands. The tough outside hulk shelters the medullary region, whose products are nerves performing as the conduits of nerve fluid, which are akin to the filamentary tubes in the plant world. Claude-Nicolas Le Cat, *Traité des sensations et des passions en général, et des sens en particulier* (Paris: Vallat-La-Chapelle, 1767), xxviii–ix.

boldens the field of microneurology by superimposing a theory of passions on the materialist foundations of nerve anatomy in both polyps and higher organisms. He maintains close ties with the fluid theorists, depicting the body as a hydraulic machine of canals, liquids, and motor fluids. His mixed advocacy of conventional ideas that in time would be disproven, together with interests in irrational psychic phenomena, lend relevance to issues that would be considered important in the works of Goya and the authors of literary sensibility. In any event, by emphasizing broad principles of cerebral activity rather than closely descriptive facts, Le Cat departs radically from the interest in structural anatomy noted earlier. But his freedom profits from the speculative room encouraged by Malpighi's still respected anatomy.

A final glance at Malpighi's language reveals why his memory endured for nearly a century. His descriptive details are figurative enough to permit speculation to keep pace with information, and he presents structure in a way that fosters the image of a prepossessing, baffling maze. First, the outer cortex piles up tiny glands "where white nerve roots insert themselves or rather issue from. The glandules are so busily arranged, joined, and combined with one another within the curves and contours of the brain that you may liken them to tiny entangled bowels or winding mineral veins" (*Discours*, 91). Like the thinkers preoccupied with Chaos and labyrinths in Chapter 3, Malpighi identifies the discontinuous model but insists on adjectives that denote a connnective path. Organic and inorganic metaphors alike sustain the diversely philosophical speculation about continuity engaged by others. Whether nerve endings were "roots" was a question that remained open for future anatomists, who would use more literal language without redressing the functional relation between cortical and medullary regions. However, the indifferent stress on any one cerebral region already characterizes Malpighi's work.

Second, Malpighi moves toward discontinuity when he turns to the unifying traits of living structures. His imagery overshadows governing principles when he compares the cortical substance to an earthen pot where a tree or smaller plant takes root and draws nourishment. This analogy persisted for another half-century. But then he notes that glandules and nerve fibers are "knotted" in the manner of vine clusters, wild-fig bark, or bulbous plants like radishes and turnips. In these plant specimens "the reticular ramifications of their fibers are entirely similar to the interlacing nerve filaments of the cerebrum, cerebellum, and medulla. . . . The meshwork and interlacings form a kind of slack net" (104–5). In this metaphor, the eighteenth century receives its central model for relational continuity.

Standing apart from other English and French treatises was the sophisticated language of Haller's *First Lines of Physiology* (1766). It was a thesaurus of precise terms about the brain even though it drew facts into the familiar circle of tropes that prompted the same unanswered questions. Haller makes it clear that the brain and nervous system are a continuous network holding the secret of communication between external environment and the "mind." It is also clear that the gyri and undulated areas of the lobated hemispheres form what is only a superficial labyrinth when considered alongside the impenetrable medullary pathways that begin so plainly. Haller neatly exposes the connected parts in a brisk enumeration of cerebrum, cerebellum, crura, pons, and medulla oblongata. He applies nuanced terms to his drawings in the *Iconam anatomicum* of 1743–56, which radiated its authority westward and back across the English Channel to the Continent.

The role of such minutely rendered illustrations, important as they were for directing the reader from the abstract structure to the material thing, could not explain functional activity as well as they explain anatomical states. Illustrations fix the organ at one visible position in time, detached from the temporal process that identifies its interest to the philosophical reader.[9] All this is to say that illustrations could not assist Haller's readers, or Cullen's after him, in approaching the uncertainties that formed the hub of theoretical debates in Western Europe after mid-century. Haller lent new significance to the problem of continuity by mentioning the spatial distribution of fibers in the soft medullary pulp, where the cerebral medulla descends into the medulla oblongata. In this region, the microscope lost its sightfulness, and the fibers appeared to lie like parallel threads, lengthwise, one upon another. There was also much "oil," as noted earlier. But the fibral parallelism also meant separation in this case, and not the continuous weave that allowed the fiber model to draw the extended notice described in the preceding chapter.

9. Many careful copies of Willis's sharply detailed, annotated plates undoubtedly also circulated after publication in, among other places, the 1664 Amsterdam edition of the *Cerebri anatome, nervorumque descriptio et usus*. Haller's diagrams were improved on by those of Alexandre Briceau in France, a meticulous performance using colors and later preferred in the French Royal Academy of Medicine. Vicq d'Azyr also seemed to value iconographic materials somewhat more than his French predecessors, who must have known but seldom mention Charles Le Brun's late-seventeenth-century drawings. Vicq d'Azyr issued his own variant plates for his treatise on anatomy and physiology in 1786 and 1788, the year he succeeded Buf-

The more precisely microscopic depiction succeeded in showing connection, the less certain the submicroscopic location and mechanism of convergence and synchronization of signals. This sort of information, already assumed by the literary and artistic cultivators of "sensibility," would permit them to espouse a coordinated vision of physical action and moral knowledge. Nevertheless, the evidence was otherwise. Each of Haller's ten numbered major nerves was traceable from limbs and organs to brain, so that connectedness was a matter of individual pathways, each constituted by one kind of nerve. One pathway remained separated from the other. Haller's facts turned into unanswered questions when sensory nerves were cited. A perceived object can only present itself serially: first as a palpable shape, then as a color, then as an odor, and so forth. Where then do the separate fibral paths converge? How are these nerve messages combined and synchronized into a single impression in the brain? When, where, and how does the "mind" convert seriality into a coordinated event? Can any diagram extend the parallel threads to a sensorium that itself is diagrammable? These questions were implicit in the mode of "sensibility" that prevailed among the writers mentioned at the outset of this chapter. An artist like Goya envisioned synchronization in the dream framed in *Sepia One* with cerebral chambers; Clarissa Harlowe's dreams lay bare the integrated truth that waking moments concealed; and Diderot's "spider brain" and "clavichord man" were the natural philosopher's complementary models for the novelist's use of sensibility in fiction.

Further puzzlement accompanied Haller's inevitable recourse to picturesque words for the stripes, bands, fillets, hatchings, thin lines, and grooves that Nature's burin applies to the brain. For instance, "the taenia ends in two white striae" at the end of the hippocampus. In "the posterior horn of the ventricle," the medullary portion is "painted with transverse and palmated streaks," inviting thereby the name "psalterium or harp" (*Physiology*, 1:201). Wherever parallel nerve threads are seen in the medulla to carry the separate messages from the object, the question remains the same. These fibrous streaks may be transverse here and longitudinal there, but if they are strung out alongside one another like a psaltery, where is the hand that unites their notes into a synthesized chord?

No idle question, its metaphor also reappears in Diderot's "clavichord

---

fon in the Academy. His sixteen plates present cross-sections of the brain from various angles, together with explanations.

man" (*homme-clavecin*) of *D'Alembert's Dream*. A human psaltery replaces the horological model of the coordinated mind, a being "in whose resonant brain ideas were received, stored, associated and compared as if by innumerable 'cordes vibrantes.'"[10] Yet there is no solution to the mystery of what connective means regulated the coordination and where. Diderot depended on physiologists like Haller, Bordeu, and Le Cat, who like others did not furnish unequivocal answers. With the increasing systematization of knowledge in Diderot's period, the paradigm of linkage grew more prestigious even as the evidence of discontinuity forced basic problems to the surface. Even Haller's superlative technical contributions did not efface the subversive underside of his texts, particularly the vivid passages on the corpora striata and the hippocampus. The vagueness in turn permitted latitude in interpreting the process that relates brain and nervous system into a motor-cognitive partnership.

Cerebro-Neural Substance

It is instructive to refer to the articulate Diderot as a touchstone for the vaguer understanding intuited by other authors concerning the brain's role in nerve signaling and sensibility. Diderot's gropings in the realm of anatomy and physiology are valuable for the sharpened issues about cerebro-neural processes that emerge. An observation made earlier in this book bears repeating. Although Diderot specialists may differ as to the coherence of the *Elements of Physiology*, the very selection and ordering of material, as well as its striking stylistic embellishment and idiosyncratic questions, all contribute to producing a unique document. It is important to notice, for instance, that Diderot's aphoristic remarks often shift abruptly from simple organisms to the level of human performance. This suggests that he is closer to intuiting a unified theory of vital essence than any laboratory empiricist might have wished to attempt. His view of cerebral activity within the scheme of full organic function must be understood in this perspective: not all organisms have brains, although all organisms display vital signs that obey some language of stimulus and response. By the same token, Diderot's view of neural activity is best comprehended through the model of a communicating unit rather than as a complex net-

---

10. Aram Vartanian discusses this passage in a comparative vein. See "La Mettrie and Diderot Revisited: An Intertextual Encounter," *Diderot Studies* 21 (1983): 175.

work. This permits discussion to exclude or include the brain while also introducing the concept of signals that "connect" stimulus and response at any level of organic complexity.

From this standpoint, it is possible to read Diderot as struggling to make sense of conflicting physiological literature with a mind toward another sphere. He can be understood to reconcile diverse kinds of anatomical evidence regarding internal organic communication, or what might be termed "vital language." But at the same time, his musings unwittingly introduced the concept of "language," which stands ready to be elaborated in terms of stimulus-response processes. Insofar as these processes entail cerebro-neural activity, the higher languages of perception and of verbal signs eventually may be subsumed under the same vital principle.

As noted, Diderot's metaphor of the "clavichord man" offers coincidentally an approach to Haller's medullary "psalterium or harp," and to the agent responsible for its vibrations. So long as nobody posed the question of transforming vibrations into meaningful signals, the role of the brain could remain subsidiary. Thus Diderot could record that "the brain is nothing more than a secondary organ that never enters into action without the engagement of other organs" (*Éléments*, 9:313). Its function is secretional, and a variety of conditions mark "the white fibrilla scattered through the substance of the common sensorium" and other nerve fibers. The secretion may be "thin or thick, pure or impure, poor or rich. Hence a prodigious diversity of spirits and traits." But this observation edges Diderot away from secretion proper and into the realm of fibers, a model that will lend itself to a self-sufficient communicating network independent of the brain.

Diderot considers the simple fiber a "worm fiber," a term that represents the model of prototypical coordinating intelligence, of vitality itself. This point was noted in Chapter 6. He goes on to declare, "The simple fiber is without any cavity. I regard it as an animal, a worm," adding: "It is the principle of the entire machine" (9:279). Diderot's ability to move back and forth along the organic continuum, from complex human cognition to the most elementary life form, and to focus all the while on the same problems of mind-body duality and vital force, has the result of generalizing the partial perspectives of other natural philosophers and biologists. Regardless of the level of living matter, the same process of signal conversion and transmission takes place. And yet the paradox is, as all the writings on the brain have shown, that the vital signaling process exposes its apparent discontinuity most blatantly in the brain. The mysterious connective agent is lost in the filamentous medullary fluid. It remains for us to witness the replacement of the "worm fiber" with the polyp in Chapter 8, in order to infer that the common agent of transmission and continuity is aethereal matter, a substance that is present not only in the medulla but also throughout the Chain of Being.

Diderot's random order of statements about the brain reflects its unresolved cognitive status in eighteenth-century physiology. He coincides with Buffon in the metaphor of the brain-nerve complex as "resembling a plant bulb" and its filamentous roots, but he vacillates on the uniqueness of the brain's function. On the one hand, it seems to be incorporated somewhat passively into the system of vital functions. On the other hand, he notes "the action of the brain upon the nerves is infinitely stronger than the reaction of the nerves on the brain" (9:314).[11]

These statements reflect temporary indecision over which of two functional jurisdictions to select as the focus of an organized perspective. They belong to a sequence of statements that seem to culminate in the following decisive observation: "The nerves are the slaves, often the ministers, and sometimes the despots of the brain. Everything goes well when the brain commands the nerves; everything goes badly when the rebellious nerves command the brain" (9:316). The source of neural initiative becomes ambiguous, but the commands remain phrased in the nonverbal language of biological communication. Signals originate at either the cerebral end or the nervous end, and while Diderot considers things to go well when brain commands nerves, he nonetheless situates the nerves in a quasi-autonomous status. They are capable of rebellion, and their actions "bring to the brain singular desires, the most bizarre fantasies, affections, and fears" (9:320). More importantly, they are the "principles of sentiment and of action." Place a drop of opium on the nerve ending and it destroys or suspends sentiment as well as activity (9:318–19). The brain's secreting function is dispensable in the primary order of organic life, and, quite simply, "Life is, without the brain's presence because of loss by accident

---

11. The brain's passivity resides in being the receptacle of blood vessels that "on becoming lost in its substance, deposit a lymph." At its base, medullary sheafs that are the "origin of the nerves" make the region the "filter of a sap." Furthermore, the entire "bulbous" racination becomes a threadwork extending to virtually all points of the animal's body—and here Diderot stresses "these threads," an evocation of continuity. But when speaking of relative strength between brain and nerves, the issue is vitality itself, as instanced by the effects of inflammation, pressure, or trauma such as lesions, which produce delirium or worse. Here "the operations of the mind are vitiated," sometimes to the point of stupor or fatal unconsciousness. The contrary is also true, however. Nerve paralysis can also result in total stupor or even the cessation of vital needs (*Éléments*, 9:314–15).

or illness, or because nature denies it [to the organism]. Foetuses without heads have been seen to live" (9:312).

Why Diderot withholds primacy from the brain can be explained by the independent resilience of vital parts when they are severed from the body and from the brain's alleged control. When the heart of a living animal is pricked, it moves. Amputate the heart, says Diderot, then prick it, and it moves; cut it into pieces, prick it, and the result is the same: "On the battlefield, the separate members quiver like so many animals" (9:317). These exaggerations serve the purpose of assigning autonomous power to an agency that subsists in living matter without reference to a centralizing brain. The focus tends to emphasize the inhering power itself, rather than its accidental seat. Whatever the medullary substance is, it distributes itself uniformly, and this fact of shared-out distribution confers the same generative powers on the nerves. Their "generating fibers come from all parts of the brain. Hence it conserves its function even after one part of the brain is destroyed." The continuity leads Diderot to a startling conclusion with respect to life's primary organizing language. The plain truth is that "very little is needed to form the *common sensorium*" (9:317–18).

Thus not only is the brain expendable at the universal level of vitality, but the sensorium's function may proceed without a cerebral base. By this Diderot does not mean that humans can survive as humans without a brain. It does indicate that his erratic polar moves from micro-organic to human forms recapitulate and summarize the partial focus of other partners in brain research. Diderot's constant shifting from one extreme to another indicates an interest in synthesizing for all vital beings a concept of signalization, whether this works merely to organize matter, to deliver a motor impulse, or to convert sensory impressions into abstract thoughts. If, as Diderot suggests, "very little is needed to form the *common sensorium*," the location of the conversion process is irrelevant to finding the key to its mystery. Rather, its mediating agent would seem to be the proper object of inquiry.

Wherever brain researchers may have located the common sensorium, its "commanding" functions obey a primal language of vital transformations, ranging from simple tropisms to sensory, motor, and generative communications. Nothing in Diderot's factual statements suggests a concern with the brain in its higher "mental" operations. His word for "mind" in this context is *âme* rather than *esprit*, chosen so as to apply to all organisms that coordinate sensory data. Subsequent to this context, Diderot underplays the brain when mentioning the crayfish. Thereafter he emphasizes nerve energy. The question of the brain's essential role in abstract thinking is a separate problem.

In view of the previous qualifications, let Diderot's statement be granted: "If the brain is upset, the intellectual faculties are altered" (9:318). It is also the case, first, that the medullary filaments send impulses irrespective of the site of the sensorium, and second, that the filaments are separate and individual signal-carriers. Any intercommunicating outlets among them would result in a chaotic network: "If there is anastomoses among the nerves, there will be no order in the brain and the animal will go mad" (9:320). The crucial neural role places the brain in the rank of an organ like any other, working in a reciprocal relationship even at higher levels of organization. For instance, "the brain needs objects in order to think just as the eye needs them in order to see" (9:313). But at the other end, as quoted before, "the action of the nerves brings to the brain singular desires, the most bizarre fantasies, affections, and fears" (9:320).

The issue remains in the pre-verbal domain at this point, or what might be called *primary* language. The medullary substance is not the brain's exclusive property but is activated by the signals of the pre-verbal language. This point will be relevant to polyps in Chapter 8. Undoubtedly "the images of things sighted take form in the eye and are perceived by the brain. The intervals of sounds are gathered in the ear and grasped by the brain" (9:318). Here the context is a higher organism, although the point is still the nature of perception rather than its location at a particular level of complexity. Higher yet, the "fantasies" and "affections" carried to the human brain by the nerves comprise one class of disorder, while another class includes the "fantastic beings" that are "mixed, confused, combined and created" by the brain with the aid of memory (9:313). The perception may be grounded materially in the first case or imagined abstractly in the second. In either case, it varies in the degree of its transformation from the original neural stimulus. Diderot is too sketchy to permit a fuller explanation. His purpose, however, is hierarchical. He calls the brain a "secondary organ"—which is to say, "subject to all the vices of the other organs, as lively or as obtuse as they."

To read the century's literature on brain anatomy and physiology through Diderot is to reach a concern that cannot be formulated by empirical biology. What is the transformatory process from external stimulus to organic response? Is the process identical in its communicational code to the process reaching from sensory impression to idea? If so, what is the common ground of nonverbal and verbal language? Diderot permits his discussion to outline this sequence briefly before returning to his chief metaphor of the brain-nerve resemblance to the plant bulb. The sequence itself begins with the external objects that

> act upon the senses. The sensation in the organ has duration. The senses [organs] act upon the brain. This action has duration. No sensation is simple or momentaneous. It is, if I may so express it, a bundle. From there are born thought and judgment. But if it is impossible for the sensation to be simple, it is impossible for thought to be so. Thought becomes simple by abstraction, but this abstraction is so quick, so habitual, that we do not perceive it. What adds to our error are words, which, for the most part, designate a simple sensation. (9:313)

Here the passage breaks off to revert to the secreting brain with fibrilla floating in the medullary substance of the common sensorium. But despite the physiological details, the overriding interest seems to be in the agency that brings discontinuous elements into material and temporal unity.

There is yet another approach to evaluating Diderot's aphoristic notes on his readings in brain physiology: to follow his interest in the fiber as a mediating conduit, as indicated in Chapter 6. Diderot demotes the integral brain to the rank of a secondary secreting organ, but at the same time he is uncharacteristically decisive when writing about the medulla. And his remarks are important for what they imply about the unifying factor responsible for biological continuities at all levels of existence.

Diderot specifies that the same medullary substance exists both in the brain and throughout the nervous system. This substance is "homogeneous," a condition of prime significance and bolstered by the fact that the medulla's fibers are not separated by "enveloping bundles." None of these details suggest a major role for the brain as a structured medullary organ; what they do stress is the mediating substance itself. The medullary substance by its very composition, as distinct from its structural position in the brain or anywhere else, is a uniform medium and a continuous field. It extends from the cerebral regions and the medulla oblongata to "the prolongations of this same substance, distributed to different parts of the body" (9:315–16). The significance of its homogeneity is thus evident. Its unbroken distribution in the sentient organism guarantees an uninterrupted signal from captured external stimulus to the appropriate level of response. The problem of "connection" would seem to disappear. Nevertheless, the unbroken medullary thread does not extend explicitly to abstract thought.

Diderot says many things about the brain in shorthand notes that often blur the distinction between human and animal functions. He generalizes about the medullary substance in a statement that appears to be one more in a series of characteristically independent jottings. Understandably, he could write no differently in view of the century-long differences in emphasis and opinion among microbiologists. He remarks that the substance, both in the brain and at the sentient extremities, "is without an enveloping bundle," so that the extremities "are exposed by their position to the actions of external objects. The sense organs are adapted to these extremities, as the retina in the eye. A homogeneous medullary substance." This continuity holds profound significance because a moment earlier Diderot has mentioned the crayfish in a reference to lower organisms favored by microbiologists in their search for the secret of life. The crayfish has no eyes, but its feet are said to be diversely functioning nerves. Thus blindness is no handicap, and just as "the polyp sees without eyes," the crayfish too "is all eye" (9:331). A moment later, the turtle is mentioned for its alleged survival after decapitation with no further inconvenience than blindness.

The cognitional implications of these musings belong to another chapter, although the point about a substantive mediating continuity remains. The medulla "is fibrous or made of parallel threads; it engenders the nervous fiber." Thus Diderot stands squarely within the tactile paradigm of fibrous networks, which comprises the metaphorical thread of uninterrupted material contact throughout living matter and the impinging external universe. But he is ambiguous about abstract thought in its overall neurophysiology. Nor does he reconcile his belief that the brain is a secondary organ with his belief in the engendering power of the medulla. The ideal of continuity remains an imperfect principle.

The Secreting Brain

The brain's hegemony receives its boldest challenge from the denial by Buffon that it is the seat of sensations and sentiments. Buffon's review of the evidence coincides with Diderot's, and he types the brain as an organ of nutrition and secretion. It is an essential organ, and one without which the nerves could not maintain themselves and grow (*Histoire naturelle*, ed. Varloot, 122). However, the brain plays an unspectacular role in Buffon's larger scheme of connections. His judgment is important, for although he is not a specialist in neurophysiology, his opinions are prized by microbiologists like John Needham and are valuable precisely because Buffon is a generalist in command of staggering detail. In retrospect, Buffon's investigations relating live species and generations of individuals exhibit the master premise of his century: the idea of a unifying system true for all matter that also can coordinate, over time, the perceived external universe with the perceiving organic universe that knows it and that assigns to them both the name "reality," this totality being made manifest by an equally unified system of knowledge that rises integrally from within the perceiving universe.

With this ideal premise, Buffon makes room for linking plant and animal life at a plane superior to that of indeterminate organisms like the polyp. The bridge between plant and animal life needs a principle, which will be one that conceives the brain as "a plant that starts from the cerebellum in trunks and branches, which then divide into an infinite number of smaller branches" (Varloot, 122). In this formulation, "the brain is to the nerves what the earth is to plants: the extreme endings of nerves are the roots that, in all plants, are softer and tenderer than the trunk or branches. They contain a ductile material, suitable to make the nerve tree grow and be nourished." While the comparison is figurative, the function fits exactly. Whatever life's essence may be in the plant and animal kingdoms, this essence cannot be identified with brain function. In fact, Buffon goes so far as to cite examples of the brain's dispensability.

In Buffon's model, if the brain's nourishing function is the same for plant and animal, so too is its structure. It is fed by lymphatic arteries and in turn it feeds the nerves. The nerve fibers do not penetrate the brain, but rather abut on its surface, where they lose solidity and elasticity. These extreme endings are soft and almost mucilaginous. Just as plant roots require steamy warmth in order to decompose and absorb the cruder masses of earth and water, so the brain's moisture is rendered nutritive by the "pumping" action of the nerve roots, which supply sustenance to the branching nervous system (123). This conception separates brain from sensory and motor network in the same way that inorganic soil and live plant are discontinuous from each other. The separation depends on the same fibroid metaphor Buffon's contemporaries used. First, the medulla and cerebellum are said to comprise a barely organized mucilage into which many small arteries terminate indistinguishably. Before their dissolution, these tiny vessels appear to be long, very thin threads that carry a nutritive white lymph instead of blood. Second, and discontinuous with the amorphous mucilage, are the nerves, a closed system of correspondences so tightly connected that one strand cannot be disturbed without affecting the others violently.

This description demonstrates the inconsistencies in the fluid-vibration debate, both positions being combined in Buffon's case. But the point is that Buffon isolates the brain from this debate. In order to establish that the brain is alien to the neural network, he mentions an oft-cited effect of nerve severance. He remarks that a local irritation may be strong enough to cause general pain and convulsion, but that the reaction halts after the nerve is cut above the point of injury. Another proof of the brain's secondary status is the fact that infants have been born alive without brains and that no brain mass at all exists in some animals, despite their ability to feel and move. Buffon argues further that while it is true that pressure exerted on the brain can halt sensation, this result is mechanical, like a weight on the arm that causes swelling (Varloot, 124).

Buffon's effort to exclude the brain from an essential role in vital functions is yet another instance of the general perplexity over its amorphous nature, notwithstanding its segmentation. To include the brain in a tight system of structural correspondences would be incompatible with the overall concept of linkage. The continuist theory served by the metaphorical network of fibers holds that actual connections exist to transmit the impulse, nutrient, or generative material from one to another point in the closed network. By calling the brain a secondary support system, Buffon points by contrast to the mystery of what is the linking medium that joins the brain to nerve endings dissolved in its medullary substance. But this problem has no meaning for those who, like him, attribute a nutritive role to the brain.

Cerebral connection is important for those who follow the two-way track of impulses from the environment to the sensory-motor center. This concern is consistent with proponents of the vibrationist model of sensory communication. In contrast, the nourishing brain is a model more suited to the fluidist school dating back to Vieussens and earlier. However, the eighteenth-century fluidist argument does not minimize the brain's role in coordinating nerve messages. The important implication in fluidism is that it calls attention to the material contents of sensory connection, a connection denied to vibrationist theory. Therefore the deemphasized role of the brain is of less consequence than one might expect. Vieussens concludes, from the dissection of twenty-six sheep brains, that no sensation is possible through the action of vibrating fibers. He emphasizes the soft condition of all nerves. The brain supplies lymphatic fluid or "nervous sap," which is not the immediate vehicle of sensation (*Traité nouveau*, 1:209–10). Rather, the contents of this fluid and specifically the animal spirits, effect sensory convection.

This means that conventional brain anatomy is incidental to understanding behavior. The argument against vibrationism must be seen as negating the importance of cerebro-neural fiber connections. The negation proceeds along two fronts, one sustaining the older view of the brain's nutritive role, the other stressing the complex contents of nerve fluid. Ultimately the nature of transmitted impulses becomes the focus of attention. On this account Vieussens cites experiments to show that the external nerve bundle cannot vibrate, because its ending abuts the outer layer of the dura mater. Nor can the fibrous inner substance of nerves vibrate because even the slightest filament contains soft and spongy medullary content in the neural "pores." A taut fiber is necessary in order to produce vibration, argues Vieussens. He carries his brief to the doorstep of vision itself, where the full implication of fluidism becomes clear. Vision is commonly held to result from light-ray impingement on the retinal surface, causing the vibratile optic nerve to respond. Vieussens asserts that such activity is impossible because both retina and nerve are extremely soft and flexible. Rather, visual effect consists of the striking rays making contact with the animal spirits. The rays "paint" a surface image on the retina, and the image is communicated to the spirits in the retinal pores and carried from there to the brain. The movements of light rays and animal spirits cause transmission to the brain, without any fibral oscillation.

The belief in animal spirits is a fact of supreme importance throughout the Enlightenment. Their activity, as much as the brain's, holds the key to the cognitive-motor system. Conventional fluidist theory contends that a liquid still more fine than nerve sap exists within the medullary fibers. The subtle distillation, or animal spirits, permits what the nerve sap cannot. The nerve sap cannot alone convey sensation because its elements are too thick to "communicate movement successively." Again it is the "successive" or "connecting" power of substances that underlies this speculation. The animal spirits consist of the tiniest molecules whose minimal mass allows free movement among thicker fluids like lymph. The lymphatic fluid may clog the neural pores and prevent the animal spirits from moving through the nerves. But such blockage is pathological, while in normal health the animal spirit is an invisible liquor akin to aethereal matter. Its constitutive simplicity is such that it can form a sensory continuum from one end of the nervous system to the other. Vieussens's formula declares that the nervous sap is to animal spirit what air is to the globules composing light. The animal spirit is a liquid body composed of "fine air" that insinuates itself into the blood vessels through breathing. Its relationship to aether is thus paramount, as the context of Chapter 9 will indicate.

The fluidists devalue brain function in another respect. Their hydro-kinetic model removes the responsibility for emotional experience from brain-nerve trackings. Rather, blood circulation is the medium and cause of anger, fear, melancholy, and their contrary temperaments. The theory also undergirds the metaphor of connectedness even while deemphasizing cerebro-neural vibrations. Vieussens mentions a "liquid column" of fluid in its course through the slender canal of the nerve fiber. The tubular scheme obeys an overall principle: that a natural equilibrium of fluid movements typifies the healthy organism. A similar balance governs the elastic force of the bundles or "tunics" of the vessels that carry such fluids. The law of hydrokinetic pressure is such that no reflux of fluid in the canals is pos-sible without a greater force external to them. This mechanical fact bears on the concept of continuity, uniting both fluidists and vibrationists under the same banner of linkages. When an external object excites the sensory nerve, it suspends the flow of animal spirits within, which then form a liquid column. Vieussens compares the event to a hose blocked by a finger. That portion of the animal spirits found in the brain expands to fill the brain cavity and forms the head of the liquid column. The sensation excites the elastic nerve tunic, which then transmits its excitation by convection. If any vibrating is involved, it is the agitation of the tubular nerve against the columnar nerve fluid. But the conveyed sensory event does not entail con-duction. It is "communicated" to the animal spirits bound within the nerve in a process that reconciles differences in density of bundle and fluid. The expansion, not vibration, of animal spirits in the brain cavity then allows the impression to be traced (*Traité nouveau*, 1:235–36).

In support of Vieussens is Le Cat's refutation of vibrationist theory. Le Cat insists on a continuity of animal fluid from the brain outward, and the impossibility of a flowback of spirits to the brain from another source. He too conceives of animal spirit in aethereal terms, more subtle than light, although he also attributes its essence to fire. This orientation derives from a metamorphic doctrine of material linkages that is less occult than it might sound. Animal spirit cannot be contained as a liquid, although it flows like a sap linked to the gelatinous nerve lymph (*Traité des sensations*, xlvi). Sensory communication, as in Vieussens, occurs by convection when the contracting nervous network generates blood and serous affluences that reach the brain and trace the impression.

These explanations were as plagued by inadequacies as the vibra-tionist explanations, fully described by other scholars. But they all con-verged in their unanimous assertion of the continuist doctrine in spite of the discontinuities in transmission or conversion exposed at some level of anatomy or physiological process. Even so, it must be remembered that British adherents of Haller became embroiled with fluidists over distinctions that lose their urgency when animal spirits are understood as aethereal spirit. Haller distinguishes irritability from sensibility. Yet the debate over whether nerves are characterized by irritability, and muscles by sensibility, existed because everybody had accepted the distinction between the two kinds of impulses. The distinction may be important at the level of function, but it is irrelevant at the level of impulse-convection. Some physiologists would explain that nerve fluid flows *between* muscles and brain through the nerves. The position is strategic. We may see in retrospect that since the fluid incorporates the animal spirits, these may carry both kinds of impulses to the brain, where differentiation will take place under other auspices.

No overall theory of "communication" or connection between brain and external events existed to situate each stage of convection and impulse-conversion. The notion of a tracing process begins to anticipate the concept of a "language" that secures such communication. But a consensual theory of brain traces is thwarted by the division between fluidists and vibrationists. Among the latter, Hartley moves to reconcile animal spirits with brain secretion. He expounds the notion of glandular secretion, called nervous fluid or animal spirits, and he inserts the ubiquitous element of aether into the system. The medullary substance is "sufficiently uniform for the free propagation of vibrations," he notes. The aether residing here is of "an uniform density on account of the smallness of the pores of the medullary substance, and the uniformity of its texture, before taken notice of, will suffer the excited vibrations to run freely through it" (*Observations*, 1:22–23). Thus the nerve fibers themselves do not appear directly to be responsible for transmission. Hartley takes the argument of Boerhaave and Vieussens in favor of animal spirits and accommodates it to the Newtonian hypothesis of vibrating aether. The vibrations excited both in the aether and in the larger fluid particles are propagated along the fibers from nerve to brain. This continuity is not complete, however, as we shall see, so that the transformatory process from impression to image and then to abstractions remains an uncertainty in Hartley's work.

The fact is that hints of a threatening discontinuity brings a wrinkle to Hartley's discussions of brain anatomy. Hartley cites the different densities of aether in the medullary substance, whose result "may almost be an Interruption or Discontinuity of it" (1:23). The sensory impulses or "vibrations" are propagated "feebly and imperfectly" into neighboring regions of the brain matter, which is heterogeneous and of varying hardness. The medullary particles are thus indisposed "to receive and communicate Vibrations; and . . . only small Vibrations, and such irregular ones as oppose each other, will just begin to take place in the immediately continuous Parts, and there cease without proceeding farther" (1:23). How do the sensory data reach their cognitive destination, and in what form? The disconcerting possibility of a break in continuity brings Hartley back to face this issue in detail.

Because microscopes are not powerful enough to account unequivocally for brain impulses, Hartley considers two possibilities. Either the vibrations enter the brain and "begin to be propagated freely every way over the whole medullary substance, being diminished in strength in proportion to the quantity of matter agitated," or else "if we suppose the pia mater to make some small discontinuity in the medullary substance by its processes, as has been hinted above, then we must also suppose that the vibrations which ascend along any sensory nerve affect the region of the brain which corresponds to this sensory nerve more, and the other regions less" (1:24).

This account of the pia mater parallels Diderot's account of the meninges: the membranes are one and the same, to the same effect. Hartley's account isolates each of the five sensory faculties and postpones their final coordination. He does not explain whether the aether extended through the medullary substance transmits the vibrations to their coordinating destination in the sensorium or in some higher mental faculty. Quite the opposite, "it seems impossible to trace out these communications anatomically, on account of the great softness of the brain" (1:19). He prefers to speculate that "if there be some little impediment and confinement in certain regions, on account of some exceedingly small discontinuity, arising from this intervention of the pia mater between certain regions, it may, as it seems to me, suit this theory rather better than an absolute and perfect continuity, as before supposed" (1:9).

The debate reveals its inhibitory effect in the positions of Diderot and Haller. Diderot cannot harmonize his conception of the brain with the nervous system just outlined. As noted, he classifies the brain as a secreting gland that functions integrally among other organs, rather than as a central controlling organ. Haller's carefully organized anatomy can do no better with the debate over fluids and vibrations. He seldom hazards an opinion concerning cerebro-neural process despite abundant anatomical details. Haller's reticence, therefore, speaks the more loudly because in one instance he draws attention to a mystery. The nerve has a tender pulp that, when impinged on by an external object "conveys, by the nervous spirits, some change to that part of the brain where the impressed fibers of the nerve first arise from the arteries. We know nothing more, than that new thoughts are thus excited in the mind" (*First Lines of Physiology*, 2:32).

From Brain to Imagination

In order to examine the indecisive course neuropsychology took late in the century from a chronological standpoint, a historical note is appropriate. A historical perspective will also help to position artists and writers who became fascinated with such themes as dreaming, nightmare, madness, and the general pathology of behavior, whose Unreason they recognized as being derived from the enigmatic dualism of brain and mind. Followers of Haller, like Daniel Delaroche, abandoned the fluidist camp in a tendency that sliced the fields of anatomy and physiology into smaller technical perspectives that were not hospitable to theorization. Delaroche pinpointed the coordination of perceptual and motor responses in the sensorium of the brain, regardless of whether these responses are initiated at the nerve ends or by the will (*Analyse*, 41). But Delaroche's specialized work kept him from larger questions that move from brain to mind.

Progress toward a synthesis did occur in the end-of-century work of Pierre Cabanis, which passes over the preceding structural debate in order to make physiology the literal root of moral sentiments. Cabanis's scheme identifies a nonsensory network that, alongside the sensory and motor systems, has parallel conduits to the brain. This means that physical influences other than the sense organs modify brain behavior, whose activity derives from an internal source. Cabanis explains that "independently of the brain and the spinal column, different foyers of sensibility exist in the living body." Here "the impressions gather together somewhat like light rays, either then to be reflected immediately toward the motor fibers or else to be sent in this assembled state to the universal and common center. It is among these divers foyers of the brain that the sympathies are very lively and multiplied" (*Rapports*, 2:11). Cabanis refers here to more than the "sympathetic" or semi-autonomous communications between regions such as the gastro-intestinal or genito-urinary tracts and the brain. The internal nonsensory sympathies can affect the brain and in turn modify our moral disposition. In fact, the nervous system itself comes under the canopy that gathers internal impressions "that belong most especially to it, since their cause resides within it," in the "particular foyers" of the neural network as well as "in their common center," presumably the brain (*Rapports*, 2:13). These hints foreshadow somatic mechanisms that explain psychological states, which in fact were not specified until the nineteenth century, and in fields related to chemical reactions.

The bifurcation between psychic and somatic causes existed earlier, however, as indicated by the fifteen cases histories submitted in 1764 by Johann Friedrich Meckel of the Berlin Royal Academy. This report aimed to demonstrate that varieties of madness were caused by brain weight changes and abnormal frictional pressures. In the course of demonstration, the line between cause and symptom grew tenuous as the researcher approached the elusive psychological dimension. Here the role of imagination had prominence, but in a direction that deflated the idealist and universalist tendencies of the pursuers of continuity.

One kind of "dementia" (*démence*) studied by Meckel is also named "idiocy" (*stupidité*), the condition being defined in physiological terms and not behavioral ones. But the effects on the imagination are predicated on physiology. Meckel also invokes the standard premise of "the intimate tie between the natural action of objects on the senses" and the imagination. The irrational state is caused by "the compression of parts of brain . . . with a collapse of strength in body and mind. The tiny medullary tubes are compressed by extravasated serosity." As a result, nerve fluid is insufficiently secreted, "and consequently the impression of external objects acting upon the senses cannot pass directly to the common sensorium." In turn, the victim "cannot form distinct ideas nor judge external objects. As for the internal sense, it follows that since the impressions on the nerves and the representations in the brain are lacking, an equal weakness befalls the reproduction of ideas in the imagination or memory" (*Recherches*, 81).

While the approach to imagination is pathological, the assumptions Meckel makes about imaging and cognition are in accord with the emphasis on nerve fluid mentioned earlier. A second variety of madness, named alternately "idiocy" and "unreason" (*déraison*), is attributed to victims who are classified as insane (*insensés*). The cause of this condition is "the lightness of the brain [that] can only be attributed to the emptying of the tiny medullary tubes in the brain, since the liquid required in blood vessels was not missing in the brains examined. Thus the dryness of the tiny tubes and the lack of fluid they must contain produce the astonishing hardness of the brain that lasts even after the death of these insane subjects." The same condition marks temporary delirium in fevered patients: the heat flushes excessive blood to the brain, causing an obstruction in the tiny medullary "tubes." However, the weight and dryness factors prove to be symptoms rather than causes. As in the earlier case, the key factor is the secretion of nerve liquid and its ability to mediate an appropriate signal after external objects act on the sensory organs. The medullary "conduits" or "canals" are "blocked" or rendered "impermeable," and "the memory suffers a weakness that influences the intellectual acts."

For Meckel it was enough to describe these physical states without pursuing their substratum in "the internal representation of ideas [that] cannot be done naturally." Brain research halted at the frontier between known facts and the independent discipline not yet identified as "psychology." Even so, the pathological report on brains is deemed incomplete without reference to the psychological premises that determine madness—namely, that judgment or "reasonings need to be founded on ideas or distinct representations of objects" (75–76).

In conclusion, the bits and pieces of a unified system also existed in Meckel's nonspeculative, limited domain, as they did among his continuist counterparts. In this instance, the added dimension of madness allowed the faculty of imagination to become one of the fragments that belonged to the still unexplained continuum. This dimension gave an artist like Goya room to explore aberrational dreams for their cognitive value. The same interest in madness extended to the research in neurophysiology that sustained the fluid-vibration debate.

8. The Polyp's Mind

It seems that polyps were made to upset all of our ideas about animal economy.
                    —Bonnet, *Considérations sur les corps organisés*

"[The nervous system] can be compared to a polyp, whose roots or mouths extend to the sense organs and all else, giving each part a kind of sensibility and activity.
                    —Bordeu, *Recherches sur les maladies chroniques*

The disagreements just reviewed concerning the brain's interaction with the neural network helped to perpetuate a more important argument during the Enlightenment. This involved the larger debate over the "mind" or "soul" as a separate entity from thinking matter. The problem of "soul" has had a known historical resolution. The philosophical term has by now disappeared in favor of either "mind" or genetic molecules. Nevertheless, the soul preoccupied an era when natural philosophy mattered even while moving toward its final cleavage into modern idealist philosophy and reductionist science. Before that division, theorists of the soul and sensibility persisted in a common fluctuating perspective whose historical drift they could not anticipate. This perspective shapes the current chapter.

Historians naturally want to follow chronologically the direction taken by the individual shaping elements, both human and experimental. But when eighteenth-century research dealt with the nature of matter and organic forms, the shaping process itself pulled in several directions at the same time. The direction seems unambiguous in certain bilateral changes, such as when the soul posited by Cartesian dualism vanished in La Mettrie's monist mechanism. This particular shift seems to be compatible with, say, Diderot's conversion from deism to materialism. However, a concurrent dualist neurophysiology also persisted in France, England, and Switzerland, where conservative microbiologists like Needham, Réaumur, and Bonnet resisted drawing the materialist or vitalist inferences of their evidence—namely, that the zoophytes and polyps observed for the first time could dispense with a soul and still reproduce or regenerate themselves, whether by preformation or by epigenesis. Other protagonists coping with still other problems can also be cited to demonstrate the unresolved state of materialist-dualist beliefs about the same basic vital signs. However, this would not change the fact that at stake in all categories of research was the subsuming general principle of behavior in living matter.

To date there has been no study that disentangles the multifarious uses of the terms "force" and "soul" in the eighteenth century after the tripartite Aristotelian concept became obsolete. A loose notion of souls as separate agencies—animal, sensitive or vegetative, and rational—maintained its viability throughout the Enlightenment. The difficulty is that these adjectives often dropped out of use when the context entailed the ultimate responsibility of a "force" for organized behavior in living matter. Such behavior may involve reproduction or, ascending the ladder of complexity, regeneration, sensibility, motor response, and the use of imagination and reason. On any rung in this scale of vital behavior, the event must depend on the organism's response to a stimulus, and this is the common factor that can serve as a synthesizing concept for all competing beliefs about basic life processes. Response to stimulus is the principle governing the basic events of living and thinking matter. Another name for it would be signal-conversion, which produces signs that indicate the organism has recognized the signal.

The concept of a conversion process synthesizes for all organic levels the type of message-making that is epitomized in the neurocerebral process. However, the presence or absence of a brain or nervous system is irrelevant in contexts where the idea of a "soul" remains controversial. In these contexts, the mind-body dilemma takes over and poses the problem of explaining the discontinuity between the material signal and its implementation by some "soul" or "energy." An example at the human level is "mental" activity or thought, the most abstract kind of behavioral response by an organism to the environment. An example at the polypal level of activity is nerveless, general sensibility, whether through phototropism in response to the environment or through regeneration into an "other." Both the complex and the primitive instances reflect the fact that between the message and the response lies an interval of unknown quantity and quality that needs to be named.

Defining the Problem: From Soul to Mind

One core notion bridges eighteenth-century philosophy, science, and literature in the full context of competing Western European ideas. This idea is the changing notion of a vital force or "soul," and it blends the details of particular theories pursued by individual scientists.

In the context under discussion, the problem of soul is not theological. It relates to neurophysiological assumptions about sensibility that concern intellectual and scientific historians but also, less directly, literary scholars. The relevance of sensibility to literary criticism was already introduced in the Preface with regard to competing theories or paradigms. The contents of these paradigms and their explanations differ, but the issues and questions are the same. What frames them all is the idea of an animating force that exists either immaterially as a soul or materially as something unseen but determinate enough to satisfy those who deny immaterial agents.

Scholars today know the details of these issues with respect to individual scientists and wider comparisons, but they still have no focus that simplifies the various positions at a synthesized level of concepts. To ponder one issue is to raise questions about the others in a way that misses the hierarchical relationship of biological and philosophical problems. Their interdependency is stressed, instead of their relative importance in the mind-body duality. For instance, although the problem of sensibility is surely a master question prompted by the shift from Cartesian dualism to mechanist monism and vitalism, its subordinate issues quickly entangle the overall picture. Among these issues are: Does matter have sensibility without a soul? If so, what permits matter to develop and reproduce organically? If matter *succeeds* in developing and surviving in its environment, is this not a sensibility and a form of intelligence, that is, an intelligent process? Regardless of the answers, the questions themselves rest on four concepts whose historical development scholars have followed: matter, organic process, sensibility, and soul. The interrelatedness of these concepts is admittedly crucial and usually emphasized, but the order of their importance as general concepts and subordinate issues grows obscure.

If sensibility is the master problem in the mind-body debate, the issues related to it appear at first sight to have clear-cut boundaries. One category of issues is biological, and the other is philosophical. Nevertheless the question of how an immaterial soul can affect matter intersects both categories. As a result, a host of distracting factors arise that quickly polarize positions into dualism on the one hand and reductionist materialism on the other. To ask about reproduction and regeneration means asking not only the biological question of what regulates preformation or epigenesis, but also the philosophical question of whether a teleological intelligence engineers the generative continuity achieved from one individual to its successor. In the same vein, reproduction entails two dissimilar biological aspects: the embryological problem differs from the evolutionary one. The philosophical aspect of evolution has to do with the continuity among the species as it concerns the belief in the Chain of Being. Similarly complicated issues arise in the area of sensibility and neurophysiology.

Lost in this welter of issues regarding vital matter is a unifying fact among the specific forms of activity. Living matter rests on two foundations, generation and sensibility, and these are the key to the mystery of vitality itself. In this unifying fact lies the common assumption of a designing regulator and its immaterial or material nature. This regulator is mechanical in the dualist scheme only because a "soul" oversees it. When materialist mechanism rejects the soul, its position approaches vitalism insofar as both philosophies attribute some transcending force or animist power to matter itself. What prevails regardless of theoretical positions is an implicit common focus on the energy responsible for basic physical activity. This energy is identified with the conversion of stimulus into response, regardless of the level of activity. I shall return to this point. While it is true that activities differ widely, a common denominator governs the primitive level of conversion. Thinking matter and reproducing matter indeed perform distinct functions, but they both function under the same principle of a signaling process.

As soon as the notion of signals arises, their regulation and intelligibility become a consideration. If it is plausible to regard the conversion of stimulus into response as the factor that accounts for the very survival of a living organism, then the organism's self-regulating capability also becomes a concept to consider. This includes its manner of displaying intelligence. This regulatory competence ensures the successful maintenance of the organism's identity vis-à-vis the Other, in this instance the environment, and it ensures the organism's reproduction, which maintains the continuity among individuals in the species. The term "intelligence" may seem inappropriate for simple organisms because it connotes consciousness and teleology. Nevertheless, the ability to survive and to reproduce suggests a higher coordinating agency, and one that no eighteenth-century observer ever denied. The idea of a higher agency can take two forms, either as the "guide" or the organizing principle of lower sentient organisms, or as the sensibility of intelligent animals and human beings. In both forms, a "soul" can be spoken of so as to affirm it or refute it. This point is elaborated in the final section of this chapter.

Vital Energy

The most dramatic proof of the unresolved struggle between vitalism and, for want of a better term, natural theology is the eighteenth-century fascination with polyps, which challenged scientific understanding of matter and its generative source. The vitality of the polyp becomes an object of both the mythological and the scientific imagination because it taps the secret springs of the life force.

The polyp has its mythological counterpart in the monstrous Hydra, symbol of multifarious evil. A Hercules might lop off one of its nine heads, and two others would spring back in place. Accordingly, eighteenth-century iconology makes the Hydra an attribute of vice, as noted in Boudard's book of emblems. Relentless aggression typifies this monster, just as it does Goya's bats. The disproportionate vitality of both creatures jars the imagination into contemplating the abnormal depths of natural energy.

But Nature's monstrosity is also a scientific wonder. Cut the polyp into pieces and it multiplies. The behavior astounded one mathematician into calling it "a hydra more marvelous than the fable." Maupertuis pictured the creature as "an aquatic worm" possessed of "surprising means for multiplying. Just as a tree sprouts branches, a polyp sprouts young polyps, and when these reach a certain size they detach themselves from the trunk that produced them" (*Oeuvres*, 2:61). Research at that time into the polyp's regenerative mechanism was associated with Réaumur's experiments on leg amputations in crayfish and Trembley's on budding. Bonnet's aquatic worm was a freshwater animal in the same category, the "point of passage linking animal and vegetable realms."[1] Its rapid breeding cycle also confirmed the idea of what Needham called a "vegetative force."

Only Voltaire ridiculed the polyp, disagreeing with the *Encyclopédie*'s recognition that it is animal by virtue of having sensation. How sad to lose the illusion of an animal that reproduces itself through budding, he writes in the *Philosophical Dictionary*, but he insists on the evidence before his eyes.

---

1. See Virginia Dawson, *Nature's Enigma: The Problem of the Polyp in the Letters of Bonnet, Trembley, and Réaumur* (Philadelphia: American Philosophical Society, 1987), 167.

The polyp resembles a carrot or an asparagus more than an animal: its roots are its feet, it has branches for arms and a stem for its body, and the stem's tube is perforated at the top for a mouth. Even so, Voltaire is captivated by the phenomenon that focuses contemporary research. He offers in place of the polyp the lowly snail (*colimaçon*), which as every child knew would move for months after its head is cut off. Voltaire associates the head with the sensorium, the memory, and the soul. The real issue, however, was not the identity of the organism itself, but instead the removal of the head from its body.[2] This issue may be defined in the framing context of the debate between the two eminent physiologists of the age, Caspar Friedrich Wolff and Albrecht von Haller. Is there a separation between matter and spirit, between the nourishment and developmental growth of living matter and its capacity for sensation and thought, between the "essential force" of vegetative processes and the generative powers of the soul? In this intricate debate, the simplistic choice was between mechanist reductionism and vitalism. Wolff denied the first and was reluctant to embrace the second, objecting to the reliance on God rather than nature to explain generation. Haller objected to the idea that a *vis essentialis* can act on matter without guidance from an higher wisdom.[3]

The belief in a concealed energy owed much to Abraham Trembley's "unassailable" evidence, in Virginia Dawson's words, that matter is somehow empowered to organize itself without the interposition of an egg. The concept of force or energy permits P. J. G. Cabanis to calibrate all matter from fibroid mineral structures to vegetal and animal systems. Cabanis explained some transitional areas by the Leibnizian notion of "zoophytes." This classification vindicated earlier research on polyps because all such organisms exhibit sensory awareness, heretofore attributed only to humans and higher animals. The zoophytes respond to external stimuli like certain "irritable plants whose movements, in the manner of those in living muscular organs, correspond to particular excitations" (*Rapports*, 2:384). In Robinet's concept of matter, this sensitivity descends still lower on the scale of material bodies. Robinet's belief that basic substance is invested with the same plastic ability, potentially vital in its metamorphosis, opened Trembley's research on polyps to broader speculations. Intriguing as these creatures are, they really serve as the springboard for the unifying theory

---

2. The details are taken up by Georges Gusdorf in his *Dieu, la nature, l'homme au siècle des lumières* (Paris: Payot, 1972), 286.

3. See Shirley A. Roe, *Matter, Life, and Generation: Eighteenth-Century Embryology and the Haller-Wolff Debate* (Cambridge: Cambridge University Press, 1981), 110–13.

of vital force, the centerpiece of attention among Enlighteners concerned with problems of cognition and continuity.

At so elementary a level of organized matter, it was important to discard conventional terms of classification. Rather than "creatures," "plants," and "organisms," Robinet spoke of "bodies" or "beings," while other researchers speak of "parts." What Buffon called an "organic molecule" was simply a trope for what eventually was seen as a metaphysical problem. The factors that affect the way freshwater polyps multiply and divide are extra-taxonomical ones, according to Robinet. Whether they are plants or animals is not the issue; what counts is the nature of propagation and epigenesis, the principle of which belongs to all realms of organicity (*Nature*, 1:157). But what is organic? And does this differ from the organized matter or dead matter discussed in Chapter 6? If Robinet dismissed the literal classifications of Buffon's Nature, he could not avoid exposing the subcategories of matter to a similar fate.

Accordingly, the first and foremost constituent of any material body is what Robinet calls the "idea" of its form. All animal and vegetal matter, after death, decomposes into "vital beings." These primary beings do not by themselves constitute life, but by their combination into "the whole," as Diderot termed it, they form a living substance. Such a notion falls short of metaphysical spirit by virtue of the indwelling and transformative power of that "idea." As Robinet asserts, all matter encloses its own idea of extended form and composition. The enclosure can only consist of a "force," which takes various names at the time. Its nourishing and generating agency integrates it with the "vegetative soul." Haller notes the polyvalent agency in polyps, which have a motor-excitation capacity despite the absence of vibrating nerves.[4] La Mettrie calls this capacity a "motor force" that produces organic automaticity, inferring this from muscular irritability.[5] The polyp's self-procreating behavior proves to La Mettrie that matter needs no soul because it contains the necessary causes of generation. However, Aram Vartanian has pointed out that La Mettrie abandoned his early effort to solve the materiality of the causes related to the life principle and its entailments in feeling and thinking. These disparate factors lead back again to the riddle of fibrous essences and the fluctuations of sap or aether discussed previously.

4. See, further, François Duchesneau, *La physiologie des lumières: Empirisme, modèles, et théories* (The Hague: Martinus Nijhoff, 1982), 212, 278.

5. See Aram Vartanian, "Trembley's Polyp, La Mettrie, and Eighteenth-Century French Materialism," *Journal of the History of Ideas* 11 (1950): 259–86.

The riddle was approached through research on polyps in several ways. Robinet collapses the distinction between regeneration and spontaneous generation. Or rather, his experiments in these distinct areas lead to the theoretical identification in both of a single responsible agent—the "vegetative force." Polyps and crayfish repair their inflicted amputations by identical powers that inhere in the fermenting specimens of crushed pumpkin, peach, and almond seeds. In the first instance, the "plastic force" may be recognized by the specific structure of the polypoid body already organized. Because this agent repairs tentacular loss consistently, the agent must be a determining force. The bodily shape is always determined specifically by the "metaphysical mold" or cast (*Nature*, 1:228). In the second instance, Robinet examines the fetid specimen by microscope and records day-by-day observations of the ever more dense swarm of "animals." Following Needham's procedures, he distills the water in order to refute adversary scientists who attribute the new life to outside contamination (1:172). His procedures result in a cycle in which vegetation follows decomposition and purification of the stagnant water, until several generations exhaust themselves.

In both instances the vegetative force is said to be distributed uniformly within the body, so that it then "pushes outward" to give a determined shape. Robinet conceives this idea on the model of explosive charges in physics.[6] The outward thrust toward a determined shape is "like any projectile force that, combined with gravity, describes necessarily a certain parabolic portion of a determined form, and stops at a mathematically fixed point, or like fireworks where the explosive powers are mixed prior to setting fire, spread out externally, and produce a determined figure in advance by the will of the Artificer" (*Nature*, 1:229). The reality of these forces is undeniable, and the greater minuteness of the vegetative force in crayfish and polyps does not diminish Robinet's belief. As a professional microscopist, he is persuaded that "this invisible world is the collection of all the forces that undertake to improve existence" in minerals and plants. Underlying these lower beings "is a gradation of forces in the invisible world, like a progression of forms in the extended or visible world. These active forces are engendered in their own way, like material forms" (*Considérations*, 8, 10).

The ideal of continuism lures Robinet farther than most naturalists toward the rational conclusions of his vitalist conjectures. Whereas Trembley, Bonnet, and Needham halt at the polyp, Robinet extends the neuro-

6. Robinet's theory of "exaltation" is described in Shirley A. Roe, "John Turberville Needham and the Generation of Living Organisms," *Isis* 74 (1983): 159–84

physiology of matter to the bottommost plane of existence. After all, he reasons, Nature begins her preparations in the tiniest atom. If Nature later masterminds living machines, it is only after trying innumerable combinations. At the level of sheer matter, the metamorphic process has not begun; as yet there are no heads, arms, legs, or flesh (*Considérations*, 15). Nevertheless, just as mushrooms are plants resembling human "parts," so too the filaments and fibrous layers of mica display plantlike textures. Beneath oil formations are animalcules composed of igneous, aqueous, aeroform, and earthen constituents. Robinet offers an extensive study of stones and rocks to show how their material shapes resemble animal organs.

The polyp becomes the stepping-stone in this scheme aimed at a continuous scale of material vitality. Nature creates this singular animal, "which is nothing but a branching bowel whose tissue is uniform everywhere, and after turning the animal inside out none of its vital functions are harmed" (*Considérations*, 17). In a machine this simple, Robinet asks, what forms are adopted by its analogs of heart and lungs? There seem to be only air sacs, or tracheae, like the simple plants that are closest to the polyp. And his microscope bears this out: "upon the tissue that forms the polyp, an infinite number of tiny grains are plausibly the viscera or the principle organs of life." Further down the scale, however, "when we cannot find air-sacs or tracheae in minerals, the only thing we can legitimately conclude is that a yet simpler organic apparatus suffices at this degree of Being" (17). Do we ask what are the vital organs of gold or diamonds? They are too simple for our senses. And just because our eyes, "and our microscopes, much better than our eyes, cannot perceive them we deny their reality." This attitude is an outrage to Nature, concludes Robinet.

Here then is one moment when sober materialism balks at dismissing the possible reality of invisible phenomena. The "prototypal force" inserts itself on every rung of "the universal ladder of Beings." As this energy infuses the "practical form," it completes the conditions required so that forms may occupy that "progressive" ladder. But this progress does not end with humankind. There may be yet subtler forms, and here Robinet seconds so mathematical an eminence as Maupertuis. The scale of beings may include forms wielding more active powers than those invested in humans. Perhaps this force can strip itself of all materiality and thus become "a new world," suggests the microscopist. But he halts at this point with a cautionary word about not entering digressively into such vast regions of possibility (12).

In the microscopic region, Le Cat has no difficulty accommodating the universal ladder to the clothlike tufts of neural fibers and strands of nerve fluid. This fabric-like substance is nearly indestructible in its quality of ge-latinous tenacity. For this very reason, the polyp too is virtually immune to harm (*Traité de l'existence*, 113). The same glutinous sap in higher animals and humans is provided by the brain. And midway along the graduated scale, this nerve fluid is materially the same substance that is found in seeds, flower bulbs, and plant cuttings. This last group is significant because the substance also can germinate and produce life. It is akin to "seminal liquid," which is a brain "in embryo form" and indeed, as noted, is supplied by the brain. Therefore everything is affected by this fluid, "from polyp to whale." And in human beings, "the lymphatic-mucilaginous" nerve fluid mingles with the "animal spirit," a fusion that restores unity since "both these fluids have their source in the bosom of the Universe itself" (*Traité de l'existence*, 62–63). This spirit pervades the air, is inhaled by the lungs, and is refined while traveling in the blood.

Fluidist theory thus argues a unified field theory about life in general, which becomes identified with neural activity. Both the signaling mechanism of human fibers, and the regenerative mechanism of the gluten in seeds, polyps, and nerves, share the same debt for their vitality to the universal life force. This theory is the most comprehensive argument for continuity from the microcosm to the Absolute.

From this standpoint, it is of no consequence that an organism lacks a network of fibers. The polyp has sensations notwithstanding. Writers gravitated toward this intriguing example of the ultimate cognitive condition, one in which sensory perception is superfluous for organizing the signals required for vital needs. By comprehending the organizational capacity for this case, the Enlighteners extend models and devise metaphors that enable them also to comprehend higher signaling codes. Words like "branching," "network," "ramification," and "web" build on the lesser metaphor of "fiber" and "thread" to convert the textile image into a fabric of universal connectedness. The neural and animal spirits that together spring from the "bosom of the Universe" are the adhesive factor in all linkages:

> This chain, by which we have seen the Author of Nature to have tied together all Beings; these insensible nuances that we have observed in the links that unite the diverse species, would the supreme Being have forgotten them all in their most important connection of the organized world? (*Traité de l'existence*, 45)

The polyp is evidence that the linking power is not absent in this most crucial domain, where elementary matter is able to organize itself. Indeed, because animal spirit mingles with so primitive a fluid, the polyp may be regarded as the basic unit of life and feeling. Both of these conditions—living and feeling—are possible despite the absence of nerve fibers and brain.

The physiological context described here is not restricted to biological writings about reproduction and the cerebro-nervous system. There is also a long-standing epistemological debate over the dilemma of the "man born blind," a debate that gains impetus from biologists who repeatedly cite examples where sensory damage to complex organisms is followed by remarkable compensatory powers. The fact arises that some animals have nervous systems that do not extend to certain parts of the body even though they enjoy sensation. Cabanis ascribes this observation to the vitalist Montpellier school of Bordeu and Barthez in its dissenting position from the prevailing influence of Haller (*Rapports*, 4, and 402–3). Regardless of the disputed details, neither school states the implied questions forthrightly. How are reproductive ability and sensory knowledge really executed? Do such nerveless bodies as the lowly polyp hold a clue? If sensation in higher life forms is linked to animal or universal spirits, does some primacy attach to the mysterious spirits flowing through the nerveless polyp?

These questions involve the way that spirits produce knowledge (a subject discussed in Chapter 9). The pertinent point now is the absence of neural activity in the polyp. Although it has no optic nerve, the polyp responds to light. While this ability is called "photosensitivity" today, it is not "sensory" activity in the eighteenth-century meaning of the term. Trembley observes that the polyp reacts to light and contracts when touched. Without having "sensation," its "sensitivity" consists of obtaining information from the external world and behaving accordingly. The "animating forces [are] spread through the matter" that composes the polyp function as a primitive intelligence, or so Bonnet speculates (Dawson, *Nature's Enigma*, 162). Translated into philosophical terms, the polyp's ability to "know" presents a model of the interchange between self and world. Here the issue concerns the subject-object relationship. This commerce is wordless, but it entails some form of signal language. Such a model of interchange extends its interest beyond science to philosophically-minded writers and artists.

The cognitive model lends perspective to Goya's fascination with "Universal Language." In *Sepia Two*, the sleeper "knows" the objects that surround him even though his dream knowledge is not sensory. His extrasensory knowledge consists of the "monsters" that Goya alludes to in *Capricho 43*. But the true monstrosity is not literal. It designates the class of organisms whose abilities circumvent knowledge normally gained through sensory means. This class includes, at one extreme, certain "monsters" discussed in medical and philosophical treatises at that time: an acephalic living infant, or a freakish curtailment in animals of the sensory-motor system. The severity of aberration is not important, however, only its kind. In the same class but at the other extreme is the polyp's experiential condition. Like Goya's sleeper, the polyp occupies the equivalent of a dream-state. It is deprived of sensation, although it enigmatically "knows" when it is touched, even by light. It survives through a direct cognitive immersion in an environment that other sentient beings seek to know through the mediacy of perceptions and signs. The polyp is sensorially "asleep" in its fiberless condition, as a higher animal whose nerves are severed is insentient in its members. If Nature's norm for an organism's survival demands sensory information from the external world, then the polyp is the primordial model of monstrosity.

But does the polyp dream? The answer depends on the nature of Universal Language. The secret of its direct-access knowledge is the "universal spirit" that animates the life principle. Although Le Cat is no religious spiritualist, he and like-minded thinkers resort to terms like "soul" and "supreme Artificer" for want of better explanations. Use of the word âme to mean "mind" as well as "soul" sustains the vagueness. Even so, the recognition that a spirit or supreme Being activates physiology imposes an arcane aura on vital processes. But if spirit is an aethereal spirit, or "spirits" in the fluidist sense, then the concept regains its materialist base. The soul is "immaterial" and "pensive," responding to the Supremity that actuates everything in the universe. And yet the soul itself pervades everything. Le Cat's arcane materialism admits unashamedly that his terms are also Saint Augustine's. The soul resides nowhere, "occupies no space, nor extension, except by its force" (*Traité de l'existence*, 67, 116).

A more cautious phrasing of vitalist beliefs appears in one of Hume's dialogues on natural religion. And while Hume protects his scientific flank by using "analogy" as a qualifier, the idea of an enabling force that is common to all domains of existence strikes him, like Le Cat, as not unlikely. But Hume carefully avoids religious mystification by reasoning from the nonbeliever's viewpoint. Even atheism must concede the existence of "a certain degree of analogy among all the operations of nature." Hume can then wonder "whether the rotting of a turnip, the generation of an animal, and the structure of human thought, be not energies that probably bear some remote analogy to each other" (*Dialogues*, 86). The gathering of such disparate domains in a single utterance is a daring association for this skeptic to make, and it is more than a remote analogy for other thinkers.

Sensory Energy

Less remote is the physiological evidence for the hypothesis of a common energy. Le Cat's treatise on sensations and passions is an appropriate format for displaying the proximity of material and immaterial domains. In the same breath, he mentions fabric materials, the nervous system, and the external environment. Animal fibers are composed of the same "solid corpuscles" as cloth fabric, and these fibers transport the "universal gluten" that unites the vast material system described earlier. The spider's glue manufactures threads in the same way that the "nutritive glue" solidifies the fibroid "corpuscles." These in turn "resemble the longish bits of fluffy matter left on clothes by linen" (*Traité des sensations*, 41). Textiles, paper, nerves—all are made of the same stuff.

But the most rarefied fluid of all must also be converted. Its permeating action in the external atmosphere affects every perceivable object. Through a series of gradual transformations, the universal fluid is channeled into a particular internal, fibrous event. Expressed in terms of sense perception, this flow or passage is a communication between external object and nervous system. The universal spirit communicates with the organism's animal spirit by a process of fluid conversions that begins with respiratory and epidermal activity. The body breathes in air, which is infused with spirits that enter the bloodstream and thereafter mingle with the nervous sap, composed of the gelatinous lymph containing universal gluten (118, 184–86).

This cycle begins with vital force and terminates in sensory power. None of the technical books at this time gives a step-by-step description to account logically for every physiological organ involved in the conversion. The relation between blood and nervous sap is unclear when the activity concerns sensory events. On the one hand, fluidist theory holds that the blood globules are "spongy" or "phosphorous" substances that imbibe the transforming fluid. They contain "aethereal matter," to use Vieussens's term. On the other hand, the animal fluid needs mediatory substance in order to form the alliances that sustain it, and the brain's role in this respect is to filter the fluid in conjunction with the nerve ganglia. A further complication is the role of "vital heat," a concept that returns us to the earth fires and volcanic heat of Le Cat's and Robinet's cosmology.

Entangled in the consubstantiation of universal and nervous spirits is the question of genesis itself. The "life principle" works by animal warmth, which is derived from fire and turns chyle into blood. There seems to exist "a kind of genealogy established by the senses themselves, which the spirits precede and form the blood, just as the blood precedes and produces with them the movements of the organs" (*Traité des sensations*, 72). That is, the heart, the brain, and other organs are formed by the blood, not the other way round. This microcosmic genesis apparently duplicates the infinite magnitude of Creation itself, given the universal distribution of gluten and fluid. In short, the cosmic fire of Chaos, the earth's thermal centers, and the "vital heat" and "gentle fire" in the hen's egg represent different degrees of the same phenomenon.

In the midst of this speculative yet also experimental biology, the factors of heat and light are constants. They occupy a place that's symmetrical with the other major scientific orientation at this time, Newtonian physics. The Newtonian universe, along with the optical bias heralded by its proclaimers, associates light and aether with order and system. This symmetry makes it appear that the metaphors of scientific discourse are unable to relinquish light as a figurative concept to explain universal connectedness. Moreover, the biological and psychological writings at this time also display the occult facet just shown. More precisely, the work exemplified by Le Cat belongs to what might be called a larger illogical empiricism, made up of disparate facts that lend themselves as much to esoteric if not magical ruminations as to the rational projects of the biological laboratory. These projects presuppose certain broad principles that also undergird specific research on polyps and that spur great interest in this organism.

Behind these diverse directions is the grand enigma expressed in a question by Cabanis: Which *force* holds things together—gravitation or "sensibility"? What Delaroche calls "vital force" is described by the *Encyclopédie* in, significantly, the article on "Fibers." The contact of atoms produces cohesion by Newtonian attraction or by chemical attraction or, finally, by vegetal affinities. The popularizing and synthesizing efforts of the *Encyclopédie*, as well as those of Cabanis and Delaroche, attest to the currency of competing versions and to the unresolved status of scientific opinion as it concerns the principle and cohesion of perceived reality. Curiously enough, the *Encyclopédie* concludes this section of the fibers article with a discussion of molecules in fluids and solids.

The Polyp's Prototypal Energy

A similar preoccupation with the polyp's secret also motivates microscopic research in England. The "amazing" experiments in reproduction by the Genevan Trembley, working in Leiden, are acknowledged by Henry Baker of the Royal Society in London. While Trembley's work has been amply described by Dawson and Lenhoff, less notice is given to Baker's treatise on the natural history of the polyp in 1743, which repeats earlier attempts to evaluate dissection and is translated into French the very next year. Baker cuts the organism in every direction and describes its daily progress toward restoration into a perfect polyp. Its tenacious regenerative power makes it a paragon of "vigor and strength of life." The most unusual of Baker's observations, however, immediately opens the entire question of sensory perception, even though this subject is not his first concern. Baker comments on a suggestive detail also noticed by Trembley, Needham, and other microscopists regarding the polyp's eyeless condition. Baker remarks that the polyp is affected by light even without having eyes. Its phototropism induces Needham to expect that, like all animals, this one too must have eyes that cannot be detected even by the best microscope. In fact, however, the polyp has only a mouth and hydra-like tentacles with button-like granules on their contractile surface.

The fact that polyps are "blind" and yet respond to light strikes Baker as a vivid characteristic. Its behavior appears to compensate for nonvision by epidermal means. This detail becomes enormously significant in both Diderot's and Mérian's conception of sensory languages.[7] It suffices for Baker to note the polyp's "quivering" or "trembling" motion, and he ascribes to the polyp an extreme sensibility to pain. But he adds, more generally, that it possesses "a most exquisite sense of feeling."[8] Lacking a nerve system and even organs, the polyp masters an elementary signal code. Although a largely undifferentiated mass of organic matter, its molecules are "living" and "organized," in Buffon's meaning of the terms. But little else appears to explain its astonishing mastery of a regenerative signal code.

An additional mystery about the polyp's "strength of life" touches on the vital force discussed earlier. If a "vast gradation" stretches continuously from the most complex animals to the least visible moving atoms, as Needham claims, then the "vegetative force" inhering in them all is probably the connecting agent. Several puzzles about polyps lose their urgency in this perspective, especially Needham's question about whether they are

7. The man-born-blind problem in Diderot has been discussed at length by scholars, but less so for Mérian. Consult Denis Diderot, *Lettre sur les aveugles, Lettre sur le sourds et muets* ed. Yvon Belavel and Robert Niklaus in *Oeuvres complètes*, vol. 4: *Le nouveau Socrate, Idées 2* (Paris: Hermann, 1978); and Jean Bernard Mérian, *Réflexions philosophiques sur la ressemblance: Choix des mémoires et abrégé de l'histoire de l'Académie de Berline* (Berlin, 1767), 2:1–49.

8. Henry Baker, *An Attempt Towards a Natural History of the Polype* (London: R. Dodsley, 1743), 81.

plants or animals. He shows them to Réaumur, who classifies them as animals, but the borderline ambiguity becomes especially useful in fixing the transitional link between plant and animal domains (*Mémoires*, 19). A similar puzzle about generative processes becomes less challenging when seen against the wider issue of reproductions. Here Needham cites the polyp in evidence against germ theory and preformationism. The polyp reproduces its parts and yet has no place to lodge a preexistent germ. It vegetates and generates in the same way that the gelatinous matter of wheat "swells from an interior force" into filaments "just breaking, as I might say, into life" (*Observations*, 31). The real issue becomes the energy lodged in primary matter, whose nature Buffon terms "an ever-active organic matter, always ready to become molded, to become assimilated and produce beings similar to those that harbor it" (Varloot, 186).

Buffon speaks within the context of reproduction and development in plants and animals at every level. But his theory of the "mold" in the creation of life is patterned on a nonvitalist model, as Varloot points out. Even so, the forming mold does not behave mechanically, but is "an active, penetrating" force analogous to chemical and magnetic forces (24). The mold is also related to the idea of a forge or foundry, which casts living matter and inert matter into a fused new being. Thus situated, the polyp clarifies the nature of reality in two contrary directions, one of them encompassing the individual dimension of how that reality is perceived. This first direction begins with Diderot's well-known discussion of the mold thesis in *Thoughts on the Interpretation of Nature*. Here he inquires whether the mold is a preexisting reality—if not an ideal or supernatural cause—rather than the energy within a living molecule itself joined to dead matter. The consequence of this speculation will be clear in a moment.

The second direction inclines toward the cosmic dimension of reality as manifested in simple organisms like the polyp. Buffon is concerned with going beyond the continuity from one generation to its successor. More important than individual reproduction, the polyp's autogenesis yields a likeness so faithful that it epitomizes all of species-continuity for eighteenth-century thought. Insofar as a species requires preservation and continuity, its "power to produce its likeness" is uniquely displayed in the polyp. The chief focus now is not vital energy as such, but rather the evolutionary continuity furnished by resemblance. Buffon's polyp makes clear the "chain of successive existences of individuals that constitute the real existence of the species" (173).

Buffon elsewhere speaks theoretically without reference to specific animals or plants, but his thought regarding organic activity of all types is plain enough. Both kinds of matter contain "an inexhaustible fund of organic and living substance that is always reversible, a substance as real and durable as raw matter" (216). This substance is universally scattered, passing from the vegetal to the animal states by nutrition and returning thereto in decomposition. These details find support in Needham's comprehensive research, published in 1749 and aptly reflected by the title *Observations upon the Generation, Composition, and Decomposition of Animal and Vegetable Substances*.

But how does the "dead" matter questioned by Diderot enter into the universal vitality other than by some adjunct function of "living" matter? Logic cannot explain Buffon's scheme any more than a step-by-step account of each factor can explain the theory of universal gradation in Robinet and Le Cat. And yet even inert matter participates in the vital process through its nutritive role. It is not simply that "organic, living molecules exist in all organized bodies, combined in more or less large quantity with dead matter, more abundant in animals where everything is full of life, more rare in vegetation, where death dominates and life seems extinguished" (Varloot, 216). More fundamental than this is a pervasive influence that affects matter of all kinds: "there exists in matter a general force, different from that of impetus, a force that does not come before our senses and therefore that we cannot utilize, but which Nature employs as her universal agent." And again, "this force belongs equally to all matter, proportionate to a body's mass or real quantity" (216).

Buffon's position detaches itself from Newtonianism without denying it. The life force is neither gravity nor attraction, but belongs to an independent order. More important is the indwelling presence of this energy even in the "dead matter" that serves to nourish organic bodies. And what is reproduction or development if not a "more extended form of nutrition"? Like the swelling filaments of Needham's seed mixtures that burst into life, the generating process begins when "the parts have enough ductility to swell and extend" (186). Heat too is another type of force, subordinate but necessary to the production of living beings. The chief source of generative power is aether, which Hoffmann locates in the male seed. The subtle aethereal particles in semen have the "dynamic" capacity to activate the egg, and vital movement begins here (Duchesneau, 47–48). Vital energy, however, is the transcendent influence. By making this distinction, Buffon hints at the missing concept that sets his thought apart from the Newtonians. In addition to its belonging equally to all matter, "this force or rather its action extends to immense distances, decreasing as space increases."

The unnamed concept here is aether, and yet it leaps out from the sentence. Why cannot force itself be the element that travels immense distances instead of its action or effect? Several advantages are gained by incorporating the theory of aether into the concept of life force. The gain in terms of cosmological unity rests beyond the horizon of Buffon's interest in living forms. The immediate gain is to fuse the prototypal life energy requisite for survival with the sensory mechanism that is no less a requisite. This mechanism is the aether-determined common sensorium, which may be so dispersed that it is undetectable in its intangible microcosmic space. In fact, its composition is identical to what fills the macrocosmic space that Newton calls the immense "sensorium of God." This idea has wide currency in the eighteenth century. Bonnet repeats the identification of aether as the "divine sensorium" (Faivre, *Mystiques*, 232), while Formey calls God's sensorium "a kind of universal organ by which are executed all acts of His intelligence and will" (*Recherches*, 31).

The Sensorium as "Mind"

In contrast to Buffon, Diderot extended his horizon beyond the realm of energy in organic molecules. The same ideas about aether in the nervous system expounded by Hartley also give Diderot a springboard for speculation. If it is true that aether infuses all medullary substance, and if this substance is responsible for sensory organization, then the sensory behavior of polyps might well have a similar explanation. The subject is important and studied too little, notes Hartley. In animals of the "polypose" kind, like snakes, having comparatively negligible brain masses, Hartley finds that the sensorium may be equally diffused over the whole medullary substance. This must be inquired into more carefully, he adds (*Observations*, 1:32). Diderot's inquiry takes the sensorium as a starting point, with the polyp serving as a touchstone because its neural structure is simple to the point of blindness. But this deficiency seems not to affect its sensory performance, and the puzzle begins here.

Indeed, the polyp is observed to be photosensitive to objects external to itself even without vision. In complex organisms, the effect of light arises from the mutual impulsation of aether on optic nerve and this nerve on aether. But such impulses also involve skin friction as well as sight, tastes, smells, and sounds, says Hartley. The perceived object affects both the nerve and the aether, and these two affect each other. These events are meaningful signals to organisms equipped with a brain. The problem would now be: what about the polyp? Its sensorium, if any exists at all, is so diffuse as to demand a new functional assessment.

The sensorium was derived from the Scholastic concept of the common sensorium (*sensus communis*), located above the forehead and in front of the upper brain where the *fantasia* is situated, below which is found the *Imaginativa* (Yates, *Art of Memory*). As the material seat of the soul, the sensorium was located by Descartes in the pineal gland. For the seventeenth-century brain anatomist Thomas Willis, the common sensorium was located in the *corpora striata*, while in the early eighteenth century, François de La Peyronie (1709) and Giovanni Maria Lancisi (1712) located it in the *corpora callosum*.[9] The Lockean meaning of "sensorium," which dominates the eighteenth-century, is both physiological and psychological. It is the central receptor of sensations, functioning as a neural coordinator in the brain, and it is also the processor of sensations or impressions into higher-order perceptions and ideas. The step from sensory coordination to perceptual combination and association is material, being mediated by aethereal spirits. But no consensus existed regarding the passage from matter to mind, nor was there a clear evolution of the term in Great Britain and France. An early dissertation by Matthew Beare, *The Sensorium: A Philosophical Discourse of the Senses* (1710), states:

> *Objects* are perceiv'd by our *Senses* to move, insomuch as different parts of the *Object* striking on the same, or different Extremities of Nerves, successively cause different *Refluxes* of the *Spirits* to the *Common Sensorium*, one after another. All *Perception* is caused in the *Soul*, by the Motion which is excited in the *Nerves* and *Organs*; as likewise the *Reflux* of *Spirits* to the Brain.[10]

Much later the authoritative Hartley makes the sensorium a synonym of "sensitive soul," as John Yolton has indicated.[11] Its seat is in the brain,

---

9. This background is in Aram Vartanian, *La Mettrie's "L'homme machine": A Study in the Origins of an Idea* (Princeton, N.J.: Princeton University Press, 1960), 81, 210.

10. Quoted by John A. Dusinger, "Yorick and the 'Eternal Fountain of Our Feelings,'" in *Psychology and Literature in the Eighteenth Century*, ed. Christopher Fox (New York: AMS Press, 1987), 274.

11. The entire question of the physiology of Lockean representation has been examined

although it may be diffused in lower animals, where the medullary substance of the nerves and spinal marrow is much less than in the human brain. This suggests to Hartley that perhaps the marrow and nerves are instruments subservient to the brain, and so too the brain with respect to the soul. He gives the example of a person intent on his own thoughts who does not hear the sound of a clock—that is, sometimes a sensation is not registered when the brain is filled with something else. The implication is that Hartley is a dualist who "insisted that ideas and sensations are of a 'mental nature' while vibrations are corporeal," although the distinction is not clear (Yolton, *Thinking Matter*, 182).

The "common sensorium" for La Mettrie is anatomically mapped: "diverse territories where each one has its nerve, and receives and lodges the ideas brought via this tube" (*Histoire naturelle*, 66). Maupertuis identifies it as the place where the soul's perception takes place (*Oeuvres*, 2:207). For some philosophers, adds Maupertuis, it is the cause of perception in the "soul" or mind. Reciprocally, mental perceptions cause the sensorium to react and transmit impulses to the nerves, thus inducing motor responses. The *Encyclopédie* defines the "common sensorium" both as the place where animal spirits assemble and as the seat of emotions (15:31–32). In all such accounts, the complex system is obviously irrelevant to the polyp, where it is at best intangible, if not absent. The variables shift in their emphasis while a single factor remains constant. This factor is energy conversion, or the power to process signals bi-directionally. What then if the polyp's sensorium were radically more simplified? And what if the complex system of bidirectional external-internal signals actually depended on intangible if not immaterial factors that rendered a sensorium inconsequential altogether, present or absent? The questions are not idle because they placed Maupertuis and Hartley in different schools of opinion about the role of the sensorium. Either it functioned both in sensation and in abstract thought, or its role in the senses is as minimal as one of its definitions, which calls it a minimal "smear."

The sensorium suffered a further reduction in Diderot's flat remark that "very little is needed to form the *common sensorium*" (*Élements*, 9:318). By this fact, even a polyp appears able to dispense with that minimal medulla and still enjoy motility, phototropism, and epidermal sensitivity.

---

by John Yolton, *Thinking Matter: Materialism in Eighteenth-Century Britain* (Minneapolis: University of Minnesota Press, 1983).

In any event, the polyp lacks a brain, a fact that Diderot underscored in discussing sensory phenomena in the brain and cerebral nerves. Yet it performs, at its level of complexity, in conformity with the generally accepted model of the sensorium found in typical sources cited by Yolton. For instance, William Porterfield describes signal conversion as mediated by Newton's *materia subtilis* in the nerve fibers. An impression made on the external sensory organ produces an "undulation" or "refluctuation" of these spirits. When they reach the sensorium they produce the idea of the object that caused the impression. The commonplace example of light is usually given: it excites motions in the animal spirits, which are propagated through the fibers to the sensorium.

The polyp dispenses with the sensory process that depends on a nerve fluid diffused throughout the fibers and fibrillas. But even this relation between fibrillas and sensorium is unclear in Diderot's account. Diderot does not state plainly that the sensorium is composed of these threads filled with medullary substance, but, in reverse phrasing, says that "the state of the white fibrilla spread throughout the substance of the *common sensorium*, nerve fiber . . . varies" (9:313). The brain is merely a secreting organ that regulates the quality and amount of fluid, which in turn is the cause of diverse "spirits and characters." The unresolved relation of sensorium to filaments and fluids brings to focus the fluids themselves. The spirits are the only common element in both the polyp and the sentient organisms endowed with nerves and brain.

The dualism of Diderot's sensationalist thought carries him in opposite directions. The reason for this, it must be acknowledged, is not simply his complex and sometimes antinomial range of thought. His *Elements of Physiology* is, as mentioned earlier, a series of notes taken while reading treatises on the subject. But equally important are Diderot's commentary and stylistic quirks that modify his sources and set forth the equivocal state of physiology in its own terms. His chapter on the brain summarizes received knowledge about sensation. But his more eccentric definitions of sensory experience suit the atypical polyp better than they do organisms that function with a sensorium. His orthodox side is precise about the overall neural network. Here it seems plain that the internal-external communication is a complete circuit. Sensation "originates at the extreme of the affected nerve," and it "goes from bodily member to brain. It is necessary for the brain also to feel, where the nerves bring sensation." This receptive and perceptive capacity depends on a sensorium that is clearly cerebral. If a bodily member is affected, "its sensation goes to the brain.

If by some cause the sensation is revived when the member is missing, the sensation is carried back to its old origin and we feel pain" (9:311–12).

On the other hand, the polyp raises its head as the exception that imposes revised definitions. If Diderot repeats that sensation occurs through the nerves, he also shifts to a definition of sensory experience that subordinates structure. Pure vitality itself is the criterion, regardless of the mechanisms that give it form. Sensation now is "every operation of the soul, no matter which, that is born of its union with the body. To feel is to live" (9:311). Nerve fibres notwithstanding, the polyp lives and regenerates without them. And Diderot adds, "Life is, without the brain's presence because of loss by accident or illness, or because nature denies it [to the organism]. Foetuses without heads have been seen to live" (9:312). The secret must be discovered among less complex structures. And it must be at this level because the nerve fiber itself is nothing more than a "worm" in its structural form: "the nerve forms a whole, a complete animal with the medullary substance." This is living matter at its first stage, where it organizes itself through the "vital force that we imagine to explain organic crystallizations" (9:278). This force may be called "intelligent," in a manner of speaking. Thus it differs from the force that is active in forming mineral crystallization, as Diderot is careful to explain in a footnote. Other philosophers are still more convinced that the same force operates everywhere, as noted. The divided opinion perpetuates bafflement. When Hume mentions the subject of universal energy, he speaks of its effects without comprehending that active power. He adds that while Newton explains universal attraction by an aethereal fluid, it is only a hypothesis subject to further experiments (*Inquiry*, 84).

These descriptive facts come into conflict with one another only when they are viewed in a functional perspective. By requiring complex structures for sensory performance, an explanation saddles itself without particular jurisdictions and functions to be assigned to elusive faculties like the sensorium. However, by refocusing the perspective, many of those facts cease to interfere. In the new formulation, the terms change from structural forms to the nature of matter in the medullary substance. When the conceptual perspective involves vital force, the polyp's sensory and coordinating performance justifies Diderot's interest as much as any attention to higher organisms might.

These different organizing principles are best illustrated by Diderot's own remarks on perceptual coordination. Here the issues grow confusing and are formulated in terms of cerebro-neural activity. The sensorium is important, along with the brain as its seat, because of some coordinating ability therein. The organism's epidermis is affected by the external object, this effect is relayed to the organism's internal mechanism, and this mechanism "makes sense" of the event, which is to say it feels and responds successfully to the external event. This position, and what it implies for notions like intelligence and language, will cause little disagreement, provided they are applied to the use of sense data for organic performances that ensure life at all levels of complexity.

In this context, Diderot adduces two quite different formulations of what we might call a conceptual perspective. He is fascinated alike by animal amputations and by polyps that demonstrate successful performance despite a short-circuited or nonexistent nervous system. And he also returns to the brain and fiber theory in order to make these the responsible coordinators of the same performance. Yet the two disparate models mediate a single phenomenon of vital response. The level of activity is not at stake, but "life" itself is, and it is identified with sensation and the constituting purpose of all performance. Because the "soul" is the active operant toward that vital goal, its performance is that of a "mental" nature. The agent is "mind" as a general concept rather than as an anthropomorphic one. It emerges that a principle is needed for formulating the essential model of a mental process ascribable to all organic forms. And for this purpose it suffices to posit a coordinated performance in the organism that is fueled by assimilated sense data.

The Polyp as Sensorium

A general model of coordinated performance defers debate over the organism's complexity or lack thereof: it defers the issue of where to fix minimal levels of capability that might admit sensations, perception, idea, image, language, intelligence, and consciousness. This graduated scale is precisely what Goya violates by his concept of dreaming. Here another mode of cognitive performance becomes possible, although it need not be termed supernaturalism or the extrasensory experience of so-called unreal worlds. The Goyesque dream allegorizes the alternative to verbal language and its multisensory sources. The subject participates, as directly as the polyp does, in a vital reality that cannot be explained anatomically. The structural grounding in rational experience, sought by the philosophical naturalists, simply is irrelevant.

Insofar as this alternative relates to Diderot, it appears as a polarity. One conception puts Diderot in the cerebralist camp, while a second permits him to discount the brain in mental coordination. In the first case, "the images of things sighted take form in the eye and are perceived by the brain. The intervals of sounds are gathered in the ear and are grasped by the brain" (*Éléments*, 9:318). From this sensory centralization Diderot concludes that, "after having reflected well about it, the brain seems to me the organ that controls voice and serves as the intermediary of all the other senses" (9:318). But, he notes, experiments with this organ do not confirm any such critical role for the vital state in itself. Death should leave its imprint, and yet "we do not always perceive the brain's lesion in the corpse." The "sensibility and life" of severed bodily members survive apart from "the life and sensibility of the whole," as noted elsewhere in the battlefield image (9:322). Diderot concludes from this separation of sensibilities in parts and whole that "therefore what we call mind or spirit (*âme ou esprit*) is not the immediate motor cause either of sensibility, or of life, or of movement."

The essence of neural life—"to feel is to live"—lies elsewhere. Diderot cannot deny the usefulness of anatomical structures, but the energy they mediate has a prior urgency. This difference between structure and content is illustrated by what the fluidist theory calls nerve affluence. This concept presents difficulties for Diderot even though he accepts it, as noted earlier. Essentially he wonders where the fluid gets "its terrible energy" if the nerve is hollow. How does so limp a canal remain intact when it contains "so much violence"? There is yet another factor. If that "fluid produces sensation, where does the variety of sensations come from? What then does the form of the organ achieve?" (9:320). Diderot cannot reconcile it, except by regarding "the fiber as a worm" or an independent "whole." Here all inquiry must begin.

The simple fiber, the worm, and the polyp represent the most elementary structure known. All are basically structureless in that no smaller parts constitute the whole. The polyp demonstrates an organizing concept around "energy" rather than "form." The very intangibility of the concept, its ostensible lack of an existing substance, becomes an advantage because all types of organisms then may be judged by the same criterion. Even higher animals reveal crucial absences, invisibilities, or intangibilities that correspond to the polyp's diffuse sensorium. Delaroche's axiom is: "The movements of the nervous system communicate to one another by intervention of sensation and will." [12] No accounting of the physiology of will

---

12. Daniel Delaroche, *Analyse des fonctions du système nerveux*, 2 vols. (Geneva: Villard Fils et Nouffer, 1778), 1:57.

is given, nor can it be. Similarly, Delaroche defines the sensorium as that portion of the brain where the mind coordinates the movements of the nervous system. Yet by his own admission the mind or "soul" cannot be said to exist in a physical place because it is immaterial. Both the elusive will and the coordinating capacity defy material definitions.

The same intangible capacity demands explanation, with or without a cerebro-fibroid anatomy. It is accurate but incomplete to credit nerve endings, communicating fibers, and sensorium with making the external world intelligible to a performing organism. If the polyp is capable of responses without such an apparatus, if other mental operations such as dreaming also escape physiological grounding, and if "an immaterial and thinking substance" inheres in the body as Delaroche reports, then serious attention must be given to notions like vital force, aether, and related intangibilities that raise the status of the nerveless polyp to an important prototype (*Analyse*, 1:44–45).

The mutually exclusive polyp and sensorium clarify a problem in the hands of Diderot. Just as Hartley believes that polypoid animals may have the sensorium diffused through the medullary fluid, so Diderot conceives of the polyp as being all sensorium. Diffusion prevents neural activity from becoming differentiated and pinpointed. Because the polyp is photosensitive, its lack of organs of sight does not make it blind, and because it has regenerative powers, its lack of reproductive organs does not doom its survival. The polyp has no vital centers, but its performance manifests sheer vitality, the embodiment of the vital principle. This performative energy is the hub of a common problem for Diderot, Hartley, and scientists interested in generation. It is a vital energy inasmuch as the organism summons up the internal means to survive as living matter differentiated from external matter. And the power is a cognitive one inasmuch as the organism *knows* unconsciously how to use its material internality in the face of the external world, instead of dissolving once again into the original environment.

The concept of matter never disappears from discussion, nor does the concept of vital force that animates matter. The primary "sight" of living matter is general sensibility, and its basic unit is the polyp, the crayfish, or the fiber.[13] All such "wholes" harbor a cohesive energy that functions without fixed anatomical centers. At this primal level, discussions omit structure

13. The distinction Haller made between sensibility and irritability was of limited importance. See Chapter 7, section titled "The Secreting Brain," on the debate as it concerned function as opposed to impulse-convection by means of the animal spirits.

because the compelling issues are universality and continuity. One major concern is the vital force that pervades and connects all specificities. After that, there is the concern over the "Universal Language" that deciphers the connection between subject and object, or between the internal and the external worlds.

A special group of notes on the polyp crisscross Diderot's more ir-rationalist speculations. Diderot seldom indicates the sources of these notes, but this is not important because a pattern emerges that gains fur-ther nuance from his style. The general theme of touch intersects with the polyp's "blindness." Eyesight, in contrast, converges with the theme of imagination. And these two themes interlace with the fact that sight de-pends on the presence of a brain, which the polyp lacks. Diderot's fanciful notes push the physiology against a mythic horizon that silhouettes star-tling implications for cognitive theory. Now the polyp evokes the spider, the original thread-spinner symbolizing the universal brain that connects all things. As Robinet observes about the polyp, its metamorphic ability to assume fibrous and ductile forms makes it a nearly magical creature (*Nature*, 1:230). The spider-brain actually incorporates the universal force that preserves continuity, as we shall see. But Diderot's polyp, in his specu-lative moods, incorporates the Universal Language by which to "know" that continuity.

Remove the brain from a turtle, says Diderot, and it suffers "no other inconvenience than blindness. It lives" (*Éléments*, 9:314). Many animals have no brain at all, he adds, including the polyp, "which is indeed an ani-mal, for it seizes prey with the feet and brings it to the mouth. Moreover, the polyp's substance is not vegetal but flesh, like other animals" (9:331). The polyp's full-fledged animality must be established in order to make it a credible model for all sentient life. But the crucial power of the brainless animal derives from its alternative to eyesight. Even so, it does not sub-stitute for vision. Quite the opposite, "the polyp sees without eyes." The very concept of sight is reformulated, as if the power to see does not neces-sarily require external organs any more than verbal signs require visibility in order to be understood. Words may also be heard or inscribed as hiero-glyphs or signs, as Louis Braille later realized, just as objects may be felt, rendering readable language and vision superfluous.

This idea is repeated by Diderot. The subject-object relationship is exemplified in the animal pursuing its prey. It must know how to find the object, to make its way from the darkness of ignorance: "The polyp goes toward the light, presents itself at the place where its prey abounds. It feels the proximity of its prey. It avoids all obstacles. It is all eye" (9:331). More advantageous than having one or two eyes is to *be* an eye. Blindness for such a being is a meaningless condition. The ocular organ provides what is called "sight" to those organisms that otherwise are deprived of corporeal sign-reading power. But this dermoptic power effectuates something else, and whatever that effect may be, an organism already so provisioned has no need for an external ocular apparatus. The polyp is equipped organically with whatever constitutes the power that other organisms supply through the grace of eyesight. Thus Diderot devises the notion of *touchsight*. In his remarkable formulation, "Those who are without eyes see by the touch. An exquisite touch would substitute for all the [other] senses" (9:346).

The polyp may be eyeless but it is not sightless. The very idea of sight entails a metamorphic power of connections far removed from everyday notions of vision. Like the spider attached to the external world of its web, the polyp and its environment are connected tentacularly, in the etymological meaning of this word. It feels its way tentatively toward the light, a tactile movement through water guided by epidermal vision. But this vision is not ordinary vision. It is the product of the power of sight. Either an ocular or a tactile organ actualizes this visionary power. The result is a conversion, a true metamorphosis of sensation into a form of internalized knowledge. In its deeper meaning, "vision" relates to the eighteenth-century interest in such visionary experiences as apparitions and dreams. Phenomena of this kind are not actually sighted by the eyes but rather "seen" in the imagination. The immateriality of such in-sight opens a new chapter in the phenomenology of knowledge.

For the moment, let us observe that Diderot calls imagination "the inner eye" (9:373). In conventional terms, this is the "faculty of again seeing absent things" (9:346). At the same time, imagination suffers the limitations of eyesight. When Diderot passes from a general view of the entire object to the details of its parts, the object's clarity improves only to a certain limit before it begins to blur: "I said up to a certain limit because if attention is fixed on a very small part, the imagination experiences the same fatigue as the eye. The imagination is the inner eye. The degree (*mésure*) of imaginings is relative to the degree of sight" (9:373). It must be emphasized that studies on Diderot show that he prizes imagination, but his esteem for this value is associated primarily with the artist and aesthetician. Quite another role is imagination's function in cognitive psychology. Here the indispensable combinatory and ideational mechanisms attributed to the imagination are philosophically problematic. If eyesight and image-sight are exchangeable for touchsight, it becomes necessary to revise the concept of imagination as an image-making power—or rather, imagination does make images, but this faculty is as dispensable as eyesight for the polyp's purposes. And these purposes, to repeat, are cognitive insofar as a prototypal model for all living matter was pursued by eighteenth-century naturalists.

Required at this juncture is a physiological explanation of how the polyp's "universal language," so to speak, converts touchsight without relying on a sensorium or fibrous apparatus. Considering the deficient state of biological information at the time, the question borders on an irrationalist framework. The question is legitimately raised, however, when the context is an artistic representation, such as Goya's allegory of perception and its nonsensory alternative in dream. As the question of touchsight is addressed by Goya, it disregards the physiology of the dream process. It exposes instead Goya's own notion of a Universal Language, which is open to several interpretations, not necessarily supernatural. But there is also the scientific context for the polyp's touchsight, a context that is bolstered by the idea of a vital force. The vital energy functions as a universal web that literally connects all things by invisible but no less material threads. And if material, are they not also "tangible" threads insofar as this tangibility is apprehended by the minimal sensorium embodied by the polyp? Here too, of course, the lack of physiological data makes the scientific and irrationalist frameworks irreconcilable. Nevertheless, Diderot's characteristic versatility permits him to deal with each. His physiological notes are exact, and also contradictory, so that the final intelligible ties within his data remain a mystery. And when set alongside his disesteem for the brain's primacy, the result dampens hope for any explanatory system based on empirical evidence.

There is, however, an advantage to this irresolution for the history of ideas. It favors the Diderot who anticipates Goya, confirming one current in intellectual history that was to evolve toward radical irrationalism. Diderot confronts the polyp's monoesthesia and considers what it implies for the human analog. His verdict is rational in an important descriptive respect: "The man who is reduced to a single sense would be mad. Nothing would remain except feeling, a blind quality in the living molecule. Nothing is more mad than this" (*Éléments*, 9:375). This judgment reflects the conventional sanity that Diderot eminently personifies in his public life.

But scholars know what his private and posthumous writings signify for coherence-in-madness, and scholars know above all that madness is too nuanced a term to receive a superficial reading in eighteenth-century studies. To reduce man to a single sense would leave nothing "except feeling," expressed as *sensibilité* by Diderot. And sensibility, in its dual meaning, begins with the kinesthesics of touch—the dynamics of tactile sensation—and then extends to the physical impact felt when powerful or "touching" emotions are experienced. The blindness of "feeling" in these terms is harmful when extreme, but not entirely without insights. Madness brings its own intellectual sanity to the satirical vision of José Cadalso, to take one example.[14] Equally pertinent are the ravings in *D'Alembert's Dream* that impose their own coherence on the entire dialogue.

In Goyesque terms, the abyss of madness yawns nearer as the satirical savagery of *Capricho 43* dissolves into dream. Knowledge consorts with monsters just as the mind consorts with the chaotic elements of reality prior to their rational ordering. What the polyp knows may also be an inchoate reality. But its medium is the same spirituous matter, an aethereal substance, that produces dreams and that flows throughout the Chain of Being that is present in the Divine Sensorium. The rational order is preceded by the five coordinated senses that are regulated by organs missing in the polyp. Might this mean that something perceived less rationally is not an inchoate reality but rather another form of knowledge gained from one degree of touchsight within the gamut of subject-object relationships that ranges from monoesthesia to madness? The polyp knows an inchoate reality from its "polypose" brain, Hartley's term for a sensorium diffused all over the body. It exemplifies a possibility that Hartley never ruled out—namely, that the simplest matter can arrive at the intelligence of the human mind if matter were "endued with simple sensation" (Yolton, *Thinking Matter*, 196). The polyp's knowledge is pragmatically useless, if indeed disorder can be labeled a form of knowledge. Nevertheless it perceives light through sensory conversion, as a phototropic signal reduced to tactile language. Diderot repeats his remarkable statement: "I conceive a touch so exquisite that it would substitute for the other four senses. It would be affected diversely according to odors, taste, forms, and colors" (*Éléments*, 9:331). This time his fantasy ends with the image of the polyp that is "all eye"—which is to say, complete tactility. Its information is, to be sure, a

---

14. See Paul Ilie, "Cadalso and the Epistemology of Madness," in *Studies for I. L. McClelland*, ed. David Gies, *Dieciocho* 9, 1–2 (1986): 174–87.

minimal conversion of signals, but it belongs to the category of functional language discussed in the next chapter. At another level of conversion, Goya's nonsensory alternative whose perceptions are dream images, the information is signaled by what he calls the Universal Language.

Mind as Self-Designing Behavior

The higher significance of polyps stands out in Aram Vartanian's observation about "the intimate analogy established between the polyp's regenerative powers and the 'metaphysical' properties of matter."[15] The analogy exposes certain concepts of living form and self-organization that, for Vartanian, unfold most critically in La Mettrie. However, the materialist reduction of soul in La Mettrie coexists with a spiritualist concept of divine "guidance" in Haller that initiates what Shirley Roe calls a "preprogrammed sequence of development" in epigenesis (*Matter*, 44). While the term "soul" is avoided in Roe's treatment of Haller, the latter's belief in God makes him a spiritual vitalist when contrasted with Wolff's belief in the purely natural forces of generation. Furthermore, the concept of soul haunts both Réaumur's preformationism and Bonnet's Leibnizian explanation for the polyp's self-reproduction, as Virginia Dawson has shown. These concurrent positions make the theoretical flux in that period less decisive than the later historical resolution turns out to be.

This indecisive theoretical flux was described in the first section of this chapter, and one conclusion may be drawn from it now. It left no room for pure chance to be the generating matrix for life. Rather, some designing factor, whether mechanical or spiritual, was thought to govern organic matter. Dawson's book is important in this regard, for it shows how the larger philosophy of living beings was implicated in the discovery of the polyp. This is not to say that naturalists believed in a rational soul for the polyp. But the central question revealed by Dawson's historical trajectory is: Does sheer matter have an organizing principle? The question has repercussions that lead to fanciful speculation on the part of Diderot and Buffon, among others, before the end-of-century materialism takes root. René-Antoine Réaumur preserves the Cartesian dualism of soul and matter in his extensive study of insect life. Abraham Trembley investigates

15. Aram Vartanian, "Trembley's Polyp, La Mettrie, and Eighteenth-Century French Materialism," *Journal of the History of Ideas* 11 (1950): 508.

the polyp and makes the decade of the 1740s one of crisis and "metaphysical impasse." Charles Bonnet, Réaumur's disciple and Trembley's follower, discovers parthenogenesis. Réaumur's memoirs on the history of insects shapes the interest of an entire generation. These three protagonists contribute to what Dawson terms the "ragged Cartesian fabric of eighteenth-century biology." The fabric deteriorates under a more factual empiricism that conflicts with the older mechanism. One symptom of the conflict is Réaumur's dissent from the belief that animals lacked souls. Another symptom is Bonnet's dissent from Réaumur by seeking teleological explanations shunned by the master.

A final abstract from Dawson's research will complete the background necessary for the discussion that follows. All the biologists mentioned are "preformists," believers in the preexistence of germs. This theory of encasement varies from Malebranche to Leibniz, but it bolsters the precept of a *scala naturae*, with its denial of any lacunae or jumps from the realm of minerals to that of plants, or thence to the realm of animals and human beings. This worldview is idealist. It draws additional support from the Neoplatonist notion of plastic forces or controlling intelligences.[16] This world view is nonetheless obliged to confront the Cartesian tenet of an unbridgeable gap between brute matter and living matter, a gap produced by the doctrine of soulless animals whose generation is subject to mechanical laws.[17]

Despite the resistance to materialism's clear historical development, and despite the precise identification of individual doctrines and tenets, the historian of ideas is faced with an overarching difficulty. Which issues are dominant at the paradigmatic level and which are secondary? Most historians of science describe both kinds within the interlacing process of historical change. For this reason, the polyp is a welcome subject: it affords a framing perspective for overlapping issues. Both Dawson and Vartanian are concerned with the concept of soul in its progress toward a materialist redefinition. Thus the link between reproduction and sensible matter is observed to remain constant from La Mettrie to Bonnet; what differs is the

16. The little-recognized presence of Neoplatonism in the theory of neurophysiological signals can be found in the system formulated by Nicholas Hartsoeker, which enjoyed currency in Bonnet's Genevan milieu. See Virginia Dawson, *Nature's Enigma: The Problem of the Polyp in the Letters of Bonnet, Trembley, and Réaumur* (Philadelphia: American Philosophical Society, 1987), 163.

17. Support for refuting this doctrine exists in the works of the Jesuit Noël Régnault (*Entretiens physiques d'Ariste et Eudoxe*, 1729) and Father Ignace-Gaston Pardies (*Discours de la connaissance des bêtes*, 1672), which proposed that animals have souls capable of feelings and sensory knowledge. By 1724, Pardies's work had seven editions and by 1755 Régnault's had eight (Dawson, *Nature's Enigma*, 34).

notion of intelligence that mediates the link, whether this notion concerns the definition of matter, the dynamics of embryology, or teleology versus self-determination. Scholarly evidence addresses these and other biological and philosophical problems, which intertwine without preeminence or specific order of priority.

If any such order is possible, it will stem from the definition of intelligence or mind. Remote as the polyp may be from an ordinary definition, it becomes relevant in the philosophical context of that time. The concept of intelligence is derived from the idea of soul, but the idea of soul in lower living forms does not carry the same implications that attach to rational human beings. If rationality is a condition of conscious intelligence, the absence of rationality does not automatically exclude intelligent activity of a nonteleological kind. Intelligence in this sense need not be conscious in order to meet the requirements of a soul. At the most primitive level of organic generation, the idea of soul entails an ability to design, which is to say it reflects an intelligent ability that is not characterized by insensate, random chance. Self-reproductive matter with any degree of complexity, down to the lowly polyp, exhibits the presence of a "soul" in the semantic context of the philosophical debate.

This concept underlies diverse scholarly pursuits in the areas under discussion, as several examples will show. The concern with sensibility is shared by literary scholars and historians of science. A literary scholar who acknowledges the scientific roots of sensibility might make a preparatory study of the psychology of perception. However, a prior issue faces such a study. This issue concerns irritability and nerve anatomy, factors that circumscribe the larger debate over definitions of soul. Irritability manifests the "vital principle" that materially identifies animal life. The vital principle acts by animating otherwise inert matter, which explains why it is sometimes called "soul." Here it appears to be the intelligent agent that brings living matter to organic wholeness. But sometimes the vital principle is equated with germs said to contain the entire developmental program, as in preformationism. In that case, a Leibnizian conflation of soul and material germ in reproductive matter is implied.

Do these poorly meshed theories harbor an unstated glimpse of a contradiction—the identity between matter and soul? Whether they are identical or synonymous is a dilemma that finds a convenient locus in the polyp, a singularly apt subject of examination. The polyp's irritability and self-designing behavior returns us to the nature of matter itself, which now becomes a broad governing issue for the area under discussion. But here the intertwining issues mentioned in Chapter 6 resist logical ordering. Vartanian's study makes it clear that the polyp's importance lies in demonstrating how matter is endowed with self-determining powers of "design." But if we are further interested (as Vartanian) in the idea of evolution and its teleological distractions, the same study clarifies the polyp's role in announcing transformism and in upholding the Leibnizian scheme of continuity. The problem of matter may be related to the problem of transformism, but the historian's first concern is modification of these problems over a period of time. The logic that encompasses the lesser issue (transformism) within the greater one (matter) seems nearly metaphysical and beside the point.

A similar parity of prominence arises among issues contingent on the preceding ones. Regeneration is an issue that can be discussed either in the context of transformism and its competing theories or in the context of the nature of matter. The polyp's regenerative ability overlaps both contexts and blurs the order of discussion. The polyp is a link between animal and vegetal kingdoms, thus bringing to the fore the "scale of nature" as a valid model. Here then is the philosophical chain of beings reduced to a scientific question. But in what terms is the problem couched? Does regeneration prompt discussion of matter and its nature, or of genesis and development? When the polyp is cut into segments, it conserves its "vital principle." Which aspect of the soul must hold the conceptual foreground: the materiality implicit to the vitalizing soul, or the intelligence allowing an organic whole to "design itself"? Each aspect is an important problem for discussion, but in what order of significance? That the soul is material is suggested by the regenerating polyp whose vegetative soul seems divisible. This makes the soul constitutionally indistinguishable from the body's organization. However, matter is by definition inert, devoid of intelligence, and thus incapable of self-organization. On the other hand, suggests Vartanian, if La Mettrie and others denied that there is a supreme intelligence for such self-determination, where else but in matter could this agency reside?

These planes come into perspective in Dawson's analysis, where historical development also hints at an order of priority. Réaumur, a Cartesian tempered by Malebranche, believed that insects displayed intelligence. Bonnet attributed that display to God's providence. Pardies believed in an intermediate third substance that accounted for all such animal displays. By studying these naturalists, Dawson shows how the idea of soul advanced beyond the stages from Cartesian dualism, with its immaterial intelligence and animal automatism, to the mechanist materialism adopted by La Mettrie. For the historian, the "problem of soul" addresses the shifting relation between dualism and materialism. But as we shall see, the triumph of materialism does not eliminate the problem. The Bonnet-Réaumur dialogue revolves around two perplexing issues: generation and the soul's place in the regenerating process. These questions take a historical direction that bridges mechanist monism to the vitalism of both materialist biology and natural theology.

Here the polyp's self-restorative powers serve as a focus for different concerns. The fact of difference among these concerns needs emphasis. The polyp displays a generating life principle, and this may be attributed to a soul. But what of normal activity? The polyp also manifests a functional knowledge, an undefined ability to perform organically. In this developed condition it displays regenerative powers. Its nonrational knowledge, however, should not be confused with the generative and designing phases of development that Bonnet associated with a vestigial, Cartesian soul. The intelligence behind origins and design is a teleological problem that invites dualism at the level of divine responsibility. But the fully developed organism functions with a knowledge and intelligence that require hierarchical distinctions. Therefore the idea of a soul is expendable if such concepts as self-design, mind, and conscious reason, depending on the organism's level of complexity, are substitutes for it.

Certainly the distance between organic function and conscious intelligence makes it necessary to enforce hierarchical distinctions. Endowing the soul with materiality will not remove these distinctions. Impatience with dualism led eighteenth-century empirical thought gradually to set aside the idea of an unextended, immaterial soul. But the problem of mind remained. By abandoning the soul, science had merely replaced a metaphysical dilemma with an epistemological one.

Stated bluntly, the problem of soul was not solved by the historical trend away from the Aristotelian three-tiered soul (vegetative, sensitive, rational). The idea of a soul was tied up with a life principle. Bonnet, Réaumur, and their contemporaries also inherited the Cartesian proposition of the soul's rationality, which gave sentient organisms, polyps included, something more than vegetative functions. Intelligence was before anything else the assumption beneath design. Design merely actuated organic vitality. Behind this was an intelligence. It could be divine or natural, but its organizing ability resisted description and so seemed teleological. But then the same concept of intelligence also applied to the subsequent functioning of the organic whole. As the polyp reveals, functional behavior exhibits design both in regeneration and in irritability. Therefore, to abandon the idea of soul by endowing matter with self-organizing powers leaves the mystery of designing intelligence intact. The teleological coin merely turns over on its other face.

Teleology may be posed as a problem only if epigenetic development and mechanical function are explained by an immaterial, rational principle. Otherwise, generation and chance development are aspects of the problem of matter and its nature. The same problem of matter attaches to function insofar as function characterizes the organically designed whole. The Cartesian soul is not a suitable model for a directing, rational agent because it would be an immaterial intelligence. The explanation, rather, is that organized matter displays performative abilities. Organic performance indicates both sensory knowledge and emotive capacity, which comprise a form of prelinguistic cognition. And abundant literature in the seventeenth and eighteenth centuries affirms that animals, though deprived of reason, nevertheless express emotion and distinguish simple objects. Their constitution includes an "intermediate" third substance, in Pardies's term, that partakes of both brute matter and soul. Such intermediacy enables material souls to "feel their own existence," a belief held by Buffon though denied by Réaumur.[18] The implication is a monist one—that everything may be accorded to matter. Behavior itself then becomes the sign of intelligence. This attribution of intelligence to animals is too extreme for Réaumur and Bonnet, suggests Dawson, and their dissent perpetuates the idea of soul conflated with germ theory.

Put another way, the emergent biology as it crystallized in research on polyps entwines the principles of life and of intelligence. It posed problems more specialized than those addressed by Cartesian mechanism, thus circumventing dualism without eliminating it. Today that circumvention seems to be the "correct" component of natural philosophy that modern science would build on later. Thus scholars document how the Cartesian model became the source of mechanistic biology, and how at the same time it broke down in the path of advancing monism. Even so, the eighteenth-century impatience with metaphysics did not assist science in describing the physiology of mind and will. This is a failure that is not emphasized

---

18. Virginia Dawson, "The Problem of Soul in the 'Little Machines' of Réaumur and Charles Bonnet," *Eighteenth Century Studies* 18 (1985): 507.

by historians of science who regard the mind-body split as a philosophical issue rather than a scientific one.

In effect, to posit such a thing as a mind is to distinguish living matter from intelligent living matter. The distinction involves the mechanist capacity of matter to function as a whole, as distinguished from matter's prior capacity to organize and direct its generative development. The generative or regenerative ability, appearing to be an inexplicable power, is conventionally ascribed to a "soul." The distinction makes matter the crucial unknown in any inquiry into the living organism. And because it is preferable to begin inquiry with known factors, science formulates issues in terms of functional behavior and its physiological processes, rather than in terms of an intelligent, controlling agency. Among those processes, however, is the sensory-motor system, which is partly psychological and borders on the immaterial half of the dualism that is to be circumvented.

Here lies the implication of work on such diverse topics as Dawson's on biological continuity in Bonnet and Réaumur, Vartanian's on the polyp and on brain models in La Mettrie, Yolton's on materialism and the brain, Roe's on matter and generation, and G. S. Rousseau's on sensibility. These and related studies approach yet skirt the elusive principle of cognition in matter. Scientists were setting aside such notions as a life force and a directing soul in favor of new concepts: self-organizing design, functional unity, and motor force or sensory knowledge. These features composed a model that kept as separate unknowns the two Cartesian concepts of a life principle and a seat of intelligence. The materialists were prolonging, unintentionally, a dualism of their own.

Just how this occurred may be observed in the fact that, according to Vartanian, La Mettrie restated the problem of mind to be a problem of physics. This restatement did not shed light on how neurophysiology affects the mind. It simply imposed on psychology a mechanico-quantitative method as a *modus cognoscendi*. La Mettrie abandoned his early effort to solve the materiality of causes related to the life principle and to feeling or thinking. As Vartanian points out, he did keep the idea of a motor force, inferred from muscular irritability. In other words, he distinguished tacitly between motility and sensibility. The one relates to mechanical functions and reverts to the Cartesian model of brute conduct. The other implies sensibility but also, at higher levels, feeling and knowledge proper to the understanding and to the "mind."

In this way, materialists perpetuated dualism under a refurbished terminology, but they did not redefine Cartesian intelligence directly. Descartes had dichotomized the life principle into mechanical generation and behavior, on the one hand, and, on the other hand, an immaterial, rational soul. The idea of intelligence, synonymous with "knowledge," was reserved for human beings. In this scheme, living organisms did not require an inherent principle of intelligence in order to reproduce or to function physiologically. An external, divine mind directed that. Rather, the principle of vital functions remained separate from the principle of intelligence. Both these principles were identified nonetheless with the soul. In contrast, the materialists conflated these principles. The organism could be seen *ab ovo* as a functional unity of "selfhood" rather than as a body directed by an intelligent agent. Intelligence itself, then, could be redefined either as rational knowledge or as sensory knowledge. Whether rational *consciousness* might enter into such functional knowledge is beside the point at this stage in history, because teleological factors were dismissed.

It goes beyond this context to redefine intelligence in a way that dissociates consciousness from cognition. The essential point, perhaps requiring further argument in another context, has been overlooked. As biology grows more "scientific" in the eighteenth century, it finds a replacement for both mechanical reductionism and teleological models, and this replacement is functionalism. But functionalism permits a dualist inference: now behavior defines intelligence. Intelligence is a binary capability that embraces subrational as well as consciously human knowledge. The sensory-emotive knowledge of brutes is never explained satisfactorily by mechanical reductionism. Yet the debates that might have clarified the subject, such as the Haller-Wolff debate, took place on prior grounds in generative theory. Even here, the "source-of-organization" problem was never solved by Wolff's epigenesist successors (Roe, *Matter*, 155).

This basic point is often submerged beneath the details of generation theory. Confusion arises when the concept of soul casts its shadow across both the generating principle and the principle of unified intelligence. The historian of science describes the confusion instead of sifting the factors that set reductionism apart from the mentalist factors that elude scientific analysis. It is instructive to observe Dawson's description of variances between Réaumur and Bonnet. According to Dawson, Réaumur believed in limited insect intelligence, defined in terms of behavior. Bonnet, on the other hand, criticized the idea of such intelligence and explained mechanical behavior in animals as being providential. The disagreement did not, however, extend to the principle of life, which was not an issue here. The problem was rather the existence of a soul that directed organic functioning in an already developed vital whole. The debate was whether such self-regulating direction approximated nonconscious intelligence on purely material grounds.

But there was also another concern of Bonnet that, as Dawson documents, brought the principle of life into play. Bonnet's research displayed "voluntary movements" in worms after their heads were cut off. The question posed by Bonnet to Réaumur was where the "self" or "soul" resides in these severed parts, given the ability of a headless segment to regenerate the worm into an organic unity. At this point a subtle shift occurs. The term "self" serves in the place of "soul" to refer to the functional seat of the organic whole. More significant still is that Bonnet now also speaks of "germs" that conventionally were held to predispose matter toward the organism's design. He does not speak of the soul in this primary stage. Instead, the germs are inexplicably activated to produce a new head, which, in turn and fully developed, will house the power comparable to a soul. How this germinating activation comes about is crucial. It supposes a life principle that animates the germs. The germs in turn control general morphology, including the cephalic formation that will house the functional power of the organic whole. No longer is the question whether a soul directs behavioral intelligence, as in the previous case of Réaumur's insects, which are already fully organized living matter. Now the question becomes one of life's beginnings and the regeneration or reproduction of life. These processes concern matter still developing toward the eventual organism alleged to be functionally intelligent. It is not yet a question of the organism functioning as a unity and perhaps displaying intelligence.

The difficulty Bonnet does not recognize is the continued dual condition of matter, first as generating life, and only afterward as an organism that functions in its sensory-motor-cognitive wholeness. This distinction seems not to impress historians of science. Dawson is willing, for instance, to allow the term "soul" to characterize both conditions. For her, the issue is Cartesian, with the soul remaining apart from inert, passive matter. In this perspective, both the soul and the life principle represent the same concept. The soul is identical with the germ: both terms denote the generative agent responsible for matter's ability to organize or design itself. The term "soul" is used justifiably in this way, but the same term is also applied when the fully designed organism functions intelligently. A single concept is made to govern both the self-designing event—the source-of-organization—and the functional intelligence manifested after organic unity is achieved.

These elements are sorted out by Réaumur. It is possible "that in the germ appropriate to become a head, is a soul which will not be in a state to exercise its functions until the germ of the head has developed, has acquired the power to carry on the functions of the head, becoming that of an animal" (apud Dawson, "Problem of Soul," 515). Réaumur's hypothesis avoids Bonnet's question about the animal's unifying principle and self-hood. Dawson observes that this question revealed the weakness of the Cartesian distinction between extended matter and nonextended soul. But she asserts this weakness on the mistaken grounds of Réaumur's views of germ theory and development: "granting soul to specific parts of the animal involved a plurality of souls. No longer could one soul explain the functional unity of the whole" (516). "Functional unity" is not really the crux at this juncture. Function, as used elsewhere in Dawson's discussion, refers to the behavioral intelligence exhibited by normally organized insects and animals after they are generated. But now Réaumur is speaking of generation itself, and of whether souls are responsible for providing that wholeness and unity. The self-designing role is not equivalent to "functional unity." The latter pertains to behavior after the organism achieves unity and self-hood. The worm's sudden decapitation returns it incapacitated to the generative and developmental stage, where the soul awaits animation by the germ. In sum, regeneration is not a behavioral trait of the unified whole, but rather a property of vital matter. This point, nevertheless, could not be admitted by the conservative Réaumur or Bonnet.

The metaphysical question must be kept separate. It is true that, in human beings, an immortal soul may be posited to coexist with embryonic development, but there is no analogy with worms and polyps to warrant use of this term by those who hold that idea. Rational and subrational organisms exhibit common traits by having animate, vital functions. The degree of intelligent behavior varies in complexity, so that human intelligence may be attributed to a rational soul. But at this level, intelligence no longer involves reproduction and self-design. The musings of Réaumur and Bonnet dared not lapse into materialism. But their work permitted a later age to detach the concept of soul from generation and free it to describe behavioral intelligence exclusively. This formulation shows the true significance of research on the polyp at that time. The polyp removed the concept of "mind" from the metaphysical Cartesian soul by reclassifying "soul" under material, functional intelligence. And whereas "intelligence" and "mind" remained elusive terms, their attributes nevertheless entered the physiological field where functions were newly defined by such categories as irritability, motility, and sensibility. The close affinities among these categories have been examined in the earlier sections of this chapter. It remains for the next chapters to examine the language of sensibility, both as a signaling process and as a "universal" language that hypothetically can remove the mind-body division.

9. The Epistemology of Aether

> Between a *spiritual substance* and a *material substance* there is no difference other than the one we assign to the modifications or the ways of being of a selfsame substance. . . . What is material can insensibly become spiritual. —La Mettrie, *Histoire naturelle de l'âme*

> The Aether is a Proteus, transforming itself into everything."
> —Bussy, *L'éther ou l'Être suprême élémentaire*

The fact that a notion like that of aether, like the idea of God, persisted beyond the Enlightenment suggests that its rationale had satisfied a permanent need through centuries of changing world views. From the Pythagorean aether surrounding the astral body to the Newtonian aether filling space, the same concept of a quintessential substance validated differing cosmological and scientific systems. The belief in many diverse aethers in eighteenth-century science extends the concept's significance for intellectual history beyond any single theory. By the end of the century, a philosophical poem in five cantos was published by Martin de Bussy under the title *L'éther, ou l'Être suprême élémentaire*. The concept continued to be advocated in different forms in the nineteenth century and later still.[1]

Scholars will have to decide how seriously to regard this concept beyond its undular postulate in Newton's corpuscular or emission theory of light. Historians of science will be the most skeptical, for they must consider aether in the rigorous terms of its evolution in classical physics as the explanation for thermal, electrical, and chemical phenomena. This perspective will look askance at the epigones of Ancient Theologies and the alchemical principles propped up by philosophical animism. Nevertheless, the aethereal premise survived, *mutatis mutandis*, throughout the Enlightenment and indeed until the end of the nineteenth century. Thus the emphasis G. N. Cantor placed on the mid-eighteenth century, where the

---

1. See the articles in G. N. Cantor and M. J. S. Hodge, eds., *Conceptions of Ether: Studies in the History of Ether Theories, 1740–1900* (Cambridge: Cambridge University Press, 1981).

theories of Newton and Boerhaave attracted most attention, is explained by "the unifying role of ethereal fluids" in natural philosophy ("Theological Significance," 151). Political historians, for their part, have not ignored this "eccentric" component in the broad movement of European Freemasonry.[2] And from the standpoint of literary criticism, readers interested in the aesthetics of the creative imagination have found the survival of the aether concept a significant event for certain Romantic, occultist, and exotic manifestations in modern literature.[3]

How, then, do these varying perspectives affect the status of aether as a topic of investigation? Clearly all scholarly camps must agree that the concept is crucial to the history of ideas, if only on the grounds of a single convergence. Without aether to explain the operations of matter and spirit, science and religion were bereft of a principle that mediates two otherwise incommunicable worlds. If science repudiated dualism in its materialist ambition, and if dualists of all stripes insisted on some kind of incorporeal transcendence, then aether must count among the chief vehicles for explaining the inexplicable. The perennial mind-body problem may begin to unravel starting with this particular knot.

It is instructive to note that aether continued to have significance for physicists, biologists, and psychologists alike until the mid-nineteenth century. An experiment by Casimir Chardel reported in the journal *Psychologie physiologique* adopted the premise that fire is constituted by aether in order to report "a kind of light flame, apparently the dying man's soul united with his intelligence." This report found its way into a treatise on electricity and matter by Louis Goupy who, in 1854, brought into the same context his knowledge of Humphrey Davy, Luigi Galvani, and Franz Mesmer. The pertinent factor for eighteenth-century studies is the later blossoming of a Romantic organicism that appears to have its origins in Bonnet and, more generally, in a vitalist Chain of Being. Electricity, by its positive and negative forces, not only "has produced worlds but can once again produce them." Furthermore, it "determines the evolutions of light and fire, the life and death of plants and animals, the formation and the movement of all bodies, their conflagration and the decomposition, whether by fusion or by volatilization." In a word, the forces of electricity "animate and conduct

2. See Margaret Jacob, *The Radical Enlightenment* (London: George Allen and Unwin, 1981), 223.

3. Barbara Stafford, *Voyage into Substance: Art, Nature, and the Illustrated Travel Account, 1760–1840* (Cambridge, Mass. and London: MIT Press, 1984), 462–53.

the entire universe under God's orders, just as our entire limbs are under the orders of our will."[4]

At this juncture, what may appear to be zany physics from an empirical standpoint was at the same time both a preservation of the Mesmerist project for magnetism in the preceding century, and a "scientific" crutch for Faustian demonism among late Romantic currents.[5] The belief prevailed that "our brain transmits" the commands of our will "either by emitting electricity to our extremities or by retracting it just as quickly." Goupy's hope was that "in the name of magnetism we may learn to emit it beyond ourselves" (L'éther, 38). In terms of eighteenth-century science, Newtonian aether or "electrical fire" lost none of its material force when accounting for events in the cosmological scheme of things. Whereas empirical physics and chemistry cut away the more vitalist-prone activities of aether, the emerging neurophysiology no less than the undying Hermetic tradition did the contrary, by adhering to properties that addressed themselves to the mind-body dilemma.

These properties can be analyzed under three headings. For physiology and for brain anatomy, the evidence John Yolton presents constitutes a fund of texts that invite further analysis.[6] Because Yolton deals primarily with Great Britain, a second category of texts drawn from French thought will anchor the field of inquiry for at least Western Europe, including Spain and Portugal. Finally, the Hermetic tradition, with its Neoplatonic physiology penetrating late seventeenth- and eighteenth-century thought, can be viewed in connection with Newton in order to bridge the apparently inmiscible currents of empiricism and Ancient Theology. A brief inspection of Newton's own conjectures will also be helpful for hints of their intellectual implications rather than for their physics. Granted Newton's empirical aim of explaining gross matter by an "elastic" and "electric" spirit, his nontechnical pronouncements on aether serve as reminders that the alchemical tributary to his general cosmology is far from negligible.

4. Louis Goupy, L'éther, l'électricité, et la matière, 2nd ed. de Quare et inventis (Paris: Chez Ledoyen, 1854), 38–39.

5. Stuart Peterfreund studies the reappearance of energy as a concept both in theology and in Blake and Coleridge, the latter "an opponent of the Newtonian synthesis," in his "The Re-Emergence of Energy in the Discourse of Literature and Science," in Science and the Imagination, ed. G. S. Rousseau, Annales of Scholarship: Metastudies of the Humanities and Social Sciences 4 (Fall 1986): 22–53.

6. My approach to the issues raised by Yolton in his Thinking Matter: Materialism in Eighteenth-Century Britain (Minneapolis: University of Minnesota Press, 1983) is to analyze his quotations of primary sources in the context of related issues raised by my own sources, both British and French.

Perception and "Subtile Matter" in British Neurophysiology

Newton's theory of aether is a subject in itself, most of it generating subsequent work in mathematics and physics, such as Robinson's technical dissertation of 1743, but also affecting biblical studies. More pertinent to epistemology is Newton's integration of alchemical and Hermetic ideas with mechanical philosophy, studied at length by Betty Dobbs. By assimilating the Neoplatonic notion of air to mechanics, Newtonians could postulate aether's mediation in animal spirits. This point is discussed later in detail. The mediatory role of aether was seized on by the Enlightenment in an otherwise technical discussion of its chemistry in the *Encyclopédie* (6:51–54). The four-page article credited Newton with experimenting on heat conduction in a vacuum in order to confirm the existence of aether. Its elastic property was ascribed to a rarer and more fluid character than that of air, thereby endowing the nerve fibers with their elasticity.

The question of emphasis certainly influenced the *Encyclopédie*'s handling its entry for aether. Being bound to both precision and scope within limited print space, the article required a sense of proportion for its design to be minimally comprehensible to the intelligentsia. The significant point is that the Encyclopedist perpetuated a neurophysiological role for aether.[7] Despite the article's dominating stress on empirical science, it notes that some philosophers regard aether as a fifth element, both spirituous and subtle. Readers not trained as scientists could easily have come away impressed with the vague and barely credible status of this substance as a demonstrated reality. The article calls it "subtile matter that, according to many philosophers, begins at the confines of our atmosphere and occupies the entire expanse of the heavens" (6:51). Some thinkers limit it to the beyond, others believe that it penetrates the pores, and yet others hold that it does not exist except as air. In short, aether is a "hypothesis," and consequently "physicists take the liberty of imagining it according to their fancy." As for "the so-called philosophical aether," it is like all other matter,

---

7. The *Encyclopédie*'s article "Astrologie" reflects the idea of effluvia and planetary light determining the rarefaction and condensation of air on Earth. See Herbert Leventhal on fire, air, and aether, in his *In the Shadow of the Enlightenment: Occultism and Renaissance Science in Eighteenth-Century America* (New York: New York University Press, 1976), 61, 182–84. The closely related ideas of light and fire as fluids makes terminology in all these texts a problem framed clearly by Roger K. French's discussion of the auras, aethers, heat, and light of an earlier age, where the lessened differences among fire and spirits reflect the intermixing of unstated macro- and microcosmic premises. See French, "Ether and Physiology," in Cantor and Hodge, *Conceptions of Ether*, 111–34.

distinguished only by its "tenuousness." For the nonscientific reader, these intangible qualities would have made aether an appropriate model for any nonmechanical or immaterialist explanation of the universe and of sentient beings in particular.

The Newtonian theory summarized by the Encyclopedist also includes aether's property of exerting pressure, by which gravity occurs, as well as its well-known function in transmitting light through vibration. But these facts hold no interest for biologists, poets, or philosophers. Put another way, the technically scientific account does not eliminate the conjectural elements of an aethereal epistemology. The conjectured "philosophical aether" figures among the received ideas of the day and is respectable enough to be acknowledged by the Encyclopedist. Indeed a wider survey of texts alluding to aether in the eighteenth century reveals a scale parallel to the one displayed in the *Encyclopédie*. Those texts also reflect Newton's original proportion of allusions to the vaguer properties of aether. What is preserved in the texts pertains to cognitive processes, and more generally to organic functions and perhaps even to systemic schemes bearing vitalist overtones.

These considerations lead us to the wealth of information furnished by John Yolton's study of "thinking matter" in Great Britain. The staggering labor of reading, processing, and comparing so many sources is an achievement not easily matched for other nations. The concomitant task of synthesizing Yolton's material raises questions of method, as I shall suggest, but the issues and his conclusions seem indisputable. Of the methodological questions just hinted at, there are only two, and one of them is philosophically too sophisticated for this book. It concerns the easy interchange of the notions "physiology of thinking" and "physiology of acting." The problem posed by Yolton must be accepted on his terms—namely, that almost all authors contended that there was some material connection between thought and action. However, another philosophical issue remains unattended. Should a distinction be made between will and desire, on the one hand, and perception and ideation, on the other? This question requires a separate format for discussion, but the distinction affects the handling of Yolton's evidence.

A representative piece of evidence is Langrish's "warning against settling for vibration alone in the physiology of thinking and acting."[8] Here the terms of discussion are whether there is some connection between

8. Cited in Yolton, *Thinking Matter*, 180.

thought and action. However, Yolton's context sets aside thought as perception. His context is Langrish's belief that the aethereal matter secreted by the brain is a nervous fluid like animal spirits, and that "at the command of the will, it moves as quick as Lightening" to the muscle fiber. In sequence, Yolton speaks of a Hartleyan caution against the belief that "animal spirits carry the messages of our will," for reasons of slowness. Again, he paraphrases: "there is no time gap between my will or thought to move my arm and my arm moving" (*Thinking Matter*, 181). At no moment is sensationalist perception evoked for the purpose of describing the physiology of "thinking" in the conventional terms of reason, imagination, and memory.

If there is no time gap in the physiology of either acting or thinking, can some key to the reason be found in the concept of aether? In studying the problem of motion and its control in physiology, Roger French points out that Hartley provided a mechanical basis for associationist psychology by allowing aether to replace traditional nervous spirits in transmitting medullary changes to the soul.[9] However, the problem regarding the interaction between body and soul still remained. The dualist difficulty may be extended analogously to the conflated relation between will and ideation, or, in Yolton's terms, between the physiology of will that leads to doing, and the physiology of sense-perception that leads to thinking.

Yolton's study is important for demonstrating the link between thinking and doing required by the British materialists. None of his authors successfully explain how, by "willing and acting, by *taking thought* I cause the spirits to move in specific ways or the aether to vibrate in specific nerves and muscles" (*Thinking Matter*, 203). I italicize the phrase "taking thought" to stress the imperceptible synonymity attributed to willing and thinking. Both take place in consciousness, and both presumably are cerebral events. But in Yolton's evidence thinking usually occupies a context shaped by perceptions and ideas. Yolton's conclusions focus on the doctrine of correspondence, and the key phrases used for Priestley include "perception," "association," and "correspondence" of "sensations and ideas" with vibrations (196–97). That is, "thought" is said to arise from the sensory-ideational circuit of physiology and psychology. None of this necessarily pertains to acting, which concerns the muscular movements attributable to the "near-autonomy of physiology." Of course, Yolton understands well the distinction I am making. His final remarks avoid specifying

9. French, "Ether and Physiology," 123.

any sequence of sensation-impression-idea, but instead he refers to a generic "interference with our physiology." The generalization exposes the gap separating will from thought, and consequently the gap returns us to the texts where acting and thinking are documented interchangeably.[10]

The distinction between cerebration and motor neurology is important for reading Yolton's evidence from the standpoint of ideation. The competing models of animal spirits and vibrations (including aether-induced vibrations) coincide in the notion that a *materia subtilis* regulates nerve activity. If aether is responsible for thinking in the restricted sense I have defined, then its agency should be differentiated from the neural activity responsible for motor response. By thus differentiating, we can perhaps isolate the engrammic function of the subtle matter from other functions, such as sensory transmission and neural messages to the muscles. Yolton stresses repeatedly that no satisfactory explanations were advanced for the nature of ideas, or for the causal link between the mental and the physical (204): "no one was very clear about how intentions and volitions do fit into or help cause actions" (194–95). The uncertainties Yolton reports refer to muscular motion. In the case of Alexander Stuart, "we are not told how the mind controls the animal spirits, how its action is a substitute for the mechanical starting of the impulse" (173). In the case of Browne Langrish, "he does not think anyone has yet explained muscular motion" (173), and, "how the will gives the impetus to the animal spirits, Langrish does not know" (175).

This group of uncertainties stands against the neurology of cerebration itself. It may well be that the same cerebral mechanism controls both the act of willing, which leads to action, and the act of perceiving, which leads to thought in the standard sense of the word. Nevertheless, at least two different kinds of neural impulses are implied in Yolton's bipartite sequence for his summary statement based on Thomas Reid: "without nerves to muscles we cannot move; without nerves to sense organs we cannot perceive" (184). Reid's post-Hartleyan importance lies more in his views on perception than on motor action, or so Yolton's treatment indicates. Reid describes the "material part" of perception as a sequence "from object, to sense organ, to nerve, to brain." This physiological process results in "impressions." However, Reid cannot account for "mental perceiving," and he cannot specify the nature of the correspondence between impres-

---

10. The philosophical distinctions are taken up in detail by Yolton in *Perceptual Acquaintance from Descartes to Reid* (Minneapolis: University of Minnesota Press, 1984).

sions and the perceptions that support his sign theory of ideas (195). This aspect of "thinking matter" is surely at the heart of the subject, and I hope to show that the role of aether lurks in the background even when it is not mentioned.

In the discussion of British physiologists that follows, my purpose is to establish a comparison for French thought and not to reexamine Yolton's evidence by checking into his primary sources. Some of these I have in fact studied first hand, as in the case of Hartley and Reid, but for other sources I rely on the ample quotations in Yolton's book, trusting their thoroughness and their representative nature. English texts, therefore, are quoted in Yolton's original context, with page references to his book. Supplemental quotations from Hartley and Reid are cited in their original editions, as are all French quotations cited later.

The imprecise terminology of Yolton's very sources is responsible for the uncertainty surrounding "the physiology of thinking and acting" that Yolton quotes and paraphrases. A lexical analysis of quotations from all authors suggests that adjectives like "subtle" and "rare" are the controlling terms for all transmissive and transmissible matter, whether defined as fluid spirits or as aether. The shared terminology exposes an unnoticed kinship between the rival theories of animal spirits and aethereal vibration. A book-length study of these authors would be necessary to come up with a composite view of how they believed the brain functions either to vibrate the aether or regulate the bodily fluids. Four kinds of fluids are identified by the French physiologist Claude-Nicolas Le Cat in his treatise on sensations and passions. The two pertinent fluids are *fluide moteur* and *fluide sensitif*, the chief instrument of the soul (*Sensations*, xx–xxi). However, in some accounts the elastic fluid is aether itself. Thus, to study the British authors for their view of whether the brain "filters" from the blood the animal spirits or the aether would expose the same uncertainty that surrounds "thinking matter." Even the nerve-chord vibrationists, who discounted any medium at all, believed in a generating first impulse from a rare substance, as did George Cheyne, and if not, they conceded the possibility of nerve fluid.[11]

---

11. Yolton, *Thinking Matter* 179, 181. Such uncertainty extends to the definition of "mind" as this word was employed from Locke's day to Johnson's. The connection between "mind" and "soul" in Raleigh's definition "wins full assent" from almost every speaker in the *Dictionary* except Locke, who submits a "minority report," according to Robert De Maria. The definition entered by Bentley is typical: "There is something in our composition, that thinks and apprehends, and reflects and deliberates, determines and doubts, consents and denies. . . . [T]hese powers of *cogitation*, and volition and sensation, are neither inherent in matter as such, nor acquirable to matter. . . . Senses and perception must necessarily pro-

To repeat, an unperceived kinship seems to reconcile the rival theories of animal spirits and aethereal vibration, but this link applies notably to the "thinking matter" lodged in the brain and medullary nerves, rather than to the neural medium between brain and muscles. The most striking example is William Porterfield's advocacy of a "Refluctuation of the Spirits, or of Newton's *materia subtilis* in the Nervous Fibrils, which reaching the *Sensorium*, gives us the Ideas of objects" (171). The striking fact is that Porterfield is not a vibrationist, but joins those who explain perception by animal spirits. Yet some vibrationists also attribute a pulsating force to Newtonian aether rather than to a spirituous, liquid flow. The "vibrating motion" of "aether in the nerves" is "propagated," according to Bryan Robinson, while for Henry Pemberton there is a "Pulsation and vibratory Motion of this Spirit through the whole Nerve." What the fluidist Porterfield terms "refluctuation" is for the vibrationists a "pulsation" that is "propagated." But in all cases, aether is the medium.

The crux of these differences seems unrelated to the nature and name of the transmitting medium. The crux is rather, in this instance, the difference between a fluctuation, a pulsation, a vibration, and a propagation. Add to these the gamut of terms used by other British authorities— "undulation," "propulsion," "impulse," "tremor," and "attraction," as well as such verbs or participles as "reflected," "flying into," and "impelled toward." Undoubtedly, a vibration cannot undulate, any more than a fluctuation can pulsate, but they both can apparently be propelled or impelled like waves, and they both can propagate tremors. The confusion fills in Pemberton's belief in Newton's "elastic Spirit," which is of course aether but which achieves both "Pulsation and vibratory Motion." And the contradiction itself is blatant when Robinson allows fluid to vibrate: "vibrating Motion of a very elastic Fluid" (178). Ambiguity or worse presides among the French fluidists, as we shall see later.

The debate between vibrationists and fluidists can be reduced to the character of the motion achieved by neural matter and the velocity of this motion. The debate concerns motor response, and not perception or ideational activity. The crucial issue was the speed by which messages traveled to the muscles, and whether nerve chord vibrations better accounted for

---

ceed from some *cognitive* substance which we call spirit and soul." The minority definition by Locke considers it "suspect" to define the soul as "a substance that always thinks" because men find they spend much of their lives "away from thinking." See Robert De Maria, Jr. *Johnson's Dictionary and the Language of Learning* (Oxford: Clarendon, 1986), 93.

simultaneous willing and acting than did fluid transmission. Cheyne alone opted for vibration unaided by an intermediary, and he did so only "seemingly," according to Yolton (179). Even the anonymous book by Long or Hartley conceded probability for both explanations, although favoring chord vibrations (181). But the nouns and verbs describing the transmission and its speed were not determined by the constitution of either animal spirits or aether. Both substances were depicted as highly rarefied particles, and both were said to display instantaneous velocity, according to their advocates, who did not challenge each other with respect to perception. The problem concerned muscular motion and whether particles are "impelled" and go "flying into the Nerves" (Langrish), or whether they are "propagated" (Robinson) or simply moved as "excited Pulses" (Pemberton). Yet a final contradiction: animal spirits move "by attraction" (Stuart) while "attractive powers" also inhere in the aether of muscular membranes (Robinson).

In the last analysis, Yolton cites an ultimate agency, Priestley's "force and power," and Diderot's "energy," regardless of how they are transmitted. The same generating power is cited by Cheyne, who insists that "the first *Impulse* proceeds from the *immaterial Substance*" (179). The century ends with the mind-body problem unresolved, or resolved by a return to the age-old existence of an occult power. What this ultimate agency was, by implication, can be deduced from a lexical review that sifts the stances adopted toward animal-spirit flow and aethereal vibrations, as they are presented by Yolton's evidence.

British authors employed many names for aether, sometimes designating it as Newtonian. Thus, among the Latin names, we find Newton's *materia subtilis* (Porterfield, Cheyne), Newton's *spiritus quidam* (Cheyne), and Newton's *Spiritus Subtilissimus* (Cheyne). Newtonian "subtile matter" was also called "spirits" (Porterfield), or else a "subtile, rare, and elastic Spirit" (Pemberton). These terms are associated with the qualities of Newtonian "infinitely rare and elastic Fluid" (Cheyne). (I record the authors' nomenclature without reference to their advocacy of aether.) The same "very elastic Fluid" is equivalent to a "very Elastic Aether" (Robinson). The trait of elasticity loses prominence, however, when the rarefied quality is stressed. Thus an equivalency arises for "the *aethereal Medium* in the nerves," which is "the most Subtile Matter in the Universe" (Langrish). The context is motion in all instances except Porterfield, who discusses aether in its sensory function.

It bears repeating that a rigorous distinction between "thinking" as ideational perception and "thinking" as willing a muscular action is crucial for this review. All the terms for Newtonian aether are accompanied by their stress on its subtlety. The stress is of overriding importance in the theoretical shift from animal spirits to aether. In the case of Langrish, he rejects at first Robinson's elastic aether in preference for a "Subtile, volatile, spirituous Matter, as animal Spirits secreted from the Blood by the glands of the Brain." Later, when Langrish assimilates aether into the earlier account of animal spirits, he calls it "the most refined matter in nature" (Yolton's paraphrase). Its speed is "as quick as Lightening" (180). The equivalence of subtlety and animal spirits is commonplace: Martin calls them "the finest and subtlest Parts" of the blood in the brain, while in the nerves they move as "an exceeding fine and invisible Fluid" (171). It is therefore no surprise that Porterfield equates animal spirits with the Newtonian *materia subtilis*. It is true that Stuart speaks of "nervous fluid" as the animal spirits that are "an aqueous fluid" moving from brain to muscles (173). But Langrish, in his fluidist period, refers to the "Subtile, volatile, spirituous Matter, as animal Spirits" (174). "Subtileness" or subtlety, moreover, is compatible with fluid, as Cheyne indicates by the interchangeable "*Materia Subtilis* or *Liquidum Nervosum*" (179). Indeed, Cheyne also shifts his advocacy from animal spirits to aether in a remarkable statement that demonstrates how futile the terminology was. Cheyne declares that animal spirits are either "'a fluid contain'd in hollow Tubes,' or 'a *subtile Spirit*, or *Aura* pervading . . . solid filaments' . . . whichever, it is 'the *immaterial Substance*.'"

Because each of these authors used different terminology (i.e., matter, fluid, spirit, medium), it may seem unlikely that the notions behind these terms were essentially interchangeable. Yolton spells out the individual key terms when referring to Cheyne, who "cites the subtle matter, animal spirits, and Newton's *Spiritus Subtilissimus*" and found none of them satisfactory (179). These discriminating terms nevertheless betray a strong conceptual equivalency when the evidence is analyzed. They all coincide in arguing for neural velocity and, so to speak, for insubstantial matter—which is to say matter so rarefied that it is immaterial. A concomitant factor is the origin of subtle matter.

As noted, another name for the Newtonian "subtile matter" is "spirits," but when Porterfield speaks of perception, these spirits are identical to the animal spirits. Such spirits move by an "Undulation . . . in the Nervous Fibrils, which reaching the *Sensorium*, gives us the Ideas of objects" (171). The fact that Porterfield alone makes perception his context is significant in regard to the synonymy, for when the subtle matter is refined so pointedly in the brain, its name is irrelevant. The synonymity is also significant because Langrish too combines the competing models, and so it can be said that both authors were "anticipating what was on the horizon," in Yolton's words. Shortly thereafter Hartley, and Priestley after him, abandoned the materialist explanation of "thinking matter" in purely vibrationist terms. Hartley insisted that "ideas and sensations are of a 'mental nature,'" and Priestley echoed the dualism of Bonnet while finding the same principles of association in the rival physiologies of vibrations and animal spirits (182–83). In these contexts, muscular action is really not the issue. The process of "thinking" entails an activity localized in the brain, prior to its executing a motion and perhaps even prior to representation and semiosis.

This point does not challenge Yolton's findings, but it refines the focus of discussion in several ways. It suggests that in the eighteenth century a physiology of the brain had begun to emerge and to occupy its own terrain vis à vis motor physiology and gastrointestinal physiology—all of which coincided in shared fluidist hypotheses. And the focus also calls attention to the very different origin of "subtile matter" when the origin is cerebral aether rather than the animal spirits that function in coarser regions of the body. That is, only in the brain does the physical matter of the nerve endings seem to dissolve into the aether. It is at this discontinuous point that the mind-body division becomes an observable enigma.

The Mind-Body Link in the Aethereal Continuum

The same aethereal particles found in the living body also permeate the external world. In contrast to the animal spirits, which materialize through the chemical refinement of blood and chyle, aethereal particles had no known origin apart from Creation itself. Aether has always existed, inside and outside the percipient's neural system. It was the rarest sort of air, the "Aura" named by Cheyne and the "Archeus" named in the preceding century by Jean-Baptiste Van Helmont. The Neoplatonist framework for the Archeus should not distract us from the function assigned to this spiritual substance. Even so, a Neoplatonist link to Newton himself has been suggested by D. P. Walker, as I indicate later. Stripped of its metaphysical anchor, the Archeus represented the same "principle of *activity*" called by other names in the next century: Priestley's "force and power" and Diderot's "energy," already mentioned. The name given by Van Helmont to the "air which accompanies all future generative activity" may sound quaint in today's perspective, but the Archeus itself represented "a spiritual 'matter' serving as the locus or substrate for various vital activities, to unify them, provide continuity and direction." [12] Indeed, animal spirits were also related to the source of cosmic motion in seventeenth-century physiology. These finest of all humors were "a sort of prime mover" in a universe considered as a living body by Friederich Hoffmann (King, 189). The immaterial spirits in Hoffmann's Chain of Being were unable to move matter, except for the human mind that creates voluntary motion (French, 120). The later physiology discarded the metaphysical encasement but preserved the original generative explanation for the local region of vital activity in the nervous system.

This discarding was incomplete in the case of Newtonian aether. All such explanations needed a link to connect crude matter and pure spirit. Thus while physiologies differed in the same century and evolved over several centuries toward a heightened materialism localized in the brain, the fundamental hypothesis remained the same. What Hoffmann called the "sensitive soul" existing as animal spirits in the fluid of the brain possessed the same "power" of purposeful movement derived from God that Galen before him called a "faculty" and that the French vitalists after him called *fluide moteur* derived from the *esprit universel* (Le Cat). Little new insight into the mind-body schism was provided by the evolution of physiology. What occurred instead was "a translation from one vocabulary into another," as King suggests (191). Another perspective on Hoffmann appears in the later discussion of French thinkers.

In regard to changing vocabularies and lingering hypotheses, Hartley's remarks merit a closer look. It is often noted that Hartley "posited vibrations in the medullary [a]ether as physiological correlates" to sensations, ideas, and motions (Cantor, 145). Body and mind are incommensurable, but they must interact with each other in efforts of perception and volition. Newtonian aether thus becomes the hypothetical intermediary that permits such interaction. While Hartley is a Newtonian, he gives no evidence of sharing Newton's Hermetic inclinations in regard to natural theology. However, he assumes an external origin for aether and implies

---

12. Lester S. King, *The Road to Medical Enlightenment, 1650–1695* (London: Macdonald; New York: American Elsevier, 1970), 45.

that aether is one and the same continuous substance inside and outside the percipient. Not only does aether mediate light to affect the optic nerve and the internal aether, but the same mediation is true for the frictions of skin and for the other senses. That is, sensory data are constituted by aether in both their objective and subjective conditions. More precisely, though still approximately put, the external condition of the perceived object already is both constituted in part and mediated by aether, together with whatever additional matter inheres in the object to constitute it. Its subjective condition consists in part of that same aether internalized by the percipient. The object's perceived condition is the aether subjectivized. Hartley states that the "affections of aether" are communicated to the nerves and vice versa. The impulse or attraction or action of the external object affects both the aether and the nerves, and these affect each other. Such events are material contacts of subject and object at the level of sensation and impression, and they are peculiar to the interfacing duality of external and internal aethereal activity. This material duality characterizes the aether hypothesis; it does not seem possible in the animal-spirit hypothesis reviewed by Yolton. The same contact is also integral to the Hermetic Newtonian aether, although the mechanics yield to a more theological notion of the *sensorium*, as will be noted. Contact and continuity are thus the equivalents of immediate presence.

When Hartley discusses the internal aether, the suspicion arises that Newtonian terminology has been refashioned to accommodate the idea of immediate presence. He speaks of the "Propagation of Vibrations" with the same vagueness as his predecessors, none of whom indicates what the particles of light and aether actually look like when they cause waves and vibrations "to propagate." The verb itself can mean, variously, "to multiply," "to spread" or extend, and "to transmit." One thing is clear: some *thing* must vibrate before the nerve chords themselves do, assuming these are solid. Hartley's wording is vague enough: "Vibrations, which ascend along any sensory Nerve" (24), where "along" may denote any number of events. The nerve itself may vibrate through its entire diameter and length. Or the vibrations of another substance, corpuscular or otherwise, may travel along the length of the external sheath. Or, more penetratingly, the same vibrating matter may travel "through" the neural or medullary substance.

Hartley's contemporaries maintained the vagueness of Newton's own metaphorical language. When Newton declares that aether particles "recede from one another," the verb "recede" suggests a motion that is empirically unobservable.[13] So too the imprecise verbs "to come," "to paint," and "to propagate," in the oft-quoted *Opticks* 1, 1, axiom vii: "the light which comes from the several points of the Object is so refracted . . . as to converge and . . . to paint the Picture of the Object upon [the *Tunica Retina].* . . . And these Pictures, propagated by Motion along the Fibers of the Optick Nerves into the Brain, are the cause of Vision."[14] This propagating motion is indeed vibration, but of the aether not the nerve. Newton assumes that the capilla of the nerves are "solid and uniform, that the vibrating motion of the aethereal medium may be propagated along them from one end to the other uniformly and without interruption" (*Opticks*, 328). Vision, therefore, is "performed chiefly by the vibrations of this medium, excited in the bottom of the eye by the rays of light and propagated through the solid . . . nerve."

The Newtonian physiologists could not, however, use this model without resolving Newton's imprecise verbs by means of a conflation of aether and light into a single phenomenon. The ambiguous role of their particles tightens the interfacing dualism of external and internal aethereal activity. In fact, it is not "light" that "comes" to the eye, but "rays" of light, and the physical character of rays is unknown except that their "particles" are heavier than aether. Newton declares, "I don't know what this aether is," adding, "its Particles are exceedingly smaller than those of air or even than those of light" (*Opticks*, 326). Mathematically, aether is over 700,000

13. Nonmathematical descriptions of such events have always been highly metaphorical. Regarding quantum theory, Werner Heisenberg admits: "for Bohr and myself, the most important step was to see that our language is not sufficient to describe the situation. A word such as *path* is quite understandable in the ordinary realm of physics when we are dealing with stones, or grass, etc., but it is not really understandable when it has to do with electrons. In a cloud chamber, for instance, what we see is *not* the path of an electron but, if we are quite honest, only a sequence of water droplets in the chamber. Of course, we like to interpret this sequence as a path of the electron, but this interpretation is only possible with restricted use of such words as *position* and *velocity*. So the decisive step was to see that all those words we used in classical physics—*position, velocity, energy, temperature,* etc.—have only a limited range of applicability. The point is we are bound up with a language, . . . we must describe our experiments and . . . we know that the words we use to describe the experiments have only a limited range of applicability. That is a fundamental paradox which we have to confront. We cannot avoid it; we have simply to cope with it." And "I would say that Wittgenstein, in view of his later works, would have realized that when we use such words as *position* or *velocity*, for atoms, for example, we cannot know how far these terms take us, to what extent they are applicable. By using these words, we learn their limitations." Quoted in Paul Buckley and F. David Peat, *A Question of Physics: Conversations in Physics and Biology* (London: Routledge and Kegan Paul, 1979), 6–8.

14. Quoted in Marjorie Hope Nicolson, *Newton Demands the Muse: Newton's Opticks and the Eighteenth Century Poets* (Princeton, N.J.: Princeton University Press, 1946), 94.

times more rare than air, yet aether is also capable of varying densities, as its refracting power demonstrates. Hartley and his contemporaries apply the concept of density to the physiology of aether, and this proves to be decisive in raising the issue of what neural signals are.

What vibrates, prior to sensation? It is difficult to know Newton's answer, since he speaks of "attraction" and "force" among atmospheric and cosmic particles. A study by R. W. Home demonstrates that the aether of the late "Queries" of the *Opticks* is not the "spiritus electricus" of the *Scholium generale*. Similarly, Betty Dobbs cites Newton's manuscript *De aere et aethere* of 1680 against the Hypothesis of 1675, which calls material aether a universal matter rather than spirit.[15] These scholarly findings, however, are compatible with the general awareness among Newton's followers of his venture into animal physiology and with the suggestion that the aethereal animal spirits in human beings may be a mediator between common aether and muscular juices (Dobbs, 207). Newton's immediate readers had noted of aether that "the exceeding smallness of its Particles may contribute to the greatness of the force by which those particles may recede from one another" (*Opticks*, 326). Other kinds of particle movement include "the effluvia of magnets passing through glass" and "an emission" or "an exhalation so rare and subtle, and yet so potent," produced by the friction of an "electrick body" (327). This aether is not one and the same as the electrical "exhalation" it gives rise to, as Home suggests in a point that will become relevant again toward the end of this chapter. But these phrases must also be cited with reference to understanding vibrations in their external condition. As for internal physiology, "the power of the will" is what causes the vibrations of aether to be "excited in the brain" (328).

One critical factor is clear: Newton in 1721 held that sensory perception occurs by means of the "species of things." This pre-Lockean term preserves the mind-body separation by investing the traditional sensitive soul with a hylozoic character carrying Neoplatonic overtones. In

15. Home traces Newton's shifting concept of aether in regard to electricity without entering the alchemical cosmology that interests Dobbs. Both scholars concur that he did not abandon the concept. Newton believed that an invisible subtle matter was necessary for a mechanical explanation of gravity. His Hypothesis of 1675 called material aether a universal matter rather than spirit. See Betty J. Teeter Dobbs, *The Foundations of Newton's Alchemy* (London and New York: Cambridge University Press, 1975), 205. Newton changed his mind in *De aere et aethere* (1680) when further pendulum experiments failed to support the existence of aether. However, he continued to speculate that the whole frame of Nature "might be nothing but aether condensed by a fermental principle" (Dobbs, *Foundations*, 211, 231). More cautiously, Home confirms Newton's retention of an aethereal concept of electricity as "a universal causative agency in the micro-realm." "Newton on Electricity and the Aether," in *Contemporary Newtonian Research*, ed. Zev Bechler (Boston: Reidel, 1982), 194.

Newton's words, "Is not the sensory of animals that place to which the sensible species of things are carried through the nerves and brain, that they may be perceived by their immediate presence to that substance?" (344–45). The importance of this statement may seem unappreciable if Newton is continuing his preceding remark about the instinct in animals. However, the full paragraph orchestrates rather majestically a series of general philosophical questions on Order, Beauty, and the will, culminating in the nature of the knowledge of first causes. If Newton were attributing will to animals only, logic could not have permitted him to relate it so sequentially to animal instinct. It is more probable that his thoughts flew ahead to human perception, because the next and famous statement refers to the "Being incorporeal, living, intelligent," who "in his Sensory, sees the things themselves intimately . . . and comprehends them wholly by their immense presence to himself of which things the images only carried through the organs of sense into our little sensoriums, are there seen to behold by that which in us perceives and thinks" (344–45).

The dichotomy of "outside-inside" in Newton thus embraces two aspects of perception insofar as the issue of contact and presence faced Hartley and his contemporaries. Newton distinguished between light and aether as they concern particle activity; any such activity within the nervous system did not necessarily relate to the sensorium ("the sensible species of things are *carried through* the nerves and brain"). In contrast, eighteenth-century brain anatomy required a coherent account of the passage, so to speak, from external to internal events. Hartley's language suggests that the solution was to isolate the concept of "vibration" and use it to represent the neural signal.

If this suggestion is valid, it accounts for the negligible difference between the rival animal-spirit and aether models, as far as sophisticated explanations of the mind-body link are concerned. As I suggested earlier, proponents of both models argued for their velocity and immateriality, and these qualities determined the heart of the debate. How then does Hartley isolate the neural signal without naming it as such? The answer has two parts. First, by speaking indiscriminately of aether particles and medullary particles, he unifies inorganic external matter with organic internal matter as the single mediatory agent: "the Vibration of the Aether, and concomitant ones of the small medullary Particles" (*Observations*, 1:17). In effect, Hartley nullifies the requirement that mediatory matter originate specifically in the percipient's body. The indiscriminate function of neural particles is confirmed by the factor of density, a condition of aether and medullary substance alike, as we shall see.

And second, Hartley actually separates the vibration as a vibratory signal from the aethereal medium in which it travels: "For the Aether residing in the medullary Substance, being of an uniform Density on account of the Smalness of the Pores of the medullary Substance, and Uniformity of its Texture, before taken notice of, will suffer the excited Vibrations to run freely through it" (1:22–23). He does not declare that the aether itself vibrates, but that it is to "suffer" the vibrations located in the aether and in the particles of sensory nerves. A more general statement of separate signaling is a reference to the ability of "the Particles to receive and communicate Vibrations" (1:23). The vibrations are excited in the aether and are propagated along the course of the nerves to the brain. As Yolton says of Hartley, "he thinks that aether is the medium of transmission of motion, even inside the brain" (*Thinking Matter*, 182). The emphasis belongs on *medium*, which transmits the motion of some other entity.[16] In Hartley's own words, this entity is already vibrating before its reception by the percipient: "As soon as the Vibrations enter the Brain, they begin to be propagated freely every way over the whole medullary Substance" (*Observations*, 1:24). However, we already know that aether is the external medium of those vibrations. Now that they are received by the percipient, they continue as "Vibrations of the small medullary particles."

What has happened to the aether? Yolton interprets Hartley to mean that "the white medullary substance of the brain [acts] as the immediate instrument of sensation and motion, as well as the means by which ideas are presented to the mind" (*Thinking Matter*, 182). Indeed, the indiscriminate aether-medulla mediation continues within the pia mater, where "the medullary Substance may still remain sufficiently uniform for the free Propagation of Vibrations" (*Observations*, 1:18). The factor of density, so important to the agency of external aether, now applies to organic matter. But the point is that the same signaling phenomenon exists "outside and inside" the percipient in order to preserve the continuity of the object's presence.

The metaphorical aspect of verbal scientific description, stressed in note 13, bears repeating. The continuity just mentioned is also an uninterrupted contact. The signal uses the inorganic medium of aether in main-

16. This motion opens the door to the subject of natural signs, which Yolton takes up in his *Perceptual Acquaintance*.

taining its external presence to the object, and it preserves that presence organically by continuing to vibrate in aether fused with medullary matter. Hartley is preoccupied with this uninterrupted event, although his remarks are limited to the internal physiology of vibrations. He is concerned with possible impediments to their passage through the brain, owing to the pia mater's subdividing disposition, and terms such a condition a "discontinuity." His concern with discontinuity acquires special significance in regard to the materiality of medullary particles, because an uneven density might cause a halt in neural activity. Elsewhere in the brain, the greater and lesser hardness of the regions produces different densities in the medium, so that "there may be almost an "Interruption or Discontinuity of it," and thus to "indispose the Particles to receive and communicate Vibrations" (1:23). Hartley is satisfied nonetheless that "innumerable Communications" exist in the cerebro-neural system to circumvent "some exceedingly small Discontinuity" in a given region (1:18).

The nature of Hartley's description is both unsystematic and laden with decipherable assumptions that belong to his time. Having accepted the Newtonian explanation of vibratory optical phenomena, he extends the aether theory to the internalized organic fusion of aethereal and medullary densities in order to explain perception. It is therefore of little consequence for the theory of perception that it is "impossible to trace out these Communications anatomically, on account of the great softness of the Brain." Whereas "obscurity attends all Inquiries into the uses of the particular Shape and Protuberance of the medullary Substance," no doubt is left about what I have termed an outside-inside theory of perception based on a common aethereal vibratory signaling.

While Hartley may not have shared Newton's more esoteric ideas, others at the time saw Newton "as standing in a line of Ancient Theologians."[17] These contemporaries furnish additional evidence of the interfacing duality of external and internal aethereal activity. The issue remains that of "immediate presence" defined as a material contact between subject and object at the level of perception. For instance, the Chevalier Andrew Ramsay interpreted Newton's aether as a Neoplatonic and Hermetic *sensorium* of God or the Spirit of the World, as Walker shows. Whether Newton knowingly inclined toward this Spirit rather than toward Descartes' subtle matter is discussed in Walker's review of specialized studies, but the non-

---

17. D. P. Walker, *The Ancient Theology: Studies in Christian Platonism from the Fifteenth to the Eighteenth Century* (London: G. Duckworth, 1972), 263.

electrical nature of aether in 1717 seems to have been established by Home. The relevant point here is that Newton was perceived to return to the aether theory after 1707 and to regard aethereal spirit as electrical and material (Walker 259).

There can be no doubt about Walker's assertion that Ramsay's *Cyrus* served in part as an allegory of contemporary philosophical debates. It was recognized therefore that genuine resemblances and connections existed between ancient and modern philosophical doctrines. Other forms of esoterica evolving from Newtonianism are mentioned by Hélène Tuzet, beginning with semi-psychological forces of attraction, polarity, magnetism, and cosmic energy. She attributes to Kant's theory of the heavens and science of Nature a "restoration" of a fecundating "primitive aether" linked to a hylozoic "universal Mother" (Tuzet, 192). But a more central current of scientific dualism carrying these traces is found in French naturalists from Guillaume Lamy to Julien Offray de La Mettrie, Louis le comte de Tressan, and J. C. F. de La Perrière.

Cosmic Intelligence and French Neurophysiology

The physiology of the Enlightenment has been studied at length by François Duchesneau, whose pertinent remarks on aether are limited to Friedrich Hoffmann's *materia subtilis* in the *Fundamenta medicinae* of 1695. Duchesneau's textual analysis cannot produce an epistemology because Hoffmann's inadequate terminology for neurofibral events blurs the distinction between irritability and perceptual sensitivity. Another obstacle is Hoffmann's Aristotelian-Galenic concept of a triadic soul: vegetative, sensitive, and rational. However, Duchesneau's analysis does suggest a material continuity of external and internal spheres, and this is established by several principles. First, Hoffmann asserts the concept of energy. He uses terms like "power" and "force" to characterize all types of "motion and life (*vigorem*)." This energy is invested in "the universal aethereo-aerian fluid," whose qualities are conventional: "this very subtle material fluid" and capable of "expansive force." The aethereal presence in all organic forms as well as in the cosmos attests to the pervasive continuity of "this fluid or universal motor" (Duchesneau, 58).

A second principle of outside-inside contact is Hoffmann's hydraulic model of breathing, circulation, and cerebral activity. In this commonly accepted cycle, the aether is breathed in with the air, then circulated with the blood, chyle, and animal spirits, and finally extracted by the brain. The internalization of external aether has nothing to do with the Hartleyan factor of aether density, mentioned earlier as preserving organically the continuity of the object's presence. But the cycle has much to do with what Duchesneau calls the "architectonic" activity of Hoffmann's *vis plastica*, which is strictly determined by the inherent properties of the aether particles. Thus a generative if not epistemological groundwork is laid prior to perception. The mechanical fluidist process affects the *anima sensitiva*. The sensitive soul is material, as distinct from the *mens* or spiritual soul, thus preventing any continuity of aether activity at the level of thought. But Hoffmann does allow, regarding the nerve fluid, that "a specific relation unites the spiritual principle to the material *anima sensitiva*," according to Duchesneau (47). This relation concerns generation and subsequent vital functions. Nevertheless, the nature of the relation between spirit and matter lacks textual description.

The third principle suggesting a material continuity of outside-inside was the very definition of aether. Not only is it linked to light rays and electromagnetic phenomena, but it is also the first and basic cause of vital movement. Aether gives impetus to cosmic matter at the moment of creation. It is already there when heat and fire join to induce vortices, which in turn form the *materia coelestis*. Thereafter, Hoffmann's metaphors turn vitalist. The primordial earthly matter rotates in the form of bubbles containing particles of the *materia subtilis*: "these bubbles are the seeds of things, the tissue of species, the receptacles of aether, the basis of bodies, the cause of their cohesion. If they should fail, the aether would dissipate, expelled by the rotation of the dense bodies and, on abandoning them, would condemn our earth to death" (47).

These principles were compatible with an orthodox Christian cosmology. The mind-body split remained unresolved, despite the bilateral activity of aether prior to perception. Nevertheless, Hoffmann shared a vocabulary of "fire" and "subtle spirit" that was also utilized by the mechanist Guillaume Lamy, who in 1679 alluded to the Ancient Theologians' belief in a universally knowing pure substance.

Before turning to Lamy and later French physiology, a final observation should be made regarding Duchesneau's evidence. Duchesneau also explains Hartley's vibrationism as a synchronous action by the aether, whose densification causes oscillatory movement in the nerve fibers and in the medullary particles (211). This account has limited cognitive implications. So too the review of Haller's epistemology, where Duchesneau affirms that Haller's micro-mechanist approach to sensibility is inconclusive as to the existence of nerve fluid (233–34). Nevertheless, a key quotation allows for sensation to arise "if one prefers, in the medullary pulp penetrated by spirit" (Duchesneau, 213). More precisely,

> It is not at this place that sensation is born; but following an inherent law, this fluid returns to the brain and represents the pressure that it undergoes in the seat of the soul, whether there it strikes a solid human and sensitive *monade*, or whether divine law decrees that the pressure of this fluid will change the soul when it reaches the latter's point of fixity. (213)

My point is that an underlying dualist or vitalist assumption persists even where the dominant form of physiology strives for materialism. Indeed, even if Haller's "divine law" is rejected, there remains "an inherent law" that determines the signal transfer.

The internal law nevertheless has a physiology traceable to Lamy's late-seventeenth-century mechanics. Like Hoffmann, Lamy believes that "the sensitive soul is a very subtle body" (*Explication mécanique*, 14). Moreover, this subtle matter is linked in Lamy's system to a Neoplatonist belief in "the soul of the world" (*Discours anatomiques*, 228). But his mechanist fluidism specifies that the sensitive soul is "always in movement, its reservoir being in the brain, and the nerves that start there are so many canals filled with it, dispersed throughout the body, which is irrigated by it" (*Explication*, 14). The absence of aethereal subtle spirit obviously has not eliminated the ubiquitous adjective "subtle" from the cosmic soul. But in effect "the animal spirits enclosed in the nerves are set in motion, and this motion is communicated by continuity up to the major part of the Soul which is in the brain" (14). The question is whether and how the concept of subtle aether underpins Lamy's account of the cognitive process.

One fact should be preeminent. More than sensation and perception, Lamy is accounting for a universal cognitive process. He believes that "the world is animated by a very pure, immaterial, invisible, immortal, universally knowing substance, always in motion, and the source of every motion and every soul, which are tiny particles of it" (*Discours*, 213–14). A cosmic intelligence is at play, and its microcosmic counterpart appears in the parallel phrase "always in motion," describing both processes. Further, the individual sensitive soul is "a very subtle body," integrated within the universal chain by a continuous calibration:

> Now these souls being of a divine nature, so pure and noble, they cannot immediately attach to the gross bodies that we see; but first they unite with the finest part, the subtlest, the most tenuous and so to speak the flower of matter. These souls take therefore for their first dress a very pure flame or a very subtle body of the same nature as what we conceive to be above the air. Then they dress themselves again in a less subtle body, and then a grosser one, and thus always by degrees until they can become united with the sensible bodies of animals. (214)

The sensitive soul is constituted by a less refined degree of the Spirit of the World. It is the same aethereal substance noted previously as being the Newtonian Ramsay's sensory medium. In Lamy's physiology, this is the sensitive soul "its reservoir being in the brain." The perceptual process thus entails a cerebral materiality:

> Now, since the brain's substance is of such a consistency as to receive the trace, the vestige, or the character of this motion, even though the soul easily loses the impression made on it by the object, it can retrieve [the impression] by resorting to the vestige traced on the brain, without the need for a new impulse. These motions of the soul and these characters that remain in the brain comprise the internal senses as much as the external ones. (*Explication*, 15)

Two distinct conclusions can be drawn from these remarks. First, the resultant neural signaling resembles closely the tracing theory held by British post-Lockean thinkers. Second, the signaling also belongs to the concept of spirit in Neoplatonic cosmology held by the Newtonian Ramsay. These two conclusions may be verified by brief supporting texts.

A comparison with British post-Lockean materialists reveals the negligible progress made by the competing fluidist and vibrationist models, with respect to neural signaling. Lamy accounts for brain-tracing in terms that scarcely depart from the fluidist Samuel Colliber's "minute Images or Signatures." Similarly, Hume follows Locke on memory: "these spirits always excite the idea, when they run precisely into the proper traces, and rummage that cell." In Hartley, sensations leave traces, whereas ideas are more permanent traces caused by repetition of sensations (Yolton 170, 176, 182). Lamy's tracing process is no different from the foregoing in their common cerebral result, but his traces and characters derive from a far larger system, which can be described in the terms of Ramsay's "Newtonian" Neoplatonism. Ramsay's "Soul of the World" has as its first instrument the Spirit of the World, hypostasized in the aethereal fluid of God's *sen-*

sorium (Walker, 258). The same aethereal fluid mediates Lamy's sensitive soul, which originates in "a very subtle spirit or a very tenuous matter, . . . the greatest part of which has, so to speak, its source in the sun and the rest is spread throughout all other bodies" (*Discours*, 227).

The principle of continuity from external to internal worlds cannot be more clearly proclaimed than in this system. Lamy's fluidism remains mechanist and untrammeled by metaphysics, so that the sensitive soul emerges as "the Soul which is in the brain." As quoted, "since the brain's substance is of such a consistency as to receive the trace," the soul registers "the internal senses as much as the external ones." But at the same time, "the principle of our reasonings" flows directly out of the same spirituous continuity in a Hermetic version of the Chain of Being:

> It is assuredly the soul of the world that governs and confirms [the very subtle spirit], all of whose parts have some portion of it. It is the purest fire of the Universe, which of itself does not burn but which, being insinuated into the particles of other bodies by the different motions that it gives to them, burns and causes heat to be felt. Visible fire has much of this spirit, as does the air; water has much less, earth, very little. Among the mixed elements, minerals have the least, plants more, and animals much more. It is what constitutes their soul, which enclosed in their body becomes capable of sentiment. See now how it comes and goes, and how it multiplies. This spirit is inside the seed, and when the animal is formed. . . . In man, it is the principle of our reasonings. (*Discours*, 228–30)

In this way, the individual soul is always in communication with the Soul of the World, by virtue of its spirituous origin in the "universally knowing [*sçavante*] . . . very pure substance" cited earlier. Lamy's subtle matter infuses the brain as animal spirit while its rarefied external condition preserves uninterrupted communication through the chain of finer and coarser material unions. Where does matter end and pure spirit begin? The question is duplicated for the internal state of mind. Lamy's texts avoid neural discontinuity by placing the soul in the brain, the nerves in the (sensitive) soul, and the animal spirits in the nerves. Because the rational soul is constituted by the same spirit that is "governed" by the Soul of the World, its cognitive continuity is assured. The spirituous thread extends from the unnamed aethereal spirits to the animal spirits.

If we turn to the eighteenth-century French fluidists, the concept of neural matter appears receptive to the presence of aether. The least conclusive fluidist, La Mettrie, is nevertheless metaphysically close to Lamy. Other thinkers coincide with British findings, although with differing semantic nuance. Their work will be reviewed first, and then La Mettrie's epistemology.

Neural Signaling and the Aethereal Fire

The fourfold model of bodily fluids advanced by Le Cat was mentioned earlier in connection with Yolton's British sources. The model's enduring importance is that it presents an extraordinary metaphor. The animal fluid is compared to a "lake of light" that is susceptible to sensory data and passions (*Sensations*, xliii). The oxymoron allows for the nontactile quality of light to be conceived more tangibly, as if the definition of matter itself requires some concrete condition to be realized. Nevertheless, luminosity rather than liquidity is Le Cat's intended denotation. In a second metaphor, he explains how the animal fluid changes color like "a chameleon" according to the effects of sensations (151). The chromatism belongs to the same phenomenology of light, except that now its liquid materiality is foremost. The implicit convertibility of neural matter is plain. This conflation of qualities approaches the Newtonian dualism of a Divine aethereal flux.

Le Cat's model does not rely on optics. The communion of internal perception with externality comes about through photics. There is a direct and uninterrupted "flow" of the same photointensive substance from the object to the neural matter in the brain. What this flowing movement is, of course, poses the same problem of immateriality already observed in Yolton's evidence. The "continuity" of the movement presents the same difficulty of disruption pointed out in Hartley's external and internal aether. Here the French sources offer additional clues by virtue of their theories of fibrous substance in the nerves. In fact, related notions in Cullen and Haller tend to indicate, for Western Europe, a widespread tacit understanding concerning a universal signaling substance.

Fibrous substance and photosensitivity are linked by the overarching doctrine of the Chain of Being. And here it is inconsequential that the vibrationist rather than the fluidist model of neurology is embraced. If all things in the universe form a continuous chain, then continuity may be defined either as a direct, tactile contact of one entity with another, or as a contact realized through molecular interposition in the manner of effluvia or the aethereal medium. What counts is that a single concept of matter prevails for both models of perception. When the fluidist model recedes in prominence, the idea of a "force" will remain as the dominating explanation of how mind and body interpenetrate.

One of the earliest French discussions is also the closest to the neuro-cerebral problem discussed for Yolton's British authors. Vieussens's treatise on bodily fluids prepares for its defense of animal spirits by dividing matter into three groups of elements. The smallest and speediest elements take numerous shapes under the denomination of "igneous matter," in the tradition of the Ancient Philosophy. Middle-sized and less agile elements are round globules classified as "aethereal matter." It is this type that becomes pertinent to the fibral structure of nerves. Coincidentally, Newton attributes the origin of aether to fermentation and ignition (Dobbs, 173). The final and least pertinent group comprises large, slow-moving, irregularly shaped elements that Vieussens simply calls "earth."

The foregoing classification bears on the transformationist ideas of Buffon and Needham. There are also correspondences with Newton's transmutational conception of matter and its unity: "any body can be transformed into another, and all the intermediate degrees of qualities can be induced in it" (Dobbs, 232). But the three groups of elements subsist in a continuous flow of movements that accounts for the conversion of the tangible into the intangible, the visible into the invisible, and the substantial into the insubstantial. These indirect terms are obviously alternative ways of converging matter and spirit so as to dissolve the point of separation.

Motion of this kind applies everywhere, including the communicating mechanisms between percipient and the external world. The motion depends, first of all, on the decomposing activity of larger and smaller elements among the aforementioned groups, with the effect that the continuous flow of motion from one to the other accelerates as the particles become more refined and eventually "invisible." And motion depends, in turn, on the porosity of bodily fluids.

In nerve fluid, the tiny molecules of animal spirit move freely through fluidic pores in the neural fiber, and they are so rarefied in size that they may pass out of the membranes and out of the body itself into the external environment. In fact, Vieussens's definitions of animal spirit include one that types it as a liquid body composed of fine air, which insinuates itself into the blood vessels through breathing (*Traité des liqueurs*, 226). The intermingling of animal spirits with the aether at large in the atmosphere becomes an obvious event, in this view.

A similar notion of fibrous structure by Cullen and Haller, while not pronouncing on the theory of aether, confirms in important respects the significance of porosity in primary matter. In Haller's version, fibers are composed of earthy particles adhering longitudinally and connected by an intervening cohesive glue called "gluten." This same gluten is what Needham observes in the tiny granules of dried fiber. They are, by no small coincidence with Le Cat's photic model, "molecules" of crystal that can refract light. The fiber in Haller's account has a cellular substance with weblike spaces, and this description conforms both to the idea of porosity and to the prevailing model of network connections. Thus Cullen seems to allow a fluidist explanation for neural signaling, and at the same time a nonfluidist, refractive explanation. He detects a variability in the fibrous composition. Countless tiny scales constitute the nerve fiber, but this solid part is distinguished from other interceptive cells and a still different aqueous substance.

Animal fluid nevertheless belongs to a far more vaste flux, and Le Cat can therefore posit the fluid as being more insubstantial than fire or even light itself. Only in this way can he explain how continuity is preserved from the brain to the external atmosphere. Animal spirit can flow through fibers, but it is part of a system that extends beyond the individual organism. Because it is everywhere, the subtle flow brings all things into communication. It is here that the idea of a "lake of light" consolidates the account of perception. The cosmic network is "tied by affinity to a gelatinous fluid, to a gluten as universal as itself." This substance exists without exception in mineral, animal, and vegetal matter (*Sensations*, xxxii).

Mention of the aether is not indispensable in this circumstance, although Dobbs has alluded to Newton's cycle of aether's descent to the earth's center, from where it is sent forth again, like the generative elements of the Archeus (Dobbs, 232). Be this as it may, Needham's fibrous granule that refracts light resembles Haller's gluten and Le Cat's rarefied fire. They all mediate perception of a fluxionary universe (see note 7). The metaphor of a photic gluten also poses a not-so-outlandish question. Is the molecular activity a mechanical or an intelligent event? If the granular motion is merely mechanical when occurring in the brain, its identical activity in the Deity would hardly be possible. The governing belief in this context is that the very universe owes its movements to a primal fluid fixed by the Deity. To avoid theological complications, chemists and physicists usually call the fluid a universal "spirit" or "force." Yet one and the same knowing agent is at work, supernaturally or naturally. All derivative movements further down the fluxional scale generate intelligent acts. The minimal degree attained by such acts might be, say, that of a polyp that "knows" how to reproduce itself. This level in the Chain of Being obviously is remote from the second-order cognition derived through a language of signs invented by human intelligence. However, the issue is a more general neurophysiology whose hierarchy of complexities includes, among other things, the process culminating in brain traces prior to verbal signs. The work of Charles Bonnet considers the organic extremes, from polyp to human being.

The signaling process is a question of speed as well as medium. Both factors are brought into a unified system of hierarchical spheres by Bonnet. The astonishing speed of neural response would be explained, says Bonnet, "if one grants to the nerves a fluid whose subtlety and mobility approach that of light" (*Facultés de l'âme*, 21). With this premise, a path opens from French thought to the legacy left by Hartley. According to Yolton, Bonnet's work had been recommended by Priestley, Hartley's commentator. Given the fact that both fluidism and vibrationism display the same principles of association, Yolton finds it significant that Bonnet explained mental operations by recourse both to animal spirits and to vibrations (*Thinking Matter*, 183). However, Bonnet is not so materialist that he can dispense with the ideas of force and elementary fire cited by Le Cat. These ideas are nearly identical to the concept of aether postulated among the British materialists.

Bonnet's account of the fluidist process begins with a physiological mystery in the nerve fibers: "the incorporation of nourishing saps in the fibers is to a *Force* that is unknown to us" (*Psychologie*, 343–44). The process ends when ideas are reproduced by the imagination through "a motor force acting at will upon every point of the brain that corresponds to the senses" (*Psychologie*, 75). At the same time, Bonnet defines "intelligence" as a universal and eternal harmony of relationships in a great Chain of Being. Organic intelligence "from the polyp's province to the cherub's" is manifested because each being possesses its proportional "motor force" (*Psychologie*, 377). This unifying principle sets aside distinctions between the Divine Logos, the second-order cognitive signs in humans, the natural signs in animals, and the self-generative "knowledge" in polyps. Emphasis falls uon the nature of continuity in these spheres. Bonnet's choice of a reconciling Intelligence in matter and spirit parallels the reconciliation of Platonists and materialists made by the mythographer Antoine Banier, who while discussing Pythagorean physiology cites the fact that the materialists also "attributed this perfection [i.e., Intelligence] to the fire of Aether or the most subtle and agitated matter" (*Mythologie*, 1:410).

It should be noted that Bonnet's Christian idealism and his belief in the "chain of beings" require the physical and the moral realms to be connected in a "universal tie" through "the succession of degrees" of past and future existence of atoms and ideas (*Psychologie*, 365). The epistemological assumptions of this scheme include some connection between matter and mind. The universal liaison is also affected as a cosmological structure by the same factors of motion, medium, and contact that characterize neurophysiology. But here Bonnet speaks of "the parts of communication that I call the links [*chaînons*]. Their purpose is the communication or the propagation of motion . . . The links are made in such manner that they tend to propagate motion in the same direction that they receive it" (*Facultés de l'âme*, 511–12). Nevertheless, at the level of physiology, communication entails signaling, which in turn involves speed. Here Bonnet begins to "suspect some analogy between these [animal] spirits and electrical fluid" (22).

The term "aether" does not enter Bonnet's discussion, but as in the instances of Le Cat, Langrish, and Cheyne, the lexical substitutions leave no doubt as to the substance being "as quick as Lightening" and just as Newtonian. The convergence of fluidist and electrical models is explicit in Bonnet's indiscriminate vocabulary:

> The brain seems to separate from the blood or from more complex liquid some species of elementary fire. Perhaps it is contained in the nerves somewhat like the electric fluid is contained in the bodies which are filled with it. The action of objects or of the soul can produce in the nervous fluid effects analogous to those which heat or friction produce in the electric fluid. (*Facultés*, 21)

The granular nature of matter, as in Le Cat, secures the transmission here termed frictional. The aethereal movement apparently undergoes two progressively more subtle conditions, analogous to fire and light.

The "elementary fire" possesses or mediates the "motor force" of which all beings in the universal liaison are susceptible. As a cosmology, the idea is shared by Robinet, who comes under attack by Charles-Louis Richard for contending that an "active power" connects visible and invisible worlds (*La nature*, 384–87).[18] But as a physiology, the aether principle yields to the vaguer "force" recognized at the end of the century even by Cabanis. Robinet's idea of *enchaînement* holds that the force is material

---

18. Delisle de Sales, influenced by Robinet's first work, *De la philosophie de la nature* (1769), believes fire is trapped in the earth, where electricity reigns in labyrinthine, dome-ceiling caverns. It is as if human thought is dominated by a generating fire, an elementary fire of cognition, so to speak. See, further, Hélène Tuzet, *Le cosmos et l'imaginaire* (Paris: José Corti, 1965), 340–44.

and constitutes the foundation of being. This foundation is always a gradation of invisible forces, like a progression of forms in the visible world.
In Cabanis, "a secret force, always active, tends without respite to render
this order more general and more complete," by which he means the order
reigning in both the physical and the moral world (*Rapports*, 2–3). The
transformation of the aether concept into the vaguer principle of cosmic
force is a subject in itself. Within the scope of this study, there remains
the transition from the fluidist internal aether proper to a more general
aetherealized fire or electricity.

Electrical Aether and Fluidist Models of Signification

Bonnet's convergence of spiritual substance and material substance is affirmed as a synonymity by La Mettrie in the epigraph for this chapter. It
is significant that a materialist identifies that sameness. La Mettrie's rejection of G. E. Stahl's animism, and his preferences for the mechanization
of the soul as a "principal spring" of movement, does not exclude what
Paul-Laurent Assoun has called an "astonishing" formula that combines
physiological mechanism with a Hippocratic animism. Whatever general
physiology La Mettrie may follow, his belief in the concept of aether is undeniable. His essay *Histoire naturelle de l'âme* accepts admiringly one treatise
on the subject: "An excellent commentary by M. Quesnay has appeared on
this doctrine of the Ancients. This clever man demonstrates through every
research and every experiment of modern physics, ingeniously collected in
a *Traité de Feu*, where aether, subtly ignited, plays a primary role in the formation of bodies" (*Oeuvres*, 1:35). Although I have been unable to locate
this treatise, La Mettrie's independent remarks on fluid mechanics in the
Homme machine seem not to contradict the theory.[19]

As well known as these remarks may be, their link to the Ancient
Theologians bears repeating. La Mettrie deems the soul a "vain" notion

19. "Our ideas do not come from the knowledge of the properties of bodies, nor from
what comprises the changes experienced by our organs. . . . According to their nature and
their degrees, ideas arise in our Soul that have no relation to their occasional and efficient
causes, nor doubtless with the will, despite which they make a place for themselves in the
medulla of the brain. Pain, heat, the color red or white have nothing in common with the
fire or the flame. . . . Sensations do not in any way represent things, such as they are in themselves, since they depend entirely on the corporal parts that make way for their passage" (La
Mettrie, *Histoire naturelle*, 82–83). This point does not undermine the accuracy of perception.
The suggestion is that other properties of the object are not seized by the five senses, and that
"with other senses we would have different ideas about the same attributes" (80–81).

and a "chimera," but he replaced it with the notion of innate force in order to explain how animated bodies move, feel, and think. A principle of movement must be posited a priori, and La Mettrie cites the Ancients as having situated an innate force within the parenchyma, defined as the nondifferentiated filtering tissue formed from blood and pith (*Homme machine*, 131–33). They did not much distinguish spirituality from materiality for this reason. As we saw, La Mettrie's fluidist contemporaries postulated a force in elementary matter that generates intelligible order. Their reference to the polyp's self-organizational behavior belongs to the paradigm of La Mettrie's reference to the polyp after sectioning. In the sectioned condition, the polyp not only moves but reproduces, thus demonstrating a force inherent in matter that is mistakenly called "soul."

The problem is that La Mettrie does not succeed in separating the activities of behaving and thinking. Like the "thinking matter" of the British physiologists, his pith or sap (*suc*) is implicated not only in generative and motor physiology but also in perceptual activity. Only a few hints of this problem appear in the *Homme machine*, which mentions a "fever" that activates the "filtration" of spirits animating muscles and heart (138–39). These "forces of life" are entirely mechanical, just as the vibrating cerebral cords are said to resound or to echo in words. But the fact remains that an external agent related to fire is identified with the sap. The body-clock metaphor is advanced in terms of a heat excited by "Nature" together with the sap upon entering the body; this "fever" is required in order to filter the spirits responsible for motor action.

La Mettrie admits the enigmatic process of Nature's veil, but he wants to save the theory of a vivifying soul from absurdity. Thus his example of connecting and rebounding balls in *Vénus métaphysique* is but a mechanical counterpart of the more arcane hypothesis of preexisting fire. Accordingly, this treatise affirms the priority of soul to matter: "this substance is born like a fire lighted by another fire, the seminal liquid serving as a vehicle" (*Vénus*, 10).

All such metaphorical explanations and vestiges of a Hermetic tradition mentioned thus far have of course been fragmentary. But they seem to converge on the same notion of vital force transmitted in the self-determining process of organisms at their lowest cognitive common denominator: the "knowledge" of maintaining life. La Mettrie's physiology provides for a continuity from the internal to the external, from fluids to spirits, some of them heating and fermenting in order to make life, and others effecting signals to the brain. This continuity extends to the external world and to aether, as the *Histoire naturelle de l'âme* indicates.

This treatise declares that "the aether is an infinitely subtle spirit, a very tenuous matter always in motion, known by the name of pure and celestial fire, because the Ancients had placed its origin in the sun" (*Histoire naturelle*, 44–45). La Mettrie's source in Lamy is clear, particularly in his repetition of aethereal penetration in the four elements and, within a decreasing scale of continuity, in animals, plants, and minerals (45–46). The outside-inside link is maintained through nourishment, but the igneous quality of the spirit remains unaltered. La Mettrie does not specify the role of aether in the "common sensorium" lodged in the "sensitive soul." The animal spirits move as a "reflux of spirits" from the sensory organs via the nerves to the brain. The term "reflux" for spirituous motion is clearly fluidist, but the same ambiguity of nerve response observed earlier in Pemberton and Robinson again appears in La Mettrie's description. The organs are "roused" and the spirits "act" on the sensorium (51–52). This vocabulary permits animal spirits to coexist with vibrations and to open the door to an aether hypothesis.

The question now is whether aether intervenes at the point where the vibrations resound in the brain as words. Brain anatomy is not very detailed in the *Histoire naturelle de l'âme*, but it is specific enough to stipulate "different seats of the Soul" (90) and, most important, to declare that the soul is coextensive with the medullary seat (100). The extreme softness of "the brain's medulla," together with the confusion of innumerable nerve endings therein, is a condition that renders futile the debate between fluidists and vibrationists. The animal spirits are indeed "fluids" for La Mettrie, and they move at the slightest *choc*. They also effect "traces" or "ideas" on the brain. However, they are affiliated with aether as well, although they may or may not be constituted by aether. The traces and ideas are "all effects proving that the nervous sap is composed of globular elements that float perhaps in an aethereal matter" (73). Both models are thus retained by La Mettrie, whose affinity with the Ancient Philosophers is visible, if attenuated.

The aethereal hypothesis in La Mettrie need not be insisted on in his overall materialist physiology, nor may its place in epistemology be crucial in the face of his representational theory of knowledge.[20] However, the

---

20. Following Aram Vartanian, it must be mentioned that La Mettrie has more to say about aether in the *Histoire naturelle de l'âme* than in the *Homme machine*: "The ether does

persistence of aethereal matter carrying "globular elements" is perplexing, given his summarized account of neural signaling:

> We must therefore admit the existence and circulation of spirits. These same spirits that are set in motion by the action of the endmost bodies travel back to the soul. A single file of spherical globules, in each cylindrical fiber, will race at the slightest touch, gallop at the slightest signal from the will. (74)

This physiology would seem sufficient for transmitting the neural signal. The role of an aethereal medium ("the endmost bodies") for the globules appears to be purely mechanical. But to leave it at that does not expunge the Hermetic presence of aether in the passages discussed earlier.

Indeed, Aram Vartanian has pointed out that La Mettrie's Lockean epistemology fails to come to grips with the problem of knowledge because he equates the symbolized idea with its origin in the sensation, as if the idea existing in the understanding is exactly the idea contained in the sensation. La Mettrie treats the symbolic representation of sensations as a mechanical problem. However, cognition poses a fourfold problem of stages, which Vartanian describes hierarchically as beginning with motility and irritability in lower organisms, and culminating in the enigma of mind. Organisms behave adaptively with increasing complexity, and thus invite teleological conjectures regarding purpose or foresight. While La Mettrie's fluidism proposes an entirely mechanical explanation, the various texts just reviewed suggest an incomplete physiology.

The mind-body problem, as stated in cognitive terms by Vartanian, lies at the heart of the narrowing gap between living and nonliving thinking machines. His point is that modern cybernetics shows that self-directive behavior may be mechanically caused. Behavior explained by mechanical autoregulation and negative feedback in conjunction with a scansion mechanism is compatible with the concept of "the man-machine." This focus invites attention to the antecedents of today's model of cerebral functions based on neural loops and "reverberating circuits of electrochemical nerve impulses" (Vartanian, *La Mettrie's "L'homme machine,"* 135).

---

play a role in his materialism. There is, however, a problem of emphasis. My own impression is that, if he does not make too much of the concept, this is because it was accessory rather than general to his general thesis . . . [of] the *organisation* of matter" (personal communication to the author). As for La Mettrie's rejection of animism, the doctrine's religious groundwork appears to weigh more than the problem of motion per se in medical theory. Roger French presents the Cartesian problem historically in Newton's reformulation as follows. The inertness of matter requires an external moving force; behind the corporal machine, the force is

Again, however, the distinction between perceptual thought and motor neurophysiology must be kept in mind. Because information-processing is what makes thinking machines important, epistemology remains the framework for this discussion.

If La Mettrie simplifies the signifying process by equating symbolized idea with its sensorial origin, as Vartanian suggests, then it seems plausible to approach the more complex process through the concept of aether. As a fluidist concept, the aether functions as a carrier of the neural particles: "the nervous sap is composed of globular elements that float perhaps in an aethereal matter." This can foreshadow one of two present-day models regarding the neural signal. The nerve fiber or axon contains a gel with nourishing molecules that move in an "axoplasmic flow." The particle flow corresponds to the older wave-propagation model described by ripples in water, a description also applied to vibrationism. The second model does not involve moving particles. Instead, an "action potential" exists and is realized through a high-speed message carried by electric charge, due to change in the electric state of the membrane. Merely to introduce these terms is to imply a complex physiology as remote from La Mettrie's age as is the age of cybernetics. But just as Vartanian's purpose is to clarify by restatement the essential problem in La Mettrie's epistemology, so too here does the issue grow more precise.

In the signifying process, linguistic symbolization must be differentiated from the neural signaling. And yet signifying and signals are common to both phases. The distance between "natural" signs and "linguistic" signs is equal to distance between electrical impulse and engram. The question of measuring this distance or describing it still has no scientific or philosophical answer. La Mettrie considered symbolic representation to be a mechanical event. He suggested a duality of models in the aethereal carrier of neural "globules" that are themselves motor-sensory in nature. But within his vestigial Neoplatonist cosmology, derived from Lamy, he postponed resolution of the mind-body separation. While another expertise is required to expand on twentieth-century findings, to pinpoint La Mettrie's efforts is to restate the process in terms of a prefiguring electrical component.

---

supplied by animal spirits traveling near the speed of light, like aether; motion is characterized by a vital principle (physical or intellectual) that in the work of animists like Sauvages at Montpellier, assumes a religious or moral premise; vitalists like Haller similarly avoid mechanist reductionism but posit the ultimate principle of life in a separate vital principle instead of an immortal soul; aether is associated with this principle instead of being its agent. See French, "Ether and Physiology," 115–20, 129–31.

Contemporaries of La Mettrie focused on the electrical qualities of aether and furnished a context for simplifying the physiological basis of cognition. Perhaps the key statement of synthesis for the Enlightenment appeared in the Comte de Tressan's "Essay on the Electrical Fluid Considered as Universal Agent." Tressan is a Newtonian who is also familiar with the Ancient Theology through the writings of Kircher.

> I cannot help recognizing an exact relation, a very identity between the effects of light, the action of animal spirits, and the properties found in electrical fluid; this analogy becomes more striking to Reason as it is further pursued and better examined; and since three different principles for light, animal spirits, and electricity cannot exist in nature, we are forced to gather these three powers under a common and single principle.[21]

The implications of a single principle for all three phenomena are broad. It embraces both external and internal phenomena, thus securing an outside-inside continuity for perception. Just as important is the conservation of animal spirits as a concept, while also avoiding the confusion seen earlier in the British debate between fluidists and vibrationists. Tressan redefines the spirits as an electrical fluid affiliated with light. By transferring the concept of fluid to the realm of physics, he eliminates the entire physiological apparatus necessary to account for organic substances. Neural signals now may be described in mathematical terms as arising from "a body 700,000 times more rare and more elastic than air" (*Fluide électrique*, 1:168).

Tressan's "subtle liquid" in the medullary substance lends another meaning to the lexical ambiguities noted earlier in British accounts of "refluctuations" and "pulsations." All such terms denote the same communication of signals by a single electrical agent (1:156). The best example of synonymity is found in another treatise, by La Perrière, on electricity as a universal mechanism. One passage deals with "reflexive sensations" produced when objects are absent:

> The fibers and fibrillas of the senses, thus stimulated and with inconceivable promptness in measure with their agility and with the activity of the animal fluid that stirs them, effecting the series of oscillations, vibrations, and archetypal quivers to which they are habituated by the presence and repeated impression of objects, again imprint [the latter's] characters and modifications in the animal fluid. (*Méchanismes*, 2:12–13)

21. Louis, le comte de Tressan, *Essai sur le fluide électrique considéré comme agent universel* (1749), vol. 1 (Paris: Buisson, 1786), 171.

Other variable terms like "contraction," "mediate or immediate impulsions," "tumultuous motions of the general mass of fluid," and "direct or reflexive vibratory quivers" suggest an indifferent lexical usage that was permissible because of the unifying hypothesis underlying it. From external object to internal idea, as well as from volition to muscular movement, the neural signals are communicated by the same agent capable of photic speed. La Perrière begins his chapter on the "electrical mechanism of sensations" by separating electrical fluid from other neural fluids. The instantaneous sensory communication of an external event is proof for La Perrière of "the subtlety, elasticity, and fluidity of the immediate subject of electricity" (*Méchanismes*, 2:1–2). Internally, electrical fluid exercises the same signaling velocity for the separate functions of the bodily fluids: "the analogous speed with which the organic body mechanically executes all its motions . . . leaves no room for doubt that the immediate subject of electricity is one and the same body with the nerve, motor, sensitive, and animal fluid" (*Méchanismes*, 2:1–2).

Both La Perrière and Tressan approach fluids as if it were necessary for the first time to demonstrate their existence. Tressan insists we must "consider the animal spirits to be a kind of fire, like a fluid that escapes from the nerve endings, which the brain supplies by virtue of what it receives from the general hearth [*foyer*]" (*Fluide électrique*, 1:179). Although Tressan follows a hydraulic model of organic secretions, including hollow nerve canals filled with serous fluids, he considers animal spirits too vague a concept for the "force of translation" that causes neural activity (1:146–47). The universality of this force concerns him, especially its "vertical" impact on the human "economy" that causes all other organic fluids to move: "the active power that I assume the solar and terrestrial electricity exerts on vegetation" also extends to human beings (1:145).

The coexistence of animal spirits and electrical fluid permits Tressan to conserve the same hydraulic physiology and neuroanatomy described by Yolton for the British fluidists. Tressan devotes chapter 8 to the formation of animal spirits, and he gives a detailed account of fibral and cerebral structures in the function of the "subtle fluid." However, his governing idea cannot allow hydrostatic laws to account for bodily "emissions," "transpiration," or "a real emission by the brain to the extremities" equivalent to the speed of light (1:165). Tressan supplies exact calculations of electrical speed as a function of atmospheric layers and the globe's curvature. He calculates circulatory pressures and vesicular diameters in order to gauge the force needed for the transpiration, and he concludes that "the electricity sweeps the fluids along and agitates them through tiny holes that scarcely allow them to filtrate" (1:147). The same "accelerating agent" is present in the nerves.

Having "demonstrated" the existence of electrical fluid in the nerves, Tressan concedes that its afflux to the brain is more difficult to explain than its efflux: "we still remain in great uncertainty regarding the return of this fluid to the region of the *septum lucidem*, where the nerves must relay to the common sensorium all the impressions that the body receives from the different sensations" (1:166). At the same time, Newton's authority is invoked for the fact that light, admittedly a fluid, records its impression on the retina and sets off nerve fluid traveling to the sensorium at the same speed. The sustained propagation by the continuity of physical contact through pressure brings Tressan to focus on the tactile sense to illustrate the sensory process. This focus is significant for the epistemology of "presence" as a whole, and I shall point out the preservation of the tactile idea in a philosophical poem at the end of this chapter.

By selecting the sense of touch, Tressan illustrates his analysis at the most basic level, since "the other senses are but modifications" of neural response at the point of direct contact. He affirms, "The nerve nodule occupying the center of the tuft when extended to the length of the nerve experiences a lively jolt at the moment it touches or is touched." Vision, therefore, is nothing but touch:

> A body may not be touched except by another body. But what idea can we have of a body 700,000 times rarer and more elastic than air? It is well demonstrated that our distinct ideas cannot go beyond the reach of our senses. . . . By seeing we are touched, and we are passive before the kind of touch whose effect engraves a positive idea on our understanding. (1:168)

The "engraving" effect of nerve fluid begins the tracing process, as in the animal-spirits model. Beyond this hint of the engrammic process Tressan does not venture, owing to his interest in the electrical quality of nerve fluid itself rather than in the signaling and signifying events that issue from it. Indeed, there barely seems to be room to speak, as Hume does, of spirits that "rummage" in the brain cell.

But Tressan's approach must be assessed by the way he reviews the history of animal spirits from Plato's *Timaeus* to Newton's *Opticks*. While his earlier reference to the recipient *septum lucidum* follows the Pythagorean "subtle flesh of the soul," which is a vegetative and conserving power, he concentrates on the ancient ideas regarding elementary fire. This will lead him to emphasize the electrical feature closer to Newton's system. Thus, a network of fire extending throughout the nervous system is a point he notices in the *Timaeus*, while the emission of sparks when persons comb hair or rub legs, reported by Kircher, brings him closer to Boerhaave's chemistry than to animist physiology. On electrical emission Tressan remarks, "But the fire emanating from the nerves can alone be luminous, and the electric explosion of this fire can alone enflame the sulphurous molecules, which are rather tenuous and lively enough in their agitation to burn at the slightest sudden and violent shock" (1:182). The perspective abandons conventional animal spirits for electrostatics. The "electric explosion" can occur anywhere in the body, even as brain charges, since the current is capable of both affluent and effluent paths.

The universal fluid theorized by Tressan, La Perrière, or Le Cat did not go by the name "aether" in its internal organic form. But its Newtonian characteristic is an undeniable condition of the glutinous yet electrical fluid, regardless of its name.[22] The French theory also imposes a prior inference: that of elementary signals endowed in a substance that exerts a powerful force. This primal "language" of spirits is indeed worthy of the epithet, if language is conceded to be the means of imposing order on a meaningless mass. Regarding the oft-mentioned lowly polyp, this involves organizing a meaningless protoplasm through regeneration. Le Cat phrases the same agency so as to embrace the entire biosphere and universe: "this motor fluid becomes, at times, as the Minister of the supreme Being, through which he dispelled the Chaos and has given life to his works" (*Sensations*, xxxi). The actual signaling by means of electricity, however, cannot be explained by this cosmological evocation. In the scheme advanced by La Perrière, a metaphor of exchange or transaction is required.

At first glance, the crudeness of La Perrière's metaphor leaves signaling without an explanatory apparatus. The brain is "the general office of management," whereas "the elementary parts of the electric, nervous, motor, sensitive, and animal fluid are the stationhouses staged here and there to pass themselves along from one to the other and transmit the [parts] to their destination" (*Méchanismes*, 2:4). However, the model depends on the factor of "the instantaneousness of the commotion in the

22. In Great Britain, a student who identified Haller's "ethereal nerve fluid with Newton's universal "ether" *and* with the electrical fluid was rebuked "at surprising length" by William Smellie in the first *Encyclopaedia Britannica* (French, "Ether and Physiology," 118).

entire chain" (2:2). Brain anatomy counts less than transmission, and the slight importance attached to cerebral tracing is justified by the same motives that guide Tressan. Both theorists stress the inherent qualities of electricity. La Perrière's apparently crude transactional model of the brain also depends on a second factor. He directs himself to the signal-molding capability in the electrical fluid itself. The shaping of neural signals necessitates an elaborate vocabulary of the fluid's plastic nature, where sensory events are described by words like "imprint" "characters," "modifications."

There is no doubt that La Perrière is a vibrationist. The first-order signals, called "direct sensations," are the impressions of present objects transmitted by the animal fluid to the brain. The impression consists of "characteristic archetypal agitations" carried to and impressed on the brain by this fluid. The outside-inside continuity follows Newton: "The elastic and subtle universal fluid which is the immediate organ of solar influences and the vehicle for light and colors, agitated by the vibrations of the ignited, luminous bodies that are plunged into the sun and shrouded in its midst, carries, by a succession of vibrations in a straight line, the vibratory agitations, direct or reflected . . . into the nervous fibers and fibrillas of the organs of sight, and by their ministry into the animal fluid that fills the cavities " (*Méchanismes*, 2:7). The optical example is merely illustrative of vibrations. In contrast, fundamental signaling must be illustrated by the sense of touch. Once again the need for direct contact in describing continuity leads a theorist to this faculty:

> Although the organs of sight, hearing, taste, and smell have particular seats, the organ of touch is the basis of all the others, having its seat everywhere, and the others exercising their functions only through its ministry; it is evident that the animal, nervous, sensitive, motor, and electric fluid, which sets them going and employs them, resides in the organic body at large. (2:6)

The term "fluid" is here a plural noun, with sensitive, motor, and electrical functions determined by discrete fluids, although the term "animal fluid" is used generically most often. Within the full extension of the process, continuity is maintained by pressure, agitation, and sheer weight of the "impregnating" fluids in the nerve canals.

The corporeal plasticity of this fluid permits the "archetypal agitations" to be impressed and eventually to be retained permanently as ideas. These are the "reflected sensations" resulting from the archetypal quavers in the nerves, quavers "to which the nerves are habituated by the presence of the objects: it is only when they imprint the objects together with all their distinctive characters upon the parts of the animal fluids" that these second-order signals are formed (*Méchanismes*, 2:13). The plurality of fluids is plain in this instance. A third category of signals, called *sensations mixtes*, are related to the imagination, which can combine the "characteristic archetypal agitations" of both present and absent objects to create new impressions on the fluid (18–21).

Neither La Perrière nor Tressan reaches the juncture where aether and signification become one and the same. Therefore they cannot delve into the mind-body problem at its originating source. Further study of their treatises may dwell on the other metaphors, like violinist's finger-memory, that will supplement the account given here. Fundamentally, the contribution of these metaphors lies in an estrangement from Hermetic thought while retaining the electrical fluid as a concept abstracted from animal spirits and insulated from the skepticism of more empirically-minded physiologists. The aether-concept in these authors is distinctive by occupying the foreground of data imprinting and the formation of character signals. Put another way, electrical fluid usurps the brain's place in the process of tracing ("imprint . . . all their distinctive characters upon the parts of the fluids"). Nevertheless, the primal engrammic event discloses nothing about cognitive conversions, regardless of whether their location is cerebral or neural. The outside-inside continuity is explicit, but only a more philosophical framework can approach this subject coherently as science curtails its metaphorical permissiveness at the century's end. And here, within philosophical language, we shall discover that it is the poet rather than the scientist or philosopher who carries the aether concept forward in epistemological terms.

The Epistemic Transcendence of Aether

My discussion has proceeded under the assumption that natural philosophy can be a source of evidence for clarifying unsolved problems in eighteenth-century biology and psychology. The latter areas of inquiry derived their notions of aether from natural philosophy, thereby restating the matter-spirit dichotomy as a more general question of the material world in relation to the perceiving mind. The purely scientific history of theories of aether, outlined by Edmond Whittaker, drove out biology and philosophy by the nineteenth century. But the Enlightenment preserved the aether concept for neurophysiological functions, including cerebral events. The competing models of animal spirits and vibrations coincide in recognizing the conductive agency of an invisible elastic fluid. The aether fluid also stood in metonymic relation to electricity, and therefore became a unifying concept for discussing natural as well as mental phenomena from Descartes to early modern times.

The overlapping of physics and epistemology just before and after Newton had been broached by Whittaker and by Larry Laudan in different ways. Laudan discusses prevailing empirical epistemology in the inductive framework of scientific ideals based on demonstrable facts rather than on unobservable entities like aether. Here epistemology is defined methodologically and is the means by which aether theory is justified. Whittaker describes the perception of light in Cartesian dioptrics, which occurs through the pressure on the eye by "subtle matter" from the luminous object. Just as a blind man "sees" by using a stick that transmits pressure from object to hand, so too is vision such a transmission of aethereal force. Even Descartes' dissenting reader Pierre Gassendi replaced the Cartesian plenum with aether and explained its behavior in the same way. As for Newtonian optics, the role of vibrating particles propagated from light ray to sensorium is well known. Less spoken of is George Berkeley's linkage of light or aethereal fire to the vital spirit of the world (Leventhal, 182–84). Later pantheists such as Jean Rousset de Missy explained life and movement by their participation in the semi-material soul of the world, composed of "a very subtle fluid or a very tenuous [*déliée*] matter" that fills the universe and originates in the sun (Jacob, 223).

An eccentric turbulence emerged from the crosscurrents of empirical science and the older natural philosophy. The idea of phlogiston belonged to the class of "imponderables" that also included caloric and fluid theories, magnetism, and kinematic aether (Heimann, 61–62, 75–77). The weightless, elastic *phlogose* has its own history in Le Cat and others, but it also touches the history of aether in the fantastic voyages of Ormasis and Nadir.[23] In this anonymous work of 1775, discussions of electricity and *phlogistique* define the latter as the percussion of light. Among alchemists, the same "phlogistique" also goes by the name of pure fire, sulfur, dry water, and philosophical mercury. It seems to be the Newtonian aether under alchemical transformation, the active substance identified in the compo-

---

23. M.D.L.F. (Delafolie), *Le philosophe sans prétension, ou L'homme rare: Ouvrage physique, chymique, politique, et moral, dédié au savans* (Paris: Clousier, 1775).

sition, growth, and decomposition of all things. The anonymous author draws upon popular conceptions of scientific ideas at the end of the century, casting them in a fantastic setting for literary effect.

Less eccentric is the literary assimilation of aether by Martin de Bussy, whose philosophical poem of 1796 is wooden in the original and translates into awkward, prosaic platitudes. As a document, *L'éther, ou l'Être suprême élémentaire* may be regarded in the same way that Ramsay's earlier *Cyrus* has been regarded by D. P. Walker. The specifically metaphysical relevance of *Cyrus* and of Berkeley's *Siris* (1744) is discussed by Cantor. As for the subjectivist Bussy, it should be noted that a dream-state affects the poet's condition. He speaks first from a metaphorical abyss of irrational perception that brings the same intuitive lucidity affirmed by Goya's dream of Reason: "When my Spirit plunges into the abyss of time / Everything confounds my Reason and seems a dream" (*L'éther*, 25). This condition actually precedes inspiration, being its necessary counter-rational uncluttering of mind. The subsequent insight springs from the pervasive aether mediating the continuity that extends from human thought to all external things.

> With such agents, let us no longer be surprised,
> If bodies exists, if the bodies have senses,
> If from these senses Thought emerges,
> Which when exercised makes Man proud.
> Thought emanates from Spirit, it is said;
> But when my voice expresses it, and when my hand writes,
> Not in vain is the pure spirit in the fire that enlightens me,
> My Reason cannot see it, and sees only matter.
> Our understanding is born of the natural relation
> Between the inner sense and the real perception,
> A relation established by the reversible flux
> Of the celestial Element for which everything is possible. (44–45)

The poet affirms the same belief in the continuity of external matter and internal awareness that was implicit in the scientific texts examined earlier. The dynamics of aether ("the reversible flux") are described elsewhere in the poem and correspond to the idea that movement, space, and matter are indivisible yet different. The essential point is that "the Aether is a Proteus, transforming itself into everything" (45). It is conceded that aether is a "too misunderstood motor, but nonetheless necessary" (43). As a result of "its fluid action," it passes through the corridors and interstices of matter, permitting thought by "the alternative flux of the senses to the Inner Sense" (46). More profoundly, "it causes the birth of our tastes, feelings, and customs" (28).

This meditative if unpoetic accolade for aether claims a scientific basis insisted upon by Bussy:

> But physics teaches that it indeed directs
> Everything we see growing or breathing . . .
> And we know at last that each existing being
> Was an eminent fluid before existence;
> That a germ is but a point, an unparchable atom,
> That grows by increments and becomes palpable. (43)

The near-technical didacticism has its place in a poem of five cantos without interfering with Bussy's visionary purpose. What strikes the reader from the standpoint of intellectual history is that a prose exposition precedes the cantos themselves. This essay purports to have as its author the "editor" who received the manuscript and who now will preface it. But the contents do more than simply justify the subject and its publication.

Bussy's "Exposition" is in fact a compendium of the epistemological hypotheses touched on in this chapter. The physiology of sensation is linked to the metaphysics of a transcendent epistemic capacity. Yet the linkage avoids religious or even ethical sentiments. Instead, it implies a cognitive physics, as it were, an account of a limitless power characterized by its metamorphic substance. The infinite sphere is filled with "an elementary Being as immense as itself; made of a perfectly simple matter, essentially active and eminently elastic, which contains in it the Principle of everything that exists" (xii). This substance may be a Supreme Being, a pure spirit, a subtle matter that is invisible but real. In any event, it is a power "whose property is always to be in motion, and which by its increments, its cohesions, and its eternal combinations is transformed in everything that exists" (xi). Its epistemological function is explicitly stated: "this great Motor gives senses and organs" to all sentient beings. The biological role coexists with its role in governing all the laws of gravitation and stasis— indeed all physical antitheses such as day-night, heat-cold, and dry-moist.

In brief, Bussy presents what he calls a "Pascalian" universe filled with aethereal matter, "a substance, which is always the same, although it presents itself to our eyes in different forms" (xii). It is precisely this metamorphic quality that permits aether to touch and affect all things in all realms of being. Its pervasiveness, in fact, guarantees "touch," the very contact and continuity from one entity to another throughout the universe that other thinkers have called the ladder or Chain of Being. The outside-inside aspect of continuity is specifically delineated by the example of sensory touch, in Bussy's account. And by reverting to transcendent cognitive powers in tactile terms, the poet desacralizes at the end of the century what Berkeley at its beginning had described as a binding of soul and body. The decades in between undertook the march from natural philosophy to the empirical sciences without quite removing the ghost from the machine.

The epistemological ground traversed from Berkeley to Bussy was minimal compared with the scientific ground also covered, but this difference had no effect on the aether concept. The Newtonian system is incompatible with Berkeley's last work, *Siris*, which according to Herbert Leventhal was taken seriously in the American Enlightenment regardless of its eccentricity. However, Berkeley contended that fire, like Bussy's aether, is the starting point for all explanations in the universe, and it is the bridge between material and immaterial worlds. Fire is like spirits in the organic body, for it "connects the matter of the universe with the spiritual reality and power of the Godhead" (Leventhal, 184). Despite the theological perspective, the physics and chemistry are not alien to the scientists discussed previously. The idea was that "whatever perspires, corrupts, or exhales, impregnates the air, which, by being acted on by the solar fire [aether], produceth within itself all sorts of chemical operations, dispensing again those salts and spirits in new generations, which it had received from purifications" (183).

Aethereal fire is always restless and in motion, according to Berkeley, activating matter with so quick, subtle, and all-pervasive verve that "it seemeth no other than the vegetative soul or vital spirit of the world." What in Bussy is a "motor" is more animate in Berkeley, just as their deifications contrast by the same measure of mechanization, as we shall note. Yet Berkeley also calls "elastic" aether a "pure invisible fire, that is the first natural mover or spring from whence the air derives its power" (Leventhal, 182). There follows the cognitive link that aligns Berkeley with Bussy and Newton in the latter's Divine sensorium: "A divine Angel doth by His virtue permeate and govern the elementary fire or light, which serves as an animal spirit to enliven and actuate the whole mass, and all the members of this visible world" (184). Spirit and matter are thus joined in the divine aether in a manner that corresponds to the sensory process of animal spirits in organic bodies. That the "enlivened" visible world is present to God through this medium is implicit and compatible with Newton's divine sensorium.

In this tradition, Bussy focuses on the actual contact and touch realized through aether. At the same time, he eliminates the theological aspect of continuity and actually designates the human being as constituting the organ of the Supreme Being. The aether,

> being simple, and having no organs, cannot see, hear, wish, feel, speak, or think. It has only the power to act and the property of Touch, faculties that pertain to its Essence; enjoying no other advantages than from within the Beings that it forms from its substance and to which it gives organs and senses quite well combined for them to be able to enjoy, during a limited time and relative to their individual constitution, the precious advantages with which the human species is eminently and unequally endowed. (*L'éther*, xiii–xiv)

Thus a superior status falls upon humankind with regard to the benefits enjoyed through aether. Mortals are imbued with the transcendental substance and in this way come in touch with the unspecified divinity. But the nonreligious and materialist bias in these passages places Bussy at a distance from his predecessors, even while he shares with them a mechanistic and mediatory concept of the aethereal fluid. The conceptual advance marked here consists in removing the dichotomy of mechanistic aethers and "animate" aethers,—those intended to "despiritualize" nature and those allied to spirit (Cantor, 151).

A unifying principle joining the external and internal worlds of experience thus finds literary expression after its evolution in the speculations of French and British writers on neurophysiology. We may consider the evidence as being representative of Western Europe, including Spain and Portugal. Without multiplying examples repetitiously, a single literary instance from Goya's milieu will, however, be fitting. Goya's contemporary, Forner, proclaimed the identical mediacy of "The invisible but material Aether, / which, burning, fills and vivifies / the entire universe" (*Discursos*, 36). The Spaniard affirmed the possibility of widening knowledge within an orthodox Christian cosmology. But it was precisely Goya's "Dream of Reason" that raised epistemological doubts about such knowledge, turning attention to the occult workings of the aether in imagination and dream. This insight into the limits of Reason provides a context for Bussy's visionary dream from the abyss. Whereas Goya sets the mood for a Romanticized aether of the kind studied by Tuzet, Bussy sums up the scientific concept as the Enlightenment understood it. Thus the parting of the ways is marked, as both physics and literature delimit the idea of aether for their own experiential frameworks.

Transition
The Undermined Primacy
of Visual Perception

[Philo:] The discoveries by microscopes, as they open a new universe in miniature, are still objections, according to you, arguments [for a Deity], according to me. The further we push our researches of this kind, we are still led to infer the universal cause of all to be vastly different from mankind, or from any object of human experience and observation.

—Hume, *Dialogues Concerning Natural Religion*

The Unstable Faith in Newtonian Optics

The classical irony of the blind hero or prophet who sees more clearly than sighted people turns into a paradox in the eighteenth century. Now the situation involves Newtonian optics and the microscope, a system and an instrument emblematic of the ever-improving sight so necessary for perfecting knowledge. One paradox of this improved vision is that the closer the eye reaches pure light, symbolic of Truth, the less it can tolerate the brilliance. The source of light is blinding, and if this is the case then eyesight is the wrong faculty for achieving absolute knowledge.

Complaints about the paradox of eyesight are muffled but widespread in literature at this time. British poets using Newtonian imagery rejoice in optical vision, as Marjorie Nicolson has shown in *Newton Demands the Muse* (1946). But her evidence also reveals a strong evocation of flawed eyesight. In citing this subtheme, she treats it as a casual motif cross-stitched into the major theme of exalted power in scientific eyesight. Closer study of her examples will show momentary unease flaring up beneath the poetic surface and its comfortable familiarity with the new science. Some phenomena, like meteors and lightning, baffle rather than illuminate the poets' understanding. Walter Savage reports his intellectual reservations after the first nerve impulses are registered: "a dire deception strikes the mental eye." The physical eye has been struck, and now the mind thinks disappointedly about the recorded image. At another moment, Savage sees rather imperfectly: "Full-orb'd it shone, and dimm'd the swimming sight, / While doubling objects danced with darkling light." The allusion to "darkling light" is a contradiction that goes beyond the mere description of light. It underscores, rather, a flawed perception that not only sees double but cannot get by with the quantity of light supplied (Nicolson, 95–96).

These poets do not complain intentionally. The ocular mechanism proves feeble, yet it does not diminish their intellectual enthusiasm for the glorious spectacle. On the other hand, their emotional response is severely ambivalent. Mark Akenside's vision begins with the magnificence of light, reports Nicolson, and ends with its pain "when 'afflicted vision plung'd in vain to scan / What object it involv'd. My feeble eyes endured not.'" James Thomson reported the grandeur and terror experienced in the deprivation of light: "at one moment he experienced 'a sacred terror, a severe delight,' at another he felt the 'privation' of night with its obliteration of all that man calls beautiful" (Nicolson, 130). From the standpoint of cognitive utility, therefore, one of the eyes fails in purpose by not furnishing the perceptual data that the pair strains toward. And yet the poets put a misplaced emphasis on the intensity of light, leaving blameless the "faint vision" that results from it. As Thomson writes, "The too resplendent scene / Already darkens the dizzy eye, / And double objects dance." It is as if the fault rested with excessive light when in fact no such excess is supposed to be an obstacle in the context of the ambition for total knowledge. The empirical case is the reverse. Light in its full presence is an intolerable burden for the fallible eye to transport to the waiting intellect. Pure light, symbolizing Truth and the fount of all knowing, remains unknowable to the brain. So too the objects bathed in its brilliance: the paradoxical medium illuminates them and blinds the viewer to their presence.

A twofold inadequacy, expressed unwittingly by Thomson, is at work. When he looks on a summer evening lit dimly by a glow-worm, the "moving radiance twinkles" just enough to betray the presence of objects all around. But the insufficient light-beam prevents knowledge just as much as a too sufficient beam does in the earlier example. The radiance produces a tantalizing exposure of objects half-unseen: "A faint erroneous ray, / Glanced from the imperfect surface of things, / Flings half an image on the straining eye." Thomson ascribes poor visibility to the objects themselves, although the imperfection clearly extends to the eye that strains with limited penetration.

By the same token, Thomson reports that the straying light beam is weak. The medium that epitomizes all such conductors of intelligible data here falters in its illuminating power. But if pure light is light, how can it now be anything less? If it bears intrinsically the mediatory properties that make it superior to the sign-bearing vehicles for the other senses, why then is it susceptible to adulterating shade? The unsatisfactory "half an image" raises the question of what inherent qualities in light contribute to so variable a visibility. Without asking this question, Thomson experiences the effects of diminished lucidity and eyesight. Whichever of these latter two produces visibility, neither the medium nor the sensory organ gives suitable cognitive results: "While wavering woods, and villages, and streams, / And rocks, and mountain-tops that long retained / The ascending gleam are all one swimming scene, / Uncertain if beheld" (Nicolson, 96–97). The poet knows only that the scene is a reality composed of objects. Beyond this, another sensory faculty would be helpful.

These minor difficulties are the major philosophical stumbling blocks to a "night poet" like Edward Young, who cannot fit into the Newtonian scheme Nicolson devised for the daylight poets. Instead, in *Night Thoughts*, Young despairs at the rationally acquired thoughts first based on the slim evidence of the eyes: "Thro' chinks, styl'd organs, dim life peeps at light." [1] Another form of vision dispensing with light gains unmediated access to "true" reality. The form of dream taken in *Night Thoughts* leads directly to the troubled intuitions that prefigure Goyesque insights. But even a temperate poet like Alexander Pope mentions dreaming in a way that suggests a groping toward alternatives to the unsatisfactory optic mechanism of "imperfect vision." The dream sensibility brings nonsensory principles into poetry. Allusions especially to fancy and imagination, synonymous terms during most of the Enlightenment, mark the route toward freedom and eventual disorder. Fancy liberated from both Reason and the constraints of sensorial reality exerts a power to build another kind of knowledge that the Newtonians would deny.

To enter the dream psychology of even the controlled allusions by Pope means that we descend to the edges of disorder and discontinuity. The visual sense data passing from object to retina and optic nerve, and

1. Edward Young, *Night Thoughts*, ed. Stephen Cornford (Cambridge: Cambridge University Press, 1989), 3:450.

thence to the brain, travel an allegedly unbroken path to the place where
Reason compares and judges its images. By contrast, no such orderly process governs the arena abandoned entirely to imagination or fancy. These
images do of course originate in waking sensory experience, one axiom
of the century being that every dream image has been impressed first on
the imagination in an earlier moment of everyday perception.[2] When thus
understood, the chaotic nature of the ensuing dream no longer conceals
the moral truths that are of interest to Pope and other daylight poets. The
"internal view" brightens as comprehension grows:

> As the last image of that troubled heap,
> When Sense subsides, and Fancy sports in sleep,
> (Though past the recollection of the thought)
> Becomes the stuff of which our sleep is wrought:
> Something as dim to our internal view,
> Is thus, perhaps, the cause of most we do.

Several unspoken maxims about psychology need to be sorted out in this
"First Epistle" of the *Moral Essays*, including memory's role as image-
retriever in waking life. Memory's quiescence coincides with sensory inac-
tivity, and Pope's contrast of "subsides" and "sports" reinforces the agitation already surmised in "troubled heap."

Thinking about dreams in this way removes the scientifically informed
poet from the daylight world of knowledge. The "internal view" paradoxically recognized by the Newtonian Pope has nothing in common with
perceptual vision; its internality is almost as remote from the tranquil mode
of understanding enjoyed by rational means. Pope's orderly couplets match
the ideal of harmonies among expression, truth, and wisdom, but the ideal
of universal light seems to be challenged by sleep. And yet the darkness
of "that troubled heap" brings forth understanding in another form. How
Pope the rationalist can respect so incompatible a medium is a puzzle of
sorts, and critics have recently detected a more perturbed cosmovision in
his work. That Pope's respect is perhaps fleeting, may be confirmed by
the end of *The Dunciad*, whose "sublime" style is described by Nicolson as
characterizing the sublimity of darkness.

Further evidence of the paradox of eyesight appears in French litera-

2. Jean Henri Samuel Formey, *Essai sur les songes*, in *Mélanges philosophiques*, vol. 1 (Leiden, 1754), 192.

ture and art. The motif of blindness in Sade's *The Misfortunes of Virtue* has been discussed at length elsewhere.[3] Specialists in French literature frequently cite numerous paintings of blind persons in the eighteenth century (Chardin, Greuze), and in Marmontel's *Bélisaire* (1767), whose protagonist, having fallen from privileged authority, embodies the precariousness of sight and is a focus for the anxieties of the age. Blindness as an image of uncertainty, error, or loss offsets the general recognition of advances in optics, microscopy, and astronomy. Even the ascendancy of the spectator in writings by travelers to foreign country or by autobiographical self-observers does not suffice to negate the French authors' attraction to the idea of reversible blindness as a figure for their faith in the enlightening potential of experimental science. Indeed, they also "harbored a fear of the figural 'blindness' or 'monstrosity' which can befall those who see."[4]

Other critics of French literature of the Enlightenment stress the reader's "gaze" in the paradox of cognitive blindness. Here the notion is that rational judgments may derive unwittingly from a malformed faculty of sight that actually prevents the knower from "seeing" an object. Thus, in one deconstructionist reading, Rousseau's *Dialogues* are said to address the many "unsighted" readers who did not "see" the real man "shown" to full view by the *Confessions*.[5] More conventional is the blind man who is seldom duped, in contrast to sighted characters tricked by deceptive appearances in Montesquieu's thirty-second *Lettre persane*. Elsewhere in this work, Usbek remains blind politically despite the rational light that he gains, as the revolt in the harem indicates.[6]

One critic goes so far as to term the philosophy of *lumières* a philosophy of darkness, conjectures, and trials. In Serge Trottein's view, the question is: what is "light"? For as the article on *Clair-obscur* in the *Encyclopédie* suggests, in order to understand light it is necessary to understand the chiaroscuro technique. Inevitably the example of Diderot enters the discussion. His distinction in *Pensées sur l'interprétation de la nature* between a blindfolded experimental philosophy and a torch-bearing rational philosophy, one more useful than the other, demonstrates for Trottein the paradox of a century of *lumières* in which philosophy advances in darkness. The false

---

3. See Chapter 8 of my Volume 1, *Counter-Rational Reason in the Eighteenth Century*.

4. See Virginia E. Swain, *"Lumières et Vision*: Reflections on Sight and Seeing in Seventeenth- and Eighteenth-Century France," *L'Esprit Créateur* 28 (1988): 10–11.

5. Peggy Kamuf, "Seeing Through Rousseau," *L'Esprit Créateur* 28 (1988): 82–83.

6. See Béatrice Durand-Sendrail, "Mirage des lumières: politique du regard dans les *Lettres persanes*," *L'Esprit Créateur* 28 (1988): 73, 78.

belief that there is nothing outside of what our senses perceive, and that everything ceases to exist beyond what we see, is denounced by Diderot. The belief arises from fear of the unknown, and the frightening prospect of an infinite regress in Nature.[7]

The Purblind Microscope

In addition to the paradox of eyesight is a second paradox that involves the microscope's contribution to an improved intellectual vision. Here the significant evidence comes from natural philosophy rather than literature, but one poetic example is indispensable because its author was a sophisticated philosophical polymath who, moreover, composed his verse toward the end of the century and shared the same cultural climate as Goya. Referring to "the vain desires and studies of men," Gaspar Melchor de Jovellanos didactically describes one scene where the scientist

> grabs his microscope, equips it, and falls upon a wretched atom. How foolish is his triumph when the magic instrument offers him a slight sign of motion and life! He investigates its shape, and, demanding of the glass what his illusory imagination foresaw, he yields to deception by giving lowly matter the omnipotence denied to the great Being. Thus the ingrate raves, while another tries to scrutinize the intimate essence of the sublime spirit that animates him. (Polt, 193)

The structuring metaphors of this pessimistic verse epistle are "celestial light" and the "tenebrous chaos" approached by human reason. The wan "light of reason" seeks its illuminating source but Touch is only "shadows" in the "labyrinths of error." The microscope thus serves with apt symbolism. However, it is an extraordinary choice for a leading Spanish enlightener renowned for social reforms, who now finds his mood shifting into ideological retreat.

This is not to gloss over the incontestable advances realized by the microscope for biological knowledge, not to mention its opening a new dimension in consciousness. Its invention confronted the human mind with insects and, as Georges Gusdorf observes, created a Gulliverian experience, an epistemological space permitting the human frame to be understood by regarding the minuscule one (*Dieu, la nature*, 313). At the same time,

7. Serge Trottein, "Diderot et la philosophie du clair-obscur," *L'Esprit Créateur* 28 (1988): 108–9, 112, 117.

the experience was a vertiginous deepening of the field of vision. Scholars have noted the relativizing effect of microscopy, either for its "unsettling" metaphysical implications in regard to the polyp, as Virginia Dawson remarks, or, as Jacques Roger notes, because the vogue of the microscope turned biological study away from human anatomy and revealed the complex structure of insects to be equal to man's. Barbara Stafford has called these pioneers of an invisible perceptual reality "microscopic seers" whose instruments disintegrated the traditional concept of the body as an integral whole (*Body Criticism*, 341–61).

The paradox of microscopic discovery appears in the descriptions accorded the instrument in the *Encyclopédie*. There are two articles, one of them under the entry "Microscope" and devoted to the strictly technical optics and lens measurement. The second entry, "Microscopic," departs from the unambiguous scientism of the first by outlining the procedures for examining specimens. In this account, author Louis chevalier de Jaucourt stresses the importance of the amount of light that must be admitted in order properly to view the specimen. That is, if the object is dark, use lots of light; if it is transparent, use less. Left unsaid is the qualification that the formula depends entirely on the viewer's judgment, which must be subjective inasmuch as the specimens belong to an unfamiliar world of shapes and sizes that cannot be verified independently of the viewing instrument. The problem of truth alerts Jaucourt enough to warn that "one must take great care to obtain the necessary light, for upon it depends the truth of all our examinations; a little experience will show how objects appear differently in one position and in one kind of light from what they are in another position" (*Encyclopédie*, 10:493b).

This example illustrates the imprecise and even metaphorical quality of scientific description under the artificial circumstances of sightedness. The authority of Henry Baker is the source for Jaucourt's article, which takes verbatim a portion of Baker's chapter 13, "Of Examining Objects," from the widely circulated *Of Microscopes and the Discoveries Made Thereby*. Baker's specimen is the eye of a fly, which appears in one kind of light "like a lattice drilled through with an abundance of holes: in the sunshine, it appears like a surface covered with golden nails." Similarly, in one position it looks like a surface covered with pyramids, and in another position, covered with cones. In still other situations, the eye seems covered with yet different shapes (*Of Microscopes*, 1:54–55). Moreover, Baker (and the *Encyclopédie* after him) repeats Hooke's confession to lacking the most elementary condition for looking at the material world—that is, the three-dimensional character of height and depth: "as Mr. Hooke says, in many objects it is very difficult to distinguish between a Prominence and a Depression; between a shadow and a black stain; and in Colour between a Reflection and a Whiteness." The precision of microscopy is thus only well established by the *Encyclopédie* with regard to its optical mechanics. As to its application in discovering the truth about invisible matter, microscopy is an art like any other, vulnerable to doubt concerning the artist's judgment: "it is appropriate to turn the objects on all sides and place them under every degree of light until one is assured of their true shape." The grounds of assurance remain unreported in the face of the metamorphic instability of perception.

The spread of confidence in microscopic vision may be portrayed briefly, without attempting a detailed survey, simply by noting the kinds of books disseminated. A lavishly illustrated treatise on lens-grinding and the construction of both microscopes and telescopes appeared in Paris in 1671, under the title *La dioptrique oculaire* and written by François Lasseré, alias Cherubin d'Orléans. More than a century later, in 1787, the British scientist George Adams Jr. published a diversified book titled *Essays on the Microscope*. Between these limits, in 1747, Adams Sr. published *Micrographia Illustrata*, which includes a translation of Louis Joblot's and Abraham Trembley's accounts of fresh-water polyps. In addition, Baker's aforementioned work appeared in London around 1741, and its first volume was reprinted in 1743 and titled invitingly *The Microscope Made Easy*. In 1764, Martin Ledermüller's long technical study of 1761 in German, illustrated with lavish copper plates, appeared in translation as *Amusement microscopique tant pour l'esprit que pour les yeux*. Furthermore, the concept of microscopic detail suggests an epithet for all manner of close critical inspection. Thus it inspired the title *Le microscope bibliographique* (1771) for Maximilien Malebranche's critical survey of the French publication *Journal Encyclopédique*, and others published by Pierre Rousseau, where inaccuracies and banalities reputedly impaired the cultural climate. Finally, a noteworthy metaphor in philosophical discourse appeared in David Hume's coinage "a new Microscope" when alluding to minute operations of the mind (*Inquiry*, 74).

In her study of the microscope and English imagination, Nicolson finds no startling or immediate stimulation of poetic or religious imagination as occurred when the telescope was invented. She surveys the mixed reactions to its invention by Thomas Digges among men of science and men of letters. Nicolson admits that the paradoxical sighting of Nature's beauty and repellent ugliness elicited an undeniable pessimism among lay-men and scientists. Overall, however, the warnings against human pride and neglect of God given by Henry Power in 1663, and microscopist Baker's realization of his "incapacity for either" of the two extremes of Creation—magnitude or minuteness—are signs of a dual "conception" of both pes-simism and optimism. In the end, Nicolson opts for the contention that "the microscope led even more certainly than the telescope to optimism and to fervent praise of Man" (90).

Such was the climate of expectations in the eighteenth century. It in-fluenced the intellectual world in the generations preceding Goya, who subsequently used *Capricho 43* to submit the generally confident expec-tations to an intuitional skepticism. Nor was the author of this engrav-ing by any means alien to the world of microscopes. The versatile utility of the instrument for engravers, jewelers, lapidaries, and fine-instrument makers is emphasized in Louis Joblot's *Descriptions et usages de plusieurs nouveaux microscopes* (1718). A glance at *Capricho 43* suffices to indicate the two optical or purely visual trouble spots that interfere with a confident grasp of the picture's basic information prior to interpretation. First, the horizon behind the airborne bats and owls is dotted with unidentifiable flying specks. Second, the graphic inscription must be read to be under-stood with its meaning reinscribed imagistically. Whereas eyeglasses are not needed for the inscription, a mental telescope or microscope might be thought useful for the receding perspective of bats that presumably trail off into chiropteran specks. Yet these hypothetical optic instruments only encourage speculation about probabilities.

The behavior of lenses in microscopes, telescopes, and eyeglasses, in their early stages, depends at least as much on magnification as on re-fraction. The microscope especially comes to be considered a telescope in reverse, like a fraternal twin of different gender. Both instruments enlarge and probe depth, each in its own genre of space. But eighteenth-century science being neither masculine nor feminine in gender but, so to speak, androgynous like its protective deity Minerva and capable of omnific at-tributes, these optical instruments evolve in philosophically dissimilar di-rections. The microscope revolutionizes habits of thought that relativize objectivism, while the telescope ratifies the systematic application of cos-mological mechanism.

In this evolution, the fortune of the microscope is of historical inter-est chiefly for its unique role as detector of inconspicuous fissures of am-bivalence despite its widespread usage. An accompanying feature of this development is the book illustrations that increasingly supplemented not only scientific writing but also texts of all kinds, engravings often executed with enough imagination to create a new epistemological experience of the kind mentioned earlier in regard to the Gulliverian dimension of consciousness. For instance, published sketches sparked wonderment by depicting the strange world of near-invisible creatures like the polyp, or magnifications of epidermal and mineral specimens. The stage had already been set by the equally strange illustrations found in the natural histories of Athanasius Kircher. This neglected late-seventeenth-century Jesuit, who was among the most scientifically informed of the erudite polymaths of his time, exercised considerable influence over the Catholic sector of West European enlighteners in the next century. Kircher is an important scientific authority in Spain for Feijoo, himself a major disseminator of recent natural philosophy. We must imagine the powerful visual impact of such works as the 1709 Rome edition of the *Musaeum Kircherianum*. Its engravings supplemented the wonderland of fossil drawings that also pictured underground dragons, both biped and winged, in the *Mundus subterraneus* of 1665. Few other books of natural history were as richly illustrated, and the stunning range of sketches that depict marine plants, mollusks and shellfish, and mineral configurations—all displaying their mushroomed or dendrical shapes, coral webbings, and veined textures—must have burst on the visual awareness with the same initial shock experienced verbally by the first modern readers of free-association prose.

The modern reader who skips the Latin pages of Kircher looking only for the pictures will just pause briefly before the engravings that depict machinery and large engines devised for hydrology and mining. The same holds for optical and chemical contraptions like magic lanterns and elaborate alembics. They induct the novice of any century into an unfamiliar world that at first seems fantastic, until the gaze grows restless because these fabrications are scaled larger than life even though man-made. It is rather the natural forms in reduced scale that lend the schematic pictures in Kircher's books an odd and sometimes disconcerting reality when encountered at close range. The microscopic eye of the illustrator already is apparent in these drawings, a forecast of the approaching curiosity that turns science inward to a reality that defies naked eyesight. At the same time, the peculiar and even occult air about the pictorial ensemble indicates quite another direction that, in Goya's time, the more imaginative naturalists and supernaturalists will take.

This irrational or aesthetic effect is present even in a scientific materialist like Le Cat, who from 1739 to 1767 can speak of the "often fantastic and trick-playing images" of the microscope (*Sensations*, 13). While his physiological observations of sense-perception are level-headed, microscopic descriptions comprise in his words "the most sublime anatomy" of all. Here Le Cat feels neither poetic nor religious sentiment, only the respectful caution demanded by the "infinitely small parts of the machine" that elude precise explanation. On this scale the most "secret and essential operations" hold sway, unreachable by optics and remaining the site where the "mysteries of life" converge, nothing less than the "sanctuary of nature" (14–15).

Textual asides in life-science discussions like Le Cat's are the occasional mileposts that show where naturalist inquiry bifurcates into esoteric and rational branches. The more fantastic accounts originated in seventeenth-century traditions or earlier, but they persisted into the Enlightenment and squeezed between the hard layers of "new" science and antiquarianism like the sludge of semi-superstition that oozes both ways. A book about ancient and modern superstitions by Bellon de Saint-Quentin in 1733 reprinted a letter of 1692 by a Dr. Chauvin to his friend and patient the Marquise de Senozan. This type of carryover in time is identical to those that characterize the rigorous treatises on brain anatomy, in which the 1668 discourse by Stenon reappears in successive editions and updates. The clarity of Stenon's description seems to have been prized notwithstanding the long strides made in microscopy by 1766, the date of a late French edition of Winslow's renowned *Anatomical Exposition*. The letter salvaged by Bellon de Saint-Quentin belongs more properly to the polemics against magic, but it incorporates microscopic technique into the medical thought of its time and thus wins extended life.

The curious feature of Dr. Chauvin's letter is that it purports to defend certain uses of the divining rod by a proof that appeals to the molecular findings of the microscope. At the same time, this text is included in a compilation designed by Bellon de Saint-Quentin to disprove supernaturalism. The argument cites the microscope's recent findings that assist us in imagining bodies much smaller and harder than those perceived by the senses. According to atomistic theory, there are tiny corpuscles in the interstices of earth, water, and air, tiny bodies that are unbreakable or displaceable by larger elements. Based on this corpuscular structure, and on the "organization" of the human sensory system, Dr. Chauvin reasons that a villager with a divining rod can detect and pursue murderers. The process entails a physiological "sympathy" developed along the route of flight and pursuit, whereby the mediating rod responds to the endlessly divisible corpuscles, to the movement of the animal spirits, the diviner's inner emotions, and to the irregularity of blood and tissue fluid on both sides (Bellon, *Superstitions*, 4–5). The argument rests on creditable notions of the physical world and grows shaky when its reasoning ignores cause and effect as they apply to divining rods.

Poorly reasoned principles, protected by favored assumptions, also crept into the most serious experimental memoranda. The observations on the generation, composition, and decomposition of animal and plant substances by John Turberville Needham are such a case. Experiments with common infusions made from crushed seeds produce filaments revealed under Needham's microscope. He enlists Buffon's prestigious collaboration to confirm an assumption of a "vegetative force" behind this propagation. In a previous set of slides, Needham's microscope reveals male semen to develop first by liquifying and then by shooting out long filaments that "ramify on every side" and divide into "moving globules" that trail "filaments" or long tails after them (*Observations*, 15–16, 29). Now his brewed seed mixtures seem to corroborate the earlier work. Under magnification a "new class of beings" becomes visible, but their unknown origin also magnifies their mystery. They are "animals" that "grow upon, are produced by, and in the strict sense of the word brought forth from plants, then by a strange succession again become plants of another kind, these again animals of another, and thus on for a series, further than the utmost power of glasses can carry the most inquisitive observer."

A thin borderline of awe separates these pragmatically noted transformations from the specious reasoning that tries to vindicate divining rods on equally sound scientific principles of the day. Needham concedes the inadequacy of microscopes for a complete explanation, while Bellon de Saint-Quentin perpetuates the confident logic that argues scientific truths from abstract concepts. This exchange of roles nudges biology paradoxically toward the irrationality of wonderment even as superstition speaks in a more confident technical jargon. The "strange succession" of the animal-vegetal cycle is the fostering context of this slight shift. Nothing less than the hypnotizing process of metamorphosis is involved, a natural phenomenon so commanding that it first assumes mythic proportions in ancient culture.

The idea of metamorphosis, treated in Chapter 2, takes on new life in the eighteenth century after long being relegated to literary contexts. The metamorphic feature that simulates the sense of wonder is summed up in the "marvelous liveliness" reported in 1718 by Joblot in the microscopic changes of the common maggot. Natural transformation requires Joblot's disciplined attention. His day-to-day sightings rivet his awareness, the first step to more imaginative contexts where metamorphosis can be contemplated as a general process. Joblot's tiny brown worm is nearly round, with eleven rings and three dark-amber legs on each side. On June 10 he observes its "marvelous liveliness," and from July 10 to September 2 it produces ten tinier bugs. The worm sheds its now white skin and remains brown again for the entire winter. It is dormant in April, appearing dead. But a second shedding ensues and occasions its "metamorphosis" into a fly (*Description*, 34–36). More poetic occasions for Joblot to exalt the microscope are shown later. In the experiment just described, the noteworthy concept is the fact of metamorphosis itself, which Goya could not help but construe both for its biological elusiveness and for its philosophical implications. It is this broken line in Enlightenment biology that permitted poetic intervals to intrude precisely where the new optical technology asserted its rigor in the face of superstitious fantasy.

Much later in the century, the best example of that broken line may have occurred when Cabanis delineated the physical and moral interdependence of human behavior. Cabanis extends Le Cat's materialist psychology and also his recourse to microscopic evidence. He is no less assiduous in carrying the instrument's dramatic power to its inevitable lyrical inadequacy. Place any organic, mucilaginous substance under a microscope and let it dry, proposes Cabanis. His own sources have reported on almond specimens, which shrink in volume as they dry and can be seen transposed into myriads of "animalcules" that agitate and "pullulate" as they seek nourishment. These micro-organisms seek to devour, they perish, and their bodies may be observed to produce yet smaller animalcules. Metamorphosis is now defined as a cycle of destructions and reproductions that follow one another until the most powerful microscope can only discover "the stillness of the tomb" (*Rapports*, 2:1).

This morbid note, auditory in its allusion, combines with the visual note of an optics that now, in a descriptively weak moment, cedes its place and leans on the livelier sense of hearing, capable of detecting even silence. The poetic paradox is crucial to Cabanis's purpose in citing metamorphic evidence. The death-to-life pullulations swirl endlessly and dramatically without interrupting the "chain" of "intermediary echelons" that obey the law of the eternal movement of matter. But a comparable linkage among the senses permits the substitution that science needs for uninterrupted coherence. In both cases we are on the border of Chaos, the two-tiered edge where the natural universe still gives an organized structure to its volatile parts and where the individual mind still performs the same orderly act with respect to its perceptions.

A similar passage in Condillac's treatise on animals describes this second metamorphosis more plainly as a chaotic succession of whirling sensations. Although Condillac is referring specifically to animal psychology, his message is the comparative one of how human understanding differs from the other animals. He speaks of ideas in relation to needs, and of how memory retrieves these ideas in "whorls" as they arise with their corresponding needs. Thus each need

> is a center from which movement extends to the circumference. These whorls are alternately superior to one another in proportion to how violent the needs become. They all spin with astonishing self-interest: they press, they destroy, they take form once again. . . . From one moment to the next, the whorl trails others after it is swallowed up in turn, and they all grow confused as soon as the needs cease. One sees only a chaos. (*Animaux*, 84–85)

Condillac's vivid account cannot be supported with material evidence, but its evocative imagery gives an inkling of how tempted the life sciences were by the metaphorical crutch. Nor have we digressed very far from the suggestiveness of microscopy in this regard.

From Condillac's image of Chaos to the notion of abyss is but a short step when the main avenue of discussion continues to be organic reproduction. The much debated theory of the animalcule within the animalcule presents the scrupulous Maupertuis with the perspective of a swarming chasm whose measureless sweep is unimaginable except by microscope. The theory of preexisting germ-encasement envisages succeeding generations like so many Chinese boxes, and "what an abyss of number and tininess!" this entails, exclaims the mathematician Maupertuis. From one generation to another "the bodies of these animals diminish in the same proportion of size as that of a man to the atom which is only discoverable with the very best microscope." The image of an unbreachable distance is compounded when the succession materializes visibly into tadpoles "lost in a labyrinth," or where the successions "metamorphose" into a fetus (*Oeuvres*, 2:24, 26).

The figures of speech Maupertuis uses adhere to the philosophical ideal of the continuity of all being and thought. The microscope promises to add links to the chain of knowledge, and yet its colossal range of magnifying power betrays that power. The germ within the germ diminishes geometrically, so that the distance between each on the scale of atoms indeed is abyssal. A still more important implication concerns the philosophical assumption of continuities. The microscope reveals distances between the parts of the most compact bodies, obliging Maupertuis to conclude that no material substance is continuous. And if this is true infraspatially, it is the obvious case for the macrocosmic range of interstellar space. That Nature may be a random dispersal of parts rather than a Whole is a plausible hypothesis that Maupertuis dares to raise as a mathematician who knows his biology (2:175–76).

The advances in microscopic science per se up to 1756 are praised by Maupertuis, although he refers by name only to Needham and Buffon. He goes so far as to urge government support for further work in lens-making, with a prize to be awarded for the most sophisticated microscope. But for every Maupertuis there was a Daniel Leclerc, who urged suspension of medical judgment until the final proof is determined. Leclerc was a historian of medicine who in 1717 doubted that the instrument was properly used by most experimenters. His caution was often echoed later in the century, according to Jacques Roger, who uses Leclerc's words: "the imagination, which is joined imperceptibly to eyesight, and especially so when one believes he has found the reason for certain things he is seeing and thus becomes ever so faintly stubborn on the point, may result in his seeing, so to speak, what he does not see at all" (Roger, *Sciences*, 192). This is among the most explicit texts for corroborating Goya's "dream of Reason," because it gives weight to the interpretation that *Capricho 43* depicts Reason in the act of imagining or dreaming beyond its facultative prerogatives. Both text and etching thus inculpate scientific reason together with other human activities for the disarray of eighteenth-century life.

The tie between imagination and microscopy exists early in eighteenth-century optics and late in the history of the instrument's usage. Joblot's descriptive book of usages for the newly developed microscope in 1718 still carries a strong sense of wonder at the "marvels" to be seen. A fly regales the eye more opulently than a palace, and a droplet from a fermented concoction turns into a "vast lake" where surprisingly minute fish of all shapes are diversely motile (*Description*, 33). The lively interest in metamorphosis, reawakened in the eighteenth century, owes as much to the morphological diversity now available for study as to the reproductive theories already mentioned. Insofar as Joblot intends his book as a primer for the general public, he is overgenerous in his technical exposition of how microscopes are constructed and how viewings may be influenced either by the angles of reflecting rays or by the position of specimens. But insofar as his book is also an advocacy of versatile usage, its appeal to the aforementioned engravers and mechanical artisans of all stripes encourages imaginative applications. The appeal does not foresee that a grossly magnified object might attain a transformation unsuitable to ordinary circumstances or to science. Be this as it may, the microscope does not seem to have become a source of salon amusement in the way destined for electricity.

Among its most rigorous advocates, the microscope conserved its pragmatic role without blinding these savants to the inevitable recourse that imagination offers by enlivening their corroborations. Buffon confirms an unsuspected relation between minerals and organic matter through an argument that takes an imaginative leap of faith. His example is a salt crystal, which he calls

a cube composed of an infinite number of other cubes distinctly recognizable under a microscope. These little cubes are themselves composed of other cubes perceptible with a better microscope, and there is scarcely a doubt that the primitive parts constituting this salt are also made of cubes whose minuteness will always escape our eyes and even our imagination. (*Histoire naturelle*, ed. Varloot, 174)

This confidence permits the further conclusion that Nature has an infinite number of living or organic parts that are made up of the same organized substance as the mineral bodies just mentioned. As Maupertuis puts it, the smallest matter has a principle of intelligence (*Oeuvres*, 2:149). The ideal of continuism hovers nearby. Nevertheless, Buffon's claim that "there is scarcely a doubt" is a deductive inference. He reasons by means of correspondences that encourage a Humean "belief" in continuity, based nearly on pure fact. But the residue of doubt attracts special notice because the microscope is blind precisely at this fragile point: the "minuteness will always escape our eyes and even our imagination."

The fragility of microscopic sight is summed up in the *Encyclopédie*, whose dichotomous articles on this topic, discussed earlier, betray a discontinuous conceptual organization. The entry titled "Microscope" is a miniature treatise on optics, while the entry titled "Microscopic" shifts attention to the purpose of microscopy and the descriptive accuracy obtained for the objects intended for magnification. The fact that an object is microscopic poses the disruptive question of which methods make visible what our senses inform us to be invisible, methods that determine the "true" nature of the object. The first article deals with the technical features of an autonomous instrument whose scientific beauty leaves no room for the philosophy behind its application. Its engineering is its own end. In contrast, the second article exposes the difficulty in distinguishing spatial relationships, such as shape, elevation, and depth. Its examples, including fiber and lower animal anatomy, lure the reader to other articles on these subjects.

In its conglomerate, then, the literature on microscopic study widened the aperture of doubt with each increment of mystery attached to the undeniable new discoveries that are made. The polyp was an uncanny creature that provoked questions about the relevance of eyesight as well as the essence of neural activity, and about the nature of life's origins. These topics lead in turn to the subject of physical matter, which under microscopic study and in the form of fermentations or granules provides occasion for framing the concept of linkage. Nature's unbroken gradation is precisely the hypothesis exposed in *Capricho 43* by the airborne specks that perhaps represent the continuity between bats and owls. But the scientific basis for such a vision exists at the microscopic level of structured matter.

The mystery of universal connection had a key that was believed ultimately to lie in the microanatomy of sense perception. And this neurological dimension is the den where the monster of discontinuity raises its head. The "angiscope" is Le Cat's preferred one-lens instrument for studying nerves, a microscope he recommends for the clarity of relief it supposedly gives to fine objects. On the other hand, Needham's criterion is magnification, as he searches vainly for the eyes of his freshwater polyps. Both researchers share the intuition that the ultimate force responsible for meaningful structures—perceptual or just plain molecular—is an invisible but substantive presence. And both studies founder on the inadequacy of the microscope's capabilities. The heart of this concept remains nevertheless inscrutable at its source, which is the vital substance common to all creation and variously labeled as brain matter, aether, or divine spirit.

The Surrogacy of Touch for Sight

Microscopic vision, and therefore eyesight itself, cannot see, much less understand, the basic truths that nonetheless are believed consensually by the eighteenth century—namely, that a material object coheres because its particles hold together or are "connected," and that connectedness or continuity is the sine qua non for the Chain of Being. It cannot be demonstrated that everything in the universe *touches* something else. This belief is unprovable except by abstract Reason, and it is wholly undemonstrable to the material senses. The external world perceived by the five senses eludes positive verification of its grounding principle. On this account, the eighteenth-century preoccupation with microscopic particles persists until it can go no further in unveiling the secrets of molecular matter. Investigation will ultimately pass beyond biology and beyond the sense of sight to the realm of physics, where atoms and subatomic particles will be studied by other means.

The pervading fascination with the sense of Touch in the place of eyesight has its explanation in the context just outlined. Among its focal points is the dilemma of the man born blind, posed originally by William Molyneux to John Locke at the end of the seventeenth century. The dilemma embraces several issues, including the problem of whether the sense of "Touch" alone adequately replaces sight for the purpose of knowing the truth about the basic material status of external objects. The "basic" status comes to be defined as three-dimensional space. Other more narrowly construed problems initially motivated the philosophical consideration of the dilemma as well. But its celebrated interest thereafter, together with countless independent allusions to the primacy of Touch among the five senses, cannot be explained on technical or philosophic grounds alone. The theme enjoyed an independent status of its own in painting and engraving, where its representation is a particular irony.

For centuries, the Hermetic symbol of an eye centered in the palm of the hand appeared in numerous allegorical frontispieces of books and on title pages. The union of tactile and visual perceptions became so conventionalized at the end of the Renaissance that one representation shows a hand with its palm spread open and an eye atop each fingertip, an image used as a printer's mark in Spain.[8] At the same time, allegorization began to break away from Hermetic and religious orientations. One engraving by Adrian Collaert in the sixteenth century depicts a matron holding up a spiderweb in the right hand—an echo of the Minerva-Arachne myth— and an eagle in the left hand. While the many small scenes framing matronly "Touch" include the expulsion of Adam and Eve, the majority are

---

8. The publisher Luis Sánchez in 1595 used this image, reproduced in Francisco Vindel, *Escudos y marcas de impresores y libreros en España durante los siglos XV a XIX, 1485–1850* (Barcelona: Editorial Oribid, 1942), nos. 386, 387.

secular and naturalistic. One scene with men fishing with nets extends the spiderweb theme, while a large tortoise in the foreground stresses the reptilian and chthonic character of life that survives through tactile sensing. Memory of this iconological tradition is maintained in eighteenth-century emblematics. In one iconological manual, *Le Toucher* is depicted by a youth touching his left wrist in order to feel his pulse, and the text cites Aristotle in reference to the universality of touch among the animals (Boudard, *Iconologie*, no. 127). A similar text accompanies the figure of a young woman whose wrist is grasped by a falcon's claws (Richardson, *Iconology*, no. 105). Crawling animals like the snail and the ferret pass before a monkey, serving as an attribute for the hands in Gravelot (Fig. 14).

This tradition maintains the mythic Minervan presence in a discreet fashion. In 1760, the five senses depicted in seven engravings by Saint-Aubin reveal a sophisticated coincidence of motifs. The allegories for both "Touch" and "Sight" feature a piece of weaving as the foil for a young woman seated indoors next to a table. The woven fabric is ready for embroidering. In the allegory for "Touch" it is placed on the table, while in "Sight" it is placed in the woman's two hands. "Touch" sits with her elbow propped on the table, one hand supporting her cheek and the other resting on the knees. "Sight" sits with feet propped on a stool, looking head down at the fabric in her hands. A ball of twine in the foreground is toyed with by a cat, and nearby is the table with a workbasket and scissors. However, whereas these are the only attributes of idle "Sight," those of "Touch" include a book that rests on the table alongside the woven cloth (Bocher, *Gravures françaises*, 5:115–17). So many attributes for the senses in a manual of iconology might preclude interpretation because their role would be to permit artists to select a few such attributes according to a particular intention. But Saint-Aubin himself is an artist who has made his selection, and it encourages a disparaging interpretation of "Sight," at once idle and removed from the possibility of reading. As for "Touch," her proximity to both the woven and the written object recalls the manifold arts of the Goddess of Wisdom. Another allegory, already examined in Chapter 1, is Le Cat's frontispiece, which places "Touch" in the bottommost, darkest area, where men beat weaponry at their forge and offer their gift to Minerva. A comparable, earlier painting by Rubens after Brueghel, *El Tacto*, dedicates the entire canvas to armaments—breastplates, leg guards, spears, helmets—and tools, together with a forge and a bird of prey; in a pre-Goyesque "Touch," an owl hovers in the gloom (Prado, no. 1398). There is also a remarkable painting by Nicolas de Largillière that depicts

LE TOUCHER

Figure 14. Hubert François Gravelot. "Le Toucher" (Touch). *Iconologie*, vol. 4, p. 115. 1791. Courtesy of the Bibliothèque Nationale, Paris.

nothing but eleven hands in various poses that run the gamut of tactile activities from the most abstract (holding a letter) to the most sensual (fondling a woman's nipple).

The preceding examples, easily extendable to monographic length, document a far from shallow undercurrent that bestows independent value to the sense of "Touch" in the visual arts. Certain unverbalized ideas suggest themselves regarding this status, pointing back again to the nature of sensory knowledge and the language that expresses it. These ideas also appear in written form, sometimes indirectly through imaginative literature, and more often conceptually in the texts of natural philosophers. One passage in Buffon on the function of touch declares: "It is by touch alone that we can acquire complete and real knowledge. It is this sense that corrects all other senses, whose effects would only be illusions [otherwise]" (*De l'homme*, 213). The same text confirms Buffon's manifest attachment to palpable matter by upholding the "absolute preeminence of touch over sight," according to Roger (*Autre Buffon*, 120). The most fundamental knowledge, it will be seen, concerns the ability to ensure organic survival. But it must also be asked whether the tactile sense becomes metaphorized at much higher levels of human discourse where the definition of survival is best made in the appropriate terms of human aspiration. In social and moral terms, and in the sense of conserving the human species in time, is there evidence of an exaggerated sense of touch?

The answer begins to take shape in one example that fantasizes a race of "night-men" who resemble bats in *La découverte australe* by Restif de La Bretonne. Other anthropoid hybrids are also fantasized in this work, such the "monkey-men" and "dog-men." But the "night-men" are represented as a real species, not an accidental one, living silently in grottoes by day and using their voices only at night. One of them, observed to walk by groping with his eyes shut, is taken prisoner, and it is learned subsequently that his people hope to perfect the race by intermarriage. While the author hardly proposes to be realistic, his conception of evolutionary development emerges from a period that prioritizes eyesight and therefore makes it possible to fantasize the condition of primal man in tactile and auditory terms. A more famous example in fiction, cited by Marjorie Nicolson, is the "man born blind" who distinguishes colors by touch in the third book of *Gulliver's Travels*. This serious allusion in an otherwise satirical fiction is based on fact, Swift having found a reference to a man with this power in Robert Boyle's works. The Swiftian character Scriblerus also exerts this power: "by the delicacy of his touch, [he] could distinguish the different vibrations of the heterogeneous Rays of Light" (Nicolson, 84).

The power of tactile knowledge is a genuinely appealing notion, although the ultimate reasons for this appeal are doubtless subjective in the case of literary authors like Restif de La Bretonne and Swift. What seems clear is that their examples draw on two popularized scientific principles represented by the words "race" and "vibrations." The authors situate tactile knowledge in two frameworks of time—one evolutionary or collective, the other psychological or individual. These two perspectives, separate here, meet in Diderot's intuitive mixture of science, philosophy, and fantasy, *D'Alembert's Dream*. That the convergence occurs in so important a work confirms the preoccupation with touch as the originary and supreme faculty of perception. Diderot's text limits evolutionary time to the individual embryo, described in its development of a nervous system, while psychological time is represented by the sensory nerves, described by their intervals and successions of message-bearing sensations. It is not surprising that the dominant anatomical element is the fiber. Diderot begins by tracing human origin from a "dot" of molecules in the parents' blood or lymph to the point where it becomes "a thin thread, then a sheaf of threads."

> This bundle is a system capable of feeling sensations, and nothing more. If it continued to be just that it would be sensitive to any impression affecting sensitivity alone, such as heat, cold, smoothness, roughness. This sequence of impressions, varying in inensity and differing from each other, might perhaps produce memory, consciousness of self and a limited kind of intelligence. But this sensitivity pure and simple, which is nothing but touch, becomes modified in character in organs developed from different threads: one forms an ear and gives rise to a kind of touch that registers noise of sound; another forms the palate and gives rise to a second kind of touch that we call taste; a third, forming the nose and its lining membrane, gives rise to a third kind of touch that we call sense of smell; a fourth, forming an eye, gives rise to a fourth kind of touch we call awareness of color. (*D'Alembert's Dream*, 186–87)

The idea that memory, consciousness, and Reason might evolve on their own from the tactile sense if the fibers were left to themselves is a speculation that remains unexplored in *D'Alembert's Dream*. But Diderot's interest in the polyp, together with texts by other thinkers, reinforces the attribution of cognitive power resident in less complex matter. What might be called "dermatopsis" is precisely the sensibility to light and sound registered by the skin or external surface of lower organisms, such as the tortoise or spider that serve allegorically for the sense of touch. Significant in itself is the conversion of all sensory faculties to the single dermatoptical sensing power.

Diderot's fascination with tactile knowledge leads him to fuse the perspectives of evolutionary time and psychological time. In contrast, the naturalist's concern with time is oriented chiefly toward the past, since the history of species can be documented only in the past tense. The embryologist can do no more for an organism's prenatal history. As for the forward-looking evolutionary orientation presented by Restif's "night-men," its conception of time is an instance of what Paul Alkon has called a "futuristic fiction" containing its own scientific component. Several further kinds of discourse also dwell on the sense of touch by framing it in the temporal terms of cultural history and its moral heritage.

One painting by Hubert Robert uses tactile knowledge to evoke past history in the human scale of time. Robert's very large *Ruins. Interior of Diana's Temple at Nîmes* depicts an early moment of history represented in monumentally proportioned ruins that are inspected by diminutive human visitors to the site (Fig. 15). The spectator, when regarding canvases of this size, habitually tends to stand back and take in the whole, since the towering background—whether high stone walls, as in this case, or mountains against the horizon elsewhere—can only be seen intelligibly at a distance. But in this instance the spectator too must move up close and join the dwarfed figures in the foreground, who at eyeball range become life-size, just as the ruins they in turn wish to regard become intelligible to them as they draw near to the external surface. However, now the roles of living and painted beholders cease to be comparable. Robert's observers approach so close to the ruins that they appear to be not so much looking as touching the graven stone surfaces. Like groping figures, they point at and finger the ancient inscriptions they cannot read. The vision provided by eyesight does not help them understand history, and they resort instinctively to a more "primitive" form of cognizance, as children might finger or handle strange objects in order to familiarize themselves with their nature. Indeed, in the group at the right, one member already leans an elbow familiarly on a slab and thus joins the iconological convention of allegorical sightlessness that may be witnessed either in Saint-Aubin's rendition, mentioned earlier, or in Goya's unseeing dreamer of *Capricho 43*.

Robert's visitors among the ruins enact the tactile acquisition of historical values. The knowledge of history is a requisite for the organism's survival in its highest cultural form. But that knowledge reaches an im-

Figure 15. Hubert Robert. *Ruines* (Interior of Diana's Temple at Nîmes). Courtesy of La Réunion des Musées Nationaux, France.

passe—the abyss of time described in Chapter 3—that the tactile sense can circumvent, if imperfectly, according to Robert's representation of time's material reality. There remains the social and moral knowledge that perhaps is the subtlest level of all for eighteenth-century creators of sensibility. Here too, rather dramatic examples reveal touch to be the controlling metaphor. The works of Sade present the libertine acts of touching and handling that gratify beyond the power of sight. The destructive nature of libertinism transgresses the licit bounds of tactile sensuality, although its negative example also serves as a form of moral knowledge. Indeed, even when a character repents of carnality, as in the early version of *Justine*, the word "maceration" is used to evoke its plastic nuances as the operative term for a spiritual purge achieved by physical means. In Laclos's *Liaisons dangereuses*, the most dramatic moments as well as the epiphanies of awareness occur when messages transpire by the squeezed hand, the heartbeat felt in a brief embrace, the feeling of weight on one's stomach. Although this novel of sensibility thematizes appearances that depend on the gaze and physiognomic signs, its sensual vocabulary is austere except for the type of kinesthetic allusions just mentioned. Similarly, the dizzying spatial spectacle in Piranesi's *Carceri* transcends the visual impasses that bewilder the eye. The incarcerated subject in these engravings stands surrounded by sinister chains, pulleys, toothed wheels, spiked beams, and other frightening artifacts of the torture chamber. They inspire their terror through the tactile imagination. The prisoner can conceive of the menace only by mentally anticipating the palpable press of these devices on his body. But then, in the victim's desire to escape the secret dungeon, the grilled windows, iron grids, and stone-walled staircases become palpably physical barriers against the hands and feet, whereas their effects on the spectator are merely visual.

The Idea of "Tactile Knowledge"

The preliminary evidence offered here suggests that "haptonomy," or the science of affectivity through material contact, becomes articulated verbally and pictorially in the eighteenth century.[9] The haptonomic gesture is as old as placing hands on a human being to impart a sense of security or

---

9. The neologism is coined by Bernard This in keeping with the prefix *hapto*—attach, knot, touch, make contact ("Le sentiment océanique et l'haptonomie," in *Art et fantasme* [Paris: Editions du Champs Vallon, 1980], 235–51).

confidence. It is linked by Bernard This to the so-called "oceanic feeling" evocative of the maternal amniotic fluid but also of eternity. In any case, the psychological roots of the tactile motif lie in human nature and go beyond the present scope of discussion. What seems undeniable is that the widespread preoccupation with touch exists both in its own right and in the absence of eyesight.

Running parallel to this interest seems to be a comparable fascination with dreams. In *Capricho 43* the fact that Goya's bats cannot see and yet are perfectly cognizant, or that his dreamer cannot actually see them and yet envisions them by dreaming, imply alternate forms of perception, material or otherwise. The *Encyclopédie*'s article on "Songe" reminds the reader that the ultimate test of reality is that people touch themselves to know if they are awake or dreaming (15:357). The process of falling asleep to dream is described by Spanish alchemist and mathematics professor at the University of Salamanca, Diego de Torres Villarroel, who writes, "instant by instant I kept losing the touch of my eyes and the sight of the other three and a half senses" (*Visiones*, 16).

It is axiomatic among scholars that the phenomenon of light is the metaphor for Truth among philosophers as well as writers and artists in the eighteenth century. By extension, eyesight and Reason were metonymically fused in the context of understanding (e.g., "I see what you mean"). The condition of blindness acquires a conceptual status of its own in iconology, where it appears with its own emblematic attributes (Gravelot, *Iconologie*, no. 5). While countless examples abound in writing, it is noteworthy that Hume abandons the metaphor of light at a given moment in exchange for the metaphor of touch. Hume's allusion to light evokes the context of microscopes mentioned earlier:

> These impressions are all strong and sensible. They admit not of ambiguity. They are not only placed in a full light themselves, but may throw light on their correspondent ideas, which lie in obscurity. And by this means we may perhaps obtain a new microscope or species of optics by which . . . [to enlarge the minute, finer operations]. (*Inquiry*, 74)

Soon after, Hume discusses the means of connecting these "correspondent ideas," and he resorts to the metaphor of contact or touch, like the effect of his billiard ball that leads to conjunction. He says that the mind always conjoins similar previous causes to similar previous effects. Then, "we only learn by experience the frequent conjunction of objects, without being ever able to comprehend anything like connection between them" (81).

In a similar vein, one example from poetry is noteworthy because it illustrates a comprehensive argument about the fundamental insubstantiality of things that mortals blessed with eyesight may find incomprehensible. In *Fragments of Ancient Poetry* (1760), James Macpherson describes the sightless Ossian lamenting the dead through the pessimistic theme of ubi sunt?—"I feel their tombs with my hands"—, effected while listening to the river's murmur of the lost past. In citing this passage, Fredric Bogel comments on "a curious desubstantializing of past, present, and almost of temporal location itself" (Bogel, 99). It may be recalled in this regard that the best compensation Minerva can devise for having punished Tireisias with blindness, in the hymn by Callimachus, is to grant him the wisdom denied to sighted mortals (*Hymns*, 148–54).

The tactile surrogacy for sight understandably is a disputed endeavor in the century of light. The wavering between the primacy of touch and sight extends to the neurophysiological sections of books on psychology and natural history. Perhaps the author least impressed by the sense of touch is the eminent biologist Claude-Nicolas Le Cat, who devotes virtually his entire treatise on the senses to the faculty of sight. Le Cat believes that touch is the crudest of the faculties, and he devotes fifteen pages to it, and as many for the other three senses. What he reports, nevertheless, includes the history of a blind man with a remarkable sense of touch, the sculptor Ganibasius of Voterre, who reputedly could make a clay replica of an object after touching it (*Traité*, 211). The divergence between Le Cat and other colleagues more bemused by touch reflects the disparity between a shallow regard that conceives of this faculty by the conditions abiding at its perceptual externality, and a more thoughtful regard that conceives of touch as a language internal to the mind. It is nonetheless the case that there can be no tactile signal without the epidermal activity that is eventually internalized through the perceptual mechanisms.

One limitation to further research on touch becomes obvious through the limitations of the microscope. In his description of the origin of the tactile sense in the cutaneous papillae of the skin, Haller observes that the round papillae are "seated in cavities of the cuticle and receiving nerves very difficultly seen" (*First Lines*, 1:245). The microscopic eye dims as it attempts to observe the "cellular network whose fibers and plates are closely compacted and interwoven together in an intricate manner, which renders it porous" (1: 244). Thus Haller remains at the external end of nerve activity without mentioning what manner of path the neural message travels along. In view of the importance granted to fibers, he misses the issue of discontinuity that announces itself in the porousness detected in the cellular network. Le Cat provides a similar description, except that in keeping with a fluidist conception of signaling, he refers to "the nervous capillaries," which, after having "converged by their interlacing to the formation of the skin, terminate at its external surface and there shed their first inner lining (*paroi*), that is, the lining furnished it by the dura mater," thereafter going on to form the reticulated epidermis (*Traité*, 209). In this observation, all relations with cerebral matter become vestigial and the internalized touch passes without comment.

A more open ambiguity appears in Bonnet's assignment of touch to the lowest order of the senses (*Essai de psychologie*, 68–74). Despite this ranking, Bonnet concedes that the only way to distinguish a real globe from a painted one is to touch it: "the mind (*âme*) cannot distinguish here between the appearance and the reality except by touch." Furthermore, when it comes to explaining the phenomenon of sight, he cannot avoid the tactile metaphor:

> The light that reflects upon an object can be considered as a solid body, like a bundle of tiny darts that rest one end on the object and the other end on the retina. The mind touches so to speak the eye's object, as it would touch it with the finger or a rod, but this kind of touch is infinitely more delicate than touching proper. (81)

The group of observers who regard touch more respectfully include La Mettrie, Diderot, Condillac, and Delaroche, among others. The fact that La Mettrie links touch to the organs of generation, owing to the pleasure felt in sexual activity, betrays the originary character attributed to touch mentioned earlier. But his more pertinent observation aligns La Mettrie with those who remark that "the blind have a fine sense of touch," later described as "exquisite," and being constituted by the "nervous tufts ('houpes') that extend not perpendicularly . . . but parallel and longitudinally," a disposition that enables them to acquire ideas about shape and distance in compensation (*Histoire*, 350–51). This text, according to Aram Vartanian, is the point of departure for Diderot's analysis in *Letter on the Blind* to the effect that "Saunderson sees by his skin" (Vartanian, 1983). Regarding Diderot's widely discussed conception, scholars have approached it from so many viewpoints that an attempt to summarize them would be futile. Many of Diderot's salient remarks are quoted throughout this study in other contexts, and his position is perhaps best abbreviated here in the present context of physiology. He coincides with Buffon in observing that touch corrects eyesight and that the touch is per se indeed an eye for several reasons. First, the medullary substance is common to both mechanisms, as demonstrated both by new research on crayfish and by standard anatomy. Second, although each sense has its own alphabet and "burin," with the brain functioning as a wax page, an "exquisite" touch can replace all other senses. Diderot also conceives of a touch so exquisite that it can detect colors, this idea arising in the context of polyps but also plainly while he was thinking of the human brain (*Éléments*, 9:316, 345–47, 368).

Diderot's ambivalence toward sight and the light of Reason, notwithstanding many texts emphasizing both and favored by scholarly studies, remains confirmed by his own irrationalist style and ambiguous genres. The lure of tactile cognition in Diderot exists and fits pertinently into its general theme at that time, if not dominating his own philosophy of knowledge. The issue of scholarly emphasis is less serious here than when one deals with the role of touch in Condillac, whose work coheres more recognizably as a consistent set of principles. The changes in outlook from the *Essai sur l'origine des connaissances* to the *Traité des sensations* are unidirectional, in contrast to the fluctuating weight of interests in Diderot's more varied and more numerous works. Condillac's earlier treatise challenges the privileging of touch that Berkeley advances in his essay proposing a "new theory of vision," and this point has been noted by Jacques Roger. On the other hand, the later *Traité des sensations* abandons the idea of vision's self-sufficiency, defining the central issue to be "perceptual order," as Isabel Knight has indicated. Condillac continues to maintain that touch is no more credible than the other senses, and that while touch may suggest an external world it does not establish this as fact. The particular point now is that no single sense reveals to the statue anything outside itself (Knight, 100, 105).

At the same time, two more elementary principles build the foundations of Condillac's philosophy, one of them identified by Knight as "the genetic priority of sensation." The second principle is that "the fundamental physical experiences of pleasure and pain is the root, the true source, of the development of the mind" (Knight, 88). Both principles define the rooted essence of knowledge in biological terms. They generalize for all living organisms the corporeal awareness that inheres prior to sight, smell, taste, and hearing. This is to say, the knowledge acquired through kinesthesia is anterior even to specific touch. It must be stressed that, for the eighteenth century, knowledge of this kind did not require self-consciousness in order to qualify as authentic cognition. Here cognition means an all-embracing capability circumscribed only by its utility to the organism in its particular rank within the scale of beings. Thus not only the cognitive act but also its mediating language may be said to fall within the range of capabilities shared by all sentient beings from polyps to higher animals and finally to the reasoning human being. These definitions of cognition and language are a necessary perspective if the intellectual historian is to be able to speak globally about the development of such concepts.[10]

The sameness of animal and human thinking mechanisms is made plain in Condillac, inasmuch as both beast and man are shown to process information, understand it, and thereby survive without the use of Reason or eyesight. Revealing evidence of this indistinction appears in Condillac's use of the statue, an illustration that he modifies significantly at a crucial moment. As noted, no single sense reveals to the statue anything outside itself. Because this is the case, it must be asked why Condillac initiates the statue's sensory awareness with the sense of smell in the *Traité des sensations*. His statue is an example designed to expose man's originary experience by considering the progressive steps taken by the statue as a gradually awakening sentient being. But Condillac does not follow all the possible permutations of progressive sensory acquisition. The bulk of his attention eventually focuses on sight anyway, in keeping with the overt tenor of privileged notions at that time. This quantitative fact makes it imperative to keep in mind the subordinate role accorded to sight as Condillac establishes the operative groundwork of information processing and abstraction. He first describes the statue as being equipped only with the olfactory nerve and a corresponding brain receptor. A rose is presented to the awakened statue, and the analysis commences. However, in the *Traité des animaux* the very same example is varied for the sake of brevity by coupling smell with the sense of touch. In this instance, the statue appears already capable of many concrete and abstract operations without the aid of the other three senses, including sight. Moreover, the final sense to be described is sight, whereas touch is the final sense described in the *Traité des sensations*.

---

10. This perspective will be located within a Neoplatonic context in my Volume 3, *The Universal Dream Language of Minerva*.

The order in which the senses impinge on the statue therefore does not seem to be a crucial factor in Condillac. Whether the order is a crucial reality in the evolution of life or in the scale of beings is of course beyond debate. The polyp cannot see, but its epidermal sensitivity permits it to "know" by touch-sight. The point, however, is that Condillac himself reveals the statue to be capable of a remarkable range of concrete and abstract notions without sensory aids other than smell and touch. In the *Traité des animaux*, the statue's sensations and judgments occupy different categories of awareness, comprising a knowledge that dispenses with eyesight. The price of this knowledge, to be sure, is to forgo a more complicated series of mental operations. On this account, Condillac describes the statue by means of anticipation, foreshadowing vision's simplifying role by alluding to vision in contrast to the described complication. Nevertheless, the statue's cognitive ability as such is unrestricted when endowed only with touch and smell. Had Condillac wanted to devise further examples of tactile cognition, he could have extended this chapter to the length he evidently intended to reserve for the climactic chapter, which bestows sight on the already well-equipped statue.

No genuine contrast exists in the *Traité de sensations*. Although touch is the last of the five senses described, the analysis posits touch as being endowed in the statue unaccompanied by other senses. The statue awakens, and its primal experience is its sensation of selfness ("moi")—its breathing and the parts of its body. This can of course be construed as a kinesthetic form of touch, akin to the previously mentioned self-knowledge experienced physiologically by the personages in *Les liaisons dangereuses*. Condillac's statue feels nothing outside the self except heat and cold. The next degree of sensation comes with the addition of arm movement, in which the hand is the principle sensory organ. Mobility is thus essential, together with flexibility of the fingers. By these tactile means, the statue may know space, extension, shape, solidity, fluidity, hardness, softness, motion, rest, heat, and cold. Perhaps most essential of all for continued success in maintaining its life, the statue may know pain, pleasure, and desire. This cognitive array makes it irrelevant that Condillac considers the sense of touch last. As noted, he begins describing the statue by limiting it to the sense of smell. Even at this primitive level, the statue proves capable of all mental operations: it can compare, judge, remember, make connections, and have the affective experience of all this in the form of pleasure, pain, and desire. The virtual parity with touch does not, however, diminish the latter. On the contrary, diminished in both instances is the privileged status enjoyed by sight when invoked unanalytically outside such systematic contexts. What proves to settle the question of hierarchy is Condillac's assertion that the strongest sensations are those enumerated as being derived from touch: "the memory of ideas that arrive through touch must be stronger and last much more than that of ideas that arrive through the other senses" (*Sensations*, 1:210–11).

As Condillac suggests, the primary condition of awareness occurs when the statue becomes conscious of its breathing and bodily members. Prior to any external stimulus, an incipient sense of touch already exists in the form of kinesthetic sensation. The importance of this detail cannot be overestimated. There is no knowledge without a previous base of knowledge. As Condillac explains in the very first preface of *Sensations*, we cannot remember ever being ignorant. The state of ignorance leaves no trace in the mind, and so we cannot recapture the origin of our ideas. These ideas are already a given, and if that is the case, the fact that they are kinesthetic and inwardly tactile rather than derived from one or another external sense is a crucial determinant in building the foundation of knowledge. By inference, touch must precede and coordinate the activity of each of the other four senses in their meaningful processing of information:

> For touch, having instructed them, continues to act with them every time that it can be of some assistance. It takes part in everything that may concern them, teaches them to help one another reciprocally, and it is to [touch] that all of our organs, all of our faculties owe the habit of relating to the objects entailed in our conservation. (*Sensations*, 2:147–48)

A conclusive element of the statue's lesson is its final self-assessment, which Condillac designates under the rubric "The reunion of each sense with touch." Fully constituted, the sentient statue possesses a "general notion of sensation," which means

> that it will only form one class from all the impressions that bodies make upon it. And this idea is more general. . . . Deprived of touch, [the statue] is powerless to exercise alone any of the other senses . . . [without] its imagination acting with a force capable of rendering them present to it. . . . Thus these senses gain by their reunion with touch and compensate the statue even more for what it has lost on the side of imagination. (1:143–45)

In other words, while a past experience of the sensory world may be retrieved through imagination without the assistance of touch, the world's most "real" characteristic is its materiality, and this can be obtained only through touch. The point is made indirectly but it places tactile knowledge at the constitutive center of any experience of immediate external reality.

The conclusion that the sense of touch is the designated unifying principle of reality seems unavoidable. This is held without fanfare by eighteenth-century psychology. The conclusion is emphatically made in the domain of neuroanatomy by Daniel Delaroche, who sets touch apart from the other senses by defining its unifying property as the essential difference between it and other senses. Quite simply, the other senses furnish no idea of what might be the nature of the object that stimulates them, this nature being nothing other than an individual mass of matter configured uniquely in space. Yet whatever other of its qualities might be known to the perceiver, he could not know them to exist independently of himself unless the distance between him and the object were established: "Without touch, these four kinds of sensations would for us only be different manners of existing; we would attribute them entirely to ourselves" (*Analyse*, 1:93–4). Touch reveals the material condition of the object, separating its body from the perceiving body. Without touch, all qualities of the other would be applied to the self. Touch establishes the difference between self and other:

> But if we know a few of the properties constituting the essence of bodies, it is to touch alone that we are indebted. It is this which teaches us to distinguish what is not us from what is us. It is this which makes us perceive the resistance of a body at rest or its thrust when moving; and it is in consequence of this resistance and this thrust that we come to know the inertial force of that body. We soon learn that this very force is exerted equally, whether the external body acts upon ours at rest, or whether being at rest it undergoes the action of our body. The sensation that it excites varies with the direction of the thrust, the duration of the impression it creates, the number of parts in the body that are affected at the same time, or because the expression is felt with more or less vivacity upon the different parts. In this way we acquire the notions of size and consistency of bodies, as well as notions of extension and solidity, which are inseparable from the idea that we form to ourselves of matter. (*Analyse*, 1:98–9)

The explanation appears to be couched in terms of standard physics, but close analysis reveals the author's fidelity to his chosen subject, *Analyse des fonctions du système nerveux*. The terms employed belong to the psychology of perception ("sensation," "impression," "expression," "vivacity"). Furthermore, the nature of tactile phenomena resides in the modes of contact among masses, including the weight and thrust of the percipient's fingers pressing on the object, no less than conversely. While these modes share the vocabulary of physical dynamics, the text emphasizes sensation in its initial, external phase as a contact between surfaces, one of which is always neurally awake.

Any objections to the primacy of touch made by those who privilege sight are taken up by Delaroche and parried with several arguments: first, an allusion to Buffon's testimony of being blinded by looking at the sun and having his knowledge restored through the other senses, and second, an allusion to Cheseldon's blind younger life. Delaroche concludes by reaffirming that the tactile experience is the indispensable prerequisite for acquiring information through other senses. Our first ideas of distance are obtained not by seeing but by touch while stretching out the arms: "The idea that we form of a body's extension when it is beyond the reach of our hands is entirely relative to that of other bodies surrounding it, and it cannot be exact unless we know its distance" (*Analyse*, 1:100). This treatise on the nervous system of 1788 looks back over nearly a century of discussion of the "man born blind" dilemma and concludes that tactile knowledge is an a priori component of any notions that sight might furnish regarding the solidity and spatial status of objects.[11]

Epilogue

This chapter has suggested that the primacy of visual perception in the eighteenth century was undermined by themes that evoked an alternative: tactile cognition. Just as the poetic complaint of "faint vision" dissented from the Newtonianist revel in light's intensity and its verities, so did the philosophical theme of cognitive blindness denounce the illusory reality constituted by the world's external surface. There was, furthermore, an inverse side to microscopy's augmented sight. This was a spatial ambiguity in the unfamiliar sighted landscapes that were exposed without prior means of orientation. Invisible matter made suddenly visible showed ordinary perception to be as unstable as the metamorphic appearance of perceived reality.

These untrumpeted findings sustained an "internal view" of reality, a nonempirical boding of light's full presence grown unbearable to the

11. Delaroche's treatise complements identical arguments proposed by the philosopher Mérian in his historical survey of the Molyneux problem, commented on by Francine Markovits.

sensory eye's quest for Truth. A half-articulated unease gestated behind the writings and images under discussion, an intimation that some absent plenary faculty existed. Such expressions of incomplete knowledge sub- sisted at the same time that the new optical technology gave prominence to irrational processes such as metamorphosis. While Newtonian science carried ambivalent undertones, the ideal of universal light was challenged by such insights as Pope's conceit of a sporting fancy that explains reality through the "stuff of which our sleep is wrought." The microscope's aug- mented power of sight paradoxically heightened awareness of Nature's invisible mysteries, thus lending support to esoteric science as well as em- pirical science. Among the responses to the limitations of eyesight were imagination's wonderment over Nature's marvels and a fascination with the sense of touch. The idea of "tactile knowledge" underwent a surrep- titious gestation; it did not come fully into existence so much as it was an unnamed possibility confirmed by iconographical and literary evidence. The primacy of kinesthetic sensation in Condillac, and the primacy of tac- tile experience in Delaroche, together responded to the absence of that plenary faculty.

The suggestive role played by touch points back to earlier chapters of this book that discussed the polyp's "touchsight" and the overall dilemma of discontinuity in the face of the continuist and connectiveness ideals. The mystery of universal connection was thought ultimately to be solved by the microanatomy of sense perception. Le Cat's study of nerves, and Need- ham's search for the eyes of his freshwater polyps, shared the intuition that the ultimate force responsible for meaningful structures—perceptual or just plain molecular—was an invisible but substantive presence. And both studies foundered on the inadequacy of the microscope's capabilities. The heart of this concept remained in any event inscrutable at its source, which was the vital substance common to all creation and variously named as brain matter, aether, or divine spirit.

The wider scientific context involved the idea of a vital force. Vital energy was believed to function as a universal web that literally connected all things by invisible but no less material threads. And if material, they were also "tangible" threads insofar as this tangibility was apprehended by the minimal sensorium embodied by the polyp. Lacking a nervous system, the polyp nonetheless mastered an elementary signal code. Although a largely undifferentiated mass of organic matter, its molecules were "living" and "organized" in Buffon's meaning of the terms. But little else appeared to explain its astonishing mastery of a regenerative signal code.

The polyp also provoked questions about the relevance of eyesight as well as the essence of neural activity and the nature of life's origins. These topics led in turn to the subject of physical matter, which under microscopic study and in the form of fermentations or granules provided occasion for framing the concept of linkage. Nature's unbroken gradation was also the hypothesis revealed in *Capricho 43* by the airborne specks that perhaps represented the continuity between bats and owls. But the scientific basis for such a vision existed at the microscopic level of structured matter.

Required at this juncture was a physiological explanation of how the polyp's "universal language," so to speak, converted touchsight without relying on a sensorium or fibrous apparatus. Considering the deficient state of biological information at the time, the question bordered on an irrationalist framework. The question may be legitimately raised, however, when set against the comparative context of an artistic representation, such as Goya's allegory of perception and its nonsensory alternative in dream.

The link to Goya consists of his depiction of dream-space, which presented the brain as a trope for the continuity-discontinuity axis that shaped the problem of cognition. Brain anatomists had found it impossible to trace out the neural communications because of the brain's softness. They described neural disjunctions when investigating the connective mediatory substance akin to aether. This fissure between organic matter and mental acts paralleled the philosophical dilemma of the spirit/matter division. Again it was Goya's *Capricho 43* and related works that enabled a broad analysis of this discontinuously perceived reality.

The same problem of discontinuity appeared in concepts of knowledge that reflected a disparity between linear or continuous models and labyrinthine ones. Scientific writings used obsessive images like the fiber and the spiderweb to evoke connectedness and continuity, whereas cognitive discontinuity in other types of discourse appears in the themes of Chaos and metamorphosis. Here my earlier chapters built on the lexicon of Unreason described in my previous study of "counter-rational Reason" (Volume I). The evidence showed that the terms used in physiological treatises and natural philosophy included metaphors for the cognitive process, metaphors that glimpsed yet avoided the organic discontinuity of sense-perception and thinking. I suggested that eighteenth-century physiological terminology betrayed a subliminal unease regarding the organic discontinuity of sense-perception and thinking. Words like "branching," "network," "ramification," and "web" amplified the lesser metaphors "sheaf," "fiber" and "thread." These textile terms wove a compensating conceptual fabric of universal connectedness. Between the organic microcosm and the Absolute, the neural and aethereal fluids that together streamed from the "bosom of the Universe" were the glue of continuity.

By calling the eighteenth century "the Age of Minerva," my study identifies the quest for knowledge in a rational age with the symbolic attributes of the goddess Minerva. Most thinkers and artists in eighteenth-century Western Europe (France, Spain, England) shared the ideals of unbroken harmony, cognitive synthesis, and universal continuity. But their ideals dissolved in the face of a reality that they perceived as the aforementioned discontinuous experience. The disparity took paradigmatic expression in Minerva's appearance and disappearance in several key works by Goya. My point of departure, therefore, was "The Sleep/Dream of Reason Produces Monsters," on the assumption that a great artistic work often expresses the unstated preoccupations of an age. One such preoccupation in the eighteenth century, as indicated, was with the discontinuous nature of knowledge. Despite Reason's efforts to organize knowledge of "reality," the ideal of universal continuity dissolved in the face of empirical Nature, which thinkers perceived as a discontinuous experience. Indeed, the problem of discontinuity stemmed from Reason itself, whose multiple faces wrought the counter-rational effects described in Volume 1.

Yet another aspect of discontinuity was the dichotomy of spirit and matter. In order to reach the crux of the mind-body dilemma, this book has suggested that the flux of aether in the nervous system was the key to overcoming the division both at the level of primordial Nature and at the level of human cognition. The aethereal, spirituous, neural energy investigated by physiologists found an analogy in Goya's pictorial conceit about dream knowledge and how thought-mechanisms function. Appositely, biological research on polyps related these same functions to vital energy. The natural philosopher's fascination with polyps was a mirror of Goya's preoccupation with the bat; both creatures seemed to draw on Nature's metamorphic power, and both addressed the issue of what defines cognitive activity. All these activities and functions hinged on what I have called "the epistemology of aether." That is, the consubstantiation of universal and nerve spirits constitutes a language of signals needed for vital functions. The structure of knowledge stems from this language, whose sophistication varies with the organism's complexity.

The epistemology of aether attempted to explain how the polyp's "language" can exchange eyesight for touchsight without relying on a sensorium or fibrous apparatus. The polyp betrayed cognition in that its activities presented a prototypal model of successful organic functions in living matter. Insofar as its functional success depended on aether, it shared in a Universal Language. Cognitive success in humans is exponentially more complex but analogous. The chief instrument of higher human behavior is the imagination, which springs from the neurophysiology of aether but, like the polyp, also dispenses with eyesight. The imagination strives to overcome discontinuist flaws in the structure of knowledge. Here the abstractive process aspires to the all-connecting knowledge of Minerva. The relation of aether to Minerva remains to be described. Their immediate link is the replacement of sensory vision with the tactile connectedness figured by Diderot's spiderweb. In another figure, Goya's symbolic bat, the vision becomes the oneiric immanence of primordial materiality.

Goya's dream scenario epitomizes the Minervan symbolism of touchsight by reenacting the waking life's eidetic or imaging abstraction. In this perspective, "The Sleep/Dream of Reason Produces Monsters" invites an allegorical interpretation. The scene elaborates Goya's idea of a "Universal Language," which answers the need to overcome discontinuity. It promises to glimpse the primordial reality shared by the bat and the polyp, a reality where fundamental matter, being perpetually metamorphic, resists empirical representation and rational understanding. The dream mechanism, to be studied in Volume 3, dispels cognitive discontinuity through the workings of aether.

In Volume 1, *Counter-Rational Reason in the Eighteenth Century*, I described how eighteenth-century Reason exposed its alter ego, Unreason to be capable of protean powers and often monstrous results, in both the political and the moral realms as well as in scientific inquiry. I cited Minerva's presence and disappearance in several works by the artist Goya, interpreting "The Sleep/Dream of Reason Produces Monsters" as the paradigm of philosophical, social, literary, and psychological unease beneath the optimistic surface of eighteenth-century intellectual life. Goya's etching provided the occasion for analyzing the Enlightenment's rational assumptions about "reality" and its deformations. What I called "counter-rational Reason" is the opposite of a uniform center of rationality in representative thought. Goya's concern was the nuanced spectrum of all rational individualities. Rather than any hypothetical core of Enlightenment discourse, he called attention to the extended Minervan rippling generated by an indefinable rational impetus. The authors cited in support of this thesis displayed in their writings a special lexicon of Unreason that coped with the spiritual aberrations intuited in Nature and mental activity. Volume 1 ended with a discussion of irrationality within the cognitive process, which opened the way to the subject of the present volume.

Here in Volume 2 I have pursued the means by which Reason disrupts continuity in experience and knowledge. I have contended that the Minervan ideals of unbroken harmony and cognitive synthesis prevailed only at the Enlightenment's surface. A deeper unease was to be found in most philosophical and scientific texts, and in metaphors that exposed the discontinuity of sense-perception and thinking, or matter and mind. The title *Cognitive Discontinuities in Eighteenth-Century . . . Physiology and the Arts* is intended to designate the models in natural history that organized perceptions of reality. These metaphors have dealt with the idea of Chaos, theories of matter, brain anatomy, and the polyp as a prototype of cognitive process. The themes emerging in the writings of natural philosophers and neurophysiologists have illustrated the uncertain progress toward overcoming discontinuity, especially its most persistent form in the mind-body dichotomy. Here the division between spirit and matter promised to be resolved through the role of aether in neural signaling. Such a resolution implicated the eighteenth-century vestiges of the Ancient Philosophy, and its identification of aether with the Neoplatonic Minerva. This point concludes the present study without elaboration, for it opens a new framework for future discussion.

Volume 3, *The Universal Dream Language of Minerva*, will argue that a vestigial Neoplatonist aura surrounding Minerva survived in the subliminal consciousness of Western Europe. I shall explore Minerva's symbolic meaning and the belief that true Reality is knowable because an aethereal process mediates between spiritual light and human enlightenment. The spiritual and empirical modes of knowing Reality are discontinuous without Minerva, who provides the mediacy of aethereal cognition. However, the obstacle to such cognition is its lack of a language that, by partaking of both spirit and matter, can apprehend the elusive continuity. At the same time, Reality also embraces the multiple forms of Unreason. These include not only human irrationalities but also the primordial realm of being.

The argument will be therefore that "primary reality" is the metamorphic ground beneath perceived phenomena that ordinary language organizes rationally. This pre-linguistic reality is a domain beyond Reason that Goya depicted through symbolic monsters and glimpsed through dream. To capture it and have knowledge of its being is to possess a transcendent truth that belongs to the realm of Minerva. Access to Minervan Truth is gained through the aethereal cognition that achieves a communion of the spiritual and the mundane. This is the Universal Language depicted by Goya, who extended the idea to dream language. It will be necessary to survey eighteenth-century linguistic theories, and also the concept of dreams in treatises of physiology, in order to develop this point. Then it may be possible to link the neurophysiological view of dream mechanisms to the universal aether associated with Minervan language. The inference of this discussion will be that cognition may best be understood in more elementary and intuitive terms than conventional approaches allow by empirical reasoning.

Bibliography

PRIMARY SOURCES

Alciati. See Daza.

Alembert, Jean Le Rond d'. *Preliminary Discourse to the Encyclopedia of Diderot.* Trans. and ed. Richard N. Schwab and Walter Rex. Indianapolis, Ind. and New York: Bobbs-Merrill, 1963.

——. *Seconde lettre à M^{rxxx} conseiller au Parlement de^{xxx} sur l'état du roi d'Espagne, pour l'expulsion des Jésuites.* n.p., n.d. [Paris, 1767].

Baker, Henry. *An Attempt Towards a Natural History of the Polype.* London: R. Dodsley, 1743.

——. *Of Microscopes and the Discoveries Made Thereby*: (1) The Microscope Made Easy, (2) Employment for the Microscope. London: R. & J. Dodsley, n.d.

——. *The Microscope Made Easy.* London: R. Dodsley, 1743.

Banier, Abbé Antoine, *Explication historique des fables.* 2nd ed. 3 vols. Paris: Le Breton, 1735.

——. *La mythologie et les fables expliquées par l'histoire* (1711). 3 vols. Paris: Briasson, 1738–40.

Baumé, Antoine. *Dissertation sur l'aether dans laquelle on examine les différens produits du mélange de l'Esprit de Vin avec les acides minéraux.* Paris: Jean-Thomas Hérissant, 1757.

Bellon de Saint-Quentin, J. "Lettre de M. de Sal . . . médecin, à M. l'abbé de M. D. L." (1731). In *Dissertation critique sur l'apparition des esprits*, 2:90–95. Amsterdam: Jean-Frédéric Bernard, 1736.

——. *Superstitions anciennes et modernes, préjugés vulgaires, qui ont induit les peuples à des usages et à des pratiques contraires à la religion.* 4 vols. Amsterdam: Jean-Frédéric Bernard, 1733–36.

Bénard, A. *Éloge de l'enfer.* La Haye: P. Gasse, 1759.

Bergier, Nicolas. *L'origine des dieux du paganisme.* 4 vols. Paris: Humblot, 1767.

Boisard, J. J. F. M. *Fables.* Paris: Lacombe, 1773.

Bolzani, Valeriano and Giovanni Pierio. *Hieroglyphice overo commentari delle oculte significationi* . . . 2 vols. Venice: G. de Franceschi, 1602.

Bonnet, Charles. *Considérations sur les corps organisés.* Vol. 2. Amsterdam: M.-M. Rey, 1762. Facsimile edition by Francine Markovits. Paris: Fayard, 1985.

——. *Contemplation de la nature.* 2 vols. Amsterdam: M.-M. Rey, 1764.

——. *Essai de psychologie, ou considérations sur les opérations de l'âme, sur l'habitude et sur l'éducation.* Londres, 1755.

——. *Essai analytique sur les facultés de l'âme.* Copenhagen: Philibert, 1760.

Bordeu, Théophile de. *Recherches sur les maladies chroniques....* Paris: Ruault, 1775.

Boudard, Jean Baptiste. *Iconologie* [Vienna 1766] Facsimile edition by Stephen Orgel. New York and London: Garland Publishing Co., 1976.

———. *Iconologie, tirée de divers auteurs.* 3 vols. Parma and Paris: Tilliard, 1759.

Brooke, Henry. *Universal Beauty.* London, 1735.

Buffon, Georges-Louis Leclerc de. *Un autre Buffon.* Ed. Jacques Roger. Paris: Hermann, 1977.

———. *De l'homme.* Ed. Michèle Duchet. Paris: François Maspero, 1971.

———. *Histoire naturelle.* Ed. Jean Varloot. Paris: Gallimard, 1984.

———. *Histoire naturelle de l'homme.* Vol. 4 of *Oeuvres complètes.* Paris: Imprimerie Royale, 1774.

———. *Histoire naturelle des oiseaux.* Paris: Imprimerie Royale, 1749–67. *Supplément*: 1789–.

———. *Oeuvres philosophiques de Buffon.* Ed. Jean Rivetau. Paris, 1954.

Bussy, Martin de. *L'éther, ou l'Être suprême élémentaire. Poème philosophique et morale à priori, en cinque chants.* Paris: Imprimerie de la rue des Petits Augustins, 1796.

Cabanis, Pierre J. G. *Rapports du physique et du moral de l'homme.* Vol. 2. Paris: Crapelet, 1802.

Callimachus. *The Hymns of Callimachus, / Translated from the Greek into English Verse, / with Explanatory Notes, / To which are added, / Select Epigrams and the Comua Berenices of the Same Author, / Six Hymns of Orpheus, / and / The Encomium of Ptolemy by Theocritus. / By Wm. Dodd B. A. / Late of Clare-Hall, Cambridge.* London: T. Waller & J. Ward, 1755.

Calmet, Dom Augustin. *Dissertation sur les apparitions des anges, des démons et des esprits, et sur les revenants et vampires de Hongrie... Journal de Trévoux,* October 1746. Enlarged edition: *Traité sur les apparitions des esprits et des vampires ou revenants de Hongrie.* 2 vols. Paris: Debure, 1751.

Caramuel y Lobkowitz, Juan. *Laberinto.* Ed. Victor Infantes. Madrid: Visor, 1981.

Caylus, Comte de. *Mémoire sur la peinture à l'encaustique et sur la peinture à la cire.* Geneva: Possot, 1755.

Cheselden, William. *The Anatomy of the Human Body.* 4th ed. 1730. 9th ed., London, 1768.

Chompré, Pierre. *Dictionnaire abrégé de la fable.* Paris: Foucault, 1727. 12th ed., 1777.

Condillac, Abbé Etienne Bonnot de. *Essai sur l'origine des connaissances humaines* (1746). In *Oeuvres philosophiques,* vol. 1. Parma, 1792.

———. *Traité des animaux.* Amsterdam and Paris: Debure, 1755.

———. *Traité des animaux.* Ed. François Dagognet. Paris: Vrin 1987.

———. *Traité des sensations.* 2 vols. London and Paris: Debure, 1754.

Cueto, Leopoldo Augusto de, ed. *Poetas líricos del siglo XVIII.* Madrid: Los Sucesores de Hernando. Biblioteca de Autores Españoles 61 (1921); 63 (1917); 67 (1922).

Cullen, William. See Haller.

D'Alembert. See Alembert, Jean Le Rond d'.

Daza Pinciano, Bernardino. *Los emblemas de Alciato. Traducidos en rhimas españolas, añadidos de figuras y de nuevos emblemas en la tercera parte de la obra.* Lyon: G. Rovillo, 1549.

Delaroche, Daniel. *Analyse des fonctions du système nerveux.* 2 vols. Geneva: Villard Fils & Nouffer, 1778.

Diccionario [de Autoridades] de la lengua castellana . . . Compuesto por la Real Academia Española. 3 vols. Madrid: Francisco del Hierro, 1726–37.

Diderot, Denis. *Correspondance.* Vol. 9. Ed. Georges Roth. Paris: Éditions de Minuit, 1963.

————. *Éléments de physiologie.* Ed. Jean Mayer. Paris: Didier, 1964.

————. *Éléments de physiologie.* Vol. 9 of *Oeuvres complètes,* ed. J. Assézat and M. Tourneux. Paris: Garnier Frères, 1875.

————. *Lettre sur les aveugles à l'usage de ceux qui voient.* Ed. R. Niklaus. Paris and Geneva: Droz, 1963.

————. *Lettre sur les aveugles, Lettre sur le sourds et muets.* Ed. Yvon Belavel and Robert Niklaus. In *Oeuvres complètes,* vol. 4: *Le nouveau Socrate, Idées 2.* Paris: Hermann, 1978.

————. *Oeuvres complètes.* Ed. J. Assézat and M. Tourneux. Paris: 20 vols. Garnier Frères, 1875–77.

————. *Oeuvres philosophiques.* Ed. Paul Vernière. Paris: Garnier Frères, 1956.

————. *Rameau's Nephew, D'Alembert's Dream.* Trans. L. W. Tancock. Baltimore: Penguin Books, 1966.

————. *Le rêve de d'Alembert.* Ed. Jean Varloot. Paris: Éditions Sociales, 1971.

————. *Salon de 1765: Essais sur la peinture.* Ed. Else Marie Bukdahl, Annette Lorenceau, and Gita May. Vol. 14 of *Oeuvres complètes,* ed. Herbert Dieckmann and Jean Varloot. Paris: Hermann, 1984.

————. *Salon de 1767, Salon de 1769.* Ed. Else Marie Bukdahl, Michel Delon, and Annette Lorenceau. Vol. 16 of *Oeuvres complètes,* ed. Herbert Dieckmann and Jean Varloot. Paris: Hermann, 1984.

Encyclopédie, ou Dictionnaire raisonné des sciences, des arts, et des métiers. New facsimile printing of the 1st edition of 1751–1780. Slatkine Reprints. Stuttgart-Bad Cannstatt: Friedrich Fromann Verlag, 1967.

Formey, Jean Henri Samuel. "Considérations sur ce qu'on peut regarder aujourd'hui comme le but principal des Académies, et comme leur effet le plus avantageux. Second Discours." In *Histoire de l'Académie Royale des Sciences et Belles Lettres, Année 1768,* 357–66. Berlin: Haude et Spener, 1770.

————. *Recherches sur les éléments de la matière.* n.p., 1747.

————. "Essai sur le sommeil." In *Mélanges philosophiques,* 1:127–73. Leiden: E. Luzuc fils, 1754.

————. *Essai sur les songes.* In *Mélanges philosophiques,* 1:174–204. Leiden: E. Luzuc fils, 1754.

Forner, Juan Pablo. *Discursos filosóficos sobre el hombre.* Madrid: Imprenta Real, 1787.

Gamaches, P. Étienne Simon. *Astronomie physique, ou Principes généraux de la nature, appliqués au mécanisme astronomique et comparés aux principes de la philosophie de M. Newton.* 2 vols. Paris: Charles-Antoine Jombert, 1740.

Goupy, Louis. *L'éther, l'électricité et la matière.* Paris: Ledoyen, 1854.

Gravelot (Hubert-François Bourgignon, dit). *Almanach iconologique.* 17 vols. Paris: Lattré, 1765–81.

———. *Almanach iconologique ou des arts.* 2 vols. Paris: Lattré, 1763–73.

———. *Almanach iconologique pour l'année 1772: L'homme.* Paris: Lattré, [1772].

———. *Iconologie par figures, ou Traité de la science des allégories, emblèmes, etc., en 350 figures gravées.* 4 vols. Paris: Lattré, n.d. [1791].

Haley, William. *The Triumph of Temper.* 9th ed. London: Jones & Co., 1796.

Haller, Albrecht von. *A Dissertation on the Sensible and Irritable Parts of Animals.* Introduction by Owsei Temkin. Baltimore: Johns Hopkins University Press, 1936.

———. *Dissertation sur les parties irritables et sensibles des animaux.* Translated from the Latin. Lausanne: Marc-Michel Bousquet, 1755.

———. "Of the Brain and Nerves." In *First Lines of Physiology, Translated from the Corrected Latin Edition,* "Printed under the Inspection of William Cullen, M.D., and compared with the edition published by H. A. Wrisber, M.D." (1766), 1:178–226. 2 vols. Edinburgh: C. Elliot, 1786.

Hartley, David. *Observations on Man, His Frame, His Duty, and His Expectations.* 2 vols. London: S. Richardson, 1749.

Hume, David. *Dialogues Concerning Natural Religion.* Ed. Henry D. Aiken. London and New York: Hafner, 1969. also ed. Norman Kemp Smith (Indianapolis, Ind.: Bobbs-Merrill, 1981).

———. *An Inquiry Concerning Human Understanding.* Ed. Charles W. Hendel. Indianapolis and New York: [Bobbs-Merrill] Liberal Arts Press, 1955.

———. *A Treatise of Human Nature.* Ed. L. A. Selby-Bigge. 3 vols. Oxford: Clarendon Press, 1941.

Joblot, Louis. *Description et usages de plusieurs nouveaux microscopes.* Paris: Collombat, 1718.

Kircher, Athanasius. *Mundus subterraneus.* 2 vols. Amstelomi: Johannem Janssonium & Elizeum Weyerstaaten, 1665.

———. *Musaeum Kircherianum.* Rome: G. Plachi, 1709.

Knight, Richard Payne. *An Account of the Remains of the Worship of Priapus Lately Existing at Isernia . . . to which is added A Discourse on the Worship of Priapus, and its Connexion with the Mystic Theology of the Ancients.* London: T. Spilsbury, Snowhill, 1786.

La Mettrie, Julien Offray de. *Histoire naturelle de l'âme.* ["Traduite de l'anglais de M. Charp"]. The Hague: J. Néaulme, 1745.

———. *L'homme machine.* Ed. Paul-Laurent Assoun. Paris: Denoël-Gonthier, 1981.

———. *Oeuvres philosophiques.* Vol. 1. Berlin, 1754.

———. *Vénus métaphysique, ou Essai sur l'origine de l'âme humaine.* Berlin: Voss, 1752.

Lamy, Guillaume. *Discours anatomiques.* Brussels: Henri Fricx, 1679.

———. *Explication mécanique et physique des fonctions de l'âme sensitive, ou Des sens, des passions, et du mouvement volontaire.* 2nd ed. Paris: Lambert Rouilland, 1681.

La Perrière, J. C. F. de. *Méchanismes de l'électricité et de l'univers.* 2 vols. Paris: Brocas, 1756.

La Peyronie, François de. *Mémoires de l'Académie de chirurgie*. Paris: C. Osmont, 1743.

Le Cat, Claude-Nicolas. *Traité de l'existence de la nature et des propriétés du fluide des nerfs, et principalement de son action dans le mouvement musculaire*. Berlin, 1765.

———. *Traité des sensations et des passions en général, et des sens en particulier*. Paris: Vallat-La-Chapelle, 1767.

Lully, Raymond. *Liber chaos*. Mainz: Häffner, 1722.

Malpighi, Marcello. *Discours anatomique sur la structure des viscères, sçavoir du foye, du cerveau, etc*. Paris: D'Houry, 1683.

Maupertuis, Pierre-Louis Moreau de. *Essai sur la formation des corps organisés*. Berlin, 1754.

———. *Oeuvres*. 4 vols. Lyon: Bruyset, 1756.

M. D. C. de l'Académie Française. *Le dictionnaire des arts et des sciences* (1688). New ed. 2 vols. Paris: Rollin Père, 1732.

M. D. L. F. (Delafolie). *Le philosophe sans prétension, ou L'homme rare: Ouvrage physique, chymique, politique, et moral, dédié au savans*. Paris: Clousier, 1775.

Meckel, Johann Friedrich. *Recherches anatomico-physiologiques sur les causes de la folie qui viennent du vice des parties internes du corps humain*. In *Histoire de l'Académie Royale des Sciences et Belles Lettres, Année 1764*. Berlin: Haude et Spener, 1768.

Meléndez Valdés, Juan. *Obras en verso*. Ed. Juan Polt y Jorge Demerson. 2 vols. Oviedo: Centro de Estudios del Siglo XVIII, 1981, 1983.

Mérian, Jean Bernard. *Réflexions philosophiques sur la ressemblance*. In *Choix des mémoires et abrégé de l'histoire de l'Académie de Berline*, 2:1–49. Berlin and Paris: Rozet, 1767.

———. *Sur le problème de Molyneux*. Afterword by Francine Markovits ("Mérian, Diderot, et l'Aveugle"). Paris: Flammarion, 1984.

Needham, John Turberville. *Nouvelles découvertes faites avec le microscope*. Leiden: Luzac fils, 1747.

———. *Nouvelles observations microscopiques* (1745). Paris: Goneau, 1750.

———. *Observations upon the Generation, Composition, and Decomposition of Animal and Vegetable Substances*. London, 1749.

Newton, Isaac. *Opticks, or A Treatise of the Reflections, Refractions, Inflections, and Colours of Light*. 3rd ed. London: William & John Innys, 1721.

Pernety, Dom Antoine-Joseph. *Dictionnaire mytho-hermétique dans lequel on trouve les allégories fabuleuses des poètes, les métaphores, les enigmes, et les termes barbares des philosophes hermétiques expliqués*. Paris: Deladain l'aîné, 1787; reprint, Paris: Denoël, 1972.

———. *Les fables égyptiennes et grecques dévoilées et réduites au même principe, avec une explication des hiéroglyphes et de la guerre de Troye*. 2 vols. Paris: Delalain l'aîné, 1786. Reprint, 1982, 1991.

Quarles, Francis. *Emblems Divine and Moral. Together with Hieroglyphics of the Life of Man* (1635). London, 1777.

Restif de la Bretonne, Nicolas-Edmé. *La découverte australe* (1776–81). Ed. Paul Vernière. Paris and Geneva: Slatkine, 1979.

———. *Les nuits de Paris, ou Le spectateur nocturne*. London, 1788–89.

————. *Le paysan perverti.* 4 vols. The Hague and Paris: Esprit, 1776.

Richard, Charles-Louis. *La nature en contraste avec la religion et la raison.* . . . Paris: J. F. Peyre, 1773.

Richard, Abbé Jérôme. *La théorie des songes.* Paris: Frères Estienne, 1766.

Richardson, George. *Iconology* (1779). 2 vols. Introduction and notes by Stephen Orgel. New York and London: Garland Publishing Co., 1979.

Robinet, Jean Baptiste. *Considérations philosophiques de la gradation naturelle des formes de l'être.* Paris: Saillant, 1768.

————. *De la nature.* 2 vols. Amsterdam: Van Harrevelt, 1761.

Robinson, Bryan. *A Dissertation of the Aether of Sir Isaac Newton.* Dublin: George Ewing & William Smith, 1743.

Songe patriotique. N.p. 1790.

Torres Villarroel, Diego de. *La suma medicina o piedra filosofal.* Salmanca, 1752.

————. *Visiones y visitas de Torres con don Francisco de Quevedo por la corte.* Introduction and notes by Russell P. Sebold. Madrid: Espasa-Calpe, 1966.

Trembley, Abraham. *Mémoires pour servir à l'histoire d'un genre de polypes d'eau douce, à bras en forme de cornes.* Leiden: Verbeek, 1744.

Tressan, Louis, le comte de. *Essai sur le fluide électrique considéré comme agent universel.* 2 vols. Paris: Buisson, 1786.

Valeriano. See Bolzani.

Valois, Nicolas. *Les cinque livres, ou La clef du secret des secrets.* Précédés de Nicolas Grosparmy. *Le trésor des trésors.* Ed. Jean Roger. Paris: Retz, Biblioteca Hermetica, 1975.

Vieussens, Raymond. *Histoire des maladies internes . . . Neurographie. . . . Traité des vaisseaux.* 3 vols. Toulouse: J.-J. Robert, 1774–75.

————. *Traité nouveau des liqueurs du corps humain.* In *Oeuvres françaises de M. Vieussens.* 2 vols. Toulouse: J. Guillemette, 1714–15.

Voltaire [François-Marie Arouet]. *Oeuvres complètes.* Ed. Louis Émile Dieudonné Moland. 52 vols. Paris: Garnier Frères, 1877–85.

Winslow, Jacques-Benigne. *Exposition anatomique de la structure du corps humain.* Paris: Desprez & Desessartz, 1732.

Young, Edward. *Night Thoughts.* Ed. Stephen Cornford. Cambridge: Cambridge University Press, 1989.

————. *Night Thoughts, or The Complaint and the Consolation.* Illustrated by William Blake. Text by Edward Young. Ed. Robert Essick and Jenijoy La Belle. New York: Dover Publications, 1975.

SECONDARY SOURCES

Assoun, Paul-Laurent. "Présentation" to *La Mettrie: L'homme machine,* 9–80. Paris: Denoël-Gonthier, 1981.

Bateson, Gregory. *Steps to an Ecology of Mind.* New York: Ballantine, 1972.

Bocher, Emmanuel. *Les gravures françaises au XVIIIe siècle.* 6 vols. Paris: Damascène Morgand & Charles Fatout, 1875–82.

Bogel, Fredric V. *Literature and Insubstantiality in Later Eighteenth-Century England*. Princeton, N.J.: Princeton, University Press, 1984.

Bono, James J. "Science, Discourse, and Literature. The Role/Rule of Metaphor in Science." In *Literature and Science Theory and Practice*, ed. Stuart Peterfreund, 59–89. Boston: Northeastern University Press, 1990.

Bord, Janet and Jean-Clarence Lambert. *Mazes and Labyrinths of the World*. London: Latimer New Dimensions, 1976.

Bremner, Geoffrey. "Les 'Éléments de la physiologie' et le sens de la vie." In *Diderot: Les dernières années, 1770–1784*. Ed. Peter France and Anthony Strugnell, Edinburgh: Edinburgh University Press, 1985: 81–91.

Broch, Hermann. *The Death of Virgil*. San Francisco: Northern Lights, 1983.

Buckley, Paul and F. David Peat. *A Question of Physics: Conversations in Physics and Biology*. London: Routledge & Kegan Paul, 1979.

Byrd, Max. "Pope and Metamorphosis: Three Notes." *Modern Philology* 85 (1988): 447–59.

Cantor, G. N. "The Theological Significance of Ethers." In *Conceptions of Ether: Studies in the History of Ether Theories, 1740–1900*, ed. G. N. Cantor and M. J. S. Hodge, 135–55. Cambridge: Cambridge University Press, 1981.

Cantor, G. N. and M. J. S. Hodge, eds. *Conceptions of Ether: Studies in the History of Ether Theories, 1740–1900*. Cambridge: Cambridge University Press, 1981.

Casini, Paolo. "La revanche de l'inconscient: d'Alembert vu par Diderot." In *Dix-Huitième Siècle*, 17–25. Paris: Presses Universitaires de France, 1984.

Clarke, Edwin. "The Doctrine of the Hollow Nerve in the Seventeenth and Eighteenth Centuries." In *Medicine, Science, and Culture*. Ed. L. G. Stevenson and R. P. Multhauf. Baltimore; Johns Hopkins University Press, 1968.

Crocker, Lester. "L'analyse des rêves au XVIII⁰ siècle." *Studies on Voltaire and the Eighteenth Century* 23 (1963): 271–310.

David, Madeleine. *Le débat sur les écritures et l'hiéroglyphe au XVII⁰ et XVIII⁰ siècles, et l'application de la notion de déchiffrement aux écritures mortes*. Paris: SEVPEN, 1965.

———. "Un témoin des espoirs du XVIII⁰ siècle. Kalmar et sa langue philosophique, 1772." *Revue historique* (April–June 1956): 283–89.

Dawson, Virginia. *Nature's Enigma: The Problem of the Polyp in the Letters of Bonnet, Trembley, and Réaumur*. Philadelphia: American Philosophical Society, 1987.

———. "The Problem of Soul in the 'Little Machines' of Réaumur and Charles Bonnet." *Eighteenth Century Studies* 18 (1985): 503–22.

De Maria, Robert, Jr. *Johnson's Dictionary and the Language of Learning*. Oxford: Clarendon Press, 1986.

Derrida, Jacques. *De la grammatologie*. Paris: Éditions de Minuit, 1967.

Dobbs, Betty J. Teeter. *The Foundations of Newton's Alchemy*. London and New York: Cambridge University Press, 1975.

Duchesneau, François. "D'Alembert et la physiologie." *Dix-Huitième Siècle*, 81–91. Paris: Presses Universitaires de France, 1984.

———. *La physiologie des lumières: Empirisme, modèles, et théories*. The Hague: Martinus Nijhoff, 1982.

Duchet, Michèle and Michèle Jalley, eds. *Langue et langages de Leibniz à l'Encyclopédie*. Paris: Union Générale d'Éditions. 1977.

Durand-Sendrail, Béatrice. "Mirage des lumières: Politique du regard dans les *Lettres persanes*." *L'Esprit Créateur* 28 (1988): 69–81.

Dusinger, John A. "Yorick and the 'Eternal Fountain of Our Feelings.'" In *Psychology and Literature in the Eighteenth Century*, ed. Christopher Fox, 259–76. New York: AMS Press, 1987.

Engell, James. *The Creative Imagination: Enlightenment to Romanticism*. Cambridge, Mass.: Harvard University Press, 1981.

Faivre, Antoine. *L'ésotérisme au XVIIIe siècle*. Paris: Seghers, 1973.

——. *Mystiques, théosophes, et illuminés au siècles des lumières*. New York: Georg Olms, 1976.

——. "Magia Naturalis: Théologie de la lumière et de l'électricité dans la 'Naturphilosophie romantique.'" In *Lumière et cosmos: Courants occultes de la philosophie de la nature*, ed. Antoine Faivre, 191–216. Paris: Albin Michel, 1981.

Falvey, John. "The Aesthetics of La Mettrie." *Studies on Voltaire and the Eighteenth Century* 87 (1972): 397–479.

Fellows, Otis. *Diderot*. Boston: Twayne, 1977.

Foucault, Michel. *Les mots et les choses*. Paris: Gallimard, 1966. Translated as *The Order of Things: An Archeology of the Human Sciences*. New York: Vintage Books, 1966.

Frank, Robert G., Jr. "Thomas Willis and His Circle: Brain and Mind in Seventeenth-Century Medicine." In *The Languages of Psyche: Mind and Body in Enlightenment Thought*, ed. George S. Rousseau, 107–46. Clark Library Lectures, 1985–86. Berkeley and Los Angeles: University of California Press, 1990.

French, Roger K. "Ether and Physiology." In *Conceptions of Ether: Studies in the History of Ether Theories 1740–1900*, ed. G. N. Cantor and M. J. S. Hodge, 111–34. Cambridge: Cambridge University Press, 1981.

Gay, Peter. *The Enlightenment, an Interpretation*. Vol. 1: *The Rise of Modern Paganism*. New York: Vintage Books, 1968.

Gusdorf, Georges. *Dieu, la nature, l'homme au siècle des lumières*. Paris: Payot, 1972.

Hagstrum, Jean. *The Sister Arts*. Chicago: University of Chicago Press, 1958.

Hankins, Thomas. *Science and the Enlightenment*. Cambridge: Cambridge University Press, 1985.

Harman, P. M. *Metaphysics and Natural Philosophy. The Problem of Substance in Classical Physics*. Totowa, N.J.: Barnes and Noble, 1982.

Heimann, P. M. "Ether and Imponderables." In *Conceptions of Ether: Studies in the History of Ether Theories 1740–1900*, ed. G. N. Cantor and M. J. S. Hodge, 61–83. Cambridge: Cambridge University Press, 1981.

Hetzer, Theodor. "Francisco Goya and the Crisis in Art around 1800." In *Goya: The Origins of the Modern Temper in Art*, ed. Fred Licht, 92–113. New York: Universe Books, 1979.

Hill, Emita B. "The Role of 'le monstre' in Diderot's Thought." *Studies on Voltaire and the Eighteenth Century* 77 (1972): 149–261.

Himelblau, Jack. "Tohil in the Popul Vuh of the Maya Quiche: Role Versus Implied Identity." *Journal of Latin American Lore* 12 (1986): 3–24.

Home, R. W. "Newton on Electricity and the Aether." In *Contemporary Newtonian Research*, ed. Zev Bechler, 191–213. Boston: Reidel, 1982.

Iglesias, María del Carmen. "Los monstruos y el origen de la vida en la Francia del siglo XVIII." In *Homenaje a Julio Caro Baroja*, ed. Antonio Carreira et al., 617–30. Zaragoza: Pórtico Librerías, 1978.

Ilie, Paul. "Cadalso and the Epistemology of Madness." *Studies for I. L. McClelland*, ed. David Gies. *Dieciocho* 9, 1–2 (1986): 174–87.

———. "Goya's Teratology and the Critique of Reason." *Eighteenth Century Studies* 18 (1984): 35–56.

———. "El templo de Minerva en la España del XVIII." *Hispanic Review* 59 (1991): 1–23.

Jacob, Margaret. *The Radical Enlightenment*. London: George Allen and Unwin, 1981.

Jones, William Powell. *The Rhetoric of Science: A Study of Scientific Ideas and Imagery in Eighteenth-Century Poetry*. Berkeley and Los Angeles: University of California Press, 1966.

Kamuf, Peggy. "Seeing Through Rousseau." *L'Esprit Créateur* 28 (1988): 82–93.

Kern, Hermann. *Labirinti: Forme e interpretazione. 5000 anni di presenza di un archetipo. Manuale e filo conduttore*. Milano: Fetrinelli, 1981.

King, Lester S. *The Road to Medical Enlightenment, 1650–1695*. London: Macdonald; New York: American Elsevier, 1970.

Knight, Isabel. *The Geometric Spirit: The Abbé de Condillac and the French Enlightenment*. New Haven, Conn. and London: Yale University Press, 1968.

Korshin, Paul. *Typologies in England, 1650–1820*. Princeton, N.J.: Princeton University Press, 1982.

Kouidis, Apostolos P. "The Praise of Folly: Diderot's Model for *Le neveu de Rameau*." *Studies on Voltaire and the Eighteenth Century* 185 (1980): 237–66.

Koyré, Alexandre. *From the Closed World to the Infinite Universe*. Baltimore: Johns Hopkins University Press, 1957.

———. *Newtonian Studies*. Chicago: University of Chicago Press, 1965.

Kuhn, Thomas S. *The Structure of Scientific Revolutions* (1962). 2nd ed., enlarged. Chicago: University of Chicago Press, 1970.

Lafuente Ferrari, Enrique. *Los Caprichos de Goya*. Barcelona: Gustavo Gili, 1978.

———. *Goya en sus dibujos*. Madrid: Urbión, 1979.

———. *Los desastres de la guerra y sus dibujos preparatorios*. Barcelona: Instituto Amatller de Arte Hispánico, 1952.

Laudan, Larry. "The Medium and Its Message: A Study of Some Philosophical Controversies About Ether." In *Conceptions of Ether: Studies in the History of Ether Theories 1740–1900*, ed. G. N. Cantor and M. J. S. Hodge, 157–85. Cambridge: Cambridge University Press, 1981.

Lenhoff, Sylvia G. and Howard M. Lenhoff. *Hydra and the Birth of Experimental Biology, 1744: Abraham Trembley's Memoires Concerning the Polyps*. Pacific Grove, Calif.: Boxwood Press, 1986.

Leventhal, Herbert. *In the Shadow of the Enlightenment: Occultism and Renaissance Science in Eighteenth-Century America*. New York: New York University Press, 1976.

Levitine, George. "Some Emblematic Sources of Goya." *Journal of the Warburg and Courtauld Institutes* 22 (1959): 106–31.

Licht, Fred. *Goya: The Origins of the Modern Temper in Art*. New York: Universe Books, 1979.

López-Rey, José. *Goya's Caprichos. Beauty, Reason, and Caricature*. 2 vols. Princeton, N.J.: Princeton University Press, 1953.

Markley, Robert. *Fallen Languages: Crises of Representation in Newtonian England, 1660–1740*. Ithaca, N.Y. and London: Cornell University Press, 1993.

Markovits, Francine. *Sur le problème de Molyneux*. Afterword by Francine Markovits ("Mérian, Diderot, et l'Aveugle"). Paris: Flammarion, 1984.

Marx, Jacques. "Le concept d'imagination au XVIIIe siècle." In *Thèmes et figures du siècle de lumières: Mélanges offerts à Roland Mortier*, ed. Raymond Trousson, 147–59. Génève: Droz, 1980.

Mazzolini, Renato G. and Shirley A. Roe. *Science Against the Unbelievers: The Correspondence of Bonnet and Needham, 1760–1780*. Oxford: The Voltaire Foundation, 1986.

McClelland, I. L. *Ideological Hesitancy in Spain, 1700–1750*. Liverpool: Liverpool University Press, 1991.

McGuire, J. E. "Force, Active Principles, and Newton's Invisible Realm." *Ambix* 15 (1968): 154–208.

Moli Frigola, Montserrat. "La ciudad ideal de Carlos de Borbón. Proyectos urbanísticos para las ciudades de Roma y Nápoles en las fiestas de la hacanea (1738–1759). In *Actas del Congreso Internacional sobre "Carlos III y la Ilustración,"* 3:305–70. Madrid: Ministerio de Cultura, 1989.

Nicolson, Marjorie Hope. *Newton Demands the Muse: Newton's Opticks and the Eighteenth-Century Poets*. Princeton, N.J.: Princeton University Press, 1946.

Nordstrom, Fölke. *Goya, Saturn, and Melancholy. Studies in the Art of Goya*. Stockholm: Almqvist and Wiksell, 1962.

Peterfreund, Stuart. "The Re-Emergence of Energy in the Discourse of Literature and Science." In *Science and the Imagination*, ed. G. S. Rousseau. *Annales of Scholarship: Metastudies of the Humanities and Social Sciences* 4 (Fall 1986): 22–53.

Polt, John H. R., ed. *Poesía del siglo XVIII*. Madrid: Castalia, 1975.

Proust, Jacques. "L'article 'Bas' de Diderot." In *Langue et langages de Leibniz à l'Encyclopédie*, ed. Michèle Duchet and Michèle Jalley, 245–78. Paris: Union Générale d'Éditions, 1977.

———. "Raison, déraison dans les articles philosophiques de l'*Encyclopédie*." *Saggi* 18(1979): 423–48.

———. "Diderot et la philosophie du polype." *Revue des Sciences Humaines* 182 (1981): 21–30.

Rigotti, Francesca. "Biology and Society in the Age of Enlightenment." *Journal of the History of Ideas* 47 (1986): 215–33.

Ritterbush, P. C. *Overtures to Biology: The Speculations of Eighteenth-Century Naturalists*. New Haven, Conn. and London: Yale University Press, 1964.

Roe, Shirley A. "John Turberville Needham and the Generation of Living Organisms." *Isis* 74 (1983): 159–84.

——. *Matter, Life, and Generation: Eighteenth-Century Embryology and the Haller-Wolff Debate*. Cambridge: Cambridge University Press, 1981.

Roger, Jacques. *Les sciences de la vie dans la pensée française du XVIIIe siècle: la génération des animaux de Descartes à l'Encyclopédie*. Paris: Armand Colin, 1963.

Rossi, Paolo. *The Dark Abyss of Time: The History of the Earth and the History of Nations from Hooke to Vico*. Trans. Lydia G. Cochrane. Chicago and London: University of Chicago Press, 1984.

Rothstein, Eric. "Epistemology and Poetry in the Mid-Eighteenth Century." In *Poetry and Epistemology: Turning Points in the History of Poetic Knowledge*, ed. Roland Hagenbückle and Laura Skandera. Regensburg: F. Pustel, 1986.

——. "Organicism, Rupturalism, and Ism-Ism." *Modern Philology* 85 (1988): 588–609.

——. *Restoration and Eighteenth-Century Poetry, 1660–1780*. Boston and London: Routledge & Kegan Paul, 1981.

Rousseau, George S. "Nerves, Spirits, and Fibres: Towards Defining the Origins of Sensibility." In *Studies in the Eighteenth Century 3: Papers Presented at the Third David Nichol Smith Memorial Seminar, Canberra, 1973*, ed. R. F. Brisenden and J. C. Eade, 137–57. Toronto and Buffalo: University of Toronto Press, 1976. Reprinted with postscript in *The Blue Guitar* (Messina) 2(1976): 125–53.

Saint Amand, Pierre. *Diderot. Le labyrinthe de la relation*. Paris: Vrin, 1984.

Stafford, Barbara. *Body Criticism: Imaging the Unseen in Enlightenment Art and Medicine*. Cambridge, Mass.: MIT Press, 1990.

——. "Conjecturing the Unseen in Late Eighteenth-Century Art." *Zeitschrift für Kunstgeschichte* 48, 2 (1985): 329–65.

——. *Voyage into Substance: Art, Nature, and the Illustrated Travel Account, 1760–1840*. Cambridge, Mass. and London: MIT Press, 1984.

Starobinski, Jean. "Fable et mythologie aux 17e et 18e siècles: Dans la littérature et la réflexion théorique." In *Dictionnaire des mythologies et des religions des sociétés traditionnelles et du monde antique*, ed. Yves Bonnefoy, 1:390–400. Paris: Flammarion, 1981.

——. "Goya." In *Les emblèmes de la raison* (1973), 123–35. Paris: Flammarion, 1979.

——. *Jean-Jacques Rousseau: La transparence et l'obstacle*. Paris: Plon, 1957.

——. "Le mythe au 18e siècle. *Critique* no. 366 (November 1977): 975–97.

——. "Remarques sur l'*Encyclopédie*." *Revue de métaphysique et de la morale* 75 (1970): 284–91.

Swain, Virginia E. "*Lumières et Vision*: Reflections on Sight and Seeing in Seventeenth- and Eighteenth-Century France." *L'Esprit Créateur* 28 (1988): 5–16.

This, Bernard. "Le sentiment océanique et l'haptonomie." In *Art et fantasme*, 235–5. Paris: Éditions du Champs Vallon, 1980I.

Tonelli, G. "The Law of Continuity in the Eighteenth Century." *Studies on Voltaire and the Eighteenth Century* 27 (1963): 1619–38.

Tort, Patrick. *L'ordre et les monstres: le débat sur l'origine des déviations anatomiques au XVIIIe siècle*. Paris: Le Sycamore, 1980.

Toulmin, Stephen. *Human Understanding: The Collective Use and Evolution of Concepts*. Princeton, N.J.: Princeton University Press, 1977.

Trottein, Serge. "Diderot et la philosophie du clair-obscur." *L'Esprit Créateur* 28 (1988): 107–19.

Tuveson, Ernest Lee. *The Imagination as a Means of Grace: Locke and the Aesthetics of Romanticism*. Berkeley and Los Angeles: University of California Press, 1960.

Tuzet, Hélène. *Le cosmos et l'imaginaire*. Paris: José Corti, 1965.

Van Lennep, Jacques. *Alchimie*. Brussels: Crédit Communal, 1985.

——. *Art et alchimie: Étude de l'iconographie hermétique et de ses influences*. Brussels: Éditions Meddens, 1966.

Varloot, Jean. "Préface" to *Buffon: Histoire naturelle*, 7–31. Paris: Gallimard, 1984.

Vartanian, Aram. *Diderot and Descartes: A Study of Scientific Naturalism in the Enlightenment*. Princeton, N.J.: Princeton University Press, 1953.

——. "La Mettrie and Diderot Revisited: An Intertextual Encounter." *Diderot Studies* 21 (1983): 155–97.

——. *La Mettrie's "L'homme machine": A Study in the Origins of an Idea*. Princeton, N.J.: Princeton University Press, 1960.

——. "The 'Rêve de d'Alembert': A Bio-Political View." *Diderot Studies* 17 (1973): 41–64.

——. "Trembley's Polyp, La Mettrie, and Eighteenth-Century French Materialism." *Journal of the History of Ideas* 11 (1950): 259–86. Reprinted in *Roots of Scientific Thought*, ed. Philip P. Wiener and Aaron Noland, 97–516. New York: Basic Books, 1957.

Vindel, Francisco. *Escudos y marcas de impresores y libreros en España durante los siglos XV a XIX, 1485–1850*. Barcelona: Editorial Oribid, 1942.

Walker, D. P. *The Ancient Theology. Studies in Christian Platonism from the Fifteenth to the Eighteenth Century*. London: G. Duckworth, 1972.

Warnock, Mary. *Imagination*. Berkeley and Los Angeles: University of California Press, 1976.

Wellman, Kathleen. *La Mettrie: Medicine, Philosophy, and Enlightenment*. Durham, N.C.: Duke University Press, 1992.

Whittaker, Sir Edmund Taylor. *A History of the Theories of Aether and Electricity*. 2 vols. London: Thomas Nelson & Sons, 1951.

Wilbanks, Jan. *Hume's Theory of Imagination*. The Hague: Martinus Nijhoff, 1968.

Yates, Frances A. *Giordano Bruno and the Hermetic Tradition*. London: Routledge & Kegan Paul, 1964.

——. *The Art of Memory*. London: Routledge & Kegan Paul, 1966.

Yolton, John. *Perceptual Acquaintance from Descartes to Reid*. Minneapolis: University of Minnesota Press, 1984.

——. *Thinking Matter. Materialism in Eighteenth-Century Britain*. Minneapolis: University of Minnesota Press, 1983.

Name Index

Subject Index

abyss, 63, 71, 77, 85, 101, 130, 332–33
Absolute, the, 22, 31, 92, 138, 140, 143, 146,
  153, 241, 297, 300–301, 311, 316. *See also*
  sensorium, Divine; the Whole
aether, ch. 9; 1, 84, 86, 111–12, 131, 136, 159,
  160, 172, 173, 174, 177n, 188–89, 201, 214,
  227, 228, 246, 250–51, 262, 355–56, 357. *See
  also* fluidism
allegory, 19–22, 63, 65, 93–98, 293, 336–39,
  341. *See also* iconology
Ancient Philosophy or Theology. *See* occultism
animal spirits, 1, 11, 104, 156–58, 173, 185,
  189, 207, 227, 228, 246, 254, 277–85, 289,
  295–300, 309. *See also* fluidism
Archeus, 186, 285, 300

bats: blind, 344; classification of, 41; and
  continuity, 33–34; energy of, 128, 135;
  metamorphosis of, ch. 2; mentioned, 327,
  335, 354, 355
blindness, 48, 115–16, 137–40, 148–49, 195n,
  224, 248, 251, 258–60, 314, 323, 334, 339,
  341, 345, 346, 352
brain, ch. 7; 102–4, 123–34, 180, 193, 194, 255,
  296, 311. *See also* medulla

Capricho 43: and bats, 344, 354; and discontinuity, 30–31, 33–34, 46–49, 125, 128; and
  dream of Reason, 333; and madness, 262;
  perception of reality in, 164; skepticism
  in, 327. See also *Sepia One*; *Sepia Two*
Chain of Being, 14, 17, 42, 55–56, 63, 80,
  106–7, 109, 113, 118, 121, 140, 163, 165, 176,
  220, 237, 262, 275, 297, 298, 301, 317, 336
Chaos, ch. 3; 38, 43, 47, 51–52, 63, 69, 140,
  215, 247, 311, 332
chiaroscuro, 323
classification, 56–57, 68, 106–7, 110, 117,
  118–19, 130
cognition: and aether, 86, 156–57, 313, 356,

357; allegorized, 30, 143; and the Absolute,
  22, 31, 92, 138, 140, 143, 146, 153, 297, 301;
  and (dis)continuity, 44, 46–50, 102, 104,
  159, 354–55; and dream, 1, 37, 52, 210, 321–
  22; and empirical order, 61; functional,
  8, 9, 267–70; and Humean belief, 32–33,
  36, 40, 146, 155; and ideation, 280; and
  knowledge, 26, 100, 124–25, 143–44, 267–
  70, 320, 354–55; pre-linguistic, 7, 107, 306;
  and regeneration, 172; tactile, 115–16, 138,
  339–52
communication. *See* continuity; language
connection. *See* continuity
consciousness, 28, 52–53, 86, 125, 148–49, 270,
  279; Gulliverian, 324, 328
continuity: and the Absolute, 241, 300–
  301, 311, 316; and aetherial continuum,
  285–93; of being and thought, 332; and
  causality, 79; connectedness in, 23, 29, 133,
  152, 223, 227; and communication, 23–24,
  134, 146, 226–29; correspondence in, 134,
  241, 279; and cosmic soul, 295–97, 300,
  311; dependent on discontinuity, 107–08,
  145; and harmony, 200–201; liaison in, 25–
  26, 40, 43, 44–45, 109–10, 113, 131, 159, 302;
  gradation in, 120, 123, 169, 175, 178, 241–42,
  248, 264; in fibers, 183, 189, 226; levels of,
  25, 27, 31, 41, 100, 111, 243; and linearity,
  45, 100, 120, 133; and organicity, 159; and
  Reason, 14, 196; from sensation to sign,
  183, 224, 229, 231. *See also* the Whole
continuism, ideal of, 14–17, 30, 37, 50, 105,
  108, 113, 123, 151, 159, 174–82, 241

dermatopsis, 340–41. *See also* touchsight
designing intelligence. *See* intelligence
difference. *See* identity
Divinity. *See* cognition, and the Absolute;
  continuity, and the Absolute
discontinuity: ch. 1, ch. 5; in knowledge,
  102, 354; levels of, 14–17, 92, 104, 269–70;

This book has been set in Galliard. Galliard was designed for
Mergenthaler in 1978 by Matthew Carter. Galliard retains many of the
features of a sixteenth-century typeface cut by Robert Granjon but
has some modifications that give it a more contemporary look.

Printed on acid-free paper.